Wings of the Weird & Wonderful

Wings of the Weird & Wonderful

Captain Eric 'Winkle' Brown
CBE DSC AFC RN

First published in Great Britain as two volumes
in 1983 & 1985 by Airlife Publishing Limited

Revised and updated in 2010 by Blacker Design and
Hikoki Publications

ISBN 9 781902 109162

A CIP record for this book is available from
the British Library

Printed in China

Crécy Publishing Limited
1a Ringway Trading Estate, Shadowmoss Rd,
Manchester M22 5LH
www.crecy.co.uk

Publisher's note: First published in two volumes in
1983 and 1985. This new combined edition has been
greatly revised and expanded and now covers 53 of
the world's most weird and wonderful aircraft.

This book would not have been possible without the
generous assistance of the following people who
supplied artwork and photographs: Richard Caruana,
Philip Jarrett, Bundesarchiv, Barry Ketley, *The
Aeroplane*, The RAF Museum Hendon.

Contents

Foreword

The unusual and unorthodox in aircraft design or operation has always intrigued me; the superlative performance and handling has always excited me. Occasionally fortune smiles and combines all these characteristics in one rare bird – to offer the thrill of a lifetime.

I have been lucky enough to experience both the weird and the wonderful, and have selected some examples of these to put on record. This book describes them from a totally subjective standpoint, in the hope that aviation enthusiasts can capture some of the impressions these aircraft made on me, and thus some animation may be given to their statistical data.

It is an odd collection, including some outstanding examples of aeronautical development such as the Grumman F8F Bearcat, combined with some almost dangerous experiments like the General Aircraft GAL/56.

I was privileged to be a test pilot at RAE during one of the most extraordinary periods of aviation history. The variety of aircraft being tested at Farnborough at any one time was staggering and the number of different types flown there in 1946, is unlikely ever to be beaten. We were testing early airliners, alongside a new breed of turbo-prop fighters, the first generation of jet aircraft, and experimental rocket-equipped naval aircraft.

The type of tests carried out at Farnborough varied enormously from stalling tests at 50mph on a Miles Libellula, through transonic testing in a Spitfire XIV at Mach 0.86 to supersonic dives in a North American F-86 Sabre.

We were also involved in the development of a number of ground-breaking innovations, such as rocket propelled launchers for carrier aircraft, the first flexible deck for aircraft carriers and, probably most importantly, the all-moving tailplane which played a vital role in the race to break the sound barrier.

I have never been able to regard aeroplanes as inanimate objects, for they breathe life through their engines, and beauty or ugliness through their forms. They portray their characters through their controls, and can be as gentle as a lamb or as spiteful as a vixen. One thing they can never be is dull. Hopefully readers will feel the same about this book.

Eric Brown

Aircraft flown by Eric Brown

This is a complete list of the 490 aircraft flown by Eric Brown, which was produced and checked for the *Guinness Book of Records*. It comprises just the 'basic' types (not marks or models, e.g. Eric Brown flew fourteen marks of the Spitfire, but there is only one entry for Spitfire).

A

Aeronca Grasshopper
Aerospatiale Alouette
Aerospatiale Ecureuil
Aerospatiale Twin Squirrel
Agusta 109
Aichi Val
Airspeed Ambassador
Airspeed Envoy
Airspeed Horsa
Airspeed Oxford
Arado 96B
Arado 196A
Arado 199
Arado 232B
Arado 234B
Arado 240
Armstrong Whitworth Albemarle
Armstrong Whitworth Whitley
Auster Aiglet
Avro Anson
Avro Athena
Avro Lancaster
Avro Lancastrian
Avro Lincoln
Avro Manchester
Avro Shackleton
Avro Tudor
Avro Tutor
Avro York

B

B.A. Swallow
B.Ae 125
B.Ae 146
B.Ae Hawk
BAC Lightning
Baynes Carrier Wing
Beagle B.206
Beagle Pup
Beech Baron
Beech Bonanza
Beech Super King Air
Beech Traveller
Beechcraft Expediter
Bell AH-1 Huey
Bell 47
Bell 204
Bell 222
Bell Airacobra
Bell Airacomet
Bell HTL-5
Bell Jet Ranger
Bell Kingcobra
Bell Long Ranger
Blackburn Beverley
Blackburn Botha
Blackburn Buccaneer
Blackburn Firebrand
Blackburn Firecrest
Blackburn Roc
Blackburn Shark
Blackburn Skua
Blohm & Voss 138
Blohm & Voss 141B
Blohm & Voss 222 Wiking

Boeing Fortress
Boeing Superfortress
Boeing Vertol Chinook
Boulton Paul Defiant
Boulton Paul P.108
Boulton Paul Sea Balliol
Brantly B-2
Bréguet Alizé
Bréguet Atlantic
Brewster Buffalo
Bristol Beaufighter
Bristol Beaufort
Bristol Blenheim
Bristol Bombay
Bristol Brigand
Bristol Britannia
Bristol Buckingham
Bristol Bulldog
Bristol Freighter
Bristol Sycamore
Britten-Norman Islander
Bücker Bestmann
Bücker Jungmann
Bücker Jungmeister
Bücker Student

C

Cant Z1007
Caprioni 309
Caprioni 311
Caprioni Ca 135 bis
Cessna 150
Cessna Cardinal
Cessna Skymaster

Cessna Skywagon
Chance-Vought Corsair
Chance-Vought Cutlass
Chilton D.W.1
Chrislea Ace
Comper Swift
Consolidated Catalina
Consolidated Liberator
Consolidated Vultee Privateer
Convair 240-5
Curtiss Commando
Curtiss Helldiver
Curtiss Kittyhawk
Curtiss Mohawk
Curtiss Seamew
Curtiss Tomahawk

 D

Dassault Étendard
Dassault Mirage
Dassault Mystère
De Havilland 86B
De Havilland Beaver
De Havilland Chipmunk
De Havilland Comet
De Havilland Devon
De Havilland Don
De Havilland Flamingo
De Havilland Fox Moth
De Havilland Gipsy Moth
De Havilland Heron
De Havilland Hornet Moth
De Havilland Leopard Moth
De Havilland Mosquito
De Havilland Otter
De Havilland Puss Moth
De Havilland Rapide
De Havilland Sea Hornet
De Havilland Sea Mosquito
De Havilland Sea Vampire
De Havilland Sea Venom
De Havilland Sea Vixen
De Havilland Swallow
De Havilland Tiger Moth

De Havilland Vampire
Dewoitine 520
DFS 230
DFS Kranich
DFS Weihe
Dornier 17
Dornier 18
Dornier 24
Dornier 26
Dornier 27
Dornier 217
Dornier 335
Douglas Boston
Douglas Dakota
Douglas Dauntless
Douglas Devastator
Douglas Invader
Douglas Skymaster
Douglas Skynight
Douglas Skyraider
Druine Turbulent

 E

Elliott Newbury Eon
Embraer Bandeirante
English Electric Canberra
Enstrom F28
Enstrom Shark
Erco Ercoupe

 F

Fairchild Argus
Fairchild Cornell
Fairchild XNQ-1
Fairey IIIF
Fairey Albacore
Fairey Barracuda
Fairey Battle
Fairey Firefly
Fairey Fulmar
Fairey Gannet
Fairey Gordon
Fairey Primer

Fairey Seal
Fairey Spearfish
Fairey Swordfish
Fiat B.R.20
Fiat C.32
Fiat C.42
Fiat G.50
Fieseler Storch
Focke-Wulf 189
Focke-Wulf 190
Focke-Wulf 200
Focke-Wulf 58 Weihe
Focke-Wulf Ta.152
Focke-Wulf Ta.154
Folland 43/37
Fouga Magister
Fournier Milan

G

General Aircraft Cygnet
General Aircraft Hamilcar
General Aircraft Hotspur
General Aircraft L./56
Gloster E.28/39
Gloster Gauntlet
Gloster Gladiator
Gloster Javelin
Gloster Meteor
Gloster Sea Meteor
Gotha 244
Grumman Ag-Cat
Grumman Albatross
Grumman Avenger
Grumman Bearcat
Grumman Cougar
Grumman Goose
Grumman Guardian
Grumman Hellcat
Grumman Panther
Grumman Tigercat
Grumman Widgeon
Grumman Wildcat

H

Handley Page Gugnunc
Handley Page Halifax
Handley Page Hampden
Handley Page Hastings
Handley Page Hermes
Handley Page Marathon
Handley Page Sparrow
Hawker Fury
Hawker Hart
Hawker Hector
Hawker Henley
Hawker Hunter
Hawker Hurricane
Hawker Nimrod
Hawker Osprey
Hawker P.1040
Hawker P.1052
Hawker P.1127
Hawker Sea Fury
Hawker Sea Hawk
Hawker Siddeley 748
Hawker Siddeley Gnat
Hawker Tempest
Hawker Typhoon
Heinkel 111
Heinkel 115
Heinkel 162
Heinkel 177
Heinkel 219
Henschel 123
Henschel 129
Heston Phoenix
Hiller HTE
Hitachi T.2
Horten IV
Hotspur Glider
Hughes 300
Hughes 500
Hunting Percival Jet Provost
Hunting Percival Provost

 I

Ilyushin 2
Ilyushin 4

J

Jodel Ambassadour
Jodel Club
Jodel Excellence
Jodel Grand Tourisme
Jodel Mascaret
Jodel Mousqetaire
Junkers 52
Junkers 86

Junkers 87
Junkers 88
Junkers 188
Junkers 290
Junkers 352
Junkers 388

 K

Kamov 26
Kawasaki Tony
Klemm 26
Klemm 35D
Klemm L25
Klemm L27

 L

Lavochkin 7
Le Vier Cosmic Wind
Ling Temco Vought Crusader
Lockheed Constellation
Lockheed Electra
Lockheed Hercules
Lockheed Hudson
Lockheed Lightning
Lockheed Neptune
Lockheed Shooting Star
Lockheed Starfighter
Lockheed Ventura
Luton Minor

M

Macchi C.202
Macchi C.205
Martin Baker MB 5
Martin Baltimore
Martin Marauder
MBB Bo 105
McDonnell Banshee
McDonnell Douglas Skyhawk
McDonnell Phantom II
Messerschmitt 108
Messerschmitt 109
Messerschmitt 110
Messerschmitt 163
Messerschmitt 262
Messerschmitt 410
MIG-3
MIG-15
Mil-1
Mil-2
Mil-4
Miles 18
Miles 20
Miles 28

Miles 38
Miles 48
Miles Aerovan
Miles Falcon
Miles Gemini
Miles Hawk
Miles Hobby
Miles Libellula
Miles Magister
Miles Martinet
Miles Master
Miles Mentor
Miles Mohawk
Miles Monarch
Miles Monitor
Miles Sparrowhawk
Mitsubishi Betty
Mitsubishi Dinah
Mitsubishi Zeke
Mooney M20
Morane-Saulnier 406
Morane-Saulnier Paris
Morane-Saulnier Rallye
Muntz Youngman-Baynes

 N

N.S.F.K. S.G.38
Nakajima Frank
Nakajima Oscar
Nipper III
Noorduyn Norseman
Nord 262A
Nord Noralpha
Nord Piingouin
North American Harvard
North American Mitchell
North American Mustang
North American Sabre
North American Savage
North American Super Sabre
North American Texan
Northrop 24 Gamma
    Commercial
Northrop Black Widow
Northrop F-5

 O

Orlikan Meta Sokol

 P

Percival Gull
Percival Pembroke
Percival Prentice
Percival Proctor

Percival Q6
Percival Vega Gull
Petlyakov PE-2
Piaggio P.136
Piaggio P.166
Piasecki Retriever
Piel Emeraude
Pilatus Porter
Piper Apache
Piper Aztec
Piper Comanche
Piper Cub
Piper Cub Special 90
Piper Grasshopper
Piper Navajo
Piper Pawnee
Piper Seneca
Piper Supercruiser
Piper Tripacer
PiperCherokee
Pitts Special
Polikarpov I-15
Polikarpov I-16
Portsmouth Aerocar Major

R

Reggiane 2000
Reggiane 2001
Reid & Sigrist Desford
Republic Seabee
Republic Lancer
Republic Thunderbolt
Republic Thunderjet
Republic Thunderstreak
Robin Royale
Robinson R-22
Rollason Condor
Ryan Fireball

S

Saab 21
Saab 29
Saab 105
Saab Lansen
Saab Safir
Saunders-Roe P.531
Saunders-Roe Skeeter
Saunders-Roe S.R./A.1
Savoia-Marchetti SM79
Savoia-Marchetti SM82
Savoia-Marchetti SM95
Scheibe Motorspatz
Schmetz Olympia-Meise
Schneider Baby Grunau
Scottish Aviation Bulldog

Scottish Aviation Pioneer
Scottish Aviation Twin Pioneer
Short S.31
Short Sealand
Short Skyvan
Short Stirling
Short Sturgeon
SIAI-Marchetti S.F.260
Siebel 204
Sikorsky HRS
Sikorsky R-4B Hoverfly
Sikorsky R-6A Hoverfly II
Sikorsky S-58T
Sikorsky S-61
Sikorsky S-76
Sipa S.903
Slingsby Capstan
Slingsby Kirby Cadet
Slingsby Motor Tutor
Slingsby Prefect
Slingsby Swallow
Slingsby T.21
Slingsby T.31
Socata Diplomate
Stampe et Vertongen SV-4
Stearman Caydet
Stinson Junior R
Stinson Reliant
Stinson Sentinel
Sud-Aviation Djinn
Supermarine Attacker
Supermarine S.24/37
Supermarine Scimitar
Supermarine Sea Otter
Supermarine Seafang
Supermarine Seafire
Supermarine Seagull
Supermarine Spiteful
Supermarine Spitfire
Supermarine Walrus
SZD Bocian

T

Taylorcraft Auster
Taylor J.T.1 Monoplane
Taylor J.T.2 Titch
Thruxton Jackaroo
Tipsy S.2
Tipsy Trainer
Tipsy Type B

V

Vertol 107
Vickers Valiant
Vickers Vanguard

Vickers VC10
Vickers Viking
Vickers Viscount
Vickers Warwick
Vickers Wellington
Vickers Windsor
Vought-Sikorsky Chesapeake
Vought-Sikorsky Kingfisher
Vultee Vengeance

W

Waco CG-3
Waco Hadrian
Westland Aerospatiale Gazelle
Westland Aerospatiale Lynx
Westland Lysander
Westland Sikorsky S-51
  Dragonfly
Westland Sikorsky S-55
  Whirlwind
Westland Wasp
Westland Welkin
Westland Wessex
Westland Whirlwind
Westland Wyvern
Winter Zaunkönig

Y

Yakovlev-1
Yakovlev-9
Yakovlev-11
Youngman-Baynes High Lift

Z

Zlin Akrobat

1 AVRO LANCASTER

**Just to sit in the cockpit was a sheer joy.
It exuded self-confidence.** ERIC BROWN

WHENEVER I am asked which were the great British aeroplanes of the Second World War, I name the Spitfire, Mosquito and Lancaster. I have put them in ascending order of size, but I would be hard put to choose the greatest of the three, although I had a long and intimate association with each of these marvels of aeronautical design.

The Lancaster was one of those aeroplanes which imbued an instantaneous feeling of confidence in a pilot entering its cockpit. The all-round view was superb, the instrument layouts logical and simple, and the 'sit' of the whole machine was right. This same feeling did not come instantly with the Spitfire and Mosquito, but required a spell of flight familiarisation to acquire, although the fact that all three were Merlin-engined gave a reliability factor that greatly aided the confidence-making process.

The handling qualities of the Lancaster were unbelievably docile, and it can truthfully be said that it exhibited no flying vices. For its normal operational task of night bombing it was both easy to fly on instruments and gave a stable platform for bomb-aiming. Its controls were all pleasant in cruising flight, the elevators being relatively light and effective, and the ailerons positively light and effective, while the rudders were moderately so. However, in evasive action such as the corkscrew manoeuvre, used to escape the attentions of searchlights or night fighters, the elevators became heavy in turns and the ailerons heavied up above 260mph (418km/h), as did also the rudders. The pilot had a tiring task on his hands, although he knew he could throw this large aircraft around with impunity because of its incredibly gentle stalling characteristics.

The Lancaster was very easy to land at 110mph

Lancaster 'H for Harry' taking off on a bombing raid from an RAF station in Lincolnshire.

(177km/h), and it also had good engine-out asymmetric handling qualities, although with two engines dead on one side the rudder foot load was very heavy. These were comforting points for crews returning with aircraft damaged by enemy action, and they gave the Lancaster a considerable edge in popularity with aircrews over the contemporary Stirling and Halifax.

Although this star of the bombers was a delight to fly, I was privileged to fly two versions of the Lancaster that put it in the superstar class. The first of these was a Lancaster I, fitted with hydraulic power-boosted controls, which relieved the pilot of about 60% of the normal control forces. The rate of control application was optimised after some trial and error at 30°/second on all three controls, although a maximum designed rate of 45°/second was provided. At 30°/second the harmony of control was perfect and the powered controls had in effect converted the Lancaster into an overgrown Spitfire.

This was all good stuff, but the Lancaster was not stressed to fighter standards, so an hydraulic 'g' restrictor had to be fitted to prevent the build-up of dangerously large wing loads by providing a stick force which built up progressively with increasing 'g'. However, despite the restriction of wing loading, dangerous values of tail load could still occur due to sudden movements of the elevator, so a further preventative in the form of a tail load restrictor was installed.

This latter device was operated by deflection of the tailplane spar, which was dependent upon tail load. The tail load restrictor acted as a rigid lock on the elevator movement in the following way. On obtaining a predetermined tailplane spar deflection in either direction, a microswitch was operated which closed an electrical circuit energising an electromagnetically operated hydraulic valve. Operation of this valve prevented the flow of fluid to and from the elevator power unit jack, thus rigidly locking the piston in the jack.

The application of powered controls gave the Lancaster rather the same borderline stability of the skittish Spitfire. So artificial spring feel was incorporated to provide control self-centering and restore some of the original ladylike qualities to the bomber.

It must be appreciated that this work at RAE Farnborough on the Lancaster took place in the immediate post-war years as part of a research programme aimed at getting Britain back into the civil transport game. However, to me the most enjoyable part of that programme was when the noble Lancaster was in the guise of a fighter. I can imagine that a daylight low level raid over Germany in that particular version would have been a truly exhilarating experience.

Following close on the heels of the powered-controls Lancaster I, PP755, came the RAE designed servo-tab control Lancaster II, DS708. Servo-tab controls are a possible alternative to powered controls on very large aircraft and were satisfactorily used on the American Douglas B-19 and B-36 heavy bombers and on the German Bv 222 and Bv 238 large flying boats.

Perhaps the simplest way to appreciate the principle of this method of control is to remember that it is possible to release the controls of a normal aircraft and fly it (within limits) on the trimmers. Using large and more powerful tabs makes this method more practicable. If the con-

Aero Flight, RAE Farnborough, with a servo-tab Lancaster II in the background. Eric Brown is in naval uniform in the front row.

Avro Lancaster 1
Four 1280hp Rolls-Royce Merlin XX Motors

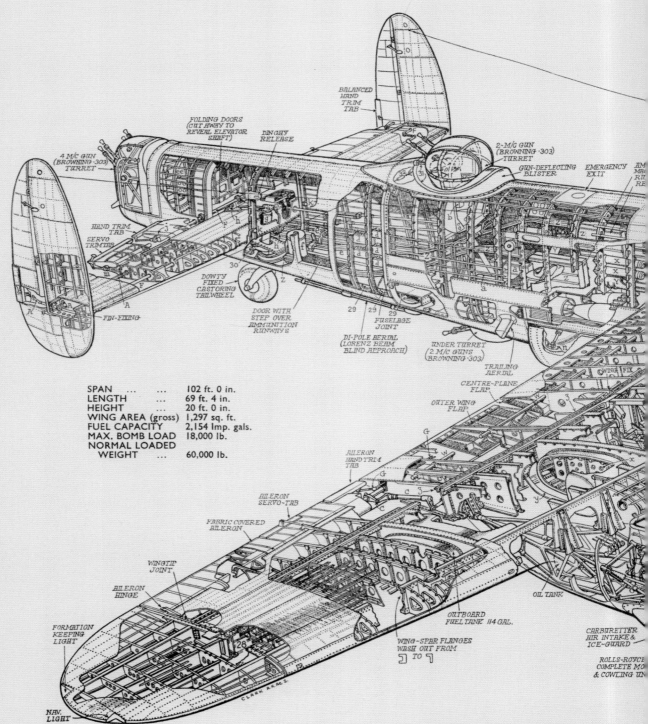

SPAN	102 ft. 0 in.	
LENGTH ...	69 ft. 4 in.	
HEIGHT ...	20 ft. 0 in.	
WING AREA (gross)	1,297 sq. ft.	
FUEL CAPACITY	2,154 Imp. gals.	
MAX. BOMB LOAD	18,000 lb.	
NORMAL LOADED		
WEIGHT ...	60,000 lb.	

A. Rudder and elevator trim.
B. Control column **stops and** seat raising cam.
C. Aileron control.
D. Throttle controls.
E. Rudder bars.
F. Rudder and elevator control rods.
G. Aileron trim cables to screw rod.

H. Service piping along bomb bay.
J. Parachute stowage (end of Nav. Table).
K. Oxygen bottle stowages.
L. Observer's window blister.
M. Bomb lock units in floor.
N. Longeron joint flanges and holes.
P. Spar flange reinforcement.
Q. Hydraulic reservoir.
R. Signal pistol.
S. Armoured doors.
T. Rest bunk and 15 oxygen bottles underneath

U. Spar webs extended into former frames.
V. Spar flanges.
W. Flap op. cylinder and op. rods.
X. Reconnaissance flares.
Y. Flare chute shown stowed *and in position*.
Z. Tail gun ammunition magazine and runway.
a. Under-turret magazines.
b. Top turret magazines.
d. Vacuum flasks stowages.
e. Dead-man's handle (puts rear turret fo
    and aft to extricate gunner throu
    sliding door).

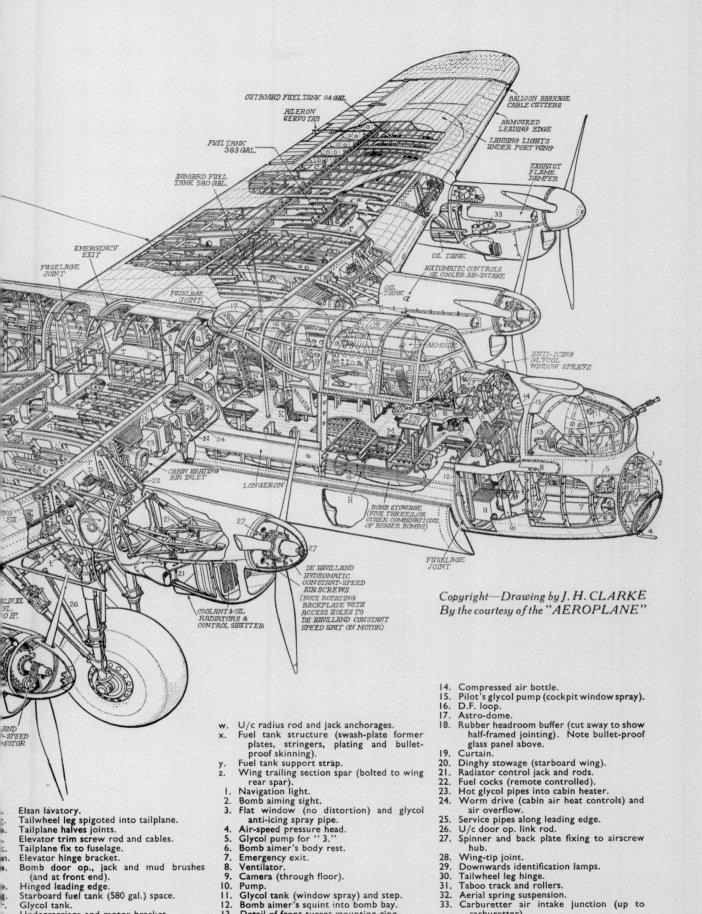

OUTBOARD FUEL TANK 114 GAL.

AILERON SERVO TAB

FUEL TANK 383 GAL.

INBOARD FUEL TANK 580 GAL.

BALLOON BARRAGE CABLE CUTTERS

ARMOURED LEADING EDGE

LANDING LIGHTS UNDER PORT WING

EXHAUST FLAME DAMPER

EMERGENCY EXIT

FUSELAGE JOINT

FUSELAGE JOINT

OIL TANK

AUTOMATIC CONTROLS OIL COOLER AIR-INTAKE

OIL TANK

ANTI-ICING GLYCOL WINDOW SPRAYS

ARMOUR

2ND PILOT

CABIN HEATING AIR INLET

LONGERON

BOMB STOWAGE (FIVE THREES, OR OTHER COMBINATIONS OF BIGGER BOMBS)

FUSELAGE JOINT

DE HAVILLAND HYDROMATIC CONSTANT-SPEED AIR SCREWS (NOTE ROTATING BACKPLATE WITH ACCESS HOLES TO DE HAVILLAND CONSTANT SPEED UNIT ON MOTOR)

COOLANT & OIL RADIATORS & CONTROL SHUTTER

MERLIN XX CYL. O H.P.

Copyright—Drawing by J. H. CLARKE
By the courtesy of the "AEROPLANE"

w. U/c radius rod and jack anchorages.
x. Fuel tank structure (swash-plate former plates, stringers, plating and bullet-proof skinning).
y. Fuel tank support strap.
z. Wing trailing section spar (bolted to wing rear spar).
1. Navigation light.
2. Bomb aiming sight.
3. Flat window (no distortion) and glycol anti-icing spray pipe.
4. Air-speed pressure head.
5. Glycol pump for "3."
6. Bomb aimer's body rest.
7. Emergency exit.
8. Ventilator.
9. Camera (through floor).
10. Pump.
11. Glycol tank (window spray) and step.
12. Bomb aimer's squint into bomb bay.
13. Detail of front turret mounting ring.

Elsan lavatory.
Tailwheel leg spigoted into tailplane.
Tailplane halves joints.
Elevator trim screw rod and cables.
Tailplane fix to fuselage.
Elevator hinge bracket.
Bomb door op., jack and mud brushes (and at front end).
Hinged leading edge.
Starboard fuel tank (580 gal.) space.
Glycol tank.
Undercarriage and motor bracket.

14. Compressed air bottle.
15. Pilot's glycol pump (cockpit window spray).
16. D.F. loop.
17. Astro-dome.
18. Rubber headroom buffer (cut away to show half-framed jointing). Note bullet-proof glass panel above.
19. Curtain.
20. Dinghy stowage (starboard wing).
21. Radiator control jack and rods.
22. Fuel cocks (remote controlled).
23. Hot glycol pipes into cabin heater.
24. Worm drive (cabin air heat controls) and air overflow.
25. Service pipes along leading edge.
26. U/c door op. link rod.
27. Spinner and back plate fixing to airscrew hub.
28. Wing-tip joint.
29. Downwards identification lamps.
30. Tailwheel leg hinge.
31. Taboo track and rollers.
32. Aerial spring suspension.
33. Carburetter air intake junction (up to carburetter).

trols are to be left free all the time they can be disconnected from the control wheel and rudder pedals, which may be used instead (since they are more convenient to use than trimmer controls) to control the operating circuits.

Servo-tab controls are actually spring-tab controls with the spring omitted. Hence the experience gained in the development of spring tabs, especially as regards prevention of flutter, could be applied directly to servo-tab systems.

The servo-tab control surfaces designed for the Lancaster differed from the standard controls in that they were all of metal construction; that the trailing edge of the rudder, the nose of the ailerons, and the outboard tip of the elevator, had been slightly modified; and that all were fitted with large tabs extending over about 80% of the control span.

These tabs, not the main control surfaces, were connected to the cockpit controls. The main control surfaces were quite free to move between the limits set by their shock-absorbing stops. Since fitting the large tabs produced a slight decrease in control effectiveness, the control travels were increased to compensate for this.

On an aircraft of Lancaster size, tab-operating forces were so small that they were quite inadequate to provide the pilot with feel, this being swallowed up in the control circuit friction. Artificial feel was therefore provided in the form

of centering springs on the pilot's controls. This spring feel was trimmable by means of the ordinary trimmer box, so that the aircraft could be flown hands off with the controls in any desired position. Provision was also made for pre-loading the springs to offset the frictional resistance to control self-centering. This artificial feel varied only with control displacement, not with speed, so that the controls felt very much lighter than usual at high speeds and care had to be exercised to avoid coarse use of the controls under these conditions.

On 19 December 1947 I made the first flight on DS708, fitted with servo-tab rudders. The follow-up ratio of tab to rudder was 1 : 1 and the lightest spring feel available was used with the introduction of a 120lb (54.4kg) centering spring on the pilot's control. I chose this spring loading to offer the lightest foot load to combat possible engine-cut at take-off.

This was a most successful flight and little subsequent alterations to the system on this control had to be made except to change the follow-up ratio to 0 : 1, thus having a pure servo-tab system with no mechanical relationship at all between pedal and rudder positions, and the tab angle being a function only of pedal movement.

On 27 July 1948 I made the first flight with the servo-tab ailerons fitted, and on 1 April 1949 the first flight with the servo-tab elevators. Thus this

Avro Lancaster II (LL735) Beryl testbed in flight, 25 March 1948. *RAF Museum Hendon.*

Avro Lancaster B.I (PP687). *RAF Museum Hendon.*

Lancasters forming up on the way to attack targets in Germany.

17

Pilot's notes: Avro Lancaster I

Fig 1:
Instrument Panel

1 Instrument flying panel
2 DF indicator
3 Landing light switches
4 Undercarriage indicator switch
5 DR compass repeater
6 DR compass deviation card holder
7 Ignition switches
8 Booster gauges
9 Rpm indicators
10 Booster coil switch
11 Slow-running cut-out switches
12 IFF detonator buttons
13 IFF switch
14 Engine starter switches
15 Bomb containers jettison button
16 Bomb jettison control
17 Vacuum change-over cock
18 Oxygen regulator
19 Feathering buttons
20 Triple pressure gauge
21 Signalling switchbox (identification lamps)
22 Fire-extinguisher push-buttons
23 Suction gauge
24 Starboard master engine cocks
25 Supercharger gear change control panel
26 Flaps position indicator
27 Flaps position indicator switch
28 Throttle levers
29 Propeller speed control levers
30 Port master engine cocks
31 Rudder pedal
32 Boost control cut-out
33 Signalling switchbox (recognition lights)
34 Identification lights colour selector switches
35 DR compass switches
36 Auto controls steering lever
37 P4 compass deviation cardholder
38 P4 compass
39 Undercarriage position indicator
40 ASI correction card hold
41 Beam approach indicator
42 Watch holder

Fig 2:
Port side of cockpit

43 Bomb doors control
44 Navigation lights switch
45 D switch
46 Auto controls main switch
47 Push-button unit for TR 1196
48 Seat raising lever
49 Mixing box
50 Beam approach control unit
51 Oxygen connection
52 Pilot's call light
53 Auto controls attitude control
54 Auto controls cock
55 Auto controls clutch
56 Brake lever
57 Auto controls pressure gauge
58 Pilot's mic/tel socket
59 Windscreen de-icing pump
60 Flaps selector
61 Aileron trimming tab control
62 Elevator trimming tab control
63 Rudder trimming tab control
64 Undercarriage control lever
65 Undercarriage control safety bolt
66 Portable oxygen stowage
67 Harness release lever

Fig 3:
Flight engineer's panel Lancasters I & III

68 Ammeter
69 Oil pressure gauges
70 Pressure-head heater switch
71 Oil temperature gauges
72 Coolant temperature gauges
74 Fuel contents gauges
75 Inspection lamp socket
76 Fuel contents gauge switch
77 Fuel tanks selector cocks
78 Electric fuel booster pump switches
79 Fuel pressure warning lights
80 Emergency air control
81 Oil dilution buttons

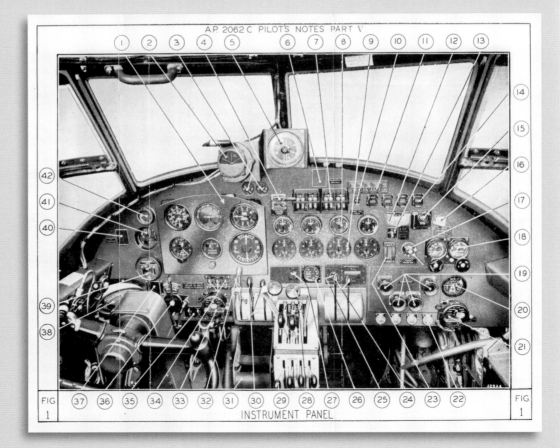

A.P. 2062 C PILOT'S NOTES PART V

FIG 1 INSTRUMENT PANEL FIG 1

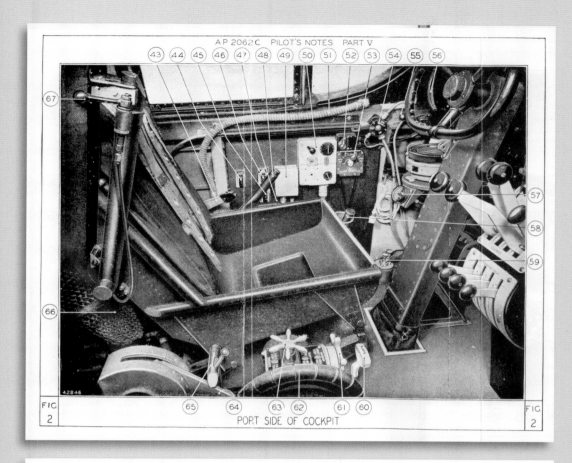

PORT SIDE OF COCKPIT

FIG 2

FLIGHT ENGINEER'S PANEL, LANCASTERS I AND III

FIG 3

The Bristol Brabazon. Early in 1949 Eric Brown started work on the new control system for the giant plane. It was tried out at RAE for the first time on a Lancaster I.

latter was the first flight of the fully servo-tab equipped Lancaster.

Again this was a totally successful experiment and like the powered-controls Lancaster gave an important benefit besides light and effective controls. This was a reduction of some 10mph in safety speed for dealing with an outboard engine failure on take-off – a critical factor in meeting civil airworthiness requirements.

How then did the two systems compare? There was little to choose between them, but to my mind the powered controls had the edge over the servo-tabs. Both gave superb harmony of control but caused a deterioration in stability; the latter could be improved artificially. It was obvious that the powered-controls hydraulic system would have to be duplicated or even triplicated for civil

use, because its failure in the Lancaster meant a reversion to manual control. This necessitated the pilot moving the hydraulic jacks and so gave him a very heavy work load, which made control marginal in turbulent air conditions, particularly for landing.

In the event the powered controls were chosen for the Bristol Brabazon, Britain's first major post-war venture into civil air transport design. In May 1949 I flew Lancaster III RE131, which was the powered controls test bed for the very large Brabazon.

Actually, my only regret is that the powered controls could not have been fitted to the Lancaster II, which was my favourite mark of Lancaster. Then one would have been having the best of both worlds, an aeroplane without peer in its class.

Avro Lancaster B.II, DS626/KO•J, No.115 Squadron RAF, Wretham, March 1943. © *Richard Caruana* (scale 1:144).

2 AVRO TUDOR

The spark of genius that produced the magnificent Lancaster failed to ignite in the Tudor, which exacted a grim penalty for that failure.

ERIC BROWN

Britain's preparations for a return to civil air transport operations after the Second World War were broadly based on the conversion of military types of aeroplane in the short term and some new designs, such as the Bristol Brabazon, in the longer term.

The North Atlantic had been a busy ferry route for large bombers, flying boats, and coastal reconnaissance aircraft during the war, and its potential as a commercial civil air route largely dictated the design of the Brabazon. But the latter was still a little way off and so an interim type was likely to be needed, specifically tailored to the route. Thus it was that the Tudor was born, making its first flight on 14 June 1945.

The Tudor I was the first British pressurised transport, and from the start it was in trouble. It suffered from directional and longitudinal instability, pre-stall buffeting at a relatively high speed, violent rudder oscillation at moderate angles, severe take-off swing, loss in performance from that estimated, and a tendency to bounce on landing.

The instability troubles were solved by fitting a larger fin and rudder and larger tailplane and elevators. But the real crunch was the performance loss which reduced the still air range from an

Avro Tudor IV (G-AHNN), of British South American Airways, in flight, 9 February 1948. *RAF Museum Hendon.*

estimated 4,000 (6437km) miles to an actual 3,600 (5793km) miles and so made the Tudor a non-starter for the Atlantic route.

It was at this point that the RAE Farnborough was called in to help, and Tudor I, G-AGRD, arrived there in the summer of 1946. This aircraft had already been fitted with the large tail empennage when I first flew it on 20 July. In addition it had been deep tufted at the RAE for airflow investigation, i.e. wool tufts were placed on masts at set distances from the aircraft skin on the whole upper surface of both wings, on one side of the body from the position of the wing maximum thickness down to the tailplane, including the fin-tailplane junction, on the top and bottom surface of the tailplane and elevator, and on one side of the fin and rudder. A trailing static was also fitted – this is like a small bomb on the end of 100ft (30m) of tubing, which transmits an airspeed reading free from all turbulence created by the aircraft.

In the next few days I carried out intensive stalling tests and encountered such violent pre-stall buffeting that the trailing static was beaten to pulp – but not before we discovered that the stall previously reported by the A&AEE, Boscombe

Down, was not the true stall. I found that by being extremely careful to prevent the pre-stall porpoising from building up, the speed could be lowered much below the previously reported minimum speeds, through intense and almost dangerous buffeting until a wing drop occurred.

Our observations showed that the apparent stall was caused by a deep and violent wing root breakaway of airflow, the resultant violent wake passing over the tail end of the aircraft. It was considered by RAE that the obvious cure was to improve the wing root filleting. A new and large fillet, designed by Avro, was therefore fitted to another Tudor, G-AGST, which I first flew at Farnborough on 8 August 1946 on stall tests.

The qualitative tests seemed to indicate that the large fillet had been successful in curing the premature buffeting trouble in that there was now only 2–5mph (1.2–3km/h) between the onset of buffeting and the stall as indicated by the wing drop. Quantitative measurements, however, showed a very different state of affairs, because the stalling speeds had increased up to 10mph above those recorded before. It thus became clear we were dealing with two separate effects, viz. changes in inner wing condition lead-

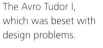

The Avro Tudor I, which was beset with design problems.

The ill-fated prototype of the Tudro II which crashed on take-off on 23 August 1947, killing Roy Chadwick and Bill Thorn. In the background is the Tudor I.

ing to changes in the speeds at which buffeting occurred, and changes in outer wing condition leading to changes in the speed at which the wing drop stall occurred.

The inner wing problem involved considerable trial and error before it was pinpointed to a very small airleak around the leading edge of the wing root causing a breakaway of flow, the resultant wake of which hit the tailplane.

The early wing-tip stalling cause was easier to locate as due to small malfitment of the wing leading-edge de-icers spoiling the aerofoil contour.

The rudder oscillation phenomenon was first experienced during tests on G-AGRD to determine the adequacy of the directional control in the engine cut condition. As rudder angle was increased, especially when trimmer was wound on to trim out the rudder pedal loads, at a certain rudder angle violent kicking occurred on the rudder pedals. This had the effect of raising the engine cut safety speed, as rudder angles above those at which kicking started could not be used.

The problem was soon traced to bad flow, initiated by sharp edges at the rear of the three hinge cut-outs projecting out into the airstream, as rudder was applied. Modifications to G-AGST cured the trouble and reduced the engine cut safety speed from 150mph (241km/h) to 115mph (185km/h) at 80,000lb (36,288kg) all-up weight.

The difficulty in controlling take-off swing, especially in a cross-wind, was mainly during the initial period of the take-off run which was long, due to poor acceleration, and aileron snatch and elevator buffet were experienced. Examination of the deep tufting on G-AGST during a take-off run showed clearly that the whole wing was completely stalled in the ground attitude; the ground incidence was 14½°. Once the tail lifted, the airflow over the rear body began to clear. These flow conditions accounted for the poor initial ground acceleration, but the root cause of the trouble was the insufficient rudder power available for corrective action.

The cure for the take-off swing problem was a shortened undercarriage to decrease wing incidence on the ground, and increase in rudder power resulting from the modifications to the rudder hinge cut-outs.

The deep tufting technique revealed another trouble spot on the Tudor, whose original inner-engine nacelles had been of the Lancaster type, extending to the trailing-edge of the wing. But these had been shortened to finish at the flap hinge to eliminate vibration troubles. The new nacelles were observed at RAE to have a complete breakaway of flow round their rather bluff ends.

The turbulence of flow occurred over the whole speed range, and obviously the drag would adversely affect performance. RAE then extended the inner nacelles some 18–24in (46–61cm) behind the trailing edge. These showed no sign of any flow breakaway over the speed range from slow cruising to top speed, and the vibration level was lowered appreciably from either of the other two nacelle designs.

On the 24 October 1946 I flew G-AGST back to the Avro airfield at Woodford. Although it had all the improvements recommended by RAE fitted to it, I sensed instinctively that we had only patched up an inherently bad design, and that the Tudor was a loser. In the event British Overseas Airways Corporation shared this view and rejected the type by cancelling their order. Four of the cancelled aircraft were taken over by British South American Airways Corporation.

In April and May 1947 I was again engaged on tests on G-AGRD to see if the new wing de-icing system had improved the stalling characteristics.

Since the Tudor I only carried 12 passengers, its commercial viability on that score alone was in question, so a stretched version was built to carry 60 passengers. This Tudor II was the largest aircraft so far produced in the United Kingdom, but the increase in structural weight resulting from the stretching process reduced performance drastically, in spite of uprated Merlin 600 Special engines.

The Tudor II had an inauspicious start when the prototype G-AGSU crashed on take-off from Woodford on 23 August 1947, killing Roy Chadwick, the Avro Chief Designer, and Bill Thorn, the Avro Chief Test Pilot. The crash was due to the incorrect assembly of the aileron circuit, whereby movements of the control wheel gave the reverse wing movement to that normally expected.

The next accident in the saga of Tudor disasters was the unexplained loss of the BSAAC Tudor 4 *Star Tiger* north-east of Bermuda on the night of 29/30 January 1948.

Meanwhile I renewed acquaintance with the Tudor I when G-AGRI came to Farnborough in July 1948 for a series of compressibility dives to assess the suitability of the airframe for fitting with jet engines. There were a few grim faces around the RAE at the prospect of doing a job reserved for high-speed fighters to date, but I must admit the challenge rather intrigued me.

It had been estimated that a Tudor fitted with four Nene engines for high altitude research purposes could have a maximum cruising speed of 435mph (700km/h) true air speed at 40,000ft (12,192m), equivalent to a Mach number of 0.654. It might therefore experience some of the compressibility phenomena such as large changes of trim, tail buffeting, pitching, oscillations, etc. As the ceiling of the Merlin-engined Tudor I was limited to about 31,000ft (9,449mm) the combination of lift coefficient and Mach number required could only be obtained by diving to reach the appropriate Mach number and apply-

ing 'g' in a pull out to attain the required lift coefficient. At an all-up weight of 61,000lb (27,670kg) for the tests the estimated ultimate breaking 'g' was 4.35.

For the tests I had a co-pilot, flight engineer, and a flight test observer. The drill I adopted was to find the trimmer settings which would trim the aircraft at the maximum indicated air speeds of the dives when flying at 5,000ft (1,524m). The aircraft was climbed to 31,000ft (9,449mm) and cruised at maximum continuous power until airspeed had built up to a steady value and the predetermined trim values set on the trimmers. The aircraft was then eased into a dive and the flight engineer set the engines to 2,850rpm with the supercharger in FS gear and the radiator shutters closed.

During the dive through several thousand feet, the co-pilot had his hands lightly on the control wheel to assist if I experienced any unmanageable control loads, either due to compressibility effects or to execute the required pull-out 'g'. In the event the Tudor behaved perfectly up to a maximum true Mach number of 0.67 and a subsequent pull-out of 2.25'g'. These values well exceeded what was required of the tests, so for once the Tudor had excelled itself.

Bad luck still dogged this unfortunate aircraft with the loss of *Star Ariel* between Bermuda and Jamaica on 17 January 1949 – again in unexplained circumstances. As a result BSAAC converted its Tudor 4s to freighters for the Berlin Air Lift and did 261 sorties on this operation, while seven Tudor 5s flew 3,167 sorties in the tanker role.

These latter aircraft were refurbished for passenger work after the Berlin crisis and G-AKBY crashed at Llandow on 12 March 1950 when approaching to land after a charter trip from Dublin with a load of Welsh rugby supporters. The loss of 80 lives made this the biggest air disaster in the UK up to that time. The accident cause was determined to be incorrect loading.

This was virtually the end of a history of tragedy surrounding an aircraft that came from the same design team responsible for the magnificent Lancaster. The spark of genius failed to ignite in the Tudor, which exacted a grim penalty for that failure.

3 BELL AIRACOBRA

Not very popular with the masses, but the Russians and I loved it for our own quirky reasons. ERIC BROWN

THE AIRACOBRA was produced by the Bell Aircraft Corporation in 1939 and incorporated many engineering innovations. The fighter's single twelve-cylinder liquid-cooled engine was located behind the pilot and drove the airscrew through an extension shaft beneath the pilot to a reduction gear box in the nose. A 20mm cannon fired through the hollow airscrew shaft. The aircraft was also fitted with a tricycle undercarriage, which was an unusual feature for those days.

When I joined Naval Aircraft Flight at RAE Farnborough in 1944 I came across Airacobra, AH574, with an arrester hook fitted to investigate the reactions of arresting a tricycle aircraft. This was because on picking up an arrester wire there is a considerable forward pitching movement which would have to be absorbed by the long stalky nose-leg of the undercarriage. At that time there were no British tricycle naval aircraft.

I first flew AH574 on 13 April 1944. This was to be the beginning of a long association with the Airacobra, because it virtually became my own private hack – as well as contributing its own little pieces to naval aviation history.

The cockpit was unusual in that it had car type doors and windows, a non-adjustable pilot's seat and a lot of armour plating. Because of the fixed seat I found the view ahead was poor for a pilot of my stature, but in spite of this I developed a deep affection for the Airacobra and we flew all over the UK and the Continent, often in filthy weather and over long stretches of sea. It never gave me a moment's trouble. Certainly it attracted a lot of attention wherever it went for, as a naval aircraft, it was unique.

The Bell Airacobra I, a type used extensively by Eric Brown as a personal transport.

Pilot's notes: Bell Airacobra I

Fig 2:
Top half – Instrument panel

1 Altimeter
2 Compass correction card holder
2A Altimeter correction card holder
3 Turn indicator
4 Rate of climb indicator
5 Gun charging handles (.30 calibre port plane guns)
6 Airspeed indicator
7 Fuselage .50 calibre gun
8 Gun sight rheostat
9 Turn and bank indicator
10 Artificial horizon
11 Gun charging handles (.30 calibre starboard plane guns)
12 Compass
13 Gun sight
14 Armourglass
15 Ring sight
16 Rear vision mirror
17 .50 calibre gun charging handle
18 Gun selector switch
19 Alighting gear switch
20 Flap switch
65 Light
66 Light

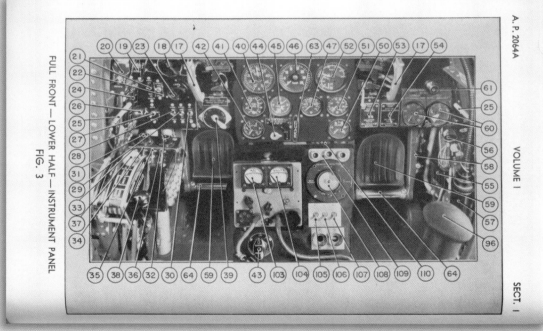

STARBOARD FRONT VIEW — INSTRUMENT PANEL
FIG. 5

PORT SIDE OF COCKPIT
FIG. 6

Fig 3:

Lower half – Instrument panel

17 .50 calibre gun charging handle
18 Gun selector switch
19 Alighting gear switch
20 Flap switch
21 Airscrew master switch
22 Cannon hydraulic pump switch
23 Ammeter
24 Alighting gear and flap travel indicator
25 Cabin door emergency release
26 Throttle
27 Airscrew automatic or manual selector switch
28 Cabin heater switch
29 Pitot head heater switch
30 Oil dilution valve switch
31 Formation light, rheostat
32 Directional instrument rheostat
33 Instrument lights

34 Cabin lights
35 Navigation lights
36 Landing light
37 Mixture control lever
38 Airscrew speed control
39 Ignition and battery switch
40 Engine manifold pressure
41 Fuel gauge unit (electric)
42 Suction gauge
43 Engine fuel primer pump
44 Cannon charging control
45 Clock
46 Tachometer
47 Reduction gear oil pressure
50 Fuel pressure (engine)
51 Engine coolant temperature gauge
52 Engine oil temperature and pressure gauge
53 Selector valve (pitot tube) alternate pressure source

54 Selector valve (bank and turn indicator); alternate vacuum source
55 Recognition flare release (damped rate control)
56 Identification light switch
57 Fluorescent lamp
58 Rudder pedal adjustment latch
59 Brake pedal
60 Oxygen regulator valve and indicator
61 Heater damper control
63 Parking brake handle
64 Rudder bar
96 Control column grip
103 Milli-ammeter
104 Voltmeter
105 Switch to power supply
106 Switch to radio
107 Switch to contactor
108 Contactor – remote type
109 Fuse panel
110 Fuses (spare)

Fig 5:

Starboard front view – Instrument panel

13 Gun sight
25 Cabin door emergency release
55 Recognition flare release (damped rate control)
56 Identification light switch
57 Fluorescent lamp
60 Oxygen regulator valve and indicator
62 Mixture control release
66 Light
78 Wobble pump control
95 Door handle
96 Control column grip
97 Control column trigger switch
98 Control column
99 Engine starter switch
100 Flare release control
111 'ON' connector
115 Socket, WT, telephones

Fig 6:

Port side of cockpit

67 Map case
68 Radio aerial mast
69 Radio control plug (stowed)
70 Cabin ventilator control damper
71 Pilot's safety harness
72 Safety harness control mechanism
82 Trim tab control mounting
85 Plug for radio control
86 Light

Bell Airacobra Mk I (P-400), AH576/UF, No. 601 Squadron RAF, while it was detached to Reid & Sigrist Ltd for trials, August 1941. © *Richard Caruana* (Scale 1:48).

Bell P-39D Airacobra AH574 was one of the first received under Lend-Lease. Originally used for airflow trials, it was essentially redundant until fitted with an arrester hook from a Grumman Martlet. It was used for catapult trials at Farnborough in 1944 in connection with early naval jet fighter development; during these it was successfully landed on HMS *Pretoria Castle*. *Barry Ketley.*

The features I remember most about this little fighter were its neat self-contained electric engine starter. This was a rocker foot pedal pressed down with the heel for twenty seconds to energise the starter motor, then pushed with the toe to engage the engine. The subsequent vibration of the extension shaft whenever the engine was running could be constantly felt under one's seat and there was a peculiar tuck under of the nose if too much 'g' was pulled at the top of a loop. On this latter point I had been led to believe that the Airacobra could tumble head over heels if mis-handled in the vertical plane, due to the unusual weight distribution caused by a centrally situated engine.

Our first little bit of history making together occurred on 30 June 1944, when I carried out the first catapult launching of a tricycle aircraft in Great Britain. Then, on 28 March 1945, I used AH574 to start to develop the approach technique for the flexible deck project, which was aimed at landing an undercarriageless aeroplane on what was virtually a rubber carpet. The technique involved a final flat run-in to the deck at a height of five feet above its surface. In order to check with what accuracy and regularity of judgement a pilot could fly above a runway surface, I did a series of trials, flying along Farnborough's main runway with the Airacobra's undercarriage lowered in case of inadvertent ground contact. The photographs showed my height was always ±3in. of the intended height above the runway.

The next stage involved taking the Airacobra to the eventual intended scene of action – the flight deck of an aircraft carrier. Now officialdom had ruled that the Airacobra was not to be deck-landed because its car door access to the cockpit would give the pilot a slim chance of survival in the event of a ditching.

On 4 April 1945 I made a series of eight simulated flexible deck approaches to the deck of the trials carrier HMS *Pretoria Castle*. On completion of the eighth run I requested permission to make a landing in emergency. It was a measure of the understanding I had with Captain Caspar John, under whom I had served previously on *Pretoria Castle*, that I was not asked to declare what 'the emergency' was, but given immediate clearance to land on. Thus the navalised Airacobra made its first – and its only – deck landing and so fulfilled its destiny by being the first tricycle aircraft to land on a British aircraft carrier.

Without any further mention of 'the emergency' the flight deck crew released the Airacobra from the arrester wire, stowed the hook, and pushed the aircraft right to the stern so I could prepare for take-off. This was going to be the nail-biting part of the action, for the *Pretoria Castle* flight deck was only 594ft (181m) long and she was only capable of 20mph (31km/h) – and there was very little natural wind. The Airacobra had a longish take-off run, and of course had to be rotated from the ground attitude to get the lift for unstick.

The one and only carrier deck landing by an Airacobra, AH574, on 4 April 1945.

The Airacobra safely arrested on HMS *Pretoria Castle*.

I set the flaps one-quarter down, and then, with my feet firmly on the brakes, wound up AH574's slightly weary engine to its full 2,800rpm and 42in Hg. boost. The latter had to be manually controlled by throttle movement as this aircraft had no automatic boost control fitted. On releasing the brakes the Airacobra accelerated slowly and showed no great urge to reach take-off speed as the bows of the ship were approached. Indeed, I can only say that we fell off rather than took-off, and as we sank in level attitude I gently eased the stick back until, to my relief, I felt the sink change to a barely perceptible rate of climb. I have a suspicion that my relief was shared by Captain Caspar John (later Admiral of the Fleet Sir Caspar John), who had already started swinging the ship as I disappeared from sight so as not to run over me if I had ditched.

From then on my Airacobra lived a compara-

tively peaceful existence, doing occasional landings into the arrester wires at Farnborough, and transporting me around the country. However, in March 1946 a Bell test pilot visited the RAE, spotted the old product of his company and expressed a wish to refamiliarise himself with the type.

He was only airborne 15 minutes, came back visibly shaken, and said he had never flown such a clapped-out aeroplane in his life. Well, he was entitled to his opinion, which he unfortunately committed to paper and so sounded old AH574's death knell. I did manage to persuade our engineers to let me have a farewell flight on 28 March, when I had a super fifty-minute session of aerobatics over Farnborough – just to show the old lady still had a kick in her. When I landed I can truly say it was with a heavy heart that I finally parted company with my old friend.

4 BELL AIRACOMET

Dull and ponderous, but a historic
first jet for the Americans. ERIC BROWN

THE BELL AIRACOMET was America's first jet aircraft and as such deserves some historical
background. The initiative in developing the
aeroplane was taken by Major-General H.H.
Arnold, Chief of the Army Air Force, who had
seen the Whittle jet engines under test in England
in April 1941 and had also seen the Gloster
E.28/39 shortly before its historic first flight.

On returning to the USA, General Arnold
started negotiations for America to acquire the
rights for General Electric to build and develop
the Whittle turbojet. On 4 September 1941, at a
meeting at Wright Field between the USAAF and
GE, a decision was made to proceed with the construction of fifteen engines and three airframes, to
be designed by the Bell Aircraft Corporation,
unknown to the latter, who were only informed
the next day.

Bell were probably chosen because they were
not overloaded with work, were close to General
Electric's facilities, and were fairly isolated from a
security stand-point. When informed of the decision next day they accepted a deadline to com-

plete the first prototype eight months after sign-
ing of the contract on 30 September 1941.

The primary purpose of the aircraft was to
investigate jet propulsion, but it was also to em-
body suitability for use as a fighter. The preliminary drawings were prepared in offices taken by
Bell in Buffalo, and prototype construction took
place in the Ford Motor Company building in the
same town.

The design had to go ahead without full details
of the design and performance data on the Type
I-A engine as it was designated by General
Electric. Bell's Model 27 was therefore fairly con-
servative in configuration, being a mid-wing
monoplane of relatively low aspect ratio with
laminar flow wing section. The engines were fitted in nacelles beneath the wing roots and flush
against the sides of the fuselage, thus giving
straight-through airflow. The fuselage was in two
sections, the forward section comprising the
armament bay and centre section, including the
cabin. The rear section was a stressed-skin semi-
monocoque construction.

America's first jet
aircraft, the ponderous
Airacomet.

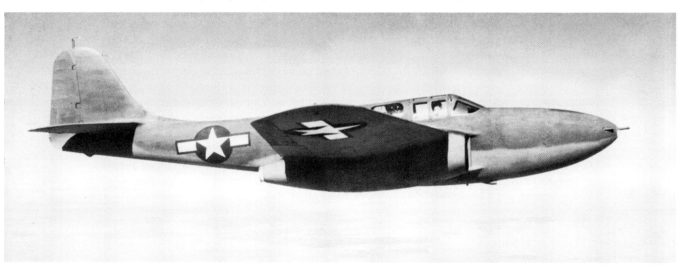

30

All control surfaces were fabric covered and manually operated, the ailerons being of the pressure-balance type with pressure seals. Aerodynamically balanced, fabric-covered flaps, located between the ailerons and the wing roots, were electrically operated. The cockpit was pressurised, and access was through a side-hinged canopy. Fuel was carried in four interconnected self-sealing fuel tanks in each wing, the total capacity being only 242gal (1,098 litres).

Before the idea of a jet fighter was mooted, Bell had a contract to build two prototypes of a twin-boom fighter with a piston-engine driving contra-rotating pusher propellers. The contract for this XP-59 aircraft was cancelled on 1 December 1941, and the designation XP-59A transferred to the jet fighter project, with the deliberate intention of misleading in order to preserve secrecy.

Construction of the XP-59A began in January 1942, and was completed in September. The aircraft was transported by rail to Muroc on 12 September, but only after a hole had been knocked out in the brick wall of the Ford building to allow the crated components to be removed in the early hours of the morning.

Muroc was located in the huge Rogers Dry Lake in a desert area of California, where aircraft could be operated without runways and in nor-

mally perfect weather conditions. This site was eventually to become the famous Edwards Air Force Base, Mecca of high speed and high altitude research test flying.

The XP-59A made its first flight on 1 October 1942 at a maximum height of 25ft (7.6m) with the undercarriage down. Altogether eight graduated flights were made on 1 and 2 October up to a maximum height of 10,000ft (3,050m). Thereafter the test programme slowed down considerably due to engine development problems with the two 1,300lb (590kg) static thrust General Electric I-A turbojets, and also by some unscheduled moves to other airfields, caused by unprecedented flooding of Rogers Dry Lake.

The second prototype flew on 15 February 1943 and the third late in April. On 26 March 1943 a batch of 13YP-59As were ordered for service tests, and these had rearward-sliding canopies and were intended to have the 1,650lb (748kg) static thrust 1-16 (J31-GE-3) engines. The first nine aircraft were to have the same armament of two 37mm M4 cannon in the nose as had been fitted to the second and third prototypes. The last four YP-59As were to have one 37mm cannon and three 0.50 inch machine-guns in the nose.

The first YP-59A reached Muroc in June 1943

The primary purpose
of the Airacomet was
to investigate jet
propulsion.

and the USAAF adopted the name Airacomet. The third YP-59A was shipped to Britain and assembled by Gloster at Moreton Valance, where it was flown by a Bell test pilot on 28 September 1943.

This Airacomet RJ362/G was transferred to RAE Farnborough on 5 November 1943. When I joined the RAE in January 1944 it was in the top secret Jet Flight, but had flown very little because of unserviceability and lack of spares. Indeed I was not even aware that such an aircraft existed until mid-1944 when I was invited to join the Jet Flight.

This high state of security at Farnborough was strictly applied to aircraft whose serial number was followed by /G (Guard). Only specially vetted flight and maintenance personnel were allowed near them, and they mostly seemed to fly in the early morning or late evening, when of course still air conditions are often at an optimum for certain types of testing. They also flew a lot at weekends when the airfield was comparatively quiet. Not only was this to keep the jets from local prying eyes on the airfield, but also to keep them from prying enemy reconnaissance aircraft. Another feature that influenced the operation of the early jets in the quiet hours, was their high incidence of

engine problems, and an inactive airfield presented an ideal emergency landing area.

Usually a special air traffic controller with a 'boffin' (scientist) at his elbow were the only personnel in the control tower during such flights, and I know that it was generally believed that they were not logged in the normal Air Traffic Control Log.

When I first saw the Airacomet I was rather disappointed with the appearance of it, which seemed to me to be of uninspiring design. The people of Buffalo, the home of the Airacomet's birth, which lies close to the honeymooning Mecca of the Niagara Falls, say that the Falls are the American bride's second disappointment. Well, flying this product of Buffalo was my second disappointment because it flew as uninspiringly as it looked.

The purpose of my being given a flight on this aircraft was ostensibly to assess its potential as a runner in the selection process for the first jet aircraft to undertake landing trials on an aircraft carrier, but I do not believe anything but a British aeroplane would have been accepted for such a prestigious event.

In the event the Airacomet proved to be badly underpowered, with an unacceptably long take-off run. In the air it had satisfactory longitudinal and lateral stability, but snaked very badly directionally. The controls were heavy although reasonably effective.

In order to burn off fuel for the landing assessment I took the opportunity to climb the aircraft to 32,000ft (9,754m), which took nearly 10 minutes. After a level full-power run with slow acceleration I put it into a 40 degree dive, but on reaching a Mach no. of only 0.74 the aircraft developed such a strong nose-up pitch it could no longer be held in the dive. Not very exciting.

At 20,000ft (6,096m) with 60% power the cruising speed was only 298mph (480km/h).

The landing characteristics were straightforward, but there was a lack of drag so that the approach at 100mph was flat and consequently a lot of float occurred before touchdown when the power was cut. The lack of drag was largely due to the absence of dive brakes, and that absence was obviously a reflection on the Airacomet's anticipated mediocre performance. The view was certainly not on a par with the other three jets in the Jet Flight stable at that time – the Gloster E.28/39, the de Havilland Spider Crab (later renamed Vampire), and the Gloster Meteor.

All four aircraft suffered from poor engine acceleration characteristics, which were attributable to the state of jet engine development in those early days. However, engine response would be a critical factor in the carrier trials both for lift control and for the baulked landing case, so the jet rpm would have to be kept in the high percentage range. This would only be possible by having a high drag configuration in the approach, but this drag should be capable of rapid disposal such as by closing of dive brakes.

The Airacomet, as expected, was therefore the least favourable choice and so was ruled out of consideration after that flight.

Obviously the Airacomet was a ponderous aeroplane. But one must consider that Bell went into this first ever design of a jet aircraft with minimal data about the power units to be used, so this historic aircraft was at least a safe test bed for a still rather temperamental form of propulsion. In that respect it served a useful purpose.

At 20,000ft (6,096m) the cruising speed of the Airacomet was only 298mph (480km/h).

5 BELL KINGCOBRA

Bell upped the ante on the Airacobra, but not by much. ERIC BROWN

THIS STABLEMATE of my Airacobra was at RAE Farnborough for a very different task; indeed they were investigating opposite ends of the speed scale. The Kingcobra, which was basically a refined Airacobra, was allocated for boundary layer investigation on its low drag wing and this was to involve high speed dives into the transonic region.

The first Kingcobra to arrive was FR408, which was on short loan to check its suitability for the experiments RAE wished to carry out. I made my first flight on the type on 18 May 1944, and the short series of tests involved stalls with a trailing static and flights to check airflow transition on the low-drag laminar flow wing section.

These latter flights involved an interesting technique. The flights were made very early in the morning on days when there was virtually no wind over 5mph (8km/h) and when it was too cool for insects to be up and about, as a squashed

fly on the leading edge of the wing caused transition to occur very far forward on the wing chord. Just after take-off a boffin popped a chlorine gas canister into the cold furnace of the tall chimney, which was an RAE landmark, and I had just enough time to line up and fly through the gas trail issuing from the chimney stack. This involved flying within a few feet of the chimney top, having the aircraft as airtight as possible and also wearing an oxygen mask. But in spite of these precautions I often finished up with a splitting headache from the chlorine gas. The Kingcobra wing had been sprayed with a special chemical, which reacted to the chlorine and delineated the boundary layer transition point on the polished wing.

Unfortunately FR408 was involved in a landing accident when being flown on a familiarisation flight by another pilot, and so had to be replaced anyway by FZ440. The tests now started in

The sleek looking Kingcobra, FR408, on short loan to RAE, was allocated for boundary layer investigation on its low drag wing, involving high speed dives into the transonic region.

earnest and incredible smoothness of wing contour was attained by a team working under Bill Gray, the boffin in charge of the tests. The ultimate achieved was a smoothness of 1/5000th of an inch, and to protect this from possible insect contamination the test section of the wing, which had a width of 3ft 3in (1m), was covered by a sheet of paper stretched tightly round the leading edge and jettisoned from the cockpit at 5,000ft (1,524m) – this being the limit at which insects are normally found. The chlorine gas was now carried by a Miles Master, so that aspect of the test had become more flexible.

The high speed dives were made to assess compressibility effects and pressure plotting was by the standard method used in high speed research. The results were then tied in with the lower speed pressure plotting.

The overall object of this rather unusual series of experiments was to demonstrate that low drag laminar flow wings lose their design efficiency if their contour is destroyed by ground crew walking on them or dragging refuelling hoses over them. Even mud spattered on the leading edge or flies collected on take-off can double the wing drag, with a reduction in range of some 30 per cent. A new lesson to the military operators in 1947.

I flew my final sortie on the Kingcobra on 3 September 1948, and had the satisfaction of producing the best transition picture we got in a series of over fifty such flights.

A good view of the Kingcobra's laminar-flow wing.

A Russian based Kingcobra.

6 BOEING FLYING FORTRESS

A gentlemanly but lumbering aeroplane, whose much vaunted ability to look after itself proved a bit of a myth over European skies, where it raised the action level to 30,000ft. ERIC BROWN

THERE CAN BE FEWER aircraft more aptly named than the Flying Fortress with its full formidable armament of thirteen .50-inch calibre machine-guns. Two were in a remotely-controlled chin turret below the plastic bomb-aimer's nose; two in cheek mountings, one on either side of the plastic nose; two in an electrically-operated turret on top of the fuselage just aft of the pilot's cockpit; one manually-operated firing through the top of the fuselage above the radio-operator's compartment; two in a Sperry electrically-operated ball turret below the fuselage; two on hand-operated mountings and firing through the side ports, one on each side of the fuselage, midway between wings and tail; and two in the extreme tail.

This eventually elegant aeroplane was designed as a four-engined high-altitude day bomber, and later modified to meet the US Army Air Corps strategy of employing mass formations, flying in daylight above 30,000ft (9144m) over enemy territory and relying for defence on their height and

Fortresses, with their tell-tale contrails, on a daylight raid over enemy territory.

the mutual support of their enormous fire power. The original specification was issued in 1934.

The first flight was made on 28 July 1935, and the B-17C Fortress I delivered to the RAF differed considerably from the later B-17E Fortress II which was so familiar in the skies over England during World War II.

I was fortunate enough to fly the Mk I to fully appreciate the tremendous improvements that were to follow in later models. This aeroplane was assigned to the RAE Farnborough for various tests connected with flight above 30,000ft (9144m). These tests included turbo-supercharger handling, oxygen flow rates, and turret heating. Armament was only seven hand-trained machine-guns of 0.30 inch calibre.

I first flew AN531 on 14 July 1944 and I was astonished how inelegant it looked in comparison with the Fortress II then flying operationally over Europe. Entry was by the forward escape hatch in the fuselage floor, or via a small door in the starboard side just in front of the tailplane, then along a nine-inch catwalk with limited headroom.

Taxying was difficult because the rudder was greatly affected by side winds and indeed was un-manageable in a wind above 25mph (40km/h). Take-off was characterised by a marked swing to the left, but once airborne it was remarkably quiet inside the aircraft. One of our tests involved a three engine take-off and climb away, and this could be done quite comfortably. Indeed in the air the Fortress handled very well with only two engines running.

The controls were light and effective in cruising flight, but the elevators heavied up at high speed and in steep turns, so it would not have been a good aeroplane in which to try corkscrew evasive manoeuvres.

The B-17E Fortress II embodied a completely new rear fuselage with enlarged horizontal and tail surfaces, greatly increased armament, protective armour, and bullet-proof fuel tanks. The B-17E was designated the Fortress IIA in Britain, the B-17F was the Fortress II, and the B-17G was the Fortress III. All were powered by four 1,200hp Wright Cyclone R-1820-65 or R-1820-97 nine-

Flying Fortress Mk I, AN530, in service with 90 Squadron.

Boeing B-17 Flying Fortress B-17G-30-DL (42-38091) levelling off for a run over target. It is a later model and fitted with a chin turret carrying .50 calibre machine-guns.

cylinder radial air-cooled engines equipped with Hamilton Hydromatic propellers and turbo-super-chargers. The Mks II and IIA differed mainly in their hydraulic systems, and the Mk III had extra fuel tanks.

My comparison flight was made in Fortress III HB778, and the aircraft was bristling with guns. The cockpit was more complex, particularly with regard to the fuel systems, and there were now carburettor air cleaners, and engine cowl gills fitted. Fuel capacity was an enormous 2,309gal (10,497 litres), and bomb load was 6,000lb (2,722kg). Electronic regulators were fitted to the turbo-superchargers, and auto-pilot was a standard fit.

The engines of the Fortress were always easy to start with their inertia type starters, but the warming up process was rather lengthy due to the setting of the turbo-supercharger regulator control on each engine.

Take-off preparations were more complex in the later models, but the take-off itself was easier, due to the lesser swing improved by a more effective rudder and the fitting of a tail wheel lock. With the elevator trim set 1½ divisions nose heavy and the engine giving 2,500rpm with 46in of boost, the unstick speed at full load was 115mph (185km/h) and the safety speed 120mph (193km/h). The tail had to be raised to improve acceleration on the runway.

The climb speed was 150mph (241km/h), using 2,300rpm and 38in of boost. At 1,000ft (305m) the turbo-supercharger regulators were closed, and then adjusted as necessary on the climb to maintain boost. The change of trim on raising the undercarriage was slightly tail heavy.

The aircraft was stable around all three axes, and the controls were quick in response and effective. The ailerons were reasonably light, the elevator slightly heavy, and the rudder extremely

Above: A formation of B-17 Flying Fortresses of US 709th Bomber Squadron, 447th Bomber Group. *RAF Museum Hendon*

Left: A Boeing B-17G Fortress III.

heavy. Cruise power up to 31,500ft (9,601m) was 2,300rpm and 33in boost, which gave an indicated airspeed of 150mph (241km/h) up to 20,000ft (6,096m) and 140mph (225km/h) above 20,000ft (6,096m).

The all-up stall occurred at 102mph (164km/h) at an AUW of 50,000lb (22,680kg) and was preceded by a slight buffeting on all controls about 3mph (5km/h) above the stall when either wing and nose dropped gently. All-down the stall at 90mph (145km/h) was preceded by more pro-

nounced buffeting and the wing dropped away faster. Recovery was straightforward and easy.

This large aeroplane was a delight to land. On the descent to the airfield circuit the turbo-supercharger regulators were cut off very slowly. In the circuit at 150mph (241km/h) the undercarriage was lowered, giving a slight nose-down change of trim. Then at 140mph (225km/h) the flaps were lowered, giving an initial nose-up change of trim, followed by a nose-down change, which required trimming out. Approach speed was 110mph

Pilot's notes: Boeing Flying Fortress

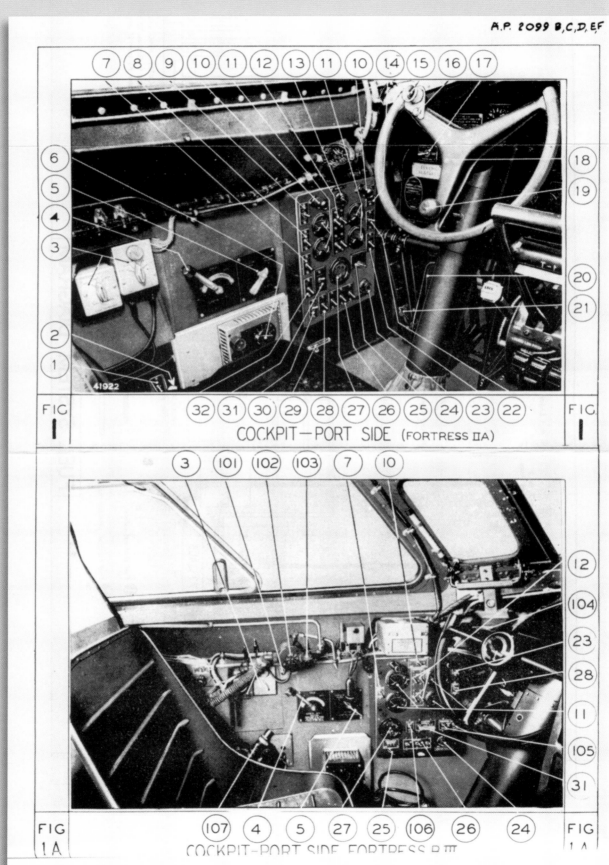

A.P. 2099 B,C,D,E,F

COCKPIT—PORT SIDE (FORTRESS IIA)

FIG 1

COCKPIT—PORT SIDE FORTRESS B III

FIG 1A

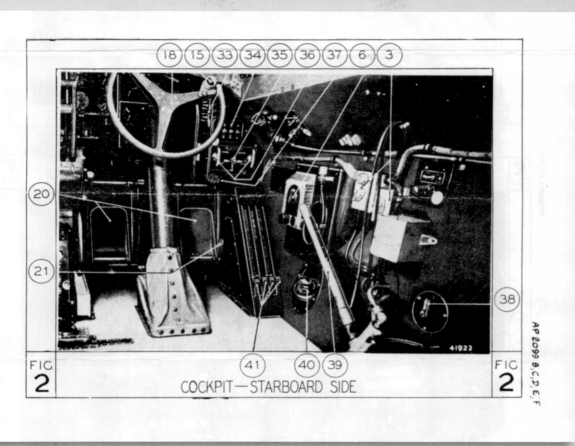

COCKPIT—STARBOARD SIDE

FIG 2   FIG 2

Figs 1, 1A, and 2:

1 Propeller anti-icer master switch
2 Floor panel
3 Intercom station boxes
4 Cabin heating and ventilating control
5 Vacuum selector valve
6 Heated clothing control
7 Bomber call light switch
8 Pass light (not in use)
9 Panel light switch
10 Panel light
11 Ammeters
12 Generator switches
13 Resin light rheostat
14 Resin light switch

15 Bomb release button
16 Throat microphone button
17 Static pressure selector valve
18 Control wheel
19 Aileron locking pin
20 Rudder pedal
21 Rudder pedal adjusting lever
22 Navigation lights switch
23 Alarm bell switch
24 Formation lights switch
25 Voltmeter selector switch
26 Battery switches
27 Voltmeter
28 Pitot heater switch

29 Bomb jettison control
30 Undercarriage warning horn cut-out switch
31 Inverter selector switch
32 Intercom call switch
33 Oil dilution switches
34 Engine starter switches
35 Fire extinguisher selector valve
36 Fire extinguisher operating buttons
37 Brake control handle
38 Hydraulic valve
39 Hydraulic handpump
40 Priming pump
41 Intercooler controls
101 Oxygen automix control

102 Oxygen demand regulator
103 Oxygen emergency knob
104 Resin light master and colour selector switch
105 Formation lights switch
106 Hydraulic pump switch (also on Fortress II)
107 Oxygen bayonet

GENERAL VIEW OF COCKPIT FORTRESS IIA

FIG 3

FIG 3

F.S.2

GENERAL VIEW OF COCKPIT — FORTRESS B III

FIG 3A

FIG 3A

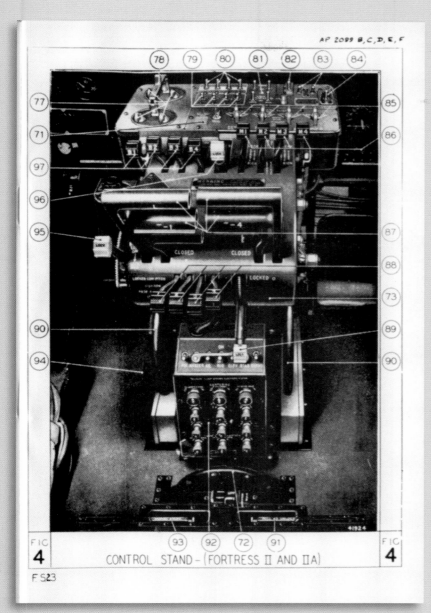

AP 2099 B, C, D, E, F

FIG 4 — CONTROL STAND – (FORTRESS II AND IIA)

F.S.23

Figs 3 and 3A:

18 Control wheel
20 Rudder pedals
37 Parking brake control
42 Telltale lights switch
43 Dimmer switch for undercarriage and tail wheel warning lights
44 Alternating current voltmeter
45 Vacuum gauge
46 Vacuum warning light
47 Bomb release warning light
48 Steering director
49 Minneapolis Honeywill PDI
50 Radio compass indicator
51 Compass light switch
52 Flight panel switch
53 IFF switches

54 IFF detonator buttons
55 Instrument flying panel
56 Fluorescent light
57 Bomber's call light
58 Undercarriage warning light
59 Tailwheel lock warning light
60 Boost gauges
61 Rpm indicator
62 Flaps position indicator
63 Fuel pressure gauges
64 Oil pressure gauges
65 Oil temperature gauges
66 Deicer air pressure gauge
67 Cylinder head temperature gauges
68 Fuel quantity gauge – inboard feeder tank (Fortress IIA only)

69 Fuel quantity gauge – inboard engine tank (Fortress IIA only)
70 Fuel quantity gauge – outboard engine tank, (Fortress IIA only)
71 Central control board
72 Rudder trimming tab wheel
73 Control stand
74 Propeller feathering buttons
75 Hydraulic pressure gauge
76 Hydraulic pressure warning light
108 Flame switch warning lights
109 Windscreen hot air control
110 DR compass (Fortress B III only)

111 Outside air temperature gauges
112 Air intake filter indicator lights (Fortress II and III)
113 Air intake filter switch (Fortress II and III)
114 Fluorescent lights rheostat
115 Liquidometer fuel gauge and selector (Fortress II and III)
116 Carburettor air temperature gauges (Fortress II and III)
117 Turbo boost selector, or manifold pressures selector
118 Radio push-button unit
119 Second pilot's oxygen blinker flow indicator, warning light, and oxygen pressure indicator
120 First pilot's oxygen blinker flow indicator, warning light, and oxygen pressure gauge

Fig 4:

71 Central control board
72 Rudder trimming tab wheel
73 Control stand
77 Magneto switches
78 Master ignition switch
79 Fuel booster pump switch
80 Fuel shut-off valve switches
81 Identification switchbox
82 Undercarriage control switch
83 Landing light switches
84 Flap control switches
85 Cowling gill switches
86 Mixture control levers
87 Throttle control levers
88 Propeller speed control levers
89 Propeller speed controls locking lever
90 Elevator trimming tab control wheels
91 Tailwheel locking lever
92 Minneapolis Honeywill automatic control unit
93 Flying controls locking lever
94 Elevator trimming tab wheel friction control
95 Throttle control locking lever
96 Mixture control locking handle
97 Turbo-supercharger regulator levers (fitted on Fortress IIA and II only; replaced on Fortress III by turbo-boost selector)

Boeing B-17G Fortress
IIIs on a raid over
Europe, 1945.

Fortress II showing the
ball turret and nose
armament.

(177km/h) at 54,000lb or 100mph (161km/h) at 47,000lb. This gave a flat attitude, so that little change of elevator angle was required for a three-point touchdown on the soft undercarriage. The aircraft ran straight with no tendency to swing.

I carried out a landing on three engines without any change in the normal landing procedure except a little extra power. This was so simple that I then tried one with two engines on one side, in which conditions the aircraft could be trimmed to fly down to 125mph (201km/h) with hands and feet off the controls.

In the circuit I used climbing power and turned with the good engines on the inside of the turn. I lowered undercarriage and flaps just before turning on to the final approach at 600ft (183m). I then eased off the power and reduced speed to 115mph (185km/h) whilst retrimming, and virtually made a glide landing which required a very mild pull force to hold off before touchdown.

It is the remarkably docile handling qualities of the Fortress that entitles it to special mention. These very qualities enabled many severely damaged bombers of this type to return safely to base when their crews had no reasonable right to hope for such salvation.

From an operational standpoint it will be a long debated point whether the USAAF high level daylight bombing over Europe was more effective than the RAF medium level night bombing. Certainly the Fortresses were more vulnerable to attack by fighters, and once the latter could reach them at height it became necessary for the bombers to have their own fighter escort. On a percentage basis therefore the daylight bomber

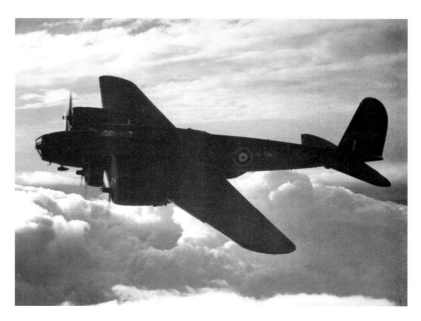

casualties were probably higher than those of the night bombers.

With regard to bombing accuracy, the odds were probably with the Fortresses with their classified Norden bomb sights. I certainly remember the pounding they gave the Renault works at Billancourt when flying cover to them in a Spitfire IX on 4 April 1943, and the incredible umbrella of fire put up by 94 Fortresses when attacked by a shoal of FW 190s. Anyone, friend or foe, who moved in on that Fortress formation was due for a very hot reception from a very great aircraft.

An RAF Fortress I which was considerably inferior to its Mk II replacement.

Seen in April 1941 at the A&AEE at Boscombe Down with a convenient 'erk to give scale, this is one of the first 'Flying Fortresses' to reach Britain. While handling and performance were exceptional, defensive armament was soon found to be pitifully inadequate. Later versions handsomely rectified this shortcoming. On account of the extremely high altitudes that this aircraft could achieve (up to 35,000 ft with full load), the undersides were painted dark PRU Blue. *Barry Ketley*

An undistinguished fighter, except in Finland.
It seemed to thrive on the cold, but withered
in the heat of the Far East. ERIC BROWN

WHEN I WAS GOING through Fighter School at the Royal Navy Air Station at Yeovilton in early 1941 there were two particularly intriguing arrivals – the Grumman Martlet and the Brewster Buffalo. Intriguing, because they were American and looked quite unlike anything in Britain. They were both tubby little single-seat fighters with a purposeful air about them, and designed from the outset for carrier operation.

The Buffalo at Yeovilton was a B-339B, one of 40 such aircraft ordered by the Belgian Government late in 1939. These aircraft had been stripped of all specialist naval equipment and ferried from Canada to Britain aboard HMS *Furious*. Arriving in July 1940 they were assembled and repainted at Burtonwood.

The F2A-2 Buffalo was a low-mid-wing aeroplane powered by a 1,100hp Wright Cyclone R-1820-G105A nine-cylinder radial engine, with a two-speed blower driving a Hamilton Standard Hydromatic propeller. It had a gross weight of 6,782lb (3076kg), borne on a wide track double-strutted undercarriage and a retractable type tail-wheel. With a span of 35ft (11m) it did not require wing folding for carrier storage.

The aircraft was designed to a 1935 US Navy specification, the very same one as that to which the Martlet (or Wildcat as it was known in the USA) was designed. The Brewster company was very inexperienced in comparison with Grumman, and when the Buffalo made its first flight in December 1937, the initial test results were disappointing. However, improvements were introduced and the first production order was given on 11 June 1938.

In July 1939 the prototype XF2A-2 was re-engined with an uprated R-1820-40 and this reduced the nose length by 5in (12.7cm). A larger fin was fitted with greater base chord, thus giving the Buffalo its very characteristic stubby appearance. The first operational F2A-2s were embarked in a US carrier in March 1941 and suffered from undercarriage failures.

In Britain the RAF rejected the Buffalo for European operations due to its lack of performance, and so 154 were sent to the Far East. This was in

A Brewster B-339B
Buffalo.

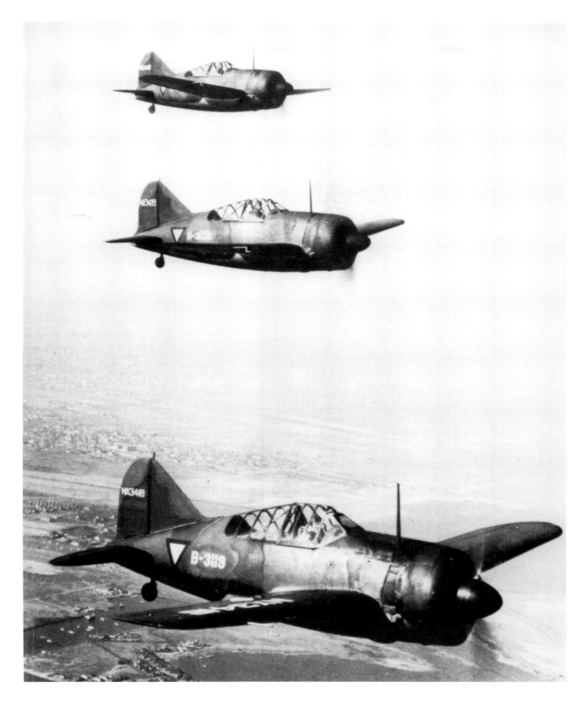

A flight of Netherlands East Indies F2A-1 Buffaloes in formation.

spite of the oil and cylinder head temperatures being unsuitable for tropical conditions.

The aircraft's initiation into combat as far as the US service versions were concerned was with the US Marine Corps in the Battle of Midway when a superior force of Japanese Zeros almost annihilated the Buffalo squadron of 19 F2A-3s. The Buffaloes of the RAF, Royal Australian Air Force and Royal New Zealand Air Force were actually earlier into action, but the pilots found the performance above 10,000ft (3,050m) to be very mediocre, so they had few successes. However, the very first Buffaloes in combat were certainly the F2A-1s supplied to Finland for their gallant fight against the Soviet Union, and these had the highest success ratio of all the Buffalo-user countries.

I had only a couple of flights in the Buffalo but made copious notes of my impressions so that I could compare the aircraft with the Grumman Martlet. Also I had very much wanted to fly the Buffalo because it reminded me of the Granville Gee Bee racer of the 1930s, which had always fascinated me.

Once in the cockpit I found the view ahead rather poor because of the aft position of the pilot

47

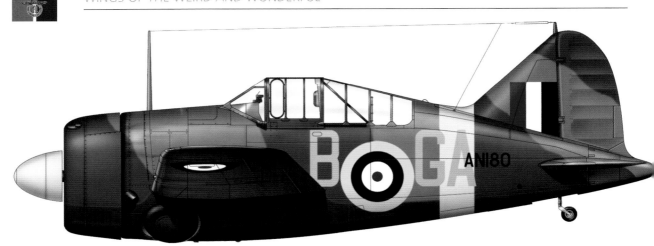

Brewster Buffalo Mk.I, AN180/GA-B, No. 21 Squadron (RAAF). © *Richard Caruana* (scale 1:48).

and the high position of the nose. In spite of this the aircraft was very easy to taxi, as the brakes were smooth and very effective.

On take-off the throttle had to be opened carefully because there was no automatic boost control, and the stick moved forward to get the tail up and improve acceleration. The rudder control was very good in keeping the aircraft straight on its short run.

The climb was steep and initially at a rate of 2,000ft/min (610m/min) but soon began to fall off noticeably as altitude increased. The longitudinal stability was decidedly shaky and would make instrument flying very difficult. It was also apparent that there were fumes coming into the cockpit, and indeed subsequent tests at Boscombe Down showed a dangerously high level of carbon monoxide contamination.

In normal cruise at 160mph (257km/h) the aircraft was longitudinally unstable, laterally neutrally stable, and directionally positively stable. Maximum speed was 290mph (467km/h) at 16,500ft (5,029m) and the service ceiling was only 25,000ft (7,620m). A not very impressive performance. However, it was a different story when it came to handling, for the ailerons were highly effective throughout the speed range, the elevators almost equally so, and the rudder very good too.

The all-up stall occurred at 76mph (122km/h) with a sudden but mild wing drop followed by the

An F2A-3 Buffalo in flight.

nose. The all-down stall was at 67mph (108km/h) with similar but slightly more pronounced characteristics.

For landing the undercarriage was lowered at 95mph (153km/h), followed by the slow moving flaps at 90mph (145km/h). An approach speed of 80mph (129km/h) gave a reasonable view, but needed almost full backward elevator trim. Touchdown occurred at 75mph (121km/h) with a good pull back on the stick to achieve a three-pointer as the power was cut. Once on the ground the aircraft could be kept nicely straight on rudder with a discreet touch of brake.

My feeling after flying the Buffalo was one of elation tinged with disappointment. It was a true anomaly of an aeroplane with delightful manoeuvrability but poor fighter performance. Indeed above 10,000ft (3,050m) it was labouring badly. It would have been mauled in the Western Europe war theatre, and it was indeed almost worse off in the Far East where climatic problems compounded the operational ones.

When compared with the Martlet, the Buffalo's only real plus sign was its ground handling characteristics during take-off and landing. It was equally as manoeuvrable as the Martlet, but thereafter all its signs were minus ones.

It is interesting to reflect on the success of the Buffalo in Finland's Continuation War with Russia. One is bound to conclude that the climate and the opposition suited the little Brewster product, which had a derated Cyclone engine for export to Finland. Of 44 F2A-1s sent to the Finnish Air Force in 1940, eighteen of these aircraft survived to fight against the German Luftwaffe in 1944 and 1945. One particular Buffalo claimed a total of 40 victories during its Finnish operational career.

Two Buffaloes remained in service in Finland until September 1948, and it is perhaps strange but fitting that a Buffalo remains preserved as an historic exhibit in this land where it found its only real glory, so far from its own homeland.

8 DE HAVILLAND SEA HORNET

Overpowered perfection.

ERIC BROWN

The DH Hornet single-seat fighter monoplane (two Rolls-Royce Merlin 130/131 engines).

O F ALL the 450-plus types of aircraft I have flown I give the accolade for sheer enjoyment to the de Havilland Sea Hornet. Of course I have flown aircraft with better individual points such as aileron control or rate of climb etc., but for getting everything together in near perfection I have found nothing to excel the superb Sea Hornet.

The exceptional operational success of the Mosquito led almost inevitably to the idea of a scaled down single-seat version to oppose the single-engined Japanese fighters in combat in the Pacific theatre. Long range was thus an essential attribute to be combined with medium altitude fighter characteristics and so de Havilland's started design work on the idea in 1942. They got Rolls-Royce to develop special Merlin power plants of minimum frontal area for the project.

The DH 103 was the private venture catalyst for Specification F.12/43 and it made its first flight in the hands of Geoffrey de Havilland Jnr. from Hatfield on 28 July 1944.

The designers of the DH 103 had not overlooked the possibility of it operating from aircraft carriers against the Japanese. They had taken heed of the lessons learned from the Mosquito deck-landing trials in March 1944, and had incorporated opposite handed engines and high drag flaps.

The Naval Staff responded by producing Specification N.5/44. Three Hornet F.Mk Is were modified by the Heston Aircraft Co. Ltd to further incorporate hydraulic-powered folding wings, a forged steel arrester hook on a flush fitting external V-frame, tail down accelerator pick-up points, and Airdraulic undercarriage legs. The weight penalty of these modifications totalled 550lb (249kg).

The first Sea Hornet flew on 19 April 1945 and, like the second aircraft, was merely a hooked Hornet without the other Heston modifications. This prototype, PX212, was delivered to RAE Farnborough on 10 May 1945, two days after VE Day. I made a flight next day as the first step in the work-up to deck-landing trials. By mid-May I had completed the type arresting proofing on the dummy carrier deck at RAE.

The next two months were spent in handling and deck landing assessment trials, and were sheer pleasure for I had a winner in my hands.

The pilot's view from the cockpit right forward

The first deck landing of a Sea Hornet prototype aboard HMS *Ocean*, 10 August 1945.

in the nose was truly magnificent all-round. The aircraft had powerful brakes and was easy to taxi as it had little weathercocking tendency.

The stalling characteristics were innocuous, with a fair amount of elevator buffeting and aileron twitching preceding the actual stall when a fore-and-aft pitch occurred simultaneously with a lateral rolling motion. At normal full load the all-up stall occurred at 130mph (209km/h) and the all-down stall at 98mph (158km/h).

For aerobatics the Sea Hornet was sheer exhilarating joy. The excess of power was such that manoeuvres in the vertical plane felt more like being in a zooming rocket than in a aeroplane. Even with one engine feathered the Hornet could loop like a normal single-engined fighter, and its aerodynamic cleanliness was such that I used to delight in demonstrating this feature by diving with both engines at full power, then feathering both propellers before pulling up into an engineless loop. Needless to say my pre-flight drill before such a demonstration was to check that the aircraft battery was fully charged and that I had two spare fuses clipped to my cockpit wall, in case I blew the unfeathering fuses at the bottom of the recovery dive.

The landing circuit was normally made at 180mph (290km/h) with the booster pumps ON, and the radiator flaps set to AUTO and the hood open. Lowering of the undercarriage at 160mph (257km/h) was followed by lowering the flaps one-third of their travel, which gave a nose-up change of trim. Speed was then reduced below

140mph (225km/h) and full flap selected, giving a further nose-up trim change. In this condition the rudder was light and effective and the elevators, though light, were not very effective for small stick movements. The ailerons, however, were unacceptable for deck-landing, being heavy and almost completely ineffective.

Throttle movement was not coarse enough in the low boost range below zero boost. The view for landing was excellent and final approach at 115mph (185km/h) was comfortable, except in turbulent air, because of the poor lateral control.

De Havilland's as usual reacted quickly to my report and soon had the lateral control problem in hand. I flew a Hornet whose ailerons had aerodynamic nose balance and this automatically increased the angle movement from 7° to 17°. These ailerons were superb in lightness and effectiveness throughout the entire speed range from 150mph (241km/h) to 450mph (724km/h), but they became progressively more sluggish at speeds below 150mph (241km/h); they were just acceptable for the forthcoming deck landing trials.

On 4 August I took PX212 with the modified ailerons up to RN Air Station Arbroath, where I teamed up with the 'batsman' for the trials. After a session of ADDLs (Aerodrome Dummy Deck Landings) I pushed on to the RN Air Station Ayr on 6 August, where my back-up aircraft, PX230, the first production night fighter, was awaiting me. The Hornet's throttle handgrips had been enlarged by the addition of the gyro gun-sight control knobs, so that it felt rather like manipu-

lating a couple of tennis balls rather than a pair of throttles.

During these ADDL sessions the engines, which were really still in experimental stage of development, were prone to give a rich cut on take-off unless cleared beforehand to a minimum boost value of +8lb, at which power setting the aircraft could just be held on the brakes.

Power stalls were carried out in the landing condition at a boost setting of -4lb, and ample warning of the stall was given by heavy buffeting on the elevator, accompanied by slight fore-and-aft pitching. The aircraft always dropped the starboard wing smartly to an angle of about 40° at the actual stall, which occurred at 80mph (129km/h). From this information, -4lb boost was chosen as the approximate engine setting for the approach and 95mph (153km/h) decided on as the final approach speed. Some approaches were made at 90mph (145km/h) but the rate of sink was too high and the ailerons twitched badly at that speed.

On 10 August I made the first Sea Hornet landings on HMS *Ocean*, steaming off Ailsa Craig on the very hour that the end of the war with Japan was announced. The landings were made at an AUW of 14,545lb (6598kg) and provided no real problems, although the use of ailerons to make corrections for line had to be assisted by differential engine handling. Take-off with the handed engines was superb and unbelievably short.

On 11 August the trials continued, although I had an hydraulic pump failure shortly after the first take-off and had to use the handpump for the remainder of the trials. This was my own choice rather than return to Ayr and pick up the spare Hornet with the 'bunch of walnuts' throttles. Anyway, all went well and I completed my stint and flew back to Farnborough that evening.

The landings were made without the use of a crash barrier as the Mosquito type barrier, although fully developed, would have entailed too much installation work in the light fleet carrier.

Deck landing is a difficult art that demands full concentration, excellent judgement and lightning reflexes. There are many variables to be dealt with and much that can go wrong, so that, even with experience, to relax concentration is to invite disaster. Yet, in the case of the Sea Hornet, I felt such absolute confidence even on these initial trials that I was mentally relaxed to a degree that was almost casual.

There was something about the aircraft that made me feel I had total mastery of it and I revelled in its sleek form and its surge of power. It was like driving a Grand Prix racing car that one instinctively knew was a winner all the way.

The success of these trials put the Sea Hornet XX into production as part of the clearance programme and I carried out the type accelerating proofing on PX214 at Farnborough on 23 January 1946. This was the first twin-engined aircraft to be launched from an accelerator and by the end of the day we had the weight up to 18,200lb (8,256kg) and I was landing at the overweight of 17,700lb (8,029kg).

Pilot's notes: de Havilland Sea Hornet

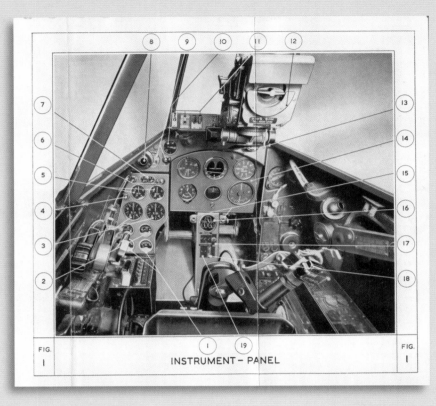

INSTRUMENT – PANEL

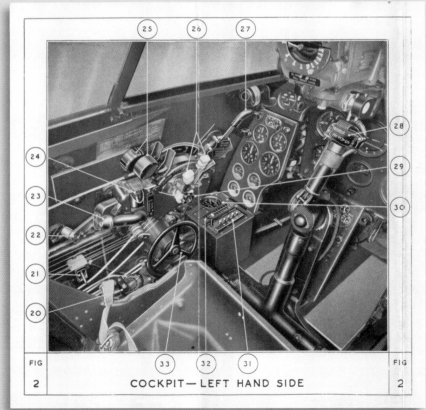

COCKPIT—LEFT HAND SIDE

Fig 1:

Instrument panel

1 Oil temperature gauges
2 Coolant temperature gauges
3 Rpm indicator
4 Arrester hook indicator light
5 Boost gauges
6 Fuel pressure warning lights
7 Oil pressure gauges
8 Cockpit ventilator control
9 Undercarriage indicator and warning light
10 Flaps position indicator
11 RP selector and GGS switches
12 Gyro gunsight
13 Propeller feathering push-buttons and fire warning lights
14 Instrument flying panel
15 Power failure warning light
16 Fuel contents gauges
17 Booster pump and cross-feed cock switches
18 Gun safety switch
19 Camera filter and camera selector switches

Fig 2:

**Cockpit –
left-hand side**

20 Rudder trim tab control and indicator
21 Undercarriage override switch
22 Undercarriage control lever
23 Flaps control lever
24 Supercharger selector switch
25 Throttle levers
26 Propeller control levers
27 Arrester hook operating lever
28 Guns and camera firing button
29 Throttle friction adjuster
30 Triple air-pressure gauge
31 RT controller
32 Elevator trim tab indicator
33 Elevator trim tab control

The Sea Hornet with night fighter radome nose.

The superlative Sea Hornet prototype, PX214, on which Eric Brown carried out the type accelerating proofing on 23 January 1946.

The first production Sea Hornet XX with slotted flaps flew at Hatfield on 13 August 1946, and incorporated the main modifications I had asked for. The first squadron formed on 1 June 1947 and embarked in HMS *Implacable* in 1949.

I have flown almost 500 types of aircraft, excluding variants of a type, and I have graded every one in a book with a terse two-line assessment. There are six that receive top grading for handling qualities – the Spitfire XII, Lancaster I with power boosted controls, the Hornet, Hawker P1040, North American Sabre and McDonnell Phantom. These six are so different in size, role and time scale, that they are difficult to compare, but for

sheer pilot enjoyment I remember the Hornet making the deepest impression. Certainly all six had good power/weight ratio, superb harmony of control, and excellent performance characteristics, but above all they inspired confidence in the pilot. The Hornet somehow had the edge on the others in my book.

Inevitably the above list will give the impression that I am biased towards British and American aircraft, but let me say that just a shade below my first choice list are the Japanese Zero, the German Fw 190, Ju 88, and Me 262. However, for tops it's still the Hornet.

DE HAVILLAND SEA MOSQUITO

Its deck-landing trials were dubbed 'Mission Impossible', but the splendid Mosquito made it and paved the way for its superb successor, the Sea Hornet. ERIC BROWN

THE STORY of the inspired design of the de Havilland DH 98 Mosquito is one of those flashes of genius that can change the course of history. The basic idea was to build an all-wood unarmed bomber that could outfly all contemporary fighters and have enough range to carry a worthwhile load of bombs to Berlin.

The prototype was built secretly in a small hanger at Salisbury Hall, London Colney, where Ronald Bishop and his design team were housed. It made its first flight at Hatfield on 25 November 1940, less than 11 months from the start of design work, and from the outset exceeded all expectations in performance and handling.

My acquaintance with the immortal Mossie started in January 1944, when I was a test pilot in 'C' Squadron at A&AEE, Boscombe Down. Early that month I was asked by the Admiralty if I thought I could deck land a Mosquito! Taken completely by surprise and although having minimal experience on twin-engined aircraft, and never having flown a Mosquito, I answered in the affirmative with all the brash confidence of youth. That reply was to refashion my whole life, and on 17 January I found myself appointed to RAE Farnborough for duties in Aerodynamics Flight. My naval predecessor had been killed in a deck-landing accident in a Seafire, hence the pier-head jump, as such a rapid move is known in the Navy.

I was told the Mosquito deck landings were planned for March, so my first priority was to pile up twin-engine time and I was pushed on to a Wellington X until the navalised Mosquito arrived. The new arrival was a Mk VI, with a Barracuda type arrester hook installed in the rear fuselage, which had been strengthened internally by reinforcing longeron ribs on either side. Experimental (non-feathering) four-bladed de Havilland metal propellers, cropped to 12ft 6in (4m) diameter, were fitted to the Merlin 25 engines operating at increased boost.

I made by first flight on this navalised prototype LR359 on 25 January, accompanied by Bill Stewart, a 'boffin' in Aero Flight, who was to be the flight

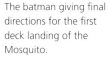

The batman giving final directions for the first deck landing of the Mosquito.

observer responsible for the conduct of the trials. Bill was a young aerodynamicist from Glasgow University; we struck up a perfect understanding and mutual confidence from the very moment of our meeting.

The project was a prestigious one, for we believed it would be the first ever landing of a twin-engined aeroplane on an aircraft carrier. The problems associated with twins were firstly the larger weight to be arrested, secondly the difficulty of coping with a single-engined landing, and thirdly the necessity for a new design of crash barrier, as the pilot would no longer have the protection of an engine ahead of him. Another problem peculiar to the Mosquito was that it had a wooden fuselage, whose strength might be suspect for the enormous retardation and side-loads involved in arresting.

The preparation for the trials involved take-off measurements, stall measurements and single-engined approaches; then a series of simulated deck landings on the airfields at Farnborough and Yeovilton, at various weights from 16,000lb (7,258kg) to 20,000lb (9,072kg).

The take-off technique found to give the shortest unstick distance was to keep the tail as low as possible throughout the ground run. The flap setting was not critical and as the swing became more serious at the greater flap settings, 25° was considered the optimum. The engines were run up to + 4lb boost on the port and + 2lb boost on the starboard; the brakes were released to prevent the tail rising, then the throttles opened to the full + 18lb and the swing counteracted by full right rudder with the stick held fully back. On unstick the stick was eased forward immediately to allow build up to single-engined safety speed.

Using this method the Mosquito unstuck in 620ft (189m) at 16,000lb (7,258kg) and 820ft (250m) at 20,000lb (9,072kg) in standard atmospheric conditions of temperature and pressure and zero wind.

The stall measurements were made with a trailing static bomb released on 100ft (30m) of tubing from the underside of the aircraft. All the stalls were made with flaps and undercarriage lowered, at various power settings, and they proved to be unexpectedly vicious. At the stall the stick would crack hard over into one corner, the ailerons locked, and the Mosquito virtually turned turtle. At a power setting of + 4lb boost the stall was so sharp that the trailing static got wrapped around the tail unit and could not be jettisoned on its parachute in the normal way at the end of the tests.

One thing was clear from all this, namely that the Mosquito's approach speed could be reduced to just 100mph (161km/h) and the touch-down speed to some 10mph (16km/h) less by keeping on power until just about three feet above the deck and then cutting the throttles. The limiting factor on approach speed was the ineffectiveness of the ailerons to assist any correction for line.

These were encouraging figures in view of the limiting entry speeds of the arrester gear in use at that time and the desirability of pushing the aircraft's landing weight up to 20,000lb (9,072kg).

The landing tests showed up the lack of drag in the Mosquito's design. Consequently the approach was made flatter than for normal naval aircraft, which were heavily flapped, and the speed range for the final approach was fairly small. The upper limit was set by the speed at which the aircraft tended to float at touch down and the lower limit by the loss of aileron control. The range set by these limits was of the order of 12mph (19km/h).

The single-engined flight tests could only be made with the 'dead' engine throttled back, as

First landing of a twin-engined aircraft on a carrier, HMS *Indefatigable,* on 25 March 1944.

The landing and take-off sequence of the Mosquito on HMS *Indefatigable*.

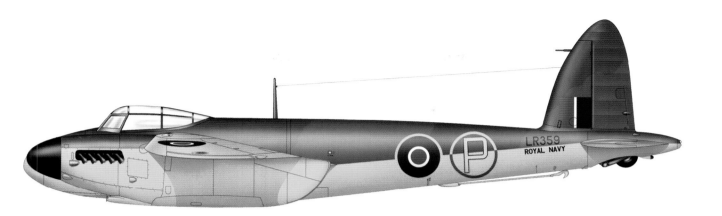

the experimental propellers could not be feathered. These tests showed it was only possible to go round again at heights above 500ft (152m), as the aircraft could only be held straight on rudder with full rudder trim, and maintain flight at a minimum speed of 170mph (274km/h).

Concurrently with the flight tests, design of a crash barrier for the Mosquito was taking place. The new design was for strips of nylon to be strung vertically between two widely separated steel wires attached to the ship's arrester gear through the normal crash barrier supports. There was a gap in the middle of the series of nylon strips to allow the nose of the aircraft to pass through untouched as the strips wrapped themselves around the wings. However, this barrier was not going to be ready for the ship trials in March, so no barrier facilities would be available. This as it transpired was to prove fortunate.

On 1 March the second navalised Mosquito, LR387, was delivered to Farnborough as the back-up trials aircraft. By the 18 March we were ready to move up to Scotland for arrester gear proofing runs at RN Air Station Arbroath. There a set of arrester wires was laid out on one of the airfield runways and we were to make familiarisation landings at East Haven airfield for Lt Cdr Bob Everett, who was to be the 'batsman' for the trials. He commanded the Deck Landing Control Officers Training School at East Haven, a Royal Naval Air Station just south of Arbroath. The 'batsman' work-up showed that he tended to disappear from view under the port engine on the final stage of the approach, so he had to stand inboard of his usual deck-edge position.

The great day dawned on 25 March and the word came that HMS *Indefatigable* was steaming off Ailsa Craig with deck ready. I took off at 13.30 from Machrihanish with only 25 minutes fuel aboard so that the weight would be down to 16,000lb (7,258kg) for the first landing. Diversion in an emergency was to be made to Prestwick or Ayr airfields.

When I arrived over *Indefatigable* she was already steaming into wind at full speed and I was told there was 46mph (74km/h) of windspeed over the deck, so after a flashing low pass I turned straight into a circuit at 400ft (122m) and came round on to finals. Bob Everett was standing midway between the port edge of the flight deck and the centre line and I remember thinking I hope he can run fast or he's liable to get tangled up with my port propeller.

Everything went perfectly and I got an OK or 'Roger' signal all the way in, holding an indicated airspeed of 80mph (129km/h), literally hanging on the props. As I crossed the carrier's stern I saw Bob give the 'cut' signal and then dart for the safety nets. The Mosquito sat down firmly on the deck, picking up No. 2 arrester wire and coming to rest in an incredibly short distance. The camera recorded a touch-down speed of 78mph (126km/h), well below our best estimates.

After refuelling the Mosquito it was ranged aft for its first deck take-off. Because of the span of the aircraft it was necessary to position it with the starboard wheel on the centre line to allow sufficient clearance from the island structure which protruded into the flight deck.

This situation brought in its train another problem for the wide track of the Mosquito undercarriage brought its port wheel very close to the port edge of the flight deck, so the swing on take-off would have to be very closely controlled.

In the event the powerful swing was easier to control then on land because initially there was a slipstream effect over the rudder from the combined ship's speed and wind speed over the deck; so the rudder control was more effective in the early stages of the take-off run. Moreover the run was so staggeringly short in the high deck windspeed that the swing never had the time to develop before the aircraft was airborne.

After two more landings the aircraft was again refuelled and a further two landings were made without any trouble. The Mosquito was then given

Navalised Mosquito FB.VI, LR359, the first twin-engined aircraft to land on an aircraft-carrier, HMS *Indefatigable*, 25 March 1944 © *Richard Caruana* (scale 1:72).

Pilot's notes: de Havilland Sea Mosquito

Fig 2:

Instrument panel

1 Coolant temperature gauges
2 Compass
3 Oil temperature gauges
4 Oil pressure gauges
5 Fuel pressure warning lights
6 Boost pressure gauges
7 Floodlights
8 RPM indicators
9 Floodlight rheostats
10 Stowage for RI compass repeater
11 Exciter button for UV lighting
12 Boost control cut-out
13 Instrument flying panel
14 Gun sight bracket
15 Radiator flap switches
16 Air intake filter switch
17 Ultra-violet lamp
18 Magneto switches

19 Rudder trimming tab and indicator
20 Electrical services switch
21 Immersed pump warning light
22 Engine starter switches
23 Booster-coil switches
24 Ventilators
25 Feathering buttons
26 Bomb doors warning light
27 Bomb containers jettison button
28 Bombs or tanks/ camera change-over switch
29 Flaps selector
30 Bomb selector switches
31 Bomb fusing switches
32 Undercarriage selector
33 Gun master switch
34 Bomb doors selector
35 Oxygen regulator
36 Triple pressure gauge
37 Flaps position indicator

38 Undercarriage position indicator
39 Landing lamp switches

Figs 3 and 4:

40 Beam approach switch
41 RI compass switches
42 Elevator trimming tab indicator
43 Engine limitations data plate
44 Machine-gun firing control
45 Bomb release button
46 Brake control lever
47 Control column
48 Throttle levers
49 Propeller controls
50 Friction controls
51 Supercharger gear change switch
52 TR 1143 push-button unit

53 Seat height-adjusting lever
54 Harness release lever
55 Socket for hydraulic hand pump
56 Air recognition lights switch
57 Identification lights switchbox and key
58 Identification lights colour selector switch
59 Voltmeter
60 Generator warning light
61 Camera gun master switch
62 Navigation lights switch
63 UV lights switch
64 Pitot-head heater switch
65 Immersed fuel pump switch
66 Reflector gun sight switch
67 Navigation headlamp switch

INSTRUMENT PANEL

FIG 2

68 IFF master switch
69 IFF detonator buttons
70 Fire-extinguisher switches
71 Fuel contents gauges, outer wing tanks
72 Fuel contents gauges, centre tank and bomb bay tank (if fitted)
73 Fuel contents gauges, inner wing tanks
74 Switch and warning light for transmitter type F
75 Master switches for R1155 and TR1143
76 Outside air temperature gauge
77 Cold air control knob
78 Windscreen wiper rheostat
79 Stowage for signal cartridges
80 Emergency door release handle
81 Stowage for hydraulic handpump handle

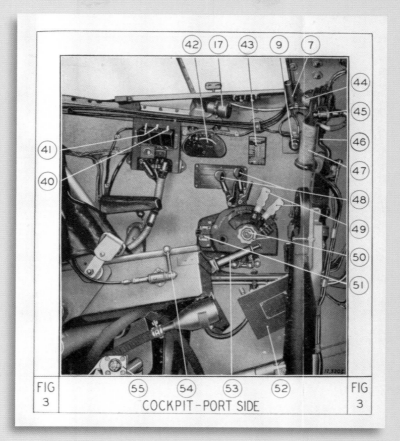

FIG 3

COCKPIT–PORT SIDE

FIG 3

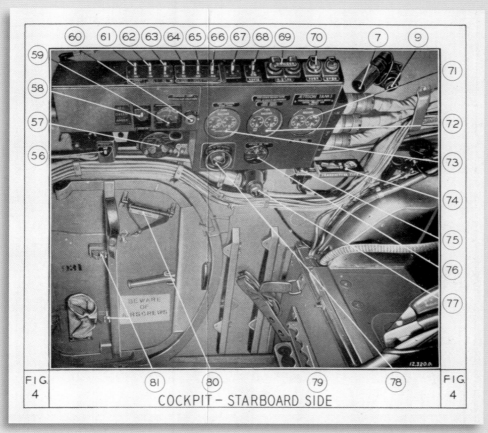

FIG. 4

COCKPIT – STARBOARD SIDE

FIG. 4

De Havilland Sea Mosquito TR.33 (TW256 593/LP) of 771 Squadron in flight, Lee-on-Solent, 27 October 1947. *RAF Museum Hendon.*

a thorough check-over and prepared for the next day's programme.

I was off in LR359 again at 08.45 next morning at a weight of 17,000lb (7,711kg) and carrying Bill Stewart as my first crew.

After landing the aircraft was refuelled to 18,000lb (8,165kg) and off we went again for a pair of landings at this weight. The first was straightforward, but on the second we picked up the arrester wire and after initial retardation there was a jolt and I instinctively knew something had gone wrong. I made a lightning assessment that either the arrester wire had failed or the hook had torn out, then waited a fraction to see if we caught another wire before opening up rapidly to full power. We accelerated rapidly but swinging to port, a tendency I did not attempt to correct fully otherwise we would be dangerously close to the island. I just managed to lift the wheels over the port edge and then we sank below deck level to within about ten feet of the sea, but picking up sufficient speed to keep us clear.

When we had started to climb I looked at Bill, who had apparently remained ice cool throughout, although I had seen him making a move to

be ready to jettison the escape hatch above our heads if we did ditch. However, the flood of relief now made itself evident and he grinned but remained silent on our way to Machrihanish.

On landing, we examined the rear end of the aircraft and found the front securing bolt of the hook claw sheared, thus releasing it from the arrester wire, and snapping the hook frame back into its housing in the fuselage. Obviously this was going to be a case of back to the drawing board.

I delivered LR359 to de Havilland's at Hatfield on 11 April. Meanwhile LR387 went to Crail, where the Navy's Service Trials Unit was based, and whose CO, Commander H.J.F. Lane was to take part in the second series of ship trials, planned for early May.

LR359 returned to Farnborough in late April with a tail wheel lock fitted to try and reduce take-off swing, but it had no significant effect. LR387 also came back via Hatfield for a last check before the trials, as it was to be the main aircraft with LR359 as the back-up. It was also used to give Commander Lane instruction and practice under RAE supervision.

On 6 May I flew LR359 to Crail while Cdr Lane

flew LR387. Next day I took LR387 to Arbroath for proofing runs into arrester wires there, and on 8 May to East Haven and thence to Machrihanish. All was set fair for joining *Indefatigable* again on 9 May off Ailsa Craig.

On 9 May, with 'Tubby' Lane as passenger, I made the first landing of the series on the carrier at a weight of 16,000lb (7,258kg) with 35mph (56km/h) of wind over the deck. After refuelling I made a further two landings at 16,000lb (7,258kg) and on the second take-off actually unstuck in 52yds (48m) in 39mph (63km/h) windspeed. I then handed over to 'Tubby' for his first crack with two landings at 16,000lb (7,258kg). Thereafter we stepped up the landing weight by 1,000lb (454kg) of fuel and alternatively made two landings each at 17,000lb (7,711kg), with 40mph (65km/h) of wind over the deck.

Next day I opened proceedings with two landings at 18,000lb (8,165kg) and then handed over to Cdr Lane to repeat one more at that weight.

'Tubby's' landing at 18,000lb (8,165kg) almost ended in disaster when he misjudged the 'cut' height and the aircraft bounced heavily over all the wires. To everyone's horror he slammed on full brakes and, amid clouds of smoking rubber, ground to a standstill a few feet short of the bows. The resultant square wheels were the only damage to the Mosquito.

After a double wheel change I was off for a 19,000lb (8,618kg) landing, followed by a 20,000lb (9,072kg) one, and Cdr Lane also did

the same. The aircraft was then bombed up for me to carry out two take-offs in excess of 21,000lb (9,526kg). I dropped the bombs live at a safe distance from the ship and carried out the final two landings at 20,000lb (9,072kg). The take-off run at 21,500lb (9,752kg), in 39mph (63km/h) windspeed, was 140yds (128m).

All in all twenty-four successful landings had been made in the two series of trials, and some invaluable lessons learned about twin-engined deck operations in general and about operating the Mosquito in particular.

The major problem encountered was take-off swing, aggravated by the small tolerances due to flight deck clearance limitations of such a large aircraft. Obviously handed engines would be the best solution, and this was indeed adopted for the Mosquito's successor, the Sea Hornet.

On 10 September 1944, a Mosquito IV, designated DZ537/G, arrived at Farnborough for type arresting proofing up to 1.9'g' retardation with an unstrengthened fuselage. After completing this test and asking what it was all in aid of, I received a lot of evasive answers which only served to whet my curiosity more. However, I got the answer early next month when I was despatched to Beccles airfield near Ipswich to instruct No. 618 RAF Mosquito IV squadron in the art of deck landing. In the hangar I saw one of their aircraft with a strange object protruding from the bomb bay and being examined by Dr Barnes Wallis. My guess was that a raid of the

The second navalised Mosquito, LR387, with wings folded. *RAF Museum Hendon.*

De Havilland Sea
Mosquito TR.33
(TW256 953/LP) of
711 Squadron, Fleet Air
Arm, 27 October 1947.
RAF Museum Hendon.

Mohne/Eder dam type made by Guy Gibson's Lancasters was being planned for somewhere.

In fact this was the preparation for Operation High Ball to be made against Japanese capital ships in harbour. I understand that 618 Squadron pilots were assigned a supply of Barracuda aircraft with which to practise ADDLs (Aerodrome Dummy Deck Landings) and then make one landing each on HMS *Rajah*. The Barracuda was one of the easiest aircraft to deck land, but in spite of this the 618 pilots damaged five. Perhaps the pilots were fortunate never to be required to attempt to deck land a Mosquito, for although 27 Mosquitoes were loaded aboard HMS *Rajah* and HMS *Striker* which sailed from the Clyde on 31 October, High Ball in fact never came to pass because the Japanese surrender occurred before the operation could be launched.

In the course of time LR387 became the first real Sea Mosquito with folding wings and nose radome. The first production TR Mk 33 flew on 10 November 1945. Folding wings were fitted from the fourteenth aircraft, which also had long-travel Lockheed oleo legs. All 50 production aircraft were fitted to carry an 18in. torpedo.

To the best of my knowledge none of these Sea Mosquitoes ever operated off a carrier, but it was apparently intended that they would for I carried out a series of RATOG tests with Sea Mosquito 33, TS449, at Farnborough in May and June 1946. At a weight of 22,560lb (10,233kg), including a torpedo and two 250lb (113kg) bombs, four rockets were used to give the necessary short carrier take-off.

These RATOG tests, including asymmetric firings, were completely successful, so the only reason I feel the Sea Mosquito was never put into carrier service was that the highly successful Sea Hornet deck landing trials occurred in August 1945. The decision was made shortly afterwards to concentrate on this superior naval aircraft to promote confidence in twin-engined carrier operations.

10 DE HAVILLAND SEA VAMPIRE

A docile but delightful little performer, which made its own niches in aviation history. ERIC BROWN

WHEN I JOINED Aerodynamics Flight at RAE Farnborough in January 1944, there was adjacent to our aircraft dispersal a small hangar, guarded by RAF Military Police with guard dogs, which housed only two or three sleek aeroplanes. These aircraft were strange sights in those days, for they had no conventional propellers and were indeed Britain's first jets.

The unique Jet Flight was commanded by Wing Commander H.J. Wilson, a former RAE Chief Test Pilot, and he was assisted by two other pilots who often came to Aero Flight to supplement their limited flying. Their stable at that time consisted of a Metro-Vickers Beryl-engined Meteor and the tiny Gloster E.28/39, Britain's first jet aircraft.

After a few crewroom chats with the Jet Flight pilots, it became my burning ambition to join this exclusive unit. This was eventually realised in May 1944 when I made a number of flights on a Welland-engined Meteor, at the invitation of Wing Commander Wilson, with the object of assessing jet aircraft for naval use. My report was enthusiastic although tempered with the realistic acknowledgement of the limitations of the early jet engines, which were both underpowered and inflexible in the matter of response to throttle movement.

By mid-1944 we had received two further prototypes in the Jet Flight; these were the Bell YP-59 Airacomet and the de Havilland Spider-Crab, later to be renamed the Vampire. About the same time my proposal to the Admiralty to carry out deck-landing trials of a jet aircraft had been received favourably, and I was asked to recommend which type should be used. The E.28/39 could not be made available for this project, so the Vampire was the obvious choice, although the twin tail-boom layout posed technical problems for catapulting and arresting.

The DH 100 Vampire was designed to specifi-

The prototype Spider-Crab, later renamed the Vampire.

63

The Bell YP-59 Airacomet was mainly designed as a testbed for America's development of jet engine technology.

cation E.6/41 as a single-seat interceptor fighter. It was an all-metal aircraft except for the ply-wood and balsa cockpit section. Powered by a 2,700lb (1,225kg) static thrust Goblin I turbojet, manufactured also by the de Havilland company, the Vampire made its first flight at Hatfield on 20 September 1943, in the hands of Geoffrey de Havilland Jnr.

The Vampire sat very low on the ground and its twin tail booms carried a tailplane set high on tall pointed fins. The profile could be seen to have given rise to the original name of Spider-Crab.

It was not until 17 May 1945 that I was sent to Hatfield to make a deck-landing assessment of prototype Vampire LZ551/G, which had been modified to give increased drag effect from the flaps and dive brakes. The standard flaps were increased by 40% in area by extending the chord and continuing them under the jet engine nacelle. The chord of the dive brakes was also extended by 8in (24cm).

For take-off the aircraft could just be held up to full power on the brakes. Using 30° of flap the nose wheel could be lifted off the ground at 60mph and with unstick at 100mph an excellent take-off distance was achieved. The change of trim on raising the undercarriage and flaps was negligible, and no sink was involved if the flaps were retracted at 150mph (241km/h).

The climb speed of 250mph (402km/h) seemed high in those days of piston fighters, but the initial rate of climb at 4,300ft/min (1,311/min) was not so startling.

In cruising flight at 5,000ft (1,524m) at 350mph (563km/h) all controls were light and effective, although the aircraft was laterally and longitudinally unstable – often the hallmark of a good interceptor day fighter.

In level flight the Vampire was slow to accelerate to its top speed of 540mph (869km/h). But in

1945 that sort of speed was worth waiting for, and it could be reached quickly by initiating a very slight dive at full throttle. The speeds which were necessary for aerobatics could be reached very comfortably in level flight and the aircraft was a real delight to handle in all aerobatic manoeuvres.

The all-up stall occurred at 106mph (171km/h) when the port wing dropped sharply and without warning, but the ensuing spiral was quite gentle and the recovery straightforward. The all-down stall occurred at 95mph (153km/h) with virtually identical characteristics except that the wing drop was a little steeper.

The enlarged dive brakes were very effective in reducing speed for landing and produced a nose-up change of trim. This was further accentuated by a strong nose-up change of trim when the high drag flaps were lowered. The total change of trim required a lot of counteracting nose-down elevator trim, but when trimmed out left a large amount of elevator control for assuming a very tail-down attitude for landing. The surprisingly high drag of the flaps necessitated a large amount of engine power, thus keeping the engine in the high thrust range of operation where the throttle was most responsive to movement. The enlarged flaps were also very effective indeed in lowering stalling speed and eliminating float. In the standard Vampire this arose from the ground effect of the low wing and short undercarriage.

These simple modifications to flaps and dive-brakes showed that the problems of deck-landing a jet aircraft were two-fold. Firstly there was the lack of propeller slipstream to control lift quickly. Secondly the lack of drag obtained from propeller braking in a piston-engined aircraft was accentuated by the high residual thrust of the jet engine on cutting the throttle.

The lowest practicable landing speed in this

Above and left: Views of the Sea Vampire's arrester-hook, flaps and dive brakes layout.

modified Vampire was 105mph (170km/h), using 9,000rpm of the total 10,000rpm available. These conditions gave a good tail-down attitude, perfect view, good lateral and longitudinal control and longitudinal stick fix stability. Although the rudders were ineffective at this speed there were no slipstream effects to be counteracted so they were adequate.

Engine response to throttle was good over the range of 8,500rpm (maximum cruising limitation) to 10,000rpm (maximum take-off limitation) without being too sensitive to prevent coarse throttle manipulation. This is an important difference between the jet and the piston engine, in that the coarse throttle response sector of the quadrant is at the high thrust end for the jet engine and at the low power end for the piston engine.

The baulked landing case was expected to be the critical factor in the Vampire's deck landing acceptability, because of the lack of lift effect from the increase of engine power until speed built up, therefore acceleration was vital. Although only 1,000rpm were available over the approach engine setting, this small increment represented a surprisingly high ratio of the total thrust available.

This, combined with a very rapidly retracting undercarriage and exceedingly rapidly retracting dive brakes which gave only a small nose-down change of trim, provided a reasonable safety margin.

My conclusion was that, subject to a satisfactory arrester hook installation being incorporated, the modified Vampire was entirely suitable for deck-landing trials.

It is interesting to reflect that I was in Germany at the time of the capitulation, and saw the German jets for the first time. I sensed how far they were in advance of ours, but I had not yet flown them when I returned to make the Vampire test a fortnight later. However, the following month I flew my first German jet and was very impressed with the performance, but not with the engine handling.

The German axial-flow engines were very sensitive to throttle in that any quick movement gave excessive jet pipe temperatures, and their life was very limited. Our centrifugal-flow engines were not insensitive in this respect but seemed much more reliable. The poor acceleration of the jet engine was of course just a matter of the stage of development. It would undoubtedly be improved

In the race to be the first jet to make a carrier deck-landing, the main American competitor was the Lockheed P-80A Shooting Star.

– and indeed would have to be – if jet aircraft were to go into carrier service.

The Americans were lagging behind both Germany and Britain in jet aircraft development, and the Bell Airacomet was a sluggish performer. However, they had the research and industrial potential to catch up. This realisation must have stung the Admiralty into a determination that the Royal Navy should make the prestigious first ever deck-landing of a jet aircraft before the US Navy. Anyway, everything started moving fast after my assessment report of the Vampire.

Certainly rumour had reached us that the US Navy was going to try and fit a P-80A Shooting Star with an arrester hook and get it aboard an aircraft carrier with all possible speed. The race was therefore on, but in fact we had got a flying start in Britain and were unlikely to be overtaken unless something went badly wrong.

By 1 October 1945, LZ551/G had arrived at Farnborough complete with the arrester hook installation, which was a faired V-frame located in the jet unit nacelle and anchored at the wing roots. The proofing of this installation, which had been designed and installed by the de Havilland factory at Christchurch, was done on the runway arrester gear at RAE and took the usual comprehensive pattern of gradually increasing entry speeds and off-centre distances. All went well until the limit was almost reached at 3.35 'g' retardation at 15ft (4.6m) off-centre, when the attachment point at the port wing root yielded. During this trial it also came to light that the damping of the hook, which dropped through the jet stream on release, was poor, so that if the aircraft landed on its three wheels simultaneously the hook tended to float in the jet stream about four inches off the ground. So it was back to the drawing board.

During its sojourn at Christchurch LZ551/G had undergone a number of further modifications other than the arrester hook installation, and the previously enlarged flaps and dive brakes. The additional modifications were: (i) fitting of a Goblin II engine of 2,000lb (907kg) static thrust; (ii) fitting of a tear drop hood; (iii) fitting of a leading edge pitot to the port wing in place of the normal pitot on the leading edge of the port fin. This latter change meant that the previous stalling speed of 95mph (153km/h) in the landing configuration now read 85mph (137km/h) in the cockpit.

By mid-November LZ551/G was ready for further arresting proofing trials and these were successful. So on 26 November I flew the aircraft to Ford airfield, carried out some ADDLs and left it there for a few days, awaiting the 'go' signal for the shipboard trials. This came on 2 December, when I returned to Ford and had one last session of ADDLs.

The all-up weight of the Vampire for the trials was 8,200lb (3,720kg). To restrict the AUW to this figure only 180gal (818 litres) of fuel were carried instead of the normal 202gal (918 litres). Unbelievably there was no compass fitted, so I wore a captured German portable compass strapped to my left wrist.

On 3 December I got the all clear to go signal and took off at 11.05. The light fleet carrier HMS *Ocean*, commanded by Captain Caspar John, was steaming off the Isle of Wight in a moderate swell. In overcast conditions I found her ploughing her way along, pitching rhythmically, and screeched over her with a low pass and a roll to announce my arrival. Unknown to me at that precise moment the ship's loudspeakers were announcing that the Vampire had been ordered to return to Ford because the boffins felt the flight deck was pitching excessively. However, Caspar John had been Captain of *Pretoria Castle*, the trials carrier, when I was in Service Trials Unit, so he knew me well and he immediately decided to accept me for landing. The combined ship's speed and wind speed over the deck was given to me by radio as 44mph (70km/h) with the flight deck pitching 12ft (3.7m) at the stern and rolling 5°.

The landing circuit was begun at 1,000ft (305m) at 200mph with the engine well throttled back, and then the dive brakes lowered when dead ahead of the ship, and the revs. increased to 7,000. As height and speed were lost the undercarriage was lowered on the downwind leg, and then at a height of 400ft (122m) at 150mph (241km/h) the arrester hook and flaps were lowered, the engine revs. increased to 8,500, and the elevator trim set 1½ divisions nose down. The final turn-in was a fairly wide sweep made in nose-down attitude at 115mph (185km/h), losing 100ft (30m) in height so that the straight approach was begun from 300ft (91m) well astern, giving a flattish approach path. The engine revs. were opened up gradually from 8,500 to 9,000 as speed was reduced gradually to 100mph (161km/h) by easing the stick progressively back, until a position about 150ft (46m) aft of the round-down and 30ft (9m) above the level of the flight deck was assumed. This position erred on the high side and aimed at pitching the aircraft into the middle of the arrester wire area, as any error on the low side meant a vastly reduced safety factor with the deck moving so much. Up to this point the excellent view made any correction for line unnecessary.

From this position the throttle was cut and no further movement on the elevators made until the round-down was crossed at 95mph (153km/h),

The world's first deck landing of a pure jet aircraft. Eric Brown landing Vampire LZ551/G on HMS *Ocean* on 4 December 1945.

The Vampire leaps into the air on its first deck take-off.

Circling HMS *Ocean* at the conclusion of the successful sea trials of the Vampire.

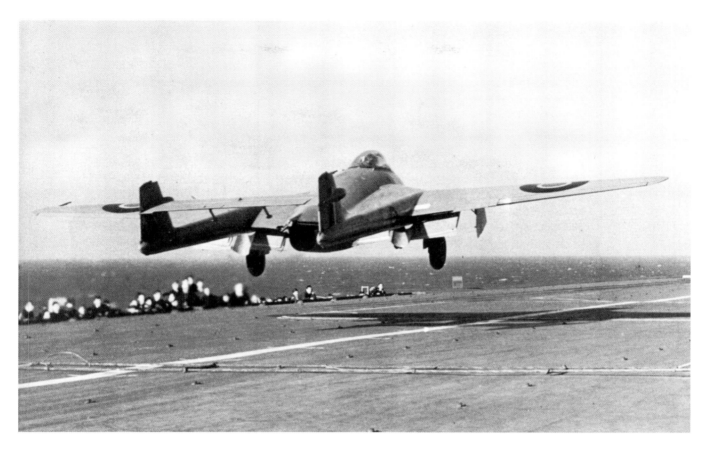

then the stick was eased back fairly sharply until the aircraft stalled completely as felt by the kick on the port aileron as the port wing dropped. The rate of fall-off in thrust was so slow that when the round-down was crossed, 6,000rpm were still registered. So in an emergency the throttle could be opened up very quickly to raise the revs to the 10,000 required for a wave-off, without exceeding jet pipe temperature limitations.

Although I had aimed for about No. 4 arrester wire, the flight deck was on the upswing of its pitch as I crossed the round-down and in consequence the hook picked up No. 1 wire and I came to a halt with astonishingly mild deceleration. As soon as the hook was felt to engage the wire I pulled back the stick to ease the force of the pitch on to the nose wheel due to deceleration, as this was considered one of the possible trouble spots with the Vampire. Examination of the photographic records revealed that the round-down had actually struck the tail booms of the aircraft, and this was confirmed by finding the tail boom pads had been slightly dented.

For take-off the flaps were set 30° down on the indicator, the elevator trimmed neutral, and the fuel booster pump switched on. The aircraft was held on the brakes until the full 10,200rpm were reached on run-up, and then released and the stick held central until 60mph (97km/h) regis-

tered on the ASI when the stick was eased back until the tail booms were estimated to be one foot off the deck. This gave a surprisingly short run in the wind conditions over the deck and I passed the island superstructure at bridge level.

After the first landing, the pitch of the flight deck combined with the gusty conditions over the round-down necessitated maintaining 100mph (161km/h) for the final part of the approach, instead of the intended 95mph (153km/h), but the maximum deceleration recorded was still only 1.7'g'. On the fourth landing, however, the trailing edge of the flaps hit the deck or a wire and sheared the hinge brackets.

As a result of the mishap to the flaps during the first series of landings it was decided to cut away 4sq ft (0.37m^2) of flap area to give a larger ground clearance, and I made a short test flight to measure the effect of this modification. It was found that the stall characteristics were unchanged, but the stalling speed had increased by 3mph (4.8km/h). The landing approach was also flatter and there was a greater tendency to float on cutting the throttle, but none of these changes were significant.

An unfaired, strengthened V-frame and arrester hook was also fitted to replace the original, which had sprung some rivets at the eye bolt attachments.

The modified Vampire, LZ551/G, taking off on 4 December 1945, during trials on HMS *Ocean*.

69

Sea Vampire being raised from the below deck service hangars.

These modifications were quickly carried out on board the carrier, and I flew ashore to the RN Air Station at Ford on 6 December, carrying out the stalls on the way. I then made a few ADDLs on the runway before returning to the *Ocean* to make another eight deck landings, finally returning direct to Farnborough.

The take-offs in this second series of trials were made with 40° of flap, but showed little improvement over the 30° setting.

The navalised Vampire, the E.6/41 as it was designated, had two major snags to acceptance as an operational naval aircraft. Firstly, the response of the Goblin II was sluggish and made lift control, which depends on speed in a jet aircraft, imprecise. Secondly, the aircraft had very short endurance. Its internal fuel tankage was 202gal, which compared very unfavourably with the contemporary German Me 262 with 586gal (2,664 litres) and the Ar 234's 834gal (3,791 litres).

The first of these snags was just a matter of technical development and since the Rolls-Royce Nene engine, which was already in existence at this time, showed vastly improved acceleration characteristics over the Goblin, it was obvious that this problem would soon be solved. But the second was an inherent design drawback, and was really the critical feature that made the Vampire unacceptable as a naval fighter.

There were two other minor faults: the abrupt wing-drop stall without warning, and the shallow approach angle after cropping of the flaps. The first of these was again an inherent design drawback, while the second could probably be improved by a compromise between the original flap area and the modified area.

The question has often been asked why the Royal Navy, which was the first in the race to operate a jet aircraft from the deck of an aircraft carrier, lost the race to introduce operational squadrons of jets into service. The answer is twofold – firstly the Vampire was unsuitable because of range and endurance limitations, and secondly the American post-war industry was geared up to a technological pitch that had been stimulated by the advanced technology discovered in defeated Germany. The UK industry, on the other hand, had understandably moved into low gear after such a prolonged period of sustained activity on which the country's very survival depended. There were thus many new American jet naval aircraft designs on the drawing board, while the UK had only one, which was once again the adaptation of a projected RAF fighter.

In the event we were perhaps the fortunate victims of circumstances, because the Korean War in the early 1950s found the US Navy largely jet equipped while the Royal Navy had mainly Sea Furies and Fireflies. It transpired that this was a war in which the task of the carrier forces was mainly ground attack with low level transit to and from targets to avoid high-altitude MIG fighter patrols. The jets suffered from low endurance and short range at low altitude, and the honours generally went to the piston-engined Sea Furies, Fireflies, and US Skyraiders for effective attacks.

I feel sure that the Naval Staff never really intended to order Vampires in quantity for carrier operations, for they obviously knew the performance limitations of the aircraft. At best I believe they hoped to have one squadron to gain experience of jet operations at sea. This belief is borne out by the meeting I attended at RAE on 11 February 1946, to discuss the Vampire trials. It was chaired by the Deputy Director of Aircraft Research and Development at the Ministry of Aircraft Production, and included the Chief and Deputy Chief Designer of de Havilland's, as well as RAE and A&AEE (Boscombe Down) representatives. Here it was stated that the Admiralty was anxious for a series of intensive deck trials to be done with jet-engined aircraft.

The decisions of that meeting are interesting in that they highlight the problems that it was felt needed examination. De Havilland's was tasked with examining the possibility of improving the engine response to throttle, especially on closing the throttle, with preparing a scheme for interconnection of throttle and enlarged dive brakes; with investigating the possibility of using improved tyres and longer stroke undercarriage oleos. RAE was tasked with preparing a scheme for interconnection of throttle and landing flap to improve lift control.

The Vampire carved its notch in aviation history and as such I shall always have a great affection for this little beauty, with which in its many marks I had a 26-year association that included other firsts, such as the first flexible deck landing with an undercarriage-less aircraft, the first catapult launch of a British jet aircraft, and the first in-flight photographic records of transonic shock waves.

The Vampire was so docile, yet so manoeuvrable and nippy, that it was the ideal introduction for many pilots of many nations to jet flying, so was therefore a great commercial success. Its lengthy service history underlines its contribution to the new post-war era of jet aviation, and I have yet to meet a pilot who did not enjoy flying it. That is perhaps the greatest accolade that any aircraft can hope for.

The flexible deck Vampire

The early jet fighters suffered from poor range and endurance, and much research was directed at improving these shortcomings. One line of investigation was that of removing the aircraft's undercarriage, which represented at least 5% of the all-up weight in land fighters and up to 7% in naval fighters.

On 11 January 1945, at a meeting at RAE, a scheme was put forward by Major Green, the former aero-engine designer, for landing an undercarriage-less naval aircraft on a rubber carpet stretched between shock absorbers to give a deadbeat deflection. The aircraft would pitch on to the carpet after picking up an arrester wire at

Sea Vampire F3, VF315, was the prototype for the F20.

Pilot's notes: de Havilland Sea Vampire F1

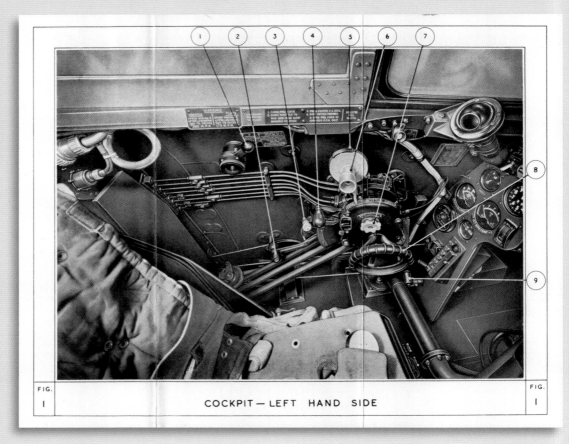

FIG.
I

COCKPIT— LEFT HAND SIDE

FIG.
I

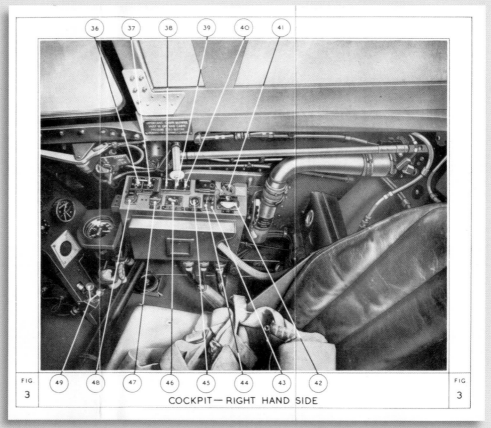

FIG
3

COCKPIT— RIGHT HAND SIDE

FIG
3

COCKPIT — INSTRUMENT PANEL

Fig 1:

Cockpit – Left hand side

1 Master switch
2 Undercarriage selector lever
3 Flaps selector lever
4 Dive brakes control
5 Canopy seal lever (hidden behind throttle lever)
6 Throttle lever
7 Friction adjuster
8 Elevator trimming tab control
9 Fuel cock lever

Fig 2:

Cockpit – Instrument panel

10 'G' switch
11 Auto manual
12 Undercarriage position indicator
13 Rear bearing temperature gauge
14 Flaps position indicator
15 Jet pipe temperature gauge
16 Burner pressure gauge
17 RPM indicator
18 Fuel tanks jettison switch
19 Oil temperature gauge
20 Undercarriage warning light
21 Elevator trim indicator
22 Gyro gunsight
23 Fuel pressure warning lamp
24 Gunsight selector dimmer control
25 RI compass indicator
26 Cabin air pressure gauge
27 Cabin altimeter
28 Cabin air pressure warning lamp
29 Oxygen regulator
30 Brakes pressure gauge
31 Generator warning lamp
32 Fire warning lamp
33 Tanks contents gauges
34 Oil pressure gauge
35 Controller TR 1464

Fig 3:

Cockpit – Right hand side

36 Interlinked starter switch
37 Interlinked master switch
38 RI compass switch
39 Pitot-head switch
40 Navigation lights switch
41 Landing lights
42 Detonator R 3121
43 Booster pump switch
44 Gunsight switch
45 Indentification lights push-button
46 Indentification lights
47 Fire extinguisher button
48 Starter button
49 De-icer pump

the rear end of the carpet. Once stopped, the aircraft could be pulled backwards by the arrester wire to a hinged flap on the aircraft carrier deck. The flap would tilt down and the aircraft would slide on to a trolley on the top hangar deck, because the height of these undercarriage-less aircraft would allow double the number to be stored at two shallow hangar levels instead of the normal single high-roofed hangar. Once the trolley cleared the flap, the latter closed up again ready for the next landing. Landings would be possible every 30 seconds. All take-offs would be by catapult launch.

The meeting concluded that the carpet scheme should be carried further, both by model experiments and theoretical work. Thus the go was given for what was to be a fascinating experiment containing all the elements of trial and error, failure and success.

As an outcome of this momentous meeting, I was given the task of working out the deck-landing technique required, and submitted my report on 27 February 1945. In essence the idea was to locate the carpet in the middle third of the flight deck with the single arrester wire in the position of what would be No. 5 wire on the *Indefatigable* class of carrier. The approach would be made in a shallow let down to the stern of the ship at 20mph (31km/h) above the stall. On crossing the stern the approach would be levelled out and the aircraft flown at some 5–10ft (1.5–3m) above the deck until the arrester hook caught the wire. Speed would then be 15mph (24km/h) above the stall. If the arrester was missed the aircraft would be accelerated away into a climb.

At this stage the responsibility for the project was put firmly in the hands of the Naval Aircraft Department at the RAE, in collaboration with Aerodynamics Department and Structural and Mechanical Engineering Department. This team launched itself straight into one-eighth-scale model experiments, whereby the aerodynamic model of a representative aircraft was launched by means of a weight-operated catapult. The aircraft arrester hook was arranged to engage an arrester wire and land on a suspended sheet.

The results of these experiments were encouraging, but they gave no information on one vital point – the determination of the stress in the carpet, especially in the immediate vicinity of the touch-down area.

As a result of these Stage I model experiments it was decided to embark on Stage II full-scale model experiments, using the carpet system supported by pneumatic tubes inflated at low pressures.

One phase of the experiments consisted of dropping from a crane the fuselage of a Hotspur glider, ballasted with concrete to a weight of 8,000lb (3,629kg). The fuselage was fitted with an accelerometer in a vertical plane and means provided for measuring the maximum penetration of the deck. Drops were made from various heights, to give contact velocities up to about 12ft/s (3.7m/s). The main point of interest was that, although penetration varied progressively with bed pressures, variation in the peak reaction did not change appreciably with pressures below 2psi.

For Stage II deck experiments it was estimated that vertical touch-down velocities of up to 16ft (4.9m) per second would be developed, and it

Right & far right: The first flexible-deck landing attempt on 29 December 1947, ends in a spectacular accident.

was therefore decided to have four layers of tubes and a carpet cover. A decision then had to be made on whether the cover should be untensioned or tensioned at 50lb/in (9kg/cm). Tests showed that the untensioned carpet reduced the penetration without a corresponding increase in reaction, and the tensioning of the carpet required a reduced tube pressure.

I was following every step in the experiments with deep interest as I would make the first full-scale flight on to the flexible deck if we ever got that far. However, my enthusiasm almost went too far on 26 March 1946, when I talked the boffins into letting me sit in the cockpit of the fuselage of Hotspur BT752, which was to be dropped on to the bed of tubes. I sat direct on the concrete ballast and was dropped at a vertical velocity of 10ft/s (3m/s). I thought my spine was coming through the top of my head as the Hotspur hit and the concrete and I seemed to be going in opposite directions at a high rate of knots. However, like the tubed bed I was fairly resilient, and so apart from the inability to enjoy sitting for twenty-four hours, no permanent damage was done.

The preliminaries having been completed, the full-scale Stage II flexible deck was now laid out at Meadow Gate, adjacent to the area where the catapults associated with the Naval Aircraft Department were ranged.

For this stage of the trials the Hotspur fuselage had wings and tail unit added so that it became a full-fledged glider. At an all-up weight of 7,000lb (3,175kg) it had a wing loading of 25½lb/sq ft (124kg/m²), and an estimated stalling speed (flaps up) of 90mph (145km/h).

The Hotspur was placed on a rocket catapult trolley sited behind the flexible deck, so that when the catapult was fired the Hotspur left the trolley at the end of the run and after less than half a second of free flight contacted the arrester wire with its arrester hook.

Thirty-four landings were made on the Stage II deck with various deck pressures and carpet tensions, and at varying heights to alter the vertical velocity at touch-down. Both on-centre and up to 15ft (4.6m) off-centre engagements of the arrester wire were made. The aircraft was launched with a datum incidence of 6° and with a speed of from 81–95mph (130–153km/h). Under action of the arresting forces it nosed over whilst dropping to deck level so that impact occurred with datum nose down from ½° to 3½°. Deck penetration varied between 14½–20¼in (37–51cm).

The overall conclusion of these Stage II trials was that the deck efficiency varied between 48½% and 75%, was not consistent but varied appreciably for identical deck conditions. However, no serious snags were met and the way ahead to Stage III was clear.

While Stage I and Stage II trials were underway I was carrying out a series of flying tests in parallel, aimed at evolving and perfecting the intended landing technique described in my report of 27 February 1945.

When the whole project was first planned the only jet aircraft which were sufficiently developed and available were the Meteor and Vampire. The layout of the former was not considered representative of the future high performance aircraft

by virtue of the engine nacelles, neither was it suitable because of its low wing. The choice therefore fell to the Vampire with its single engine in the fuselage and a mid-wing. Although the twin boom arrangement might not be representative of the future type, this feature was not sufficiently fundamental to detract from the basic requirements of the experiment.

The Vampire had to be modified to make it suitable for belly landing. A large proportion of the deck reaction comes on the engine access doors on the under-belly. These were reinforced and a transverse support provided to halve the lengthwise unsupported span of the doors. Also, the jet pipe fairing was reinforced and its fixing to its forward bulkhead strengthened. The arresting hook installation was the same as that on the Sea Vampire Mk 20 except that part-way through the trials the hook beak was modified, and the hook embodied a micro-switch. This was wired into the dive brake and flap operating system such that when the wire was engaged the dive brakes and flaps were retracted. It was specified that this should be completed in less than 0.7 seconds in order that they would not foul the deck on touchdown – especially a heavy touch-down. The specified time was handsomely achieved for the dive brakes but not fully realised for the flaps. However,

The wreckage of the Vampire after the first flexible-deck trials. There was severe damage to the fuselage which cracked laterally through the cockpit.

The rear tail booms were also badly damaged on impact with the rubber deck.

no damage resulted from this – the flaps, although not fully retracted, were sufficiently raised to clear the deck under all the conditions experienced.

For convenience of weight control the wing tip tanks were blanked off and use made only of the fuselage and stub tanks (203gal/923 litres). This corresponded to a weight of approximately 9,200lb (4,173kg), so that the landing weight was between 9,200lb and 7,600lb (3,447kg). At 9,000lb (4,082kg) (an average landing weight for Stage IV trials) the stalling speed was found to be 92mph (147km/h) EAS and an approach speed of 119mph (191km/h) TAS corresponded to 1.3Vs. To facilitate piloting, an open scale ASI was mounted level with the lower edge of the windscreen, i.e. well within the pilot's view whilst he was concentrating on the approach.

This modified Vampire 20 was designated the Mk 21 and six were allocated for the flight trials. Prior to the availability of these, two modified Vampire 3s were used – identical to Mk 21s in respect of arresting hook installation and underbelly modification, but which were lighter in weight by approximately 790lb (358kg).

Since the construction of the Stage III deck was slightly different to Stage II, and the weight/ fuselage area for the Hotspur and Vampire were different, drop tests were made with a Vampire on a sample deck of Stage III up to a maximum vertical velocity of 12ft/s (3.7m/s).

The deck and arrester gear unit for Stage III was similar in general construction and principle to that of Stage II, being 200ft (61m) long by 60ft (18m) wide. It was sited in the centre of the airfield at Farnborough, to the west of the short runway where the various types of arrester gear of Naval Aircraft Department were ranged, and just south of the main runway. The concrete raft for the pneumatic tubes was at ground level and the carpet cover was about 28in. (70cm) above the ground level. A level length of steel decking 66ft (20m) long at the same level as the carpet was provided at the approach to the deck and ramped off to ground level. A single arrester wire, supported 30in. (80cm) clear of the deck, was provided 15 feet aft of the deck. The deck was laid out for landing in one direction only (S.W.) but a second arrester wire could have been provided at the opposite end to make it two-directional.

The main difference between Stage II and III decks was in the types of pneumatic tube used. Sufficient quantity of heavy 7¼ in. diameter hose was not available for Stage III and therefore tubes were manufactured from dinghy fabric. The tubes were much lighter and had a bursting pressure of about 15psi An economical cutting of the fabric resulted in tubes with a nominal working diameter of 6⅜in. Five layers of tubes were used, necessitating about 1,800 for the deck, giving an overall depth of 28½in and an approximate working depth of 25in.

For handling the aircraft after landing it was to be dragged via the arrester hook to an after corner of the deck and lifted clear by a mobile crane using a special sling. The aircraft was thus swung clear of the deck, its undercarriage lowered and the aircraft lowered to hard ground.

To give the pilot a guide to the true centre of the deck, there was a line of four lead-in lights placed on the ground at approximately 150ft (46m)intervals from the rear ramp, and leading up to the white centre line painted on the mat. A further two lights were placed well ahead of the forward ramp.

At each side of the steel deck there were two landing signal lamps set up and backed by dark boards; it was found convenient to make the tops of these boards level with the arrester wire to act as a height datum for the pilot. The flight preparations for the first landing commenced in August 1947, using Vampire TG426.

Fly-over tests were made over a dummy deck marked out on the runway. The results obtained over four separate sets of tests (total of 20 runs) gave an average aircraft speed of 98mph (158km/h) for zero wind, and an average hook height of 10½in (27cm) above the deck.

The fly-over tests were continued over the Stage III flexible deck and gave an average aircraft speed of 102mph (164km/h) for zero wind, and an average hook height of 26in above the deck.

By the end of December 1947 everything was in readiness for the first landing, and this was attempted on the morning of 29 December, when a favourable wind of 13mph (20km/h) was blowing directly down the deck. This was somewhat lighter in strength than had been hoped for, but was very steady, and I hoped to keep the approach speed down to a minimum.

On the approach, which I made at 95mph (153km/h) the aircraft sank appreciably over the Jersey Brow site, which is an inclined gap between two sets of buildings, probably as a result of wind gradient. It did not stop sinking until it reached the height normally maintained for the level run-up, though still at some 1,000ft (305m) from the deck, whereas I usually aimed to level out at about 800ft (244m)from the deck. The subsequent drop off in speed on the run-up was greater than intended, so I opened up the throttle, but the thrust response was slow and the aircraft did not accelerate and had now sunk very near to the ground until the arrester hook was actually trailing on the soil. This dangerously low height was apparent to me, and though I attempted to gain height by easing back on the stick, the aircraft merely increased incidence and mushed forward into the arrester wire. Meanwhile the hook and tail booms struck the sharp steel ramp, and this

The sea trials of the flexible deck; the prototype Vampire, TG286, flown by Eric Brown, landing on HMS *Warrior* after two practice dummy runs over the deck.

resulted in the hook bouncing up and remaining stowed in its housing, due to failure of the supposedly fool-proof latch gear, whilst the booms were dented causing the elevators to jam hard down and the rudders jam central. Also this sharp blow to the rear end of the aircraft caused it to reduce incidence very rapidly.

Actually the aircraft crossed the wire at an airspeed of 95mph (153km/h) in a level flight attitude with the belly just scraping the arrester wire, and would almost certainly have picked up the wire if the arrester hook latch gear had not failed. However, it continued to nose over and penetrated deeply into the rubber mat in a very tail-up attitude, rode out again in a slight nose-up attitude and once more dived into the mat. As it rode out of this second impact the nose struck the steel fixing drums at the forward edge of the mat and damaged the cockpit structure badly. The aircraft was flung into the air clear of the forward ramp, and I had time to try the elevators in an attempt to climb away, but on finding them jammed I closed the throttle and the aircraft struck the ground evenly in a very shallow dive and skidded quickly to rest.

What then had gone wrong? Was it an error of my judgement, unsuitable weather conditions, application of a wrong technique, a combination of all these, or was there something we had not calculated? It was back to the drawing board.

Complete camera records of the attempted first landing allowed us at RAE to make a detailed investigation into the sequence of events leading up to the accident. The conclusions were that there was an adverse wind gradient over Jersey Brow which must be avoided, and that the approach speed must be stepped up to give the pilot a safety margin to cope with any emergency such as had just been encountered.

There were not really any serious misgivings as to this latter recommendation, because we had been working on a fairly liberal safety factor on the arrester gear performance up to this point.

As regards the avoidance of the Jersey Brow area, this could only be achieved by increasing the height of the approach at that point, which in turn meant cutting down the length of the level run-up. Actually, the run-up used was started about 800ft (244m) from the arrester wire. But this was only of such great length in order to increase the time available to get an accurate check and adjustment on airspeed, which is rather critical in regard to entry speed into the arrester gear when the relative wind speed is so low as it usually is on land. Therefore it was safe to assume this distance could be reduced adequately.

The obvious alterations to the rear ramp and arrester hook latch gear were also made, the ramp incline being reduced to 1:13 in wood. A

The Vampire touching down on the flexible deck on 3 November 1948.

safety catch was introduced into the latch gear to prevent it operating itself under the effect of a heavy blow from a bouncing hook hitting the faired hook housing.

For my part I felt there were two aids which could facilitate my task appreciably. First of these was the fitting of an open-scale ASI at windscreen level – an adaptation of my recommendation made early in 1947 – which enabled the pilot to concentrate on both height and speed without switching his eyes from the windscreen into the cockpit, as formerly.

The second aid I suggested was the adoption of a DLCO (Deck Landing Control Officer), equipped not with the usual 'bats' but with VHF talkdown equipment. His task would be to give a height check to the pilot on the run-up. For this purpose a sighting screen, with an artificial horizon level with the arrester wire, was installed at a position about two-thirds of the length of the deck, forward of the wire.

These two modifications were completed before the flight tests were recommenced on a spare Sea Vampire (serial number TG328) in the interim period – pending the preparation of the second hooked Vampire TG286 – and proved highly successful in operation.

The new series of flight tests established that a run-up distance of 600ft (183m) was acceptable and kept the aircraft out of the adverse wind gradient area. It was also decided to increase the height tolerance for the run-up by raising the arrester wire from 30–36in (76–91cm).

Further tests with the second aircraft, established an optimum final run-up speed of 106mph (171km/h), with an acceptable range from 103mph–110mph (166–177km/h). The approach speed was of course to be made at a faster speed of 115mph (185km/h) = 1.3VS.

Everything was in readiness for another attempt at landing by the middle of March 1948. A favourable wind of 12mph (19km/h) directly down the deck presented the opportunity on 17 March, and after two dummy runs (with the hook up) to establish the suitability of the weather conditions, a landing was successfully made, although the arrester gear bottomed in spite of the low contact airspeed of 104mph (167km/h). However, this trouble could be rectified by merely altering the arrester gear dome valve pressure, and in fact the setting used on that occasion was never used subsequently.

After the first successful landing it was decided to embark on an objective programme to attain zero wind and then side-wind landings.

The zero wind condition was fulfilled on the eighth landing and on the thirteenth a side-wind condition of 8mph (13km/h) at 90° to the deck was encountered.

Up to the commencement of the Stage IV trials in November 1948, I had made 33 landings, during which the following peak conditions were met:

- Minimum wind speed for landing 3mph (4.6km/h) – *tail* wind
- Minimum airspeed at contact with arrester wire 99mph (159km/h)
- Maximum airspeed at contact with arrester wire 114mph (184km/h)
- Minimum combined (arrester gear + mat friction) 3.1 'g' – retardation 'g'
- Maximum combined (arrester gear + mat friction) 4.85 'g' – retardation 'g'

By May 1948 the first batch of six Sea Vampire 21 aircraft arrived, and from that date these aircraft were used in conjunction with the hooked Vampire on the tests. The Sea Vampire 21 was in effect the fully navalised Sea Vampire 20, but incorporating all the modifications required for flexible deck landing. It differed from the hooked Vampire mainly in having square-cut wing tips, a low tailplane, rounded tip fins and rudders, and increased internal fuel tankage. With the fuel restriction of 140gal (636 litres) used throughout the Stage III this gave the aircraft an AUW of 8,400lb (3,810kg), which was an increase of 400lb (181kg) over TG286. In spite of this, the stalling speeds of both types of aircraft were found to be almost identical, and so the approved speed range remained the same also.

On five occasions in all, the arrester gear bottomed on landing due to various experimental causes, and since the arrester hook V-frame attachment bolts of 55 ton (55.9tonnes) high tensile steel showed signs of shearing, it was decided to replace them with 80ton bolts. The efficacy of this measure can be gauged by the fact that on a particularly vicious bottoming, giving a peak retardation reading of 5.6 + 'g' (accelerometer pointer went off the top of the diagram paper), the hook sheared clean off the V-frame, yet the latter only pulled at the attachment points.

The retardation 'g' and vertical reaction imposed on the pilot was almost double that to which he was subjected in a conventional deck landing. But the time interval of the peak values was so very short that there was absolutely no physical discomfort experienced, and no special harness was required. Indeed, no headrest was even fitted to the aircraft used on Stage III trials, although it was a requirement for the Stage IV trials when the Sea Vampire 21s were to make catapult take-offs.

Probably the most astounding fact that emerged from the trials was the performance of the

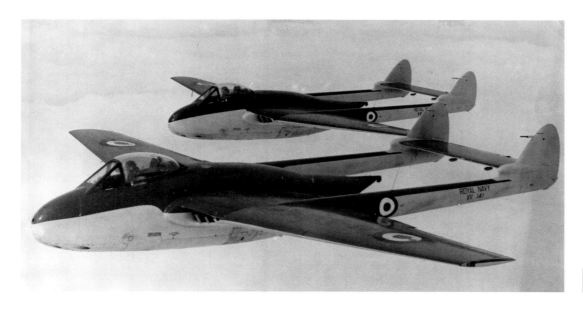

Sea Vampire F20s in formation.

arrester gear, which successfully coped with an entry speed of 109mph (175km/h) i.e. 40mph (65km/h) in excess of its designed performance.

As regards the implications of flexible deck landing for land-based operational use, I felt the project had far reaching possibilities in the near future as an answer to the advanced attack airfield and concealed defence airfield problems. This would be especially so if considered in combination with the vertical take-off experiments which were soon to be undertaken.

Ease of transportation, expediency of erection, low costs and ease of concealment, are all vital advantages offered by the flexible deck and particularly when one considered that modern high speed fighters cannot be operated off the old type wire mesh advanced airfield runway. They need very long, smooth concrete surfaces, due to their fast landing speeds and high tyre pressures.

At that time, the only type of aircraft reviewed with relation to its operation from the flexible deck was the fighter. But for the advanced airfield in particular there was a most important commitment for transport aircraft. A scheme had already been put forward to meet this by fitting an arrester hook to the freight pannier on Halifax and Hastings transports, and merely arresting the pannier as the aircraft flew low over the deck, so that it detached itself from the fuselage and the aircraft flew away free of its load.

Once the Stage III trials had progressed to a point where we were satisfied the landing technique was proven, I started training two RAF and two naval test pilots up to the full stage of actually landing on the Stage III deck. Their training curriculum comprised initial self-training practice over the airfield runways, followed by monitored practice over the actual deck. The average time

per pilot taken to complete the whole programme was 10 hours, the total being equally divided between the two training phases.

Later on it was decided to train a further four naval pilots, selected to cover the whole spectrum of pilot experience from above average to low average, and also to include a US Navy pilot. All the naval pilots and one RAF test pilot were to take part in the Stage IV trials.

Thus, at the end of October 1948, it was 'all systems to go' for the Stage IV trials in the light fleet aircraft carrier HMS *Warrior*.

The deck installed on HMS *Warrior* was that used for the Stage II trials, and it was located on the existing flight deck so that the single arrester wire was in the position of the normal No.6 wire. This brought the forward end of the rubber mat in line with the aft end of the island, where a swivelling crane was conveniently situated for handling the aircraft at rest after landing.

The whole flexible deck stood 27in. (69cm) above the steel flight deck, but the flight deck length aft of the installation had a funnel-shaped steel-plate dummy deck built up on it to the same height as the rubber mat surface. This funnel was the same width as the flexible deck at its forward end, then it tapered off aft along its 142ft (43m) length until it ended in a short curved round-down. The reason for this taper was merely to effect a saving in construction costs.

There was a 12in. (30cm) white line painted the whole length of the ship, to indicate the centre of the rubber mat, and the arrester wire centre span was painted black and white alternately in 2ft (61cm) lengths. During a visit in July 1948 to inspect the layout, I had the raised deck round-down painted all white, and 13in. (33cm) white lines painted athwartships under the arrester wire

and at a point 100ft (30m) aft of this, all to act out as markers on the approach and run-up.

The Stage VI trials commenced on 3 November 1948 and continued through to 31 May 1949, during which a total of 200 landings were made by nine pilots. Out of this total I made 26 landings, including the initial 22 and the first landing after any subsequent alteration to the deck or the aircraft.

For the first four landings the hooked Vampire, TG286, was used. This entailed free take-off from the 300ft (91m) of flight deck available forward of the flexible deck installation, and required a minimum wind speed of 43mph (69km/h) over the deck. To avoid this restriction on the operating conditions, all subsequent landings were made with the Sea Vampire 21s which were equipped for catapult take-off.

The trials themselves were not without incident in the initial stages, and indeed some might even say they were incident packed.

The first landing was made on hooked Vampire, TG286, after two practice dummy runs over the deck. This aircraft was chosen for the initial landings because of its lighter AUW and its being equipped with an auto-observer.

The arrester gear and deck was deliberately set hard for the landing, and this resulted in a short pay-out of the wire and 6.0 W vertical reaction. Such a high vertical reaction borders on the physically uncomfortable, but only for the split second of application.

When attempting the fourth landing, the deck was pitching and heaving slightly and I just failed

to pick up the arrester wire and, continuing on my flight path, struck the forward end of the flexible deck with sufficient force to record 0.4 'g' and 2.0 W on the accelerometers which were still switched on. But the aircraft bounced off into the air at a fairly steep angle of attack and remained airborne with a little forward pressure on the stick. A successful landing was made at the second attempt.

Such a contact may have resulted from continuing on a sinking run-up, but I rather feel my flight path was level and that the deck came up on the pitch of the ship and met the aircraft. Whatever the cause, the outcome was at least very reassuring.

As a result of this incident the steel fixing drums at the forward edge of the mat were removed, for the aircraft only rode out of the deck a foot before reaching them, otherwise it might have broken its back.

On the fifth landing the port wing tip of the aircraft struck the arrester wire which was rising on that side under roll. A successful landing was accomplished with minor damage to the leading edge of the port wing.

Actually the wire had ridden over the wing, then fortunately whipped clear again, but the danger was always likely to be present under conditions of roll, since the pilot keeps the aircraft level with the horizon and does not attempt to follow the movement of the rolling deck. Accordingly it was decided to reduce the width of the wire supports from 42ft (13m) to 25ft (8m), to give increased wing tip clearances for such conditions.

This modification meant that there was now only a 5ft (1.5m) clearance on each side between the flaps and the wire support for off-centre landing, but this later proved to be adequate.

The next two attempts at landing were unsuccessful, for although the arrester hook picked up the wire on both occasions, there appeared to be new whip characteristics associated with the increased tension of the shorter supported span. The wire was forced out of the hook immediately after pick-up by its whipping up and striking the aircraft booms.

Again modification action was taken to the extent of lengthening the beak of the hook and closing the angle by 18°. This was checked successfully with two landings on the Stage III deck at RAE before resuming the ship trials.

The next step in the trials was to increase the AUW for landing, and this was stepped up to a nominal 9,000lb (4,082kg) by the ninth landing. This represents a landing with centre and inboard tanks full, except for what fuel was used to complete a circuit immediately after take-off.

Thereafter, reduced wind speed, off-centre, and side-wind landings were made up to the possible limits. The minimum wind speed obtainable over the deck, with the natural wind at 16mph (26km/h) and the ship requiring 9mph (14km/h) of way on for steerage, was 25mph (40km/h), so it was decided to step up the landing speed to get a higher entry speed into the gear. This was done on the twenty-first landing and resulted in an airspeed of 123mph (198km/h) on contact with the wire. Unfortunately a high pressure pipe joint failed in the arrester gear, causing the gear to bottom violently (5.2'g') and strain the V-frame attachment bolts, so full useful data was not obtained.

The off-centre landings were made up to a maximum of 7ft (2m) to port. This meant moving the port wire support outboard to prevent it striking the flaps, and it was not possible to land more than 7ft (2m) off centre lest the wing tip strike the steel transverse mat tensioning drums.

The side-wind landings reached a maximum condition of 35mph (56km/h) at 18° from port, at which juncture on the twentieth landing the aircraft fell out of my hands just after it crossed the round-down. It sank straight on to the arrester wire which whipped up and dented the underside of the port wing and the starboard dive-brake before going into the hook. The aircraft just slid on to the flexible deck without recording any vertical reaction on the accelerometer!

There was no difficulty in coping with down draught on the approach, and since the landing speed was 112mph (180km/h) on this occasion,

it can only be assumed that the airflow pattern over the deck in this wind condition is irregular. Preliminary investigation confirmed this.

It is of incidental interest that the catapult take-offs of the Sea Vampire were the first such launches of a British jet and tricycle undercarriage aircraft from a ship.

From the twenty-second landing onwards there were no great problems encountered, so we appeared to have got it right by trial and error. The only snag remaining was that in the next 129 landings seven dive brakes were damaged, so their use was discontinued for the remainder of the trials, which had the effect of increasing the approach speed slightly.

The success of the whole experiment could hardly be in question when it is considered that after the initial set-back, 260 landings both ashore and afloat were made without any accident, by a wide cross-section of pilots. Three had never previously flown a jet aircraft before they commenced their flexible deck training, and two had only 500 hours total flying experience.

Why then was the flexible deck never adopted for operational service? The answer is twofold. Firstly, it arrived at the wrong point in time after the war was over and the impetus to military matters was waning rapidly. Secondly, the idea was a little too radical in that it meant a widespread requirement for flexible deck installations ashore and afloat for what was a comparatively small performance gain. In other words it was not cost effective.

However, the idea was so sound in technological conception that it was almost revived by the US Marines for their mobile airfield concept, which comprised a catapult installation and an arrester gear on a short light metal strip runway. The latter had limitations on high performance aircraft with high tyre pressures, hence the interest in the flexible deck. The whole concept has of course now been overtaken by VTOL aircraft such as the Harrier.

Just to round the whole thing off, some years after I left the RAE, and before the flexible deck installation was uprooted, a catapult take-off and landing was made with a Sea Hawk without the undercarriage wheels ever being lowered. A tidy way to wrap up what was undoubtedly a most spectacular thing to witness. Indeed a flexible deck landing was the standard showpiece for VIPs visiting the RAE during my time there. I enjoyed this trampoline circus act as each landing contributed some more data to our knowledge, and anyway I always found such a landing a most exhilarating experience.

11 DE HAVILLAND SWALLOW

A serial killer, which taught the aviation world some hard lessons in design. ERIC BROWN

THE DE HAVILLAND DH 108 was a post-war research aircraft built to investigate the behaviour of swept wings and the tailless layout. It was one of the crop of Allied experimental aeroplanes that were inspired by German technology, and the resemblance of the DH Swallow, as it came to be known, to the Messerschmitt 163 was no coincidence.

Design work began in October 1945 to the specification E.18/45, using the standard Vampire fuselage. The 43° swept wings were attached to the existing pick-up points and were of all wood

construction with elevons fitted outboard of the split trailing edge flaps.

The RAE Farnborough had become involved in this design from the outset because much wind tunnel testing was required to predict certain aspects of the flight behaviour. The RAE had warned that the aircraft might Dutch roll at low speeds or be likely to drop a wing severely at the stall and be difficult to recover from a spin. Thus the prototype had fixed slots extending inwards from the wing for a distance of 35% span. I therefore knew of the existence of the Swallow

DE HAVILLAND 108
(PROTOTYPE)
GOBLIN
OCTOBER 1946

before its first flight by the younger Geoffrey de Havilland on 15 May 1946. The prototype, TG283, first lifted off from the 3,500yd (3,200m) emergency runway at RAF Woodbridge and made an uneventful 30 minute flight.

Although TG283 came to be known as the slow speed version, the second prototype, TG306, was built specifically for high speed work. Its modifications included Handley Page automatic slats, which could be locked by the pilot; increased sweepback of the wings to 45°; a redesigned cockpit canopy; and a boosted Goblin 3 engine of 3,300lb (1,497kg) static thrust.

This aircraft soon showed it had the potential to beat the World Speed Record which then stood at 616mph (991km/h), so the game was on. Preparation flights began for the record attempt, and on 27 September Geoffrey de Havilland took off from Hatfield on such a trip. Over the Thames Estuary he dived from 10,000ft (3,050m) to level off at 7,000ft (2,134m) and let the Swallow have its head, when suddenly, at a Mach number of 0.875, disaster struck and the aircraft disintegrated, killing the pilot.

Nearly all the wreckage and the pilot's body was recovered and it became apparent the DH 108 had suffered structural failure due to the loads imposed at high subsonic speed. One curious aspect was that a post-mortem on the pilot's body revealed his neck had probably been broken before his body landed in the mudflats of Egypt Bay.

In spite of this setback a third prototype was built, incorporating an elongated and more pointed nose, and a streamlined cockpit canopy of lower profile. This aircraft, serial number VW120, was fitted with a Goblin 3 engine of 3,750lb (1,701kg) static thrust, and of course the wing structure was strengthened. It made its first flight in the hands of John Cunningham on 24 July 1947, and the original research programme was continued – somewhat cautiously.

After nine months a successful attempt was made on the 100km International Closed-Circuit Speed Record, when VW120, flown by John Derry, achieved 605.23mph (974km/h). On 9 September, de Havilland's claimed that the same pilot had exceeded the speed of sound for the first time in Britain in a dive from 40,000ft (12,192m) to 30,000ft (9,144m).

At this point the RAE was brought into the picture, for it had been conducting transonic research for a number of years in Aerodynamics Flight. For a variety of reasons I was the obvious choice to

Opposite: Built as part of a research programme into swept wings, dating from late 1945, the first prototype of the DH 108 was essentially the fuselage pod from a Vampire married to a vertical tail fin and swept wings. The similarity to the wartime German rocket-powered Messerschmitt Me 163 is striking. Warnings from the RAE that the design was likely to be highly unstable led to the provision of anti-spin parachutes at the wingtips, just visible here. Eric Brown's view that the aircraft was a 'killer' proved to be all too accurate when TG253 crashed not far from the RAE on 1 May 1950, killing the pilot, Sqn Leader George Genders, Eric Brown's successor as head of the Aerodynamics Flight.
Barry Ketley.

fly the DH 108 – I was CO of Aero Flight, I had flown most of the Me 163B tests, I had done transonic speed tests on the special Meteor IV *Britannia,* used for the successful World Speed Record attempt by the RAF High Speed Flight in November 1945, and had been in close contact with the de Havilland test programme on the Swallow. Accordingly, on 5 October 1948, I was despatched to Hatfield to fly TG283 and deliver it to Farnborough.

I did a familiarisation flight in the morning and then lunched at Hatfield before flying to Farnborough in the afternoon. I lunched with John Cunningham, John Derry, and Ronald Bishop, the chief designer, as I had been instructed to interview John Derry about his flight on 9 September.

I had known John Derry ever since he was a test pilot with Supermarine, and had a high regard for both his flying skill and his personal integrity. He told me that he had been doing a series of trim curves including dives in the transonic region, and these were being recorded on the automatic observer. On the last dive the aircraft had run away in the sense that the nose had continued to drop in spite of his backward control movement. The pilot's Machmeter had shown M=0.98 and then in the uncontrolled vertical dive it suddenly jumped to M=1.05 or thereabouts. Control had returned at 30,000ft (9,144m), using full-up trim flap and as much elevon as possible. The automatic observer had been switched on but had run out of film, so there was in fact no actual record of this momentous occasion.

For this reason doubts have been expressed about the authenticity of a true supersonic speed having been achieved. No one was more aware of this than John himself and I was convinced by his quiet sincerity that he had in fact exceeded the speed of sound – but in uncontrolled flight. My own subsequent flights in VW120 had confirmed this impression as I shall recount later on.

After complete re-instrumentation at RAE I began slow speed tests on TG283 on 8 December 1948, and these continued through until June 1949. They gave some demanding moments, which made it obvious this was an aircraft of high temperament.

Simultaneous with the commencement of the slow speed tests at RAE, Aero Department issued its Report, Aero 2305, on Model Spinning Tests on

The second prototype, the TG306, was built specifically for high speed work. It had a redesigned cockpit canopy and increased sweepback of the wings to 45°.

an Experimental Tailless Aircraft (DH 108 E.18/45). The report predicted that recovery from an accidental spin would take place only if the pilot took action immediately the spin started. Anti-spin parachutes streamed from the wing-tips would provide a powerful aid to recovery. Recovery from an inverted spin was good, as the rudder was not blanked by the fuselage in the inverted spin attitude.

This information was to serve me well, and of course the wing tip anti-spin parachutes had been fitted on TG283 from the outset on RAE advice. Now, in addition, a 100ft (30m) trailing static was fitted for the stall tests to be undertaken. This device was rather like an 11lb (5kg) practice bomb with a perforated spike in the nose, and 100ft (30m) of rubber tubing attaching it to the underside of the aircraft. In flight it was released from the cockpit and hung clear of all disturbed airflow, so that true airspeed reading was given on a wide-scale airspeed indicator available to the pilot and repeated in the automatic observer.

Getting into the Swallow needed external help as there was no retractable step like on the Vampire. The view, of course, was excellent and the cockpit closely resembled that of the Vampire. The brakes were very good, but during taxying there was a slight weathercocking tendency in a cross wind in spite of the tricycle undercarriage layout. Care had to be taken to ensure that the low sweptback wing tips were clear of any ground obstructions.

The Goblin 2 could be held up to full power on the brakes for take-off, and with 1½ divisions of nose-up elevator trim I lifted the nose wheel off at 100mph (161km/h), which required a fair pull force. I let the speed build up to this figure because as soon as ground effect was lost the aircraft pitched nose-up and at a lower speed might self-stall. Just after unsticking, the 108 was very sensitive to fore-and-aft control, and in a cross-wind tended to drop the down-wind wing, and it needed a large lateral stick movement to raise it. No flap was used on take-off.

Climb was made at 190mph (306km/h), at 9,700rpm, and was straightforward, although the aircraft displayed longitudinal instability if the pilot took his hands off the stick.

Cruising at 220mph (354km/h) at 15,000ft

The DH 108 Swallow was converted from a Vampire fuselage.

Opposite: The high speed Swallow, VW120, was delivered to the RAE in July 1949. After Eric Brown experienced serious problems with the plane, restrictions were placed on the test programme.

(4,572m) at 8,700rpm revealed poor stability round all three axes, and control harmony was also not very good, the rudder being too light and fore-and-aft control too heavy. The manoeuvering was restricted by a maximum permissible 'g' limit of 2.4 because of strength considerations for the full span wooden slots fitted to TG283 before hand-over to Farnborough.

The real fun and games started with the stalling trials. Once speed was reduced below 105mph (170km/h) the instability of the aircraft became apparent as it started a series of slight longitudinal oscillations, accompanied by Dutch rolling in anything but smooth air.

At 87mph (140km/h), with the nose well above the horizon, the starboard wing started to drop slowly and gently. If held up by opposite aileron at 86mph (138km/h) it snapped over almost to the vertical before one had time to react and push the stick forward. Any marked delay in taking recovery action resulted in the aircraft rolling right over on to its back and a lot of height could be lost in the ensuing steep dive. In consequence I never started stall tests below 10,000ft (3,050m).

The stall with trimmer flaps open occurred at 88½mph (142km/h) with similar characteristics, but there was also a slight buffeting tremor felt on approaching the stall.

The stall with both drag and trimmer flaps open occurred at 83mph (134km/h) – again with similar characteristics. There was more buffeting and the nose was less high above the horizon, although the stick was well back to produce the stall. The effect of lowering the undercarriage was negligible.

I have described the stall characteristics in detail because they almost caught me out and later resulted in a fatal crash to TG283. In my case the incident came near the end of an extensive series of stalling test flights. I had lowered the trailing static at 15,000ft (4,572m) and was carrying out a clean stall, attempting to find if a combination of a small amount of opposite aileron and moderate rudder could delay the wing drop. When the stall came it was a very vicious wing drop to the inverted position and before I could centralise the rudder the aircraft was in a steep right hand inverted spin. Fortunately, I had closely studied the RAE report of the wind tunnel trials of the spinning characteristics of the DH 108 and so kept a cool head. I say this because the danger to a pilot in an inverted spin is disorientation. However, I had been applying left rudder at the stall, so I kicked on rudder with my right foot but found the somewhat slow rate of rotation was not stopping as quickly as I expected. I pushed harder and then realised the rudder was jammed, probably by the trailing static wound around it. The extra push force did the trick and as rotation ceased I eased the stick back and pulled very gently through the vertical for recovery at 3,000ft (914m). The trailing static remained wrapped around the tail for landing.

The landing was rather a tricky procedure in normal circumstances. Although the view during approach was excellent, in spite of the nose-up attitude of the aircraft, the powered approach angle was very flat in order to keep the rate of descent within moderate limits, and also to prevent having to make a large change of attitude

The prototype Swallow was TG283 in which Squadron Leader Genders spun to his death on 1 May 1950.

near the ground for touchdown. Such an increase in incidence would result in the tail end of the aircraft contacting the ground.

By trial and error I found the best method for landing was to lower the drag flaps at 150mph (241km/h) on the cross-wing leg. Then, when they reached 15°, to pull up the trimmer flaps to counteract the strong nose-down change of trim. Further trimming was necessary until full flap angle was reached with full nose-up elevator trim plus a slight pull force. Turn in on the final approach leg was made at a height of 500ft (152m) and a speed of 140mph (225km/h), reducing this to 125mph (201km/h) for the straight run-in.

I kept the engine revs at about 6,000 and maintained this until I made a very slight check at 10ft off the ground, then cut the throttle. The aircraft continued to sink after the check until it was about 24in (61cm) off the ground, when a cushioning effect was experienced and it touched down gently on all three wheels at 120mph (193km/h).

A mere reduction of 5–10mph (8–16km/h) in approach speed could result in the check becoming ineffective, so that the aircraft would sink through the ground cushion to make a heavy landing. Alternatively, an early engine cut could set up a high rate of sink that would remain unaffected by any attempt to check attitude near the ground within the limits of backward stick movement one dare apply without fear of lowering the tail too far.

In spite of these rather sensitive landing characteristics, it was decided at RAE to conduct a series of dead stick landings at the then deserted Blackbushe airfield, which was adjacent to Farnborough and had a runway adequate for the purpose.

My briefing was to keep the engine throttled right back from 500ft (152m) and to progressively reduce approach speed over the series of landings. The test was made on 14 June 1949, and I got the approach speed down to 115mph (185km/h). But the hold off to reduce the high rate of descent gave a large change of attitude so that the tail cone and wing tip skids struck the runway first on touch-down at a recorded 103mph (166km/h). This jerked the aircraft violently on to its nose wheel and caused only minor damage, although the aircraft's accelerometer recorded +10½'g' and -4½'g'.

In early July the high speed Swallow, VW120, was delivered to the RAE. This aircraft differed from the low-speed version mainly in having only hydraulically lockable wing tip slats, as opposed to the full-span fixed slats of the latter. Other features peculiar to VW120 were the powered elevon controls for both longitudinal and lateral control, with variable feedback available to the pilot; a two-way range of trimmer flap movement; a strengthened metal cockpit canopy, and pilot ejection seat. Available trim flap movement was 12° up and 4° down.

On 6 July I flew it for the first time in a series of compressibility dives, and actually achieved a recorded M=0.985 in a 30° dive from 45,000ft (13,716m) with the stick fully back on the stop to hold the strong nose-down change of trim that set in at M=0.85. This, in fact, was the proof that John Derry's supersonic dive must have been in uncontrolled flight. But perhaps the most important point noted was the nasty undamped oscillation I experienced on pulling out of a dive from 38,000ft (11,582m) to M=0.94 by use of trimmer flap. This was the first real clue we had to the cause of Geoffrey de Havilland's crash.

The Goblin 4 had to be controlled on jet pipe temperature as it was very easy to overheat the engine under certain conditions. The ceiling of the aircraft, apart from lack of a pressure cabin, was therefore limited by JPT. This reached its limit of 710°C in the climb at 10,250rpm at 46,000ft (14,021m). The temperature ceiling was therefore about 47,000ft (14,326m).

Building up speed in level flight at 44,000ft (13,411m) and above was a long business, but at 45,000ft (13,716m), using 10,450rpm, I got M=0.85. However, from this speed only slight dives were needed to build up higher Mach numbers.

Using minimum fore-and-aft feedback as recommended, a slight nose-down trim change occurred from M=0.80 onwards but was gradual up to M=0.88, when it increased rapidly, reaching a very large peak pull force of some 50–60lb (23–27kg) at M=0.93. Beyond M=0.93 the pull force abated to a fairly steady 20–30lb (9–14kg). The elevons were becoming ineffective at that point, and beyond M=0.95 their effectiveness rapidly deteriorated. At M=0.98 full elevon just balanced a further nose down trim change, and beyond that point trim flap was needed to effect a recovery.

After examination of the automatic observer records it was decided to continue the compressibility dives at progressively lower altitudes to investigate the poor damping in pitch. The flight was on 8 July, a day I shall never forget. I started with a dive to M=0.88 at 25,000ft (7,620m), and then to M=0.86 at 10,000ft (3,050m), in each case deliberately inducing a longitudinal oscillation as if in bumpy air. All seemed a bit knife-edge, but I decided to push up the speed and reached M=0.88 at 4,000ft (1,219m). I then gave the stick a gentle tweak and in a flash had a run-

away divergent longitudinal oscillation on my hands. The frequency of three cycles a second was so vicious that my head was snapping back until my protective helmet hit the headrest then immediately rocketing forward until my chin hit my chest and so on all over again with lightning rapidity. Everything became a blur and I realised I was losing consciousness, so I made one last steady pull back on stick and throttle together and suddenly the oscillation stopped as quickly as it had begun.

The records obtained from this flight showed that each cycle gave +4 and -3'g' and they gave us the clue to the fatal crash of the first Swallow.

Geoffrey de Havilland's aircraft must have experienced just such a divergent oscillation in bumpy weather. He was tall and probably his head had hit the cockpit canopy with such violence that it broke his neck before he had a chance to attempt to control the oscillation that eventually snapped the wings off.

Three factors contributed to my survival. Firstly VW120 had strengthened wings; secondly I had

decided to lower my seat fully before starting the dives so that my head could not strike the cockpit hood; and thirdly I had not attempted to chase the oscillation with the stick and inevitably get out of phase with it and aggravate the divergence. In fact instinct and pre-flight analysis of just such a situation had saved the day.

As a result of this flight two restrictions were placed on the test programme. Firstly, indicated Mach number limitations of 0.87 at 25,000ft (7,620m) and 0.85 at 10,000ft (3,050m) were imposed. Secondly, the flight path angle was not to be altered above an indicated Mach no. of 0.90 at high altitude once the pilot had committed himself to it, in order to prevent violent accelerations or longitudinal oscillation being induced.

I also recommended that there should be definite values of feedback for operation of the power controls throughout the height range as a further precaution against the poor longitudinal damping characteristics of the aircraft.

I flew the DH 108 six more times before I finished my six-year tour of duty at RAE in mid-

De Havilland 108 (VW120), Hatfield, 12 April 1948. Squadron Leader Stewart Muller-Rowland lost his life flying this aircraft, when it crashed on a test flight on 15 February 1950. *RAF Museum Hendon.*

August 1949. I knew my successor as CO of Aerodynamics Flight would be Flight Lieutenant Stewart Muller-Rowland, who had been with me for two years, so I eased him into the DH 108 programme on the high speed side, and another of my senior pilots, Flight Lieutenant George 'Jumbo' Genders, on the low speed side.

Stewart and I conducted a series of manoeuvre tests with the Swallow, but since the risk of stalling and spinning was high in such a programme, it was preceded by high speed wind tunnel tests to give us an idea of the likely 'g' stall limits.

Except for take-off and landing VW120 was being flown with tip slats locked shut. There was therefore a danger of ordinary tip stalling at low speed, and at high Mach numbers the earlier tip stall could be brought on by compressibility effects.

The 'g' limitations due to Mach number were important above 20,000ft (6,096m). At M=0.88 the maximum safe 'g' at 20,000ft (6,096m) was estimated at 4.0 and at 35,000ft (10,668m) was 2.0. For rapid manoeuvering it was estimated that 5'g' could be obtained at all speeds above 380mph (612km/h) below 20,000ft (6,096m).

From a purely structural point of view VW120 had a maximum allowable 'g' of 6⅔, which with a safety factor of 1.5 gave an ultimate stress limitation of 10'g'.

I started the manoeuvre tests with an approach to the straight stall with flaps and undercarriage down, slats open. There was very little warning of the stall at 100mph (161km/h) when either wing dropped, accompanied by elevon buffet. Actually, intentional stalling of VW120 was prohibited, due to absence of wing tip parachutes.

The next step was to investigate the 'g' stalling characteristics of the slow speed TG283 in pull-outs and turns. Owing to a structural limitation of 2.4'g' on that aircraft the tests were necessarily limited to low speed 'g' stalls.

In straight pull-outs the aircraft had a marked tendency to self-stall; the right wing dropped between 80°–110° without any warning and a very steep dive ensued.

In turns there was again the marked self-stalling tendency before the aircraft flicked violently from a 60° turn in one direction to 90° in the opposite direction and finished up in a steep dive. Again there was no stall warning.

It was obvious from these tests that similar characteristics in VW120 would be serious at high altitude owing to the rapid build-up of Mach number which would occur, and to the absence of air brakes to prevent the possibility of the aircraft being precipitated into a critical compressibility dive.

At this stage I left the RAE, I had always written single-line impressions of every aircraft I flew and the following appears alongside the DH 108 Swallow: 'A serial killer. Nasty stall. Vicious undamped longitudinal oscillation at speed in bumps'. These words were tragically truer than I then imagined.

The final chapters to the story of the DH 108 were written in the next eight months. Stewart Muller-Rowland, only recently promoted Squadron-Leader, crashed to his death in VW120 on 15 February 1950 at Birkhill, Buckinghamshire. The circumstances were similar to those in which Geoffrey de Havilland had lost his life.

His place as CO of Aero Flight was taken by 'Jumbo' Genders, who was also promoted to Squadron-Leader. He, in turn, crashed to his death in TG283 on 1 May 1950, near Hartley Wintney, Hants, when he spun into the ground while conducting stalling tests.

In retrospect one must ask if this ill-fated research aircraft was worth the cost in test pilots' lives. The answer must in my opinion be in the affirmative. Aviation was in the throes of breaking the sound barrier. It was as prestigious a goal then as going into space was later to be. Aeronautics was full of new innovations like the jet engine, reheat, rockets, sweepback, boundary layer control, power operated controls, the ejection seat, and prone position piloting. Finding the correct configuration formula was the key to success. The DH 108 was a brave attempt to achieve the ultimate. It just missed by a hairsbreadth, but the formula had unknown risks. The Swallow was not without success – perhaps its greatest being the legacy of information it left – but the price it demanded will be held by many to have been too high.

12 DOUGLAS BOSTON IV

Terrific take-off acceleration. Delightfully responsive controls and thundering power, but bomb capacity rather small. ERIC BROWN

TWO FAMOUS NAMES in American aircraft engineering, Jack Northrop and Ed Heinemann, collaborated to design the Model 7A twin-engined mid-wing attack bomber in 1936, but revised it as a result of reports of the virtual invulnerability of the Dornier 17F in the Spanish Civil War. The resultant Model 7B was the first military aircraft to be fitted with a tricycle undercarriage, and made its first flight on 26 October 1938.

The French were so impressed with the 7B's performance that in February 1939 they ordered 100, but with extensive modifications, including a deeper fuselage. With the fall of France the un-delivered portion of the contract was taken over by the British Government and the DB-7 was given the name 'Boston'.

So many modifications were needed to convert the machines to British operational requirements

that these were incorporated in subsequent developments. The original Boston I was retained mainly for training, although a few were experimentally converted for night fighting and named Havoc I. It was fitted with two Pratt & Whitney Twin Wasp fourteen-cylinder radial engines.

The Havoc II had two 1500hp Wright Double-Row Cyclone 14 engines and operated as a night fighter and intruder fighter-bomber. This version was further modified to carry more fire power, and the lengthened nose was fitted with twelve .303 forward-firing machine-guns and radar when in the night fighter role.

The Boston III light bomber had modifications to the engine nacelles and tail unit, and was fitted with two 1600hp Double-Row Cyclones. Armament consisted of four .303 forward-firing machine-guns, two on either side of the trans-

The Boston IV in pugnacious mood.

Boston IV, BZ403. Its Wright Cyclone engines looked huge, yet started sweetly.

The Douglas Havoc III attack bomber was fitted with four 20mm nose cannon.

parent nose, two .303 guns on a flexible mounting in the rear cockpit, and one in the lower rear firing position.

The Boston IV was a medium bomber, with .50 calibre machine-guns replacing the earlier .303s, and dorsal power-operated turret in place of the flexible mounting. It carried four crew and an internal 2,000lb (907kg) bomb load. The Boston inspired the same feeling in me with its looks as did the de Havilland Hornet. True, one was a bomber, and the other a fighter, but both had the unmistakable look of thoroughbreds and exuded sheer power.

Entrance to the aircraft was from the port side through a door in the cockpit roof, and it was reached by steps and hand holes in the port side of the fuselage aft of the wing trailing edge. The cockpit reminded me of the Hampden; because it was a fighter type cockpit, the only concession to its bomber role was its half-wheel control column. The view all round was very good.

The engines looked huge and yet started sweetly under the impetus of their inertia starters and while testing them on warm-up the exciting surge of their tremendous power could be clearly felt. Taxying was easy, and the brakes were smooth but rather heavy in operation.

For take-off the elevator trim tabs were set four divisions nose heavy, and the rudder and ailerons set neutral. With the mixture at AUTO-RICH, fuel tank selector cocks to MAIN, booster pumps ON, flaps UP, upper gills CLOSED, lower gills half open, and superchargers LOW, the throttles were opened to 45in (114cm) of boost and 2400rpm.

The Boston took off like a scalded cat, accelerating rapidly so that the nose wheel could be lifted off early. Unstick was made at 100–110mph (161–177km/h) with a steady pull on the control column to overcome the apparent nose heaviness – which disappeared on becoming airborne – and raising the undercarriage and opening the gills.

The climb was made at 160mph using 36in. of boost and 2300rpm with the superchargers in LOW gear; when boost fell to 32in (81cm) the change was made to HIGH gear, which restored boost to 41in (104cm). The aircraft was slightly unstable longitudinally, a good fighter characteristic, and laterally and directionally stable, but the rudder hunted noticeably.

In the cruise the aircraft had to be retrimmed, for closure of the gills gave a strong nose down effect. Stability characteristics were the same as on the climb, but the rudder hunting had disappeared. The controls were delightfully harmonised and all quite light and very effective. Manoeuvrability was good for such a large aircraft, but the Boston tended to steepen up in tight turns, and the 2'g' stall occurred at 180mph (290km/h), which was rather high. Maximum speed was 310mph (499km/h) at 15,000ft (4,572m).

In a dive the aircraft had to be constantly trimmed as speed increased, and a careful watch kept on the engine boost which rose rapidly with loss of height as no automatic boost control was fitted. The rudder hunting characteristic also reappeared.

The all-up stall was preceded by buffeting commencing at 145mph (233km/h) and increasing in intensity until the nose dropped at 126mph (203km/h).

Pilot's notes: Douglas Boston IV

FIG. I — INSTRUMENT PANEL

Fig 1:

Instrument panel

1 Free air thermometer
2 ASI
3 Reflector sight
4 Altimeter
5 Radio compass indicator (overseas versions only)
6 Instrument flying panel
7 Push to mute switch
8 Gun firing switch (not visible)
9 Dual boost gauge
10 Dual revolution indicator
11 Direction indicator (inoperative)
12 Suction gauge
13 Dual oil pressure gauge
14 Dual fuel pressure gauge
15 Fuel contents gauge and selector
16 Dual carburettor air temperature indicator
17 Dual oil temperature indicator
18 Dual cylinder temperature indicator
19 Undercarriage and flap indicator
20 Undercarriage indicator lights
21 Propeller feathering buttons
22 Pilot's bomb release button
23 Upper electrical switch panel
24 Camera and gun selector switches
25 Ignition switches

Fig 2:

**Cockpit –
Left-hand side**

26 Trailing aerial
   control box (O)
27 Sliding panel
   locking lever
28 Fuel tank selector
   cocks
29 Oxygen pressure
   gauge
30 Mixture levers
31 Throttle levers
   (press-to-send
   button on inboard
   lever)
32 DR compass
   repeater
33 Propeller speed
   control levers
34 Left-hand sloping
   switch panel
35 Fuse box
36 Cockpit light
37 Throttle lever
   friction adjuster
38 Bomb door control
   lever
39 Cockpit extension
   light
40 Propeller lever
   friction adjuster
41 Supercharger
   levers
42 Carburettor air
   intake heat control
   levers
43 Cross-feed cock

(O) = Fitted on overseas
      versions only

Fig 3:

**Cockpit –
Right-hand side**

44 Radio remote
   controller (O)
45 Identification light
   and signalling
   switchbox
46 Cockpit light
47 Signalling key
   (Bendix) (O)
48 Filter switchbox
49 Radio destruction
   push-buttons
50 IFF switches
51 Sliding panel
   locking lever
52 Intercom station
   box
53 Radio compass
   controls (O)
54 Pilot's head-set
   socket
55 Trimming tab
   controls
56 Fuel dump valve
   (aircraft destruction)
   control

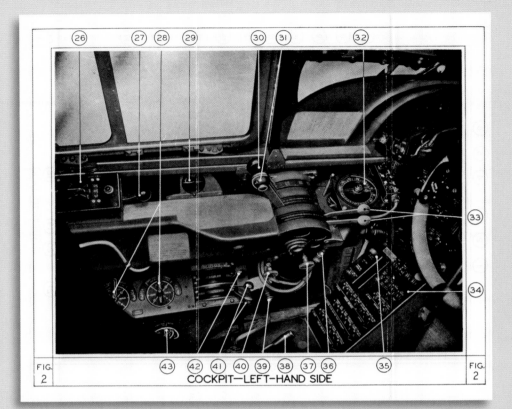

COCKPIT—LEFT-HAND SIDE

COCKPIT—RIGHT-HAND SIDE

57 Emergency air brake
   control
58 Fragmentation bomb
   switch panel
   (inoperative)
59 Boost gauge drain cock

60 Relief tube
61 Cockpit heating
   system controls
62 Radio control 'G'
   switch
63 VHF controller

64 Right-hand sloping
   bomb control switch
   panel
65 Radio remote
   controller (Bendix) (O)
66 SBC jettison switch (O)

67 UV light projector
68 P9 compass

(O) = Fitted on overseas
      versions only

The all-down stall occurred with little warning except slight aileron and elevator buffet. At the stall at 110mph (177km/h) the right wing dropped violently and very steeply, needing immediate recovery action. In this respect it was interesting to find that the flaps took 18 seconds to retract, and for this reason the half-flap (22½ degrees) setting for take-off was seldom used as it slowed the acceleration to the high safety speed of 180mph.

In single-engine flight the Boston really excelled provided the speed was kept above 155mph (249km/h) in the cruise or 165mph (266km/h) in the climb, otherwise the rudder would hunt unpleasantly. Above these speeds the controls remained light and effective and the way the aircraft handled inspired confidence. It was advisable to keep the gills closed otherwise their drag had an adverse effect on speed. The single-engine landing was aided by a fast lowering undercarriage, so this item could left until on final approach.

Normal landing was made with the gills closed, and the circuit speed was 175mph (282km/h) at which speed the undercarriage was lowered and 22½ degrees of flap selected. The booster pumps were ON and mixture set AUTO-RICH. The flaps were then fully lowered prior to turn-in at 150mph (241km/h) and gave a steep final approach at 115mph (185km/h) with excellent view. The elevator and ailerons were very positive right down to touch-down. The landing run was long but the brakes smooth and exceptionally good.

I first flew the Boston IV BZ402 on 6 December 1944 with the object of assessing the qualities that had made it such a successful low-level daylight bomber and night intruder. Certainly flying it at 275mph (443km/h) at 100ft (30m) was sheer unadulterated pleasure, with delightfully responsive controls and thundering power in my hands. At this level too the rather weakly defended underbelly is protected from ground fire by the high ground speed. As a bomber, however, the bomb load was rather small.

In night flying it had excellent qualities, the slight longitudinal instability not causing any real instrument flying problems. However, it did have that soft under-belly in the event of attack by an enemy night fighter.

The success of the Boston can be gauged by the fact that 7,097 were built for the US, British and Russian air forces. Russia received twice as many as the RAF and only some 800 less than the US Army. Certainly I rate it as a great aeroplane, being amongst the most enjoyable I have flown.

Eric Brown first flew the Boston IV in December 1944 to assess the qualities that made it such a successful low-level daylight bomber and night intruder.

13 FAIREY GANNET

A brilliant concept and a great naval
aircraft; reliable in service. ERIC BROWN

THE GANNET was built to the requirements of specification G.R. 17/45 for a two-seater anti-submarine and strike aircraft. It was the first aircraft in the world to feature a double airscrew/ twin power plants turbine unit, providing all the qualities of a twin-engined aircraft with a single-engine layout. The power egg chosen was the Armstrong-Siddeley Double Mamba, each half of which could be controlled independently, shut down and its airscrew feathered.

This configuration provided the solution to the problem of the single-engine deck-landing of a propeller-driven aeroplane. Power plants like the Double Mamba are by their nature 'full throttle' engines and operate efficiently only over a small range of turbine speeds, so shutting down of one extends range and reduces the maintenance costs.

The prototype made its maiden flight on 19 September 1949 as a two-seater, and it was the third prototype which was the first to be fitted with a third seat, also acquiring auxiliary fins on the tailplane.

The Gannet had an exceptionally capacious bomb bay and was the first British built naval aircraft in service capable of carrying all its weapons internally, other than wing-mounted rocket projectiles. The weapons load included two homing torpedoes, and aft of the weapons bay was installed a large retractable radar scanner.

The first production AS 1 flew in mid-1953, fitted with a 2,950ehp Double Mamba 100, and a little over a year later the first dual control trainer T 2 made its initial flight. The Gannet T 2 differed from the AS.1 in having no retractable radome, but dual controls in the observer's cockpit and an additional periscope, retractable when the front hood opened.

In April 1954 an Intensive Trials Unit of four AS 1s was set up and nine months later the Gannet entered service. Before entering service the aircraft had carried out intensive deck-landing trials, thereby becoming the first turbo-prop ever to land on an aircraft carrier.

Finally, an airborne early-warning version of

Fairey Gannet T.5
(XG883) in flight.
RAF Museum Hendon.

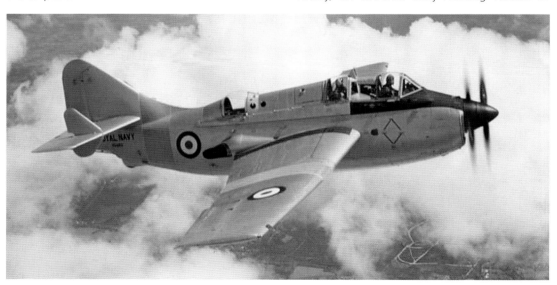

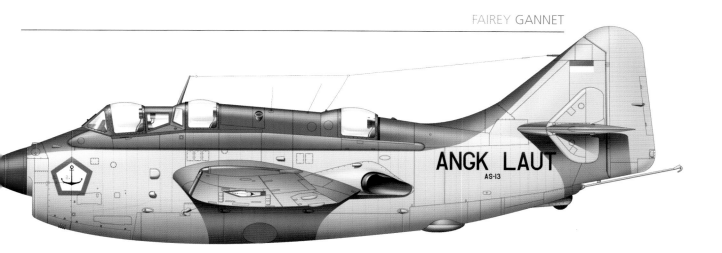

ANGK LAUT
AS-13

Fairey Gannet AS Mk 4,
AS-13 (ex-WN352),
Indonesian Navy.
© *Richard Caruana*
(scale 1:96).

the Gannet was developed and made its maiden flight in mid-1958. The AEW 3 had a large 'guppy' radome, a modified tail unit, provision for radar operators within the fuselage, and a new Double Mamba engine with short jet pipes. It entered service in 1960.

My first contact with the Gannet came when I was appointed Head of the British Naval Air Mission to Germany, tasked with training the newly formed German Naval Air Arm (Marineflieger), which was to receive fifteen AS 4s and a T 5. I therefore undertook a conversion course at RN Air Station, Eglinton, Northern Ireland, in January 1958, on the T 2 and AS 1. This involved fully exploring the single-engine flight performance envelope, and very impressive it was.

My duties with the Marineflieger involved instructional work and maintenance test flying with the AS 4 Gannets and the solitary T 5. The aeroplane imbued great confidence in both the wartime and post-war generation of German naval aviators, and was a very good advertisement for the British aircraft manufacturing industry.

The Gannet was sturdy and compact and certainly did not look what it was – a twin-engined aeroplane. The Double Mamba is basically two side-by-side propeller turbine engines, each driving one propeller through independent gear trains. The port engine drives the front propeller. Each engine is a separate unit, having its own controls and fuel and oil systems, so that each one may be operated independently of the other. A common auxiliary gear box is driven by either or both engines.

The cockpit was entered by means of a retractable footstep on the starboard side of the fuselage, and the pilot's hood was opened hydraulically by an external lever. The view was very good in spite of the rather high window ledge shields on either side of the instrument panel.

Before start-up the parking brake was put on and the LP cocks both ON. With the HP cocks OFF, the relight buttons were pressed until they squealed, thus ensuring the propellers were fined off to the 6 degree position. The throttles were closed to GROUND IDLE, the Jet Pipe Temperature control set to WARNING ONLY and the starting fuel pump master switch set ON. The appropriate HP cock was then opened and the start guard switch moved to expose the appropriate button, which, when pressed, began the starting cycle.

A twin-breech cartridge starter was fitted for each engine, and at the commencement of the start cycle the ignition light came on. Then after a two seconds delay the cartridge fired and should accelerate the engine to 4,500rpm within about four seconds.

If the engine failed to attain self-sustaining rpm of 4,500 on a single cartridge, the HP cock had to be moved to OFF until the rpm fell to 1,200, then it was moved to ON and the starter button pressed to fire the second cartridge. After start up the JPT control switch was set to NORMAL when revs. had reached 9.400 ± 200.

Normally the second engine was windmill started from the feathered position. This was done by opening up the running engine to full power, moving the HP cock of the second engine to ON to release the propeller brake, then returning the cock to OFF. Next the relight button was pressed until rpm were 1500, the HP cock moved to ON, the button released and the ignition light checked that it stayed on.

This starting procedure was the only complex thing about flying the Gannet, and once the engine idling rpm checks had been made the aircraft could be taxied away with the throttles in the ground idle position, and thereafter manoeuvred on one engine with the aid of the powerful toe brakes. The radome was housed on the ground.

Minimum take-off run was achieved by using full 40 degrees of flap, but the baulked landing flap setting of 20 degrees was gated and was used on airfields to keep the single-engine safety speed down to 126mph (203km/h). Full take-off power was checked with the parking brake applied, and with constant speeding rpm of 15,000 and an indi-

Gannet 1s of the Fleet Air Arm entering service early in 1956. It was the first turbo-prop to land on an aircraft carrier.

cated 1,250 shaft horsepower the brake was released. Unstick occurred at 86mph (138km/h) and there was a moderate nose-down trim change as the flaps were retracted.

The climb was made at 1,000shp at 160mph (257km/h) with a constant 15,000rpm. If the climb was to be made on one engine then a speed of 144mph (232km/h) was used.

In cruising flight the Gannet was stable around all three axes and the controls were well harmonised. All trimmers were very effective, the aileron trimmer being particularly powerful. There was little change of longitudinal and lateral trim when operating the undercarriage, radome,

and bomb doors, but there were some momentary directional trim changes.

The stalling characteristics of the Gannet were interesting. At FLIGHT IDLE power and everything up, there was a slight elevator buffet just before the stall at 109mph (175km/h) when the nose dropped gently against full-up elevator, together with slight lateral unsteadiness.

With the undercarriage down, and therefore the flight fine pitch stops withdrawn, and flaps fully lowered, there was no warning of the stall at 92mph (147km/h), which was again a gentle nose drop. Once again elevator effectiveness in the recovery was initially poor.

With approach power set on the throttles, the elevators retained their effectiveness throughout the stalls and the recoveries. The all-up stall occurred at 103mph (166km/h) and the all-down stall at 86mph (138km/h). Both were a gentle nose-drop, preceded by some slight aileron buffet, although the ailerons retained their effectiveness up to and during the stall.

One propeller feathered had no noticeable effect on stalling speeds.

Landing the Gannet was a delight. Using at least 200shp the undercarriage was lowered at 172mph (277km/h) and one-third flap at 155mph (249km/h), and then the turn made on to the final approach at 126mph (203km/h) and full flap lowered. Speed was then reduced to 103mph (166km/h) with 800shp on the engines. The throttles were closed to the FLIGHT IDLE gate on touch-

The airborne early warning version of the Gannet, AEW3, with its large 'guppy' radome and modified tail unit.

down and to GROUND IDLE when not intended to take-off again.

The Gannet really had solved the problem of deck landing a twin-engined aeroplane on one engine. The process was simplicity itself with the Gannet, using 20 degrees of flap and an approach speed of 109mph (175km/h). Provided the all-up weight had been reduced to below 17,900lb (8,119kg) an overshoot could be made from a baulked landing.

The Gannet AS4 had a top speed of 229mph (369km/h), and a rate of climb of 2,000ft/min (610m/min), with a maximum range of 600 (966km) miles at a speed of 150mph (241km/h) at 5,000ft (1,524m). Its endurance of 4.9 hours, was very useful for its role as an anti-submarine hunter-killer. However, that was rapidly being usurped by the helicopter.

However, the take-over bid by the helicopter was not the death knell of the Gannet, but merely heralded a change of emphasis in role to airborne early-warning. In its new capacity the Gannet 3 was a great success and gave the Royal Navy the low level defence potential against attacking aircraft and missiles it so badly needed. Indeed, the real measure of its value only became starkly evident during the Falklands campaign, when the absence of airborne early-warning cost the Royal Navy dear. It is my belief that an aircraft carrier such as the *Ark Royal*, equipped with Phantoms, Buccaneers, and AEW Gannets, in company with either *Hermes* or *Invincible*, could have sewn up the conflict in two or three weeks.

In the final analysis the Gannet must be judged both a brilliant concept and a great naval aircraft. It was very easy to deck-land, pleasant to fly, very effective in its operational roles, and in spite of its complexity it proved reliable in service.

Below: Gannet AS4 235: one of the second batch of Gannet AS4s, just about to take the wire as it lands on HMS *Centaur* in 1959. 235/C was XA473 of 810 Squadron and is seen during the aircraft carrier's deployment into the Mediterranean and Far East to Australia. On return to the UK, the squadron disbanded. *Barry Ketley.*

Left: Gannet AS4 XA430:Fairey Gannet AS4 XA430, 231/C of 810 Squadron taxies towards the lift on HMS *Centaur* sometime in 1959. *Barry Ketley.*

Pilots notes: Fairey Gannet

Fig 1:

1   Parking brake
2   Wing fold safety lever
3   Wing fold selector lever
4   LP fuel cock lever – starboard
5   LP fuel cock lever – port
6   Outside air temperature gauge
7   Engine de-icing trimmer (ground use only)
8   Engine de-icing continuity indicator
9   Harness stowage hook
10 Weapon sight selector dimmer control
11 Auto-pilot pump re-set push-button
12 Throttle lever – port engine
13 Throttle lever – starboard engine
14 RATOG firing push-button
15 Hydraulic pressure gauge
16 Fuel recuperator warning indicators
17 Oil cooler shutter switches
18 Weapon sight spare filament stowage
19 Flight instruments normal inverter failure indicator
20 Flight instruments normal inverter changeover and test push-button
21 Flight instruments inverter auto-standby switch
22 Triple brake pressure gauge
23 Ignition warning lights
24 Emergency flight fine pitch stop switches
25 Jet pipe temperature control switches

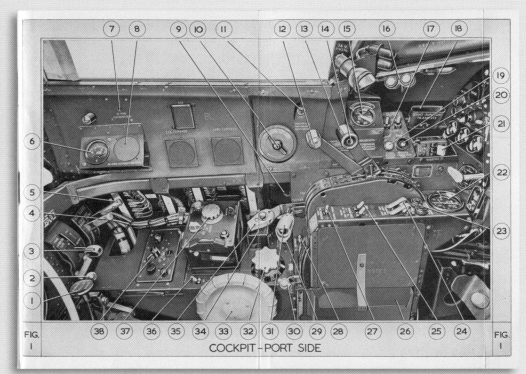

COCKPIT–PORT SIDE

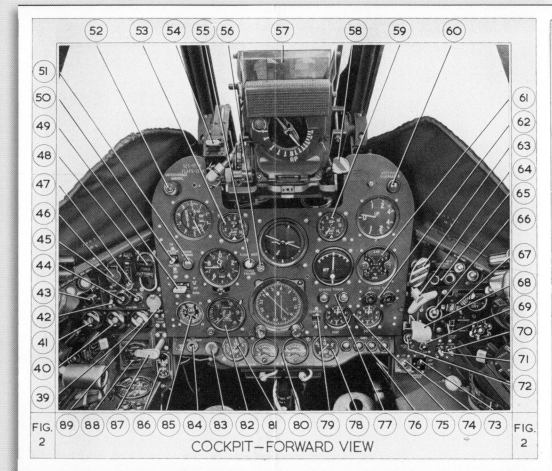

COCKPIT–FORWARD VIEW

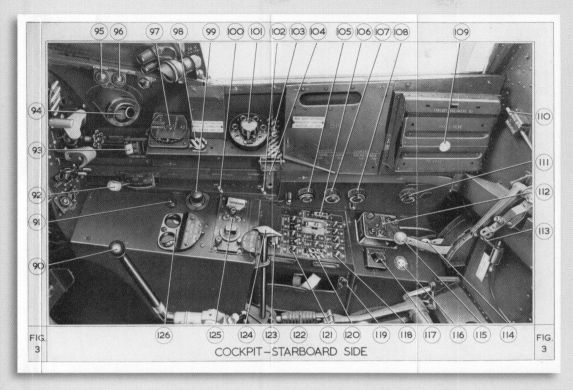

FIG. 3

COCKPIT—STARBOARD SIDE

FIG. 3

115 Flying controls
locking lever
116 Electrical socket for
servicing lead
117 ZBX/VHF mixer box
118 Switches, from top
to bottom:
2,000lb store master
switch; Engine de-
icing switch;
Alternator switch;
G45 camera ON/OFF
switch; G45 camera
SUNNY/CLOUDY switch
119 Hydraulic handpump
handle stowage
120 Switches, from top
to bottom: Radome
emergency raising
switch; Side panels
floodlamps master
switch; Instrument
panel floodlamps
master switch;
Emergency lamps
switch
121 Switches, from top
to bottom:
Navigation lights
switch – STEADY-OFF-
MORSE; Navigation
lights switch – DIM-
BRIGHT; Formation
lights switch –
STEADY-OFF-MORSE;
Formation lights
switch – DIM-BRIGHT;
Identification lights
switch – STEADY-OFF-
MORSE
122 Pilot's seat adjusting
lever
123 External lights
master switch
124 Hot air control
125 IFF control panel
126 Engine starter push-
buttons and guard
switch

26 Pilot's notes stowage
27 Engine synchroniser
switch
28 Aileron trimming switch
29 Wing locking indicator
lights test switch
30 Flap selector lever
31 HP fuel cock lever –
starboard
32 Rudder trimming control
and indicator
33 Elevator trimming
control and indicator
34 RP selector switch
35 HP fuel cock lever – port
36 Auto-pilot master switch
37 Auto-pilot controller
38 VHF controller

Fig 2:

39 Fire-extinguisher push-
button – starboard
engine
40 Fire-extinguisher push-
button – engine bay
41 Fire-extinguisher push-
button – port engine
42 Taxying lamps switch
43 Fire warning light test
push-buttons – post-
mod.329
44 Call crew push-button
45 VHF mute switch
46 RATOG jettison push-
button
47 RATOG master switch
48 Undercarriage selector
push-buttons

49 Bombs/RP selector
switch
50 Pressure head heater
override switch
51 Radome indicator
52 Undercarriage warning
light
53 Shaft horse power
gauge – port
54 Weapon sight master
switch
55 Flight instruments power
supply failure indicator
56 Horizon gyro fast
erection push-button
57 Weapon sight
58 Weapon sight emergency
retraction control
59 Shaft horse power
gauge – starboard
60 Auto-pilot 'disengaged'
indicator
61 Dual jet pipe
temperature gauge
62 Jet pipe temperature
warning lights
63 Pilot's hood jettison
control
64 Emergency hydraulic
selector
65 Generator failure
warning lights
66 Bomb doors selector
lever
67 Oxygen regulator
68 Deck hook control lever
69 Windscreen de-icing
push-button

70 Marker flare fusing
switch
71 2,000lb store selector
switch
72 Deck hood indicator
light
73 Windscreen wiper
switch
74 Fuel transfer indicator –
bomb bay tanks
75 Engine rpm indicators
76 Fuel transfer indicators –
wing tanks
77 Reverse torque
indicators
78 Oil pressure gauge –
starboard engine
79 Compass/DG change-
over switch
80 Oil temperature gauges
81 Oil pressure gauge –
port engine
82 Radio altimeter
83 Weapon sight retraction
circuit fuse
84 Fuel contents push-
button
85 Fuel contents gauge
86 Flap position and aileron
trim indicator
87 Pilot's hood control lever
88 Undercarriage position
indicator
89 Not used

Fig 3:

90 Hydraulic handpump
91 Engine de-icing overheat
warning light
92 Cold air control
93 Starting fuel pumps
master switch
94 Cold air vent
95 Sonobuoy indicator
96 Bomb door indicator
97 Bomb spacing unit
98 Bomb jettison push-
button
99 Wander lamp
100 Wander lamp switch
101 Bomb fusing selector
102 IFF master switch
103 Emergency stores
jettison push-button
104 Harness stowage fitting
105 Instrument panel UV
lighting dimmer switch
106 Battery isolating switch
107 Instrument panel
floodlamps dimmer
switch
108 Port side floodlamps
dimmer switch
109 Circuit-breakers cover-
plate
110 Hood jettison indicator
111 Starboard side
floodlamps dimmer
switch
112 ZBX controller
113 Harness release lever
114 Throttles locking lever

14 FAIREY SPEARFISH

A massive single-seat aircraft.
A real old cow. ERIC BROWN

THE FAIREY SPEARFISH was one of those rare aircraft that never went into production, there being five prototypes built and only four of these flown.

Built to the specification 0.5/43 for a multi-purpose two-seat torpedo dive bomber to replace the Barracuda, the influence of the Grumman Avenger can be seen in its design. It had the same corpulent look which came from its capacious bomb-bay, and its huge radial engine, crew greenhouse, dorsal barbette, and high tail, all reminded me of the efficient Avenger.

I first flew the Spearfish on 17 September 1947, in the form of the first prototype, RA356, at Heston to test its powered ailerons. When I saw it I thought it must be the biggest and heaviest single-engined aeroplane in the world and it possibly can lay claim to such titles, for its span was 60ft 3in (18.4m). and its overload weight in the bomber role was 22,330lb (10,129kg). The engine fitted was the 2,600hp Centaurus 57.

Later, the second prototype, RA360, came to the RAE for further powered aileron trials and deck landing assessment, and so I was able to get a good idea of its general performance. It had the more powerful Centaurus 58 with 2,800hp.

The Centaurus was started by cartridge percussion, and once it had got the huge 14ft (4.3m)

A Fairey Spearfish lined up for display to UNO delegates at Radlett, Herts, on 10 February 1946.

five-blade Rotol propeller going and was warming up, I found time to assess the cockpit view from my lofty perch some 11ft (3.4m) off the ground. In fact the view was good both forward and downward, for there was a 7° angle over the nose, which was really designed to give adequate depression of the nose for rocket aiming. This compared very favourably with the 2½° of the Avenger.

Taxying was easy with the wide undercarriage, whose massive ironmongery retracted sideways into the outer wings, but the very good brakes were essential because the rudder was quite useless in aiding taxi control. There was a lot of keel surface to react to side wind effect, but this had been recognised by the eventual fitting of a tail wheel lock. However, in a strong wind the foot loads were high to overpower the rudder against the force blowing against it.

Take-off was made with the cowl gills and oil cooler gills fully open and flaps at the TAKE-OFF setting and all trimmers at zero. With +9½lb boost at 2,700rpm, reached with the aircraft held on the brakes, the unstick was reasonably short and straightforward, with only a mild ten-dency to swing to starboard. The view on the take-off run was also improved by virtue of the fact that the tail tended to rise of its own accord as speed was gathered. The change of trim on raising undercarriage and flaps was negligible, and at a speed of 160mph (257km/h) at +6½ boost, 2,400rpm with the gills still fully open, the rate of climb was just over 1,000ft/min (305m/min). The power-operated hood was recommended to be left open until cruise height was reached, probably because of possible carbon monoxide contamination of the cockpit.

The cruising speed was far from impressive, which was not surprising as the top speed was only 292mph (470km/h) at 14,000ft (4,267m), i.e. only 40mph (64km/h) faster than the Barracuda V. The flaps had a CRUISE position to increase range.

The Spearfish had heavy controls in cruising flight and in fact the lateral control was so solid that I could barely move the ailerons with one hand at 150mph (241km/h). Inevitably, therefore, hydraulic-powered ailerons had been fitted and with the power engaged these became reasonable for an aircraft of such size. The system as I first flew it in RA356 had a 16% feedback to the

The prototype of the lumbering Spearfish, RA356, first flew on 5 July 1945, just as the war in the Far East was coming to an end.

105

Fairey Spearfish

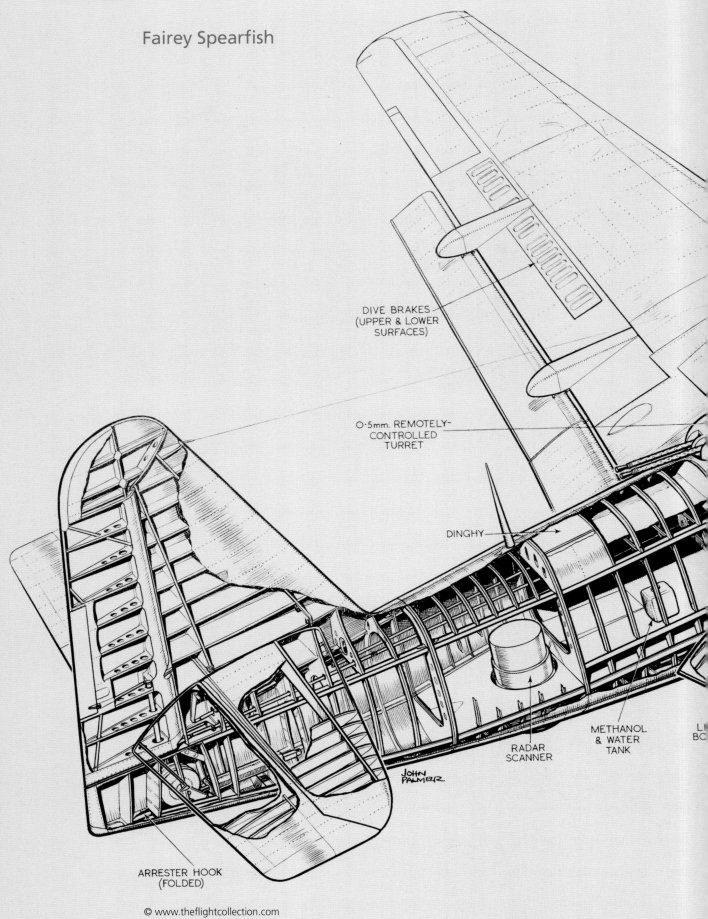

DIVE BRAKES
(UPPER & LOWER
SURFACES)

O·5mm. REMOTELY-
CONTROLLED
TURRET

DINGHY

RADAR
SCANNER

METHANOL
& WATER
TANK

L
BO

JOHN
PALMER

ARRESTER HOOK
(FOLDED)

106

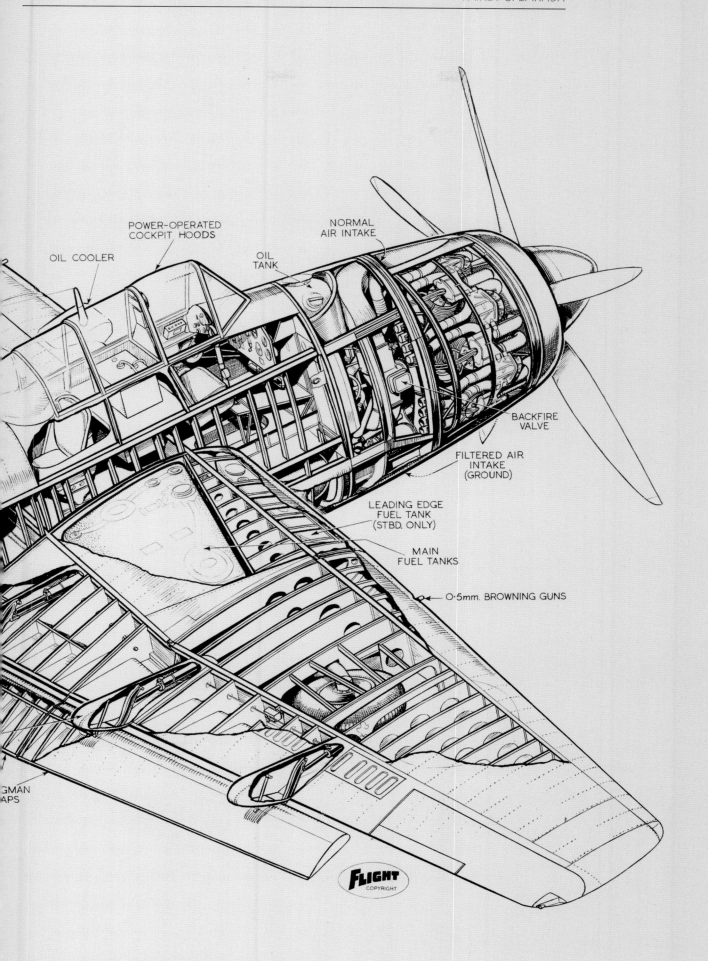

POWER-OPERATED
COCKPIT HOODS

NORMAL
AIR INTAKE

OIL COOLER

OIL
TANK

BACKFIRE
VALVE

FILTERED AIR
INTAKE
(GROUND)

LEADING EDGE
FUEL TANK
(STBD. ONLY)

MAIN
FUEL TANKS

0·5mm. BROWNING GUNS

GMAN
APS

Flight
COPYRIGHT

One of the largest and heaviest single-engined aircraft ever built, the Spearfish was meant to give the Royal Navy a heavy airborne strike capability. Unfortunately developed too late to see service in the Pacific as was intended, only a few were built before the requirement was cancelled. It did, however, contribute valuable design experience to its successor, the Gannet. This picture, taken at Radlett in 1946, is of interest as it apparently shows the remotely-powered barbette which it was thought was never fitted. *Barry Ketley.*

pilot from the hydraulic booster, and a torsion bar spring fitted to give a feel load up to 10lb (4.5kg). The spring feel could be engaged or disengaged from the cockpit. Later, in RA360, there was no feed back and the torsion bar spring gave a feel load up to 12lb (5.4kg). The latter aircraft was the less pleasant to fly as the stick continually hunted either side of neutral, and there was no build up in stick force with increase in speed.

This was meant to be an interim system until a lateral control method was developed using spoilers with small 'feeler' ailerons for later production aircraft, which of course never materialised.

The stability of the Spearfish was good longitudinally and directionally, but was laterally unstable, which made instrument flying a heavy chore.

For a carrier aircraft, where the approach speed is so close to the stall speed, the Spearfish displayed an undesirable lack of stall warning. The all-up stall occurred at 98mph (158km/h) without any warning other than an airframe judder simultaneous with the nose pitching forward. The all-down stall at 76mph (122km/h) displayed identical characteristics, and opening or closing of the cockpit hood had no noticeable effect whatsoever.

When it came to landing, the Spearfish was at its best, if that is the right word. The CRUISE flap position was selected at 190mph (306km/h), the undercarriage lowered at 160mph (257km/h) together with the flaps to TAKE-OFF position, then full LAND flap position was selected at 38mph (61km/h); each flap selection giving a progressively stronger nose-down change of trim. The engine-assisted approach was made at 92mph (147km/h) on land and 86mph (138km/h) on a carrier. The view was good, but the power of -4lb

boost had to be held on and the throttle only cut after the wheels touched the ground, otherwise the nose fell heavily and could not be held up by the elevator, although both the elevator and rudder forces had lightened considerably at approach speeds. However, even a wheels-first landing seldom caused bounce as the very soft undercarriage absorbed rebound.

After conclusion of the power aileron trials, RA360 was allocated to Naval Aircraft Department at the RAE for proofing and calibration of the new type arrester gear installed, to be carried out on the short runway at Farnborough. The high all-up weight of the Spearfish made it particularly suitable for these trials. Some of the runs and landings into the gear had to be made at overload weight. On two occasions the arrester hook did not pick up at a weight of 22,200lb (10,070kg) and I had no alternative but to open up and take-off as the short runway could never have contained the aircraft on brakes. I wrote my impression in my log book and it reads 'A real old cow'. This was largely because the baulked landing was unpleasant, because application of full power gave a fairly strong nose-up change of trim which came on rather suddenly as there was a very large incremental power increase over the last third of the quadrantal range of the throttle. This throttle arrangement was deliberate to give coarse engine control over the first two-thirds of the range of deck-landing, but had been somewhat overdone in this case.

RA360 eventually went to the Carrier Trials Unit at Ford to serve as a hack there until retired out of service in 1952 – a rather ordinary end for a very ordinary aircraft.

15 GENERAL AIRCRAFT GAL/56

They don't come much worse than this.
ERIC BROWN

OFTEN I HAVE BEEN ASKED which is the worst aircraft I have ever flown – well, this is it. I have had some exciting, and indeed frightening, moments with this tailless experimental glider, but I think for my flight observers they were mainly frightening.

General Aircraft Limited had a successful record of building military gliders during the war, such as the Hotspur and Hamilcar, and had been given contracts to build a series of experimental gliders incorporating all-wing designs. The GAL/56 had 28° of sweep on its wings, at the extremities of which were fins and rudders. It carried two crew sitting in tandem.

It arrived at the RAE in the spring of 1946, labelled as a problem child, which was certainly no exaggeration. Anyway, it became my assignment, and so the battle of wits with this capricious creature began for me on 1 May 1946.

It was a large, ungainly looking aircraft with an undercarriage of substantial proportions and oversize wheels that did nothing to improve its appearance. This was further demeaned by the yellow and black stripes paint scheme it carried on the underside of the wings, rather like a half caste wasp – and it certainly had a sting.

The GAL/56 had the registration number TS507 and was normally towed by a Spitfire LF IX to 20,000ft (6,096m) for release and subsequent testing on the glide.

With the CG in the normal position (86.8in (2.2m) aft of datum at an AUW of 4,024lb (1,825kg) take-off was a tricky procedure. The whole problem lay in the violent ground effect to which the aircraft was subject, for the cushion of air between the wings and the runway gave a strong nose-up change of trim. Thus on take-off if the aircraft was allowed to fly itself off, or worse – was pulled off, then the loss of ground effect would cause it to dart sharply back into the ground, and no amount of backward elevator movement could prevent this at speeds up to 80mph (129km/h) IAS.

By a frightening process of trial and error I found the best solution to the problem was to hold the aircraft down by hard forward pressure on the control wheel until the airspeed had built up to 100mph (161km/h). Then I gave a steady

The GAL/56 – described by Eric Brown as 'the worst aircraft he had ever flown' – was normally towed to 20,000ft by a Spitfire.

The GAL/56 was an ungainly aircraft with sweptback wings, at the extremities of which were fins and rudders. It had a large undercarriage and oversize wheels.

backward pull up through the tug's slipstream and maintained this backward pressure until the loss of ground effect evaporated, as could be felt by a sharp porpoising motion on the aircraft.

Directional control was light and effective throughout the take-off. The effect of forward or aft movement of the CG was negligible on the take-off characteristics.

On tow the glider was very pleasant to fly and could be flown hands and feet off in calm air, although it tended to corkscrew slightly in rough air. However, if the tug's slipstream was inadvertently entered, all longitudinal and directional control was lost until the glider was eventually tossed clear after a severe pounding.

In free flight, after I had released the tow rope snap gear, the aircraft appeared very stable longitudinally at forward CG, then stability fell off as the CG moved aft. On tests with the CG at the aft limit, the glider appeared stable at speeds in the middle range of about 95–130mph (153–209km/h), and unstable at the low and high ends of the speed scale.

The first stalling tests on the GAL/56 revealed very unusual characteristics, so much so that it was decided to have both wings fitted with wool tufts to show the airflow pattern. Full instrumentation and camera equipment recorded the results.

The first tests before this equipment was fitted were made at the normal weight and CG. A trailing static pitot was carried and the results recorded by auto-observer. A flight observer was also carried to take visual readings in case the auto-observer camera failed.

The first stall was made with an elevator trim setting of 1½ divisions tail heavy. From 70mph (113km/h) a nose-up pitching moment started showing itself and at 65mph (105km/h) developed into a definite self-stalling tendency which rapidly increased in backward force and move-

ment of the control wheel. The incidence rose to an alarming angle, so much so that the horizon was lost from view, and the feeling experienced by both the observer and myself was that of the possibility of the aircraft falling over on to its back.

During the nose-up pitching a distinct kick was felt on the port aileron at 64mph (103km/h), but the wings could still be held level with ease. When the stick was getting near the back stop and the airspeed had dropped to about 55mph (89km/h), and the impression was one of a tail slide having developed or at least being imminent, the wheel was pushed hard forward until a force of about 50–60lb (23–27kg) was applied. This seemed to bring it on to the forward stop, but in fact it was only about the mid-position and the stop was actually an aerodynamic one caused by the build up in control force.

The aircraft's response to this rapid forward stick movement was very sluggish. Then suddenly the nose dropped violently but squarely with very little negative 'g' effect until level with the horizon, paused and abruptly fell into a steep dive before control was regained.

The GAL/56 could be fitted either with a forward flap on the undersurface of the wing or a rear flap, and both were tried out for comparative effect. The forward flap gave a sharp nose-up change of trim for the first 10° of movement, then there appeared to be very little further trim change for the next 50°, whereas the rear flap gave a linear nose-down change of trim with increase in flap angle. With the rear flap fully down and its effect trimmed out at neutral CG there was not really sufficient backward stick movement left for a hold-off on landing at 70mph (113km/h) and consequently the landing speed was raised some 10–15mph (16–24km/h).

The all-up stall characteristics were identical with the forward flap fully lowered, but with the

Part of an ongoing research programme into tailless aircraft, this is the prototype General Aircraft GAL/56 glider, TS507. Probably seen at Farnborough in a carefully doctored official picture taken in February 1946, it proved to be yet another highly unstable British design, 'Winkle' Brown referring to it as probably the worst aircraft he had ever flown. By contrast, wartime German designers, notably the Horten brothers, had much greater success with the concept. *Barry Ketley.*

rear flap fitted the nose did not rise so steeply, and it eventually dropped in one phase instead of two. Rearward movement of the CG accentuated the steepness of the nose rise.

One impression I have firmly rooted in my mind is that the GAL/56 was undoubtedly the most difficult aircraft to land that I have ever experienced. After many hair-raising arrivals and one mild crash landing, I finally evolved what seemed to be the answer to the violent ground effect attendant on every landing.

Although a normal approach was always made, if the normal hold-off was attempted it usually managed to coincide with the onset of the ground effect. The subsequent nose-up pitch usually led to a display of the aircraft's peculiar stalling behaviour about 10ft (3m) off the ground. The subsequent dive into the runway inevitably produced an enormous bounce from the non-resilient undercarriage, plus an instinctive pullback on the control wheel to start the sequence off all over again.

However, I found that by approaching a little fast (80mph (129km/h) instead of 70mph (113km/h)) and holding off very gently so that the aircraft was floating parallel with the ground, then clamping on the control wheel and holding it rigidly central, the aircraft took up a three-point attitude on its own and sat down squarely and firmly.

This technique had to be slightly modified with change in CG position. At forward CG the aircraft would not three-point but roll on the main wheels and then the control wheel had to be moved forward to maintain that attitude until speed had dropped very low. Otherwise any premature attempt to lower the tail wheel to the ground would throw the aircraft into the air to start its antics.

At aft CG the aircraft definitely had to be landed fast (about 85mph (137km/h)). After holding off parallel with the runway the control wheel had to

be eased progressively forward and kept there to the end of the landing run, otherwise the accentuated self-stalling characteristics at aft CG tended to take charge when aided by ground effect. Moreover, with the CG 88.5in (2.25m) aft of the datum, the aircraft was out of forward elevator trim at 85mph (137km/h) so a fair push force was needed even to hold the control wheel steady as speed fell off. The inclination was to think one was moving the wheel forward when in actual fact the push force was only holding it fixed.

The RAE tests finished on 28 August 1947, when I flew the GAL/56 to Lasham airfield where I handed it over to Robert Kronfeld, the General Aircraft chief test pilot, who was going to repeat some of the tests for his own experience. Unfortunately he was caught out by the self-stalling characteristics some short time later and let the aircraft get into a spin from which it never recovered. So one of the world's most experienced glider pilots crashed to his death in what was to be one of a long list of fatal accidents to tailless aircraft. In some ways, although saddened by this news, it did not surprise me, for I had always had the instinctive feeling that the GAL/56 would one day win the eternal battle of wits with those few who flew it.

GAL/56, TS507, at Farnborough.

16 GLOSTER E.28/39

Britain's first jet, and what a little beauty. It lived up to Sir Frank Whittle's maxims of simplicity and reliability. ERIC BROWN

THE TINY LITTLE E.28/39 must rank as one of the most exciting aircraft I ever flew, for it was Britain's first jet aeroplane and a delight to fly.

The E.28/39 was primarily designed as a test bed for the Whittle W.1 engine, but based on the requirements for a fixed-gun interceptor, although the armament fit was left vague in the original specification.

The first prototype, W4041, was constructed in great secrecy in the premises occupied by Regent Motors in Cheltenham, and two sets of wings of different section were built for it. It was a beautiful looking little craft and delightfully simple. It had no trimmers, since the fabric-covered ailerons had automatic balance tabs. The small tricycle undercarriage had a steerable nosewheel, and was retracted by hydraulic pressure supplied by an accumulator which was manually charged on the ground before each flight. The hydraulically operated split trailing-edge flaps were powered by a hand pump in the cockpit. The total fuel capacity was only 81gal (368 litres).

The historic first flight at 7.45pm on 15 May 1941 at Cranwell airfield lasted 17 minutes and the Gloster test pilot, P.E.G. Sayer, had only one criticism – that the elevators were very sensitive. After some 10 hours of flying the E.28/39 was fitted with the more powerful W.1A engine and the high speed wing.

Frank Whittle shakes hands with Gloster's Chief Test Pilot, P.E.G. Sayer, after the first flight on 15 May 1941.

Gloster E.28/39 (W4041), close up port side of fuselage and (below) starboard rear view. *RAF Museum Hendon.*

W4041 was handed over to Farnborough in early 1943 and was followed in May by the second prototype, W4046, fitted with a Rover W.2B engine. The latter aircraft was lost on 30 July, when Sqn Ldr Dougie Davie baled out at 33,000ft (10,058m) when the ailerons jammed and control was lost.

Eventually W4041 was fitted with the high speed E-type wing and was sent to RAE to await delivery of a new W.2/500 engine. During this waiting period end-plate fins were fitted to the tailplane to cure some instability, and a jettison hood was incorporated. A 10-hour flying schedule set by the Ministry of Aircraft Production was begun in April 1944, and at this juncture I joined the flight test programme.

The latest W.2/500 produced 1,760lb (798kg) thrust, which was over double that of the W.1

engine of 860lb (390kg) thrust originally fitted to W4041. The loaded weight had increased to a mere 3,748lb (1700kg), and a joy indeed it was to fly, albeit somewhat temperamental with regard to the functioning of its engine.

One must of course put the relative unreliability of the engine in the context of the development state of the art, which could hardly have been earlier. However, it must be remembered that there were no aerodromes in the UK with jet fuel except Farnborough, Edgehill and Barford St John, the Gloster test airfields in Warwickshire. An engine failure in the Farnborough area meant a forced landing at Blackbushe, Odiham, or Lasham, if one could not make home base.

To cover this eventuality a Lancaster was equipped with a belly tank of jet fuel and rushed with maintenance crew and security guards to the

Britain's first jet aircraft, the Gloster/Whittle E.28/39.

Right: The original W.1 engine, outside the Power Jets engine testing site at Lutterworth.

Opposite: Four rare views of the E.28/39 being flown by Eric Brown on its last flight, on 20 February 1945.

forced landing site. The E.28/39 was extremely simple to land 'dead stick', and I got a certain relish from gliding propellerless on to an astonished RAF airfield with an aircraft bearing a large letter P (prototype) on the side, and the letter /G (guard) after the serial number, then getting out in naval uniform and asking for paraffin to refuel, well knowing there was none to be had. Always good for a laugh!

The little E.28/39's handling characteristics are interesting to record. It had a very simple cockpit layout with as many engine gauges as flying instruments, for this was primarily an engine test bed. The view was superb and almost uniquely so for a single-seat aeroplane of that era.

Taxying was delightfully simple with the steerable nose wheel, which was probably fitted because the large fin and rudder area would otherwise cause weathercocking in a cross wind. For take-off the engine had to be opened up slowly to prevent excessive jet pipe temperatures, but the full 16,700rpm could be held on the brakes. Acceleration was reasonably good and the take-off run without flaps was short.

The undercarriage retraction was a little slow, but once the aircraft was clean the rpm were reduced to 16,200 for the climb at 250mph (402km/h), which was initially good but fell off noticeably above 25,000ft (7,620m). Time to 30,000ft (9,144m) was 22 minutes.

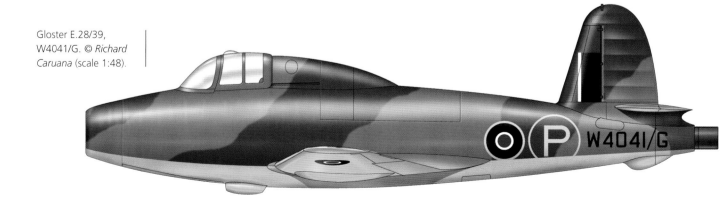

Gloster E.28/39, W4041/G. © *Richard Caruana* (scale 1:48).

Performance-wise the E.28/39 achieved its maximum level speed of 466mph (750km/h) at 10,000ft (3,050m), although the Farnborough tests were more concerned with high altitude /high Mach no. performance.

The highest height and Mach no. I personally reached were 35,500ft (10,820m) and M=0.82. From that height a dive of 40° was required to attain the Mach no., with pull out started at 20,000ft (6,096m). At M=0.82 a pull force of about 10lb (4.5kg) was required to counteract the nose-down pitch. There was a high frequency buffet, accompanied by nose-up jerking to the left and right in roll with yaw in the opposite direction.

In normal flight the controls were all quite light and effective, but the ailerons heavied up with speed. The aircraft was longitudinally unstable and marginally stable both laterally and directionally. From a handling standpoint therefore the E.28/39 would have made a good fighter, but it would have been badly underpowered and short of range with regard to performance in operational use.

There can have been few nicer aeroplanes to land than this little beauty. At 90mph (145km/h) it could be glided with undercarriage down and flaps up and the engine idling, with excellent control at that speed. The flaps had to be pumped down by hand and then speed could be reduced to 80mph (129km/h) when the E.28/39 virtually would land itself off such an approach.

Towards the end of the Farnborough test programme it was suddenly realised that practically no photographic records of this historic aircraft were in existence. A special invitation was therefore sent to the aviation press and I had a most pleasant lunchtime on 11 December 1944, beating up the RAE so that the E.28/39 in flight could be preserved on celluloid for posterity before it was retired to be put on permanent display in the Kensington Science Museum on 28 April 1946.

I can never think of this wonderful little aeroplane without thinking of the equally wonderful people I met who were associated with it – Frank Whittle of Power Jets, Gloster's chief designer George Carter, the Gloster test pilots Michael Daunt, John Crosby-Warren, John Grierson and Group Captain 'Willie' Wilson, who headed RAE's Jet Flight. All of these were pioneers in every sense of the word, for they represented the dawn of the jet age, which changed the lives of every one of us.

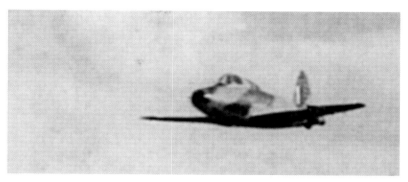

17 GLOSTER GAUNTLET

A worthy forerunner of the generation of high performance biplane fighters which graced the 1930s. ERIC BROWN

For sheer enjoyment, the Gloster Gauntlet had the edge over all other biplane fighters.

THOSE WHO WERE FORTUNATE enough to be associated with military aviation in the years immediately preceding World War II were in a vintage era of biplane fighters embracing the Gloster Gauntlet and Gladiator and the Hawker Fury. All were superb aeroplanes to fly, but for sheer enjoyment I feel the Gauntlet had the edge on the others.

It originated as Air Ministry specification F.9/26, which was in effect a challenge to the aircraft industry to build a fighter faster than the remarkable Fairey Fox light bomber of 1925. The challenge was answered by no less than nine prototypes, including the Gloster SS.18 which was the forerunner of the Gauntlet.

In spite of not winning the contest the SS.18 had such a good performance that Gloster's decided to continue its development and the SS.19B became the first recipient of the name Gauntlet and of a production specification 24/33.

The latter called for the 640hp Mercury VIS2 engine, with compressed air starting, and two Vickers Mk V machine-guns in the sides of the fuselage.

The prototype Gauntlet, to specification 24/33, recorded a maximum speed of 230mph (370km/h)

Pilot Officer Michael Lister Robinson flying Gloster Gauntlet, K5268, of 111 Squadron, 1937. *RAF Museum Hendon.*

A gaggle of Gauntlets in the 1930s. No 213 Squadron rehearsing for a display.

at 15,800ft (4,816m) and a maximum rate of climb of 2,555ft/min 779m/min at 10,000ft (3,050m). It had a service ceiling of 34,000ft and a braked landing run of 150yds (137m) in a 5mph (8km/h) surface wind.

The Gauntlet was of all-metal construction, with fabric-covered two-bay biplane wings and rear fuselage. It had a fixed undercarriage and open cockpit, so the very creditable performance was attributable to careful streamlining of all detail fittings.

The Gauntlet was built using Hawker structures and production methods, as Hawker Aircraft Ltd had taken over the Gloster Aircraft Company in 1934. By 1938 some of these aircraft had found their way into Royal Auxiliary Air Force squadrons, and this is where I had my first opportunity to fly one.

Ever since I had seen a marvellous aerobatic display with three Gauntlets of No. 19 RAF Squadron tied together, it had been my dream to fly a Gauntlet. That dream took two years to fulfil and it turned out to be superb. The version I flew was fitted with a Fairey three-blade fixed-pitch metal propeller, which gave it a lively take-off and a fair amount of swing to be counteracted. The climb angle was steep and so deliciously simple to execute – just pull back on the stick – no under-carriage or flaps to raise, no propeller pitch to change, no hood to close. However, one had to admit that the Gauntlet like all the great biplane fighters had poor forward view in anything but cruising or diving flight.

My primary aim was, however, to turn this joy-ous aeroplane inside out in aerobatics, and the sensitivity of its controls made light of loops, rolls, spins, and flick manoeuvres. Then, too, there was the exhilaration of being in an open cockpit, which makes one more aware of skid than any instrument, and also gives that extra zest to inverted flight. Perhaps the most glorious thing about an open cockpit is it allows the pilot to hear the singing of the bracing wires so that changes of speed in aerobatics become orchestrated.

Landing the Gauntlet was perhaps a little harder than flying it in any other manoeuvre, but that is a relative statement. The aircraft handled beautifully in an engine-off glide at 65mph (105km/h) and could be sideslipped to within feet of the ground with absolute confidence of precise recovery. In fact I used to deliberately approach high not just to sideslip off the excess height for the hell of it, but to improve the rather mediocre forward view in the glide. All that was required to achieve a three-point landing was a firm backward pressure on the stick at hold-off. However, on touch-down the forward view van-ished and one had to lean well to the side of the cockpit to ensure running straight.

The Gauntlet was of course not a circus stunt 'plane but a military fighter, and in that respect it was a very good gun platform, although with only two fixed synchronised Vickers Mk V .303 machine-guns, mounted in troughs in the fuse-lage sides, the fire power was not heavy.

To sum up therefore the Gloster Gauntlet was the forerunner of the generation of high per-formance biplane fighters, which in turn pointed the way to the high speed monoplanes of the late 1930s. It was a memorable aeroplane, beloved by all who were privileged to fly it, and it has carved a niche for itself in British aircraft design history. It will certainly be remembered as an aerobatic gem.

The nimble Gauntlet – an aerobatic gem.

18 GLOSTER METEOR VARIANTS

Appeared in many guises, and from the pedestrian Mk 1 went on to perform in reasonable style for a lengthy lifespan.

ERIC BROWN

THE METEOR was Britain's first operational jet, and unlike other military aircraft the Air Ministry specification F.9/40, issued in November 1949, was written around an already conceived design. The twin-engined layout was dictated by necessity, because the power available from the early jet engines was very limited.

The first Meteor flight on 5 March 1943 actually took place with de Havilland H.1 engines, instead of the intended Whittle-designed Welland engines. The next version, fitted with Metropolitan Vickers F.2 axial-flow engines, made its first flight at Farnborough on 13 November 1943. The Welland version made its maiden flight on 12 January 1944, five days before I arrived at RAE Farnborough as Chief Naval Test Pilot. By that time the Meteor had already had its first fatal crash when one of the F.2 engines burst on take-off at Farnborough.

Soon after my arrival at RAE I flew Meteor EE214/G, thus becoming the first naval pilot ever to fly a jet aircraft. Exciting as that event was for me, it could not conceal the fact that the Meteor I was a rather mediocre aeroplane from the handling standpoint. Besides being under-powered, it had heavy ailerons, suffered from directional instability, and had terrible forward view in rain.

It seems strange to reflect on some of the tests I carried out – to see if jet aircraft could be flown in formation as easily as propeller aircraft; to check how the jet engines reacted at full power when the four cannon armament was fired.

On 1 January 1943 (no public holidays in wartime) I started a most interesting series of reheat tests to augment the thrust of the jet engines in Meteor EE215/G, which had a special little cockpit installed behind mine to carry a boffin who operated the device which injected fuel into the jet pipe, and who also monitored the jet pipe temperatures.

A concurrent series of tests I made on EE212/G, EE219/G and EE227/G was to try and determine

Meteor I prototype, DG202/G.

the cause of, and the cure for, directional snaking which characterised the early jet aircraft and affected weapon aiming accuracy and made flying in turbulence difficult and tiring. These tests involved modifications to the tail unit such as fitting two auxiliary fins on the tailplane, or removing the top of the fin and rudder.

The /G for 'Guard' designation was removed from the serial numbers in April 1945. In June the prototype EE210 was introduced into the snaking tests after its return from the USA whither it had gone in 1944, in exchange for a Bell Airacomet.

In 1946 I was introduced to the Meteor III with the 2,000lb (907kg) thrust Derwent engines, and embodying a sliding canopy, increased internal fuel capacity, slotted air brakes, and a strengthened airframe. EE476 had long chord engine nacelles and it was on this aircraft I carried out an assessment of whether the Meteor III was suitable for deck landing on an aircraft carrier, having previously decided the Meteor I was unsuitable because of lack of power and non-sliding cockpit canopy.

In the event the Meteor III also proved to be a deck-landing non-starter, because of its slotted dive brakes. These increased the approach speed due to an early onset of tail buffeting, but also did not produce enough drag to keep the engine revs. above the acceleration flat spot.

Meanwhile the interminable trials to cure directional snaking continued, and EE476 was even fitted with a rudder auto-pilot. A sledgehammer to crack a nut.

My next association with the Meteor was rather a glamorous one. The new Meteor IV was fitted with the 3,000lb (1,361kg) thrust Derwent V engines in long chord nacelles, and the resultant big increase in performance necessitated a strengthened airframe and made it a potential world beater in speed. Thus it was that EE454 and I came together in May 1947 to take the aircraft through a series of transonic speed tests.

EE454 had begun life as a Meteor III but was taken off the production line to be brought up to Mk IV standard, less VHF mast and armament, and was given a high-speed finish. After establishing the Absolute World Speed Record of 606mph (975km/h) on 7 November 1945, *Britannia* as the aeroplane had been named, had its wings clipped to conform to operational fighter standard of the later Mk IVs. In this condition I found it could achieve M=0.811 in level flight at 25,000ft (7,620m) and had a limiting Mach no. of 0.84, which could be reached in a shallow dive. The compressibility characteristics displayed were a nose-up pitch with a porpoising motion, accompanied by strong wing pecking, the latter being the limiting factor. From these tests it appeared that the lengthened nacelles had made an improvement of 0.04 in Mach number.

In October 1947 I started tests on Meteor III, EE445, fitted with the suction wings invented by Dr Griffith of Rolls-Royce. The wings were perforated with holes on their surfaces and ducted to the jet-engine compressors. This allows the boundary layer of air which sticks to a wing's surface, and sets up drag, to be sucked away through the holes by suction from the engines and blown out over the ailerons through the slots near the hinges, thus improving lift and control simultaneously.

These tests continued over a year and nearly ended abruptly for me on 1 October 1948. The

The special Meteor *Britannia* on which Eric Brown did some testing, before it went on to break the world speed record, with a speed of 606mph (969kph).

underside aileron slots had been sealed over with rubber so that measurements could be made and compared with the figures obtained with the rubber removed. Although great care had been taken to make a perfect seal, all the rubber blew out on the starboard side. This set up a violent aileron oscillation and overbalance of the control so that the ailerons themselves could only be seen as a blurred mass and the wings were flexing alarmingly as the aeroplane rolled violently from side to side, sometimes going over the vertical.

I had already announced my intention of parting company with this worsening situation when another Meteor, sent to monitor my bale out, announced the seal was now coming off the other wing. So I stuck with it, since the loss of the other seal should stop the rolling motion. This fortunately proved to be the case and I regained control.

Halfway through the Griffith Suction Wing trials there appeared at Farnborough a hybrid Meteor bearing the serial number EE337. This was basically a Meteor III with the more powerful engines and stronger undercarriage of the Mk IV, together with an arrester hook, thus entitling it to be called a Sea Meteor. We made our little niche in naval aviation history when I landed the aircraft aboard HMS *Implacable* on 8 June 1948. This was the first twin-engined jet aeroplane ever to land aboard a British aircraft carrier.

By an interesting coincidence I was sent to Bitteswell airfield on 10 March 1948 to fly the world's first turboprop aeroplane, the Trent-engined Meteor, and assess its potential as a deck-landing aircraft. The airframe EE227 was an old acquaintance of mine, now powered by Rolls-Royce RB50 Trent propeller-turbines, which were really two Derwent II turbo-jet units driving

The hybrid Meteor, EE337, touches down on HMS *Indefatigable* – the first deck landing of a twin-engined jet aircraft on a British aircraft carrier.

through a .109:1 reduction gearing their 7ft 11in (2.4m) diameter five-bladed Rotol airscrews. The power rating of the Trent engine was 1,000lb (454kg) static thrust + 800 shaft horse-power.

The Meteor I airframe had side-plates fitted to the tailplane, giving in effect additional fin area, and also had a 6in (15cm) extension to the undercarriage, a 1° increase in tailplane incidence, and extra ballast located in the nose. All-up weight was 13,865lb (6,289kg).

The first striking feature of the Trent Meteor was the greater ease with which it could be taxied as compared with the pure jet Meteor. This was due of course to the much more positive thrust response to throttle movement as transmitted through the airscrews. The throttle could be operated freely without any of the detrimental effects then associated with jet engines, such as high jet-pipe temperatures and resonance over the 'flat spot' where acceleration pick up was poor. However, the tick-over speed of the Trents was rather high, necessitating occasional braking to slow down taxy progress.

Take-off acceleration was a revelation and the distance to unstick at 15,000 shaft rpm was really short. Safety speed at full power and with flaps lowered one-third was 125mph (201km/h).

The initial rate of climb at 225mph (362km/h)

was exceptionally good, and a sustained climb was made easy by an electric controller which kept constant at all altitudes any jet pipe temperature pre-selection on the throttles. The timed climb to service ceiling compared almost identically with that of the Meteor fitted with the Derwent II engines of 2,200lb (998kg) static thrust each.

In cruising flight the noise level was somewhere between that of a pure jet aircraft and a piston-engined aircraft. But I found it impossible to synchronise the engines perfectly, so that constant cockpit vibration of moderate frequency was experienced.

The most striking feature of the aircraft's performance was its remarkably low fuel consumption of approximately 40gal/h (182 litres/h per engine at 600°C JPT and 9,000rpm. These engine conditions gave 190mph (306km/h) IAS at 5,000ft (1,524m). Top speed was 440mph (708km/h) at 10,000ft (3,050m).

Acceleration on the level was marked and the throttles could be slammed fully open with complete impunity. Conversely they could be throttled fully back as quickly as one liked without fear of interrupting combustion and without any noticeable airscrew disc drag, since the blades at once coarsened pitch to reduce this effect.

EE214/G, the aircraft Eric Brown flew to become Britain's first naval jet pilot.

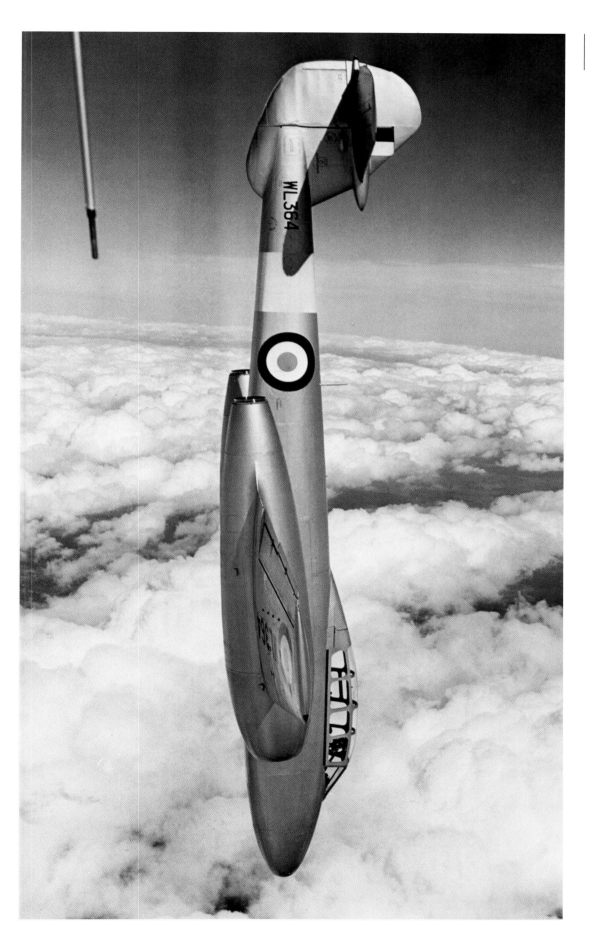

Meteor T.7 looping, in formation with photographic aircraft.

Pilots notes: Gloster Meteor 3

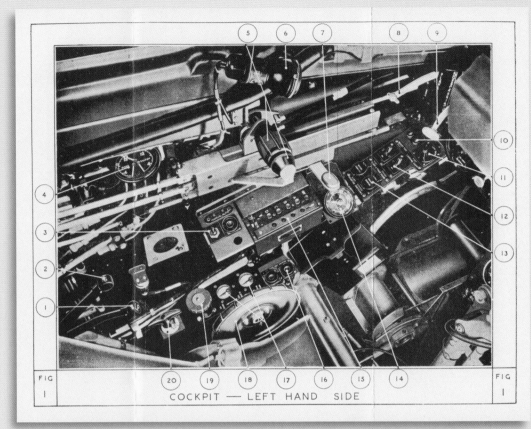

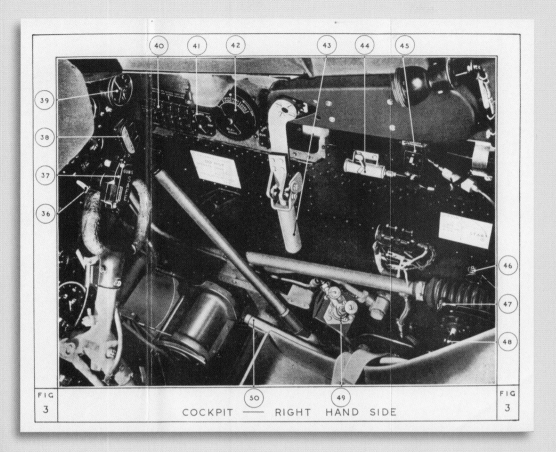

FIG 3

COCKPIT — RIGHT HAND SIDE

FIG 3

Fig 1:

Cockpit – left-hand side

1   No. 1 engine LP cock control
2   No. 1 engine HP cock control
3   'G' switches
4   Pneumatic pressure gauge
5   Throttle levers
6   Flood light
7   Air brakes control
8   Flaps selector lever
9   Undercarriage selector lever
10 Relighting switches (2)
11 Landing lamp switch
12 Low pressure pump switches (2)
13 Starter push-buttons (2)
14 Gun rounds counter (if fitted)
15 Radio controller
16 Low pressure pumps test push-buttons (2)
17 Trim indicators (2)
18 Elevator trim handwheel
19 Rudder trim handwheel
20 Fuel balance cock control

Fig 2:

**Cockpit –
Instrument Panel**

21 Undercarriage indicator
22 Flaps indicator
23 RI compass indicator
24 Instrument panel
25 Gyro gun sight
26 Instrument panel lights
27 Hood jettison handle
28 Main tank fuel contents gauges (2)
29 Oxygen regulator
30 Hydraulic emergency handpump
31 Dual jet pipe temperature gauge
32 Burner pressure gauges
33 Oil pressure and temperature gauges
34 Engine rpm indicators (2)
35 Rudder pedals adjuster release

Fig 3:

Cockpit – Right-hand side

36 Wheel brakes lever
37 Gun and camera firing switches
38 IFF demolition switches (if fitted)
39 Clock
40 Camera master, navigation lights, pressure head heater, resin lights and RI compass switches
41 Identification light selector switch
42 Gyro gunsight dimmer-selector control
43 Hood winding handle
44 Harness release lever
45 Emergency light switch
46 No. 2 engine HP cock control
47 No. 2 engine LP cock control
48 Vacuum pump change-over cock
49 Windscreen de-icing pump
50 Seat adjusting lever

A Meteor with two Rolls-Royce turbo-prop engines. This type of power plant had many advantages over the standard pure jet engines for use on naval fighters.

Under asymmetric power there was only negligible crabbing effect, requiring the slightest offset rudder trim to counteract it at as low a cruising speed as 200mph (322km/h).

Relighting of the feathered engine proved 100% reliable up to 30,000ft (9,144m).

The Trent Meteor definitely snaked less directionally than the standard pure jet version, the period of the oscillations set up in rough air being longer and the amplitude smaller than with the standard Meteor.

Stalling tests revealed that the gain in maximum lift-coefficient with power was substantial on this aircraft, a reduction of 14mph (22km/h) being recorded in stalling speed between the engine-off condition and that with the engines running at full power.

The landing speed of 120mph (193km/h) was abnormally high for a Meteor but accounted for by the greatly increased weight of this prototype. However, the high touch-down speed rapidly fell off with the airscrew disc drag as the engines were fully throttled back, and the landing run was surprisingly short.

Speed control on the approach was extremely accurate, and the rate of descent could be regu-

11 Meteor F.3, EE246/YQ-A, No. 616 Squadron, Lübeck, 1945. © *Richard Caruana* (scale 1:72).

lated almost as with an ordinary piston-engined aeroplane, due to the lift control available from the airscrew slipstream.

To sum up, the Trent Meteor was startlingly good as a first stab at the turbo prop layout, and it certainly augured well as a future application for naval aircraft.

The next Meteor variant to appear on my scene was the Mk 7 trainer. The first prototype flew on 19 March 1948 as a private venture, but the two-seater had such an impressive performance that the Air Ministry issued specification T.1/47 to cover an RAF version, and a production version VW412 arrived at RAE in January 1949. The T.7 was basically a Mk IV with the exception of the front fuselage and the reduction of the 1,000lb (454kg) of lead ballast to 300lb (136kg). In fact the T.7 proved to have a better rate of climb and take-off performance than the fighter variants, and the longer nose improved directional stability.

VW412 was fitted with an automatic dive brake system operated by Mach no. or IAS limitation, and although it worked well it was adjudged to be an unnecessary sophistication.

And finally to the Meteor F.8, although hardly in its standard form. I had been involved in prone

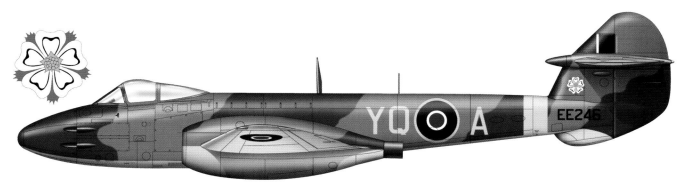

pilot trials at Farnborough, but after I left there in the autumn of 1949 these were continued to an advanced stage that involved the conversion of WK935 to accommodate a prone pilot in a new cockpit built on to the front of the nose-wheel bulkhead. This forward cockpit, forward of the main cockpit, was designed by Armstrong-Whitworth in 1952 in combination with the RAF Institute of Aviation Medicine, and contained a specially designed foam rubber couch with arm and chin rests for the prone lying pilot. A short control column was offset to starboard and the rudder was operated by hanging pedals using ankle movements. Engine and other controls were similar to those in the main cockpit to which they were connected. The tail unit had increased fin area to compensate for the extra keel surface forward.

I was invited to visit Farnborough and fly WK935 after my spell of duty at the US Naval Air Test Center at Patuxent River, and an exhilarating experience it was. It was not particularly easy to fly, mainly because of the unorthodoxy of the controls which had to be highly geared to give adequate control movement for a small wrist or ankle movement. The view was very restricted for fighter manoeuvres, but somewhat unexpectedly was good for landing in bad weather. The proximity of the pilot's face to the runway on take-off and landing took some getting used at the speeds of the Meteor. Of course the great revelation was the feeling of natural ease in performing aerobatics and the higher 'g' tolerances given by the prone position.

This experiment came to naught because Bristol Aircraft's rocket-powered interceptor project, for which the prone position research flying in the Meteor was undertaken, was cancelled.

The Meteor was a worthy holder of the title of Britain's first operational jet aeroplane, and because of its amazing adaptability survived in service in various forms for 25 years. At the outset it was hardly in the same class as Germany's counterpart, the Messerschmitt 262, but it improved to become a very snappy performer although, even at its peak, never reaching the apex of the Me 262. It was the aircraft on which many of Britain's Service pilots got their first taste of jet flying, but it was hardly a docile trainer for it had an Achilles heel – a high single-engine safety speed because its two powerful engines were too widely separated. This characteristic cost lives and gave the Meteor the reputation of an aircraft that had to be flown with respect.

Gloster Meteor F.8, converted for prone pilot position trials.

19 GRUMMAN BEARCAT

A crackerjack – the best American piston fighter I ever flew. ERIC BROWN

IN MY EXPERIENCE the name Grumman has been synonymous with excellence in naval aircraft, and so when I joined the US Naval Air Test Center at Patuxent River in 1951, I was delighted to find a Grumman F8F-2 on the inventory of Flight Test, to which I was attached. I was even more delighted to find it was kept for occasional 'chase' duties, but principally for keeping the jet jockeys in piston-engine practice by sending them off for an hour's aerobatics once a fortnight or so. These were sessions of sheer exhilaration for me and I hogged more than my fair share of them.

The Bearcat was in the true Grumman tradition in appearance, somewhat tubby and angular but exuding power and efficiency. However, it reminded me more vividly of the contemporary Hawker Sea Fury than its own family predecessors, the Hellcat and the Wildcat. It was some 3ft (91cm) shorter in span, and 7ft (2m) shorter in length than the Fury, although the folded span of the latter was some seven feet less.

Since I had just left a Sea Fury squadron and had led the Royal Navy's Festival of Britain aerobatic team equipped with Sea Furies I was in a good position to compare the two aircraft and with ample time and opportunity to do so. My interest was whetted before I flew the Bearcat by witnessing the shortest and one of the most startling aerobatic sequences I ever saw. Lt Col Marion Carl, who commanded Flight Test, took off along the lengthy Patuxent runway, holding the aircraft down for about 2,000yd (1,829m) and then, with the undercarriage still extended, pulled it up into an almost square loop and landed directly off it. This impressive display of the Bearcat's power and manoeuvrability was a sharp reminder that, at its lightest all-up weight, the pilot was allowed to apply 7.5 positive 'g' and 3.7 negative 'g'.

The 2,100hp Pratt and Whitney Double Wasp R-2800-22W had that delightful purr I have always associated with the Wasp series. As with all Grumman aircraft they somehow managed to meld this high power plant into the airframe without destroying aerodynamic line or forward view. The cockpit was roomy, but unlike most American piston-engined fighter aircraft did not make the average sized pilot feel like a pea in a pod.

The Bearcat was easy to taxi and its take-off performance was terrific, with the swing easy to control so that full power could be applied very rapidly. On the subsequent climb, with an all-up weight of only 10,400lb (4,717kg) it seemed to claw its way skyward, hanging on that four-blade propeller at a very steep angle.

Since I did no serious assessment of the Bearcat as a naval fighter, my opinion of it is based mainly on general impressions. Certainly it was a joy to throw around in the air, as it had beautiful harmony of control, aided by its spring tab ailerons. It had another hallmark of a good day fighter in that it had poor stability, rather in the manner of the Spitfire. This combination made for superb manoeuvrability which, coupled with the fact that the aircraft was overpowered, resulted in an outstanding aerobatic performer.

I do not think I have blacked myself out so consistently in an aircraft and it was just as well for peace of mind that the Bearcat was so highly stressed.

The wings of the early F8Fs were provided with 'safety tips', designed to fail when the wings were inadvertently overloaded in flight, thereby resulting in an aircraft with reduced span and greater ability to withstand high flight loads. Because of fatal accidents, resulting from violent uncontrolled motions after loss of only one of the wing tips, a wing jettisoning device was developed for service installation and was intended to ensure that when one wing tip failed the other wing tip would be shed explosively, immediately after the initial tip failure. This safety wing tip feature was eventually eliminated because of the impossibility of making and maintaining a continuously reliable installation of the explosive wing tip shedding device in service aircraft.

The Bearcat was, of course, contemporary with the early jets, and so I was interested in its transonic dive characteristics, as it was fitted with dive recovery flaps, one on each undersurface of the wing centre-section. They were hydraulically operated and controlled by a lever at the pilot's left hand, behind the throttle.

At and above M=0.75 the aircraft exhibited a tendency to oscillate longitudinally and to 'tuckunder'. These first manifestations were preceded by buffeting and were not dangerous, but were a warning of impending full loss of longitudinal control with further increase in speed which necessitated the use of the dive recovery flaps for recovery. Prior to entering the compressibility range the dive recovery flaps would pull the aircraft out of a dive without the use of the stick. But in the compressibility range the lowering of the flaps would only neutralise most of the compressibility effects, and the pilot had to use the stick for recovery, as in a normal pull-out.

For landing, the Bearcat was very reminiscent of its predecessor, the Hellcat, except that it was a bit lighter on the controls, and sat down beautifully in three-point attitude. It should have been a very good deck-landing aircraft.

I doubt whether I have enjoyed three successive fighters from the same stable more than the Grumman Wildcat, Hellcat and Bearcat. Each had the improvement in performance and handling characteristics that one would expect with the progression in time, and each was an absolute delight to fly as well as being most efficient combat aircraft.

In the case of the Bearcat I found myself inevitably comparing it with the contemporary Hawker Sea Fury, and there really was very little to choose between the two. The Bearcat probably had the edge on climb and manoeuvrability, but was not such a good weapons platform, nor as good in instrument-flight conditions as the Sea Fury. It was rather like the Fw 190 versus Spitfire IX situation – they were so evenly matched that if they met in combat the skill of the pilot alone would have been the deciding factor. Both were certainly great aircraft in their day.

The neat, but superb Bearcat – another aerobatic gem.

20 GRUMMAN COUGAR

Improved on the Panther by sweeping the wings and fitting an unconventional lateral control system. ERIC BROWN

AFTER BEING PROJECT OFFICER on the F9F-5 Panther at the US Naval Air Test Center at Patuxent River in 1951–52, it was only natural that I followed on to the F9F-6 swept-wing version known as the Cougar. I first flew serial no.126258 on 26 September 1952 for general handling, and really wrung it out for one hour and twenty minutes, during which I dived to M=1.04. Generally the aircraft made a disappointing first impression.

The F9F-6 was a modification of the basic F9F design to incorporate a 35 degree swept wing and tailplane. The F9F-5 fuselage had been modified to take the revised wings and tail and required control system changes and strengthening to provide for higher tail loads.

The wings incorporated split type landing flaps and simultaneously operating leading edge slats. Wing fences of 90in (2.2m) length and 5in (13cm) height were fitted. The lateral control system consisted of hydraulically operated flaperons and flaperettes which imparted no force feedback into the control system. The flaperons were two rec-

tangular flaps attached to the wing surfaces at their leading edges by hinges. The flaperettes were two small rectangular flaps, each of which was attached by hinges at its leading edge to the flaperon upper surface near the flaperon trailing edge. Each assembly was raised in conjunction with stick travel in its direction. After ½in (12mm) of stick travel from neutral the flaperette started opening to a maximum position of 90 degrees from the flaperon surface. Continued stick motion elevated the flaperon trailing edge to a maximum position of 40 degrees from the wing surface. The flaperettes provided a reduced amount of lateral control when the flaperon system became inoperative in the event of a hydraulic failure. The change-over to the flaperette system was by manual reversion. Artificial spring feel was provided on both the normal flaperon and the emergency flaperette system.

The horizontal tail consisted of an adjustable tailplane and horn balanced spring-tab elevators, but this arrangement was eventually replaced by a 'flying tail'.

The Cougar under test at NATC, Patuxent River.

The Cougar in planform.

The rudder pedals were linked to that part of the rudder below the tailplane, the upper portion being controlled by a yaw damper. Movement of the lower section beyond six degrees in either direction picked up the upper position of the rudder and deflected it by means of mechanical stops.

Hydraulically operated, variable position speed brakes were installed beneath the fuselage and on the inboard flap trailing edges, and had a limit extension of 75 and 40 degrees respectively. They could not be extended separately, but could be extended to any intermediate position.

The first 30 Cougars were fitted with a 6,500lb (2,948kg) static thrust centrifugal flow Pratt & Whitney J48-P-6 turbo-jet engine, but subsequent aircraft had the 7,250lb (3,289kg) static thrust J48-P-8 engine.

To my eye the Cougar was a good looking aeroplane, and I have seldom found the adage wrong that 'if it looks good it should fly good'. Now to the proof of the pudding. I felt comfortable in the cockpit, the aircraft taxied well, and with the P-8 engine took off very smartly.

Time to climb to 40,000ft (12,192m) was 10.4 minutes, and the maximum speed I recorded in level flight was 653mph (1,051km/h) at TAS at sea level. However, the impressive thing about the F9F-6 was its range of 1,322 (2,128km) miles at 495mph (797km/h) TAS at 45,000ft (13,716m) on 777gal (3,532 litres) of fuel. All the fuel was internally stowed without wing tip fuel tanks, although the internal wing fuel could be jettisoned.

The longitudinal stability left much to be desired, and the stick force per 'g' was too high (10 pounds at 402mph (647km/h) at 10,000ft (3,050m) at mid-CG), thus limiting manoeuvrability. The high altitude buffet boundary (3.3'g' at M=0.90 at 35,000ft (10,668m) at mid-CG) was just acceptable.

Lateral stability was very weak, particularly for landing, but it improved slightly with the yaw damper operating, although the lateral control forces increased under such circumstances. Controllability was marginal to recover from inadvertent entry into the jet stream of a preceding aircraft on the landing approach. Lateral stick centering was positive and the breakout force was very high, resulting in over-controlling at high speeds. The lateral trim change with speed was bad and the lateral

The Grumman Cougar undergoing its land catapult trials.

trimmer was rather ineffective. Maximum rate of roll was 300 degrees/second at 345mph (555km/h), and adverse yaw with flaperon application was satisfactory. Dihedral effect was high. Such a high rate of roll is really unusable effectively, but it pays off in the low speed range for landing by still giving a good roll rate when reduction in rolling rate is normally considerable.

Directional stability and control characteristics without the yaw damper were very poor, and rudder trimmer was really required to cope with the constant change in directional trim with change in airspeed. The yaw damper satisfactorily damped the lateral-directional oscillations, but only marginally so in the landing configuration.

The stall with slats extended exhibited a very mild nose-up pitch, but this characteristic disappeared when the slats were retracted. The stall in the powered landing approach configuration occurred at 106mph (171km/h) at an all-up weight of 12,500lb (5,670kg), and at 128mph (206km/h) in the clean configuration. These stalls occurred respectively at angles of attack of 16.8 degrees and 16 degrees, with ample aerodynamic warning. However, the accelerated stall characteristics were bad, consisting of a violent nose-up pitch and rapid wing drop – not good for a fighter aircraft.

And so from the low speed to the high speed end of the flight envelope. The high Mach number characteristics were a lateral unsteadiness starting at M=0.93, together with a longitudinal porpoising and slight buffet. These characteristics intensified up to M=0.95, then reduced moderately up to the safe flight limiting Mach number of M=1.04, where the high elevator control forces and low elevator effectiveness for recovery were marginal after a nose-down trim change occurred about M=1.0. Recovery could actually be made at M=1.04 without the use of the adjustable tailplane by reduction of power and simultaneous extension of the speed brakes. In fact it was desirable if possible to avoid use of the adjustable tailplane because its sensitivity usually resulted in 'g' overshoot when elevator effectiveness returned in the pull out.

The speed brakes were very effective compared with those of the Panther, and gave a mild nose-up pitch on extension, but they took an excessive time to extend and retract.

During deck landing trials I found the view very good except in rain. The approach speed at landing weights up to 15,700lb (7,122kg) was in the range of 127mph–132mph (204–212km/h). During approaches made using the emergency lateral control system by means of flaperettes, I found this adequate as it gave a rate of roll of 20 degree/second for a 30lb (14kg) stick force. The US Navy normally required a minimum roll rate of 15 degree/second with a stick force of less than 30lb (14kg).

Catapult launches at 18,200lb (8,256kg) with a 30mph (48km/h) windspeed over the deck, which was the minimum for safe operation, showed that adequate elevator control was available to give sufficient dynamic longitudinal rotation at the end of the catapult power stroke to ensure a clean fly-away.

The Cougar will not rate as one of the great naval aircraft, but Grumman had made a good recovery from a rather inauspicious beginning with it, and their success with their unconventional lateral control system was particularly noteworthy. However, the F9F-6 had one very serious shortcoming in that it relied very heavily on the dependable operation of the yaw damper. Without it its handling qualities deteriorated to a very marked extent, making it very difficult to fly on instruments or in turbulence, and ruining its efficacy as a weapons platform.

21 GRUMMAN HELLCAT

A rugged fighter with a daunting combat kill/loss of 19:1, the best recorded in World War II. The nemesis of the ubiquitous Japanese Zero. ERIC BROWN

One of the first Hellcat Mk Is (FN323) to reach the UK.

A S SOON as the United States entered World War II it deployed Wildcats of the US Navy to the Pacific. Here that quirky little fighter soon found it had big trouble on its hands in the form of the ubiquitous Japanese Mitsubishi Zero, which had ruled the roost in regional conflicts in the Far East since 1939. This should have rung alarm bells in both the US Navy Bureau of Aeronautics and in the Grumman Aircraft Corporation to prepare a specification and design to counter this observed threat. Reaction was initially slow,

although when it came the Grumman team demonstrated quite remarkable rapidity in translating its eventual design for a Wildcat replacement into a prototype and then bringing it to production status, all without major problems and within 18 months.

This new aircraft, named Hellcat, was conceived after distilling the experiences of fighter pilots in combat in both the Far East and European sectors of war. Their priority requirements were speed, rate of climb, firepower, armour protection, pilot

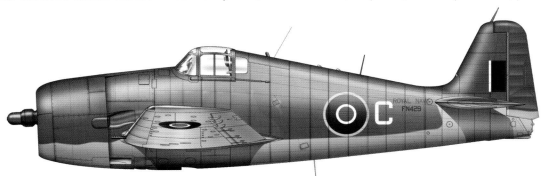

Grumman Hellcat Mk I, FN429/C, 800 Squadron, Fleet Air Arm, 1943. © *Richard Caruana* (scale 1:72).

incidence to reduce drag in level flight. A negative thrust line was adopted for the engine in order to attain the comparatively large angle of attack required for take-off, although this had a slightly detrimental effect on the view for deck landing. The thrust line produced a pronounced tail-down attitude in normal cruising flight, but considerable attention was paid to achieving the best possible view from the cockpit. This was located at the highest point amidships, resulting in a characteristic humped profile in side elevation.

The first production Hellcat flew on 3 October 1942. Of the few changes introduced on this aircraft, the principal was the replacement of the Curtiss Electric propeller by a Hamilton Standard unit, which was usually mated with the Wright Cyclone. However, that engine had been rejected in favour of the magnificent Pratt & Whitney 18-cylinder R-2800 Double Wasp. This two-stage, two-speed supercharged air-cooled radial was perhaps the best large reciprocating engine ever to be built.

Early in 1943 the Hellcat went into service with the US Navy, and shortly afterwards was made available to Great Britain under our Lend-Lease arrangements. I flew my first Hellcat on 26 July 1943 at Crail in Scotland where I was Senior Pilot in the Service Trials Unit. The aircraft, which was temporarily named the Gannet by the Royal Navy, impressed me initially by its size and pugnacious appearance, but once in the air it was immediately obvious we had a winner on our hands.

The Fleet Air Arm's Hellcats service in Europe was mainly as fighter escort covering the attacks on the German battleship *Tirpitz* in Norway, in April and August of 1944. Most of the Hellcat's FAA service, however, was with the British Pacific Fleet in the Far East. The Hellcat must be credited with changing the course of World War II in the Pacific theatre, where it arrived in the hands of the US Navy in mid-1943, at a crucial time when the Japanese Zero ruled the skies.

The Zero had acquired its formidable reputation as a consequence of its design philosophy, which staked everything on lightweight structure – even at the expense of virtually eliminating pilot protection by excluding any bullet proof windscreen, cockpit armour or self-sealing fuel tanks. This was in order to enhance performance and manoeuvrability. The end result was a fighter with an exceptional turning circle, and outstanding rate of climb, but with vulnerable structural integrity.

The US Navy's dilemma was to work out how to counter an aircraft with which it dare not dogfight. The answer lay in the Hellcat's ability to out dive the Zero, and in its devastating firepower. Therefore the scenario the US pilots sought to achieve was to approach the enemy with a height advantage and then dive into the attack, which would almost inevitably cause the Zero to go into an evasive tight turn. Because of the high speed acquired in its dive, the Hellcat could follow the Zero through some 70–80° of its turn, sufficient to

Hellcat Mk I (FN323) during pre-service trials at A&AEE, Boscombe Down, in June 1943.

get in a lethal burst of its six 0.5 calibre guns on the frail structure of its quarry. If a Zero managed to get on the tail of a Hellcat, the latter could normally elude its pursuer by diving and twisting with ailerons. With twice the engine power of the Japanese aircraft it could pull away in level flight. Even if fired on by the Zero, the Hellcat's rugged structure stood up well to such attack.

The Hellcat's two years of combat in the Pacific theatre of operations yielded an incredible 5,156 victories against Japanese aircraft; 4,948 downed by carrier-based F6Fs and 208 by land-based Hellcats. The Fleet Air Arm's contribution to this American tally in the Far East was a further 47, raising the Pacific figure to 5,203. In the European

theatre the British Hellcats claimed 13 German aircraft, thus bringing the grand total of Axis victims to 5,216. On the debit side some 270 Hellcats were lost in aerial combat, so the superb end result was a kill:loss ratio of 19 to 1, the highest of any fighter aircraft in World War II.

When this amazing record is analysed, does it show the Hellcat to be almost faultless in its design? – by no means. Although this big fighter was stable about all axes, there were marked changes of lateral and directional trim with changes of speed and power. The controls heavied-up at high speeds, particularly the ailerons, and in the clean condition the stall occurred with little warning and either wing could drop, but recovery

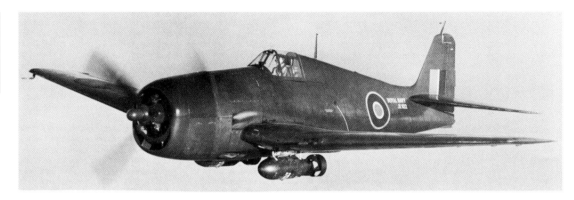

A Hellcat Mk II (JX 822), equivalent to the F6F-5, under test at Boscombe Down, late 1944, with two 454-kg (1,000lb) bombs.

A Hellcat FR Mk II (JV270), equivalent to the F6F-5P, with a camera in the lower aft fuselage, seen here with a rocket launching rail test installation.

A Hellcat Mk I (JV131). The Royal Navy received 252 F6F-3s as Hellcat Mk Is.

Hellcat NF Mk II (JX965), equivalent to the F6F-5N, with ANN/APS-6 radar, housed in a pod on the starboard wing.

was straightforward and easy. Buffeting of the tail surfaces heralding a stall was particularly pronounced in a steep turn, continued back pressure on the control column then causing the aircraft to flick out of the turn. But recovery was immediate when this pressure was released.

In a dive it was necessary to reduce rpm to 2,100 or less in order to reduce vibration to acceptable levels. The Hellcat had to be trimmed into the dive and became tail-heavy as speed built up, some left rudder being necessary to counter yaw.

In deck landing at 92mph (147km/h) the Hellcat was as steady as a rock, with precise attitude and speed control. Its immensely sturdy undercarriage possessed very good shock-absorbing charac-

teristics. These were exactly the features that tipped the balance in favour of the Hellcat over the much vaunted Chance-Vought F4U Corsair, which was faster, had a higher ceiling and greater payload, but was a handful to land on a carrier.

Conceived primarily as an air superiority weapon with the range to seek out the enemy and bring them to battle, but as the emphasis switched to an offensive capability, the Hellcat showed its great versatility in carrying both bombs and rockets.

The Fleet Air Arm received in total 252 Hellcat Is (F6F-3s) and 930 Hellcat IIs (F6F-5s with spring-tab ailerons), as well as 80 F6F-5N night fighters with AN/APS-6 radar, housed in a pod under the right wing-tip. Altogether 12,275 Hellcats were produced, and their influence on World War II was immense.

The American Hellcats had a triumphant finale to World War II when 450 US Navy and Marines carrier aircraft flew in a gaggle (it could hardly have been described as a formation) over the battleship *Missouri* in Tokyo Harbour on 2 September 1945, where General MacArthur formally accepted Japan's surrender. For the British Hellcats it was a different ending. Under the terms of the Lend-Lease arrangements they were taken aboard our carriers into open waters where they were unceremoniously pushed over the stern to a watery grave, but to a farewell salute from their grateful pilots. Ashore, two Fleet Air Arm squadrons of Hellcats managed to survive until April and August 1946 respectively. *Sic transit gloria!*

22 GRUMMAN TIGERCAT

Potentially a fine fighter, but only found an operational niche in the all-weather/night role. ERIC BROWN

A S A DEVOTEE of the Grumman company's products, I had always wanted to fly their exciting looking Skyrocket twin-engined fighter. However, it may be just as well that I did not, since it was not a great success, so I had to base my judgement of their twin design capability on the later F7F Tigercat.

Although initially used by land-based US Marine fighter squadrons, it was designed for shipboard use on the new 45,000ton *Midway* class aircraft carriers.

For a single-seat fighter it was considerably bigger than the Sea Hornet, but it was aimed at solving one of the problems associated with deck landing twin-engined aircraft – namely the recovery of the aircraft when flying on one engine only.

This was the reason the Tigercat came to RAE Farnborough in April 1946. Although the Tigercat did not strike me as beautiful when I first saw it, there was something very attractive about its lines, and those two Pratt and Whitney R-2800-22W Double Wasp engines simply shrieked of power.

To start these power plants the petrol cock was set to RESERVE, the engine master cock to BOTH ENGINES, the fuel booster pump ON, and then the engines primed from the cockpit. Starting was by the internal direct cranking method, and the starboard engine was started first to obtain brake pressure. Before taxiing the rudder boost was switched on.

The view from the cockpit was very good and the combination of tricycle undercarriage and powerful brakes made the aircraft easy to taxi even in a cross-wind. There was, however, very small airscrew ground clearance and harsh braking on the deck. The resultant nose wheel compression could have brought the airscrews within striking distance of the spring bows, which supported the arrester wires on a carrier's deck.

Tigercat, TT439, was at an all-up weight of 21,425lb for take-off, which was made with the cowlgills set to AUTO, the oil coolers set about one-quarter open as seen on the upper surface of the wings, flap selected 15° down, and all trimmers set neutral. The engines could be revved up to full power on the brakes and yet on release there was no swing, which was fortunate as the rudder was fairly ineffective at low speeds. Acceleration was excellent and the aircraft could be pulled off at 80mph in a surprisingly short distance. The climb away was very steep after such an unstick and the stick had to be eased forward to gain single-engine safety speed rapidly, especially as retraction of the undercarriage also gave a nose-up change of trim. Flap retraction had a negligible effect on trim.

The exciting Tigercat shows off its powerful profile.

The Tigercat, folded up for shipboard storage.

The Tigercat had an impressive initial rate of climb at a steep angle, and stability was satisfactory, especially laterally, which augered well for instrument flight.

The aircraft was fast in the cruise, and a full power run gave a good top speed of 427mph (687km/h) at 19,000ft (5,791m), which was some five mph slower than the Sea Hornet.

The power-boosted rudder had a geared tab fitted, while the ailerons and elevators had spring tabs. I had therefore expected good harmony of control, but this was not the case. The rudder was much too light, the elevators just about right, and the ailerons surprisingly heavy.

The ailerons heavied up with speed so much that at the limited dive speed of 518mph (834km/h) they felt almost solid and rate of roll was virtually dependent on rudder displacement.

The elevators were delightfully light, and the stick force per 'g' remained approximately constant with speed. This made manoeuvres in the looping plane very pleasant to execute.

The all-up stall with full petrol load occurred without warning at 120mph (193km/h) and was characterised by a gentle nose drop, If the fuel was used in accordance with the proper operational procedure, i.e. in the order of the main tank-auxiliary-reserve, it was impossible to effect a stall, since the CG moved forward and left insufficient backward elevator travel.

The all-down stall occurred at 89mph (143km/h) with full petrol load, and there was warning of its approach from an elevator judder, which seemed to arise from the tab vibrating at large upward elevator angles. At the stall the nose dropped gently.

The application of power even in small increments reduced the stalling speed considerably. At 15in Hg. boost the all-down stall occurred at about 70mph and still displayed mild characteristics, with a tendency to fall away unevenly laterally to starboard as the ailerons were so ineffective at that speed that the wing could not be held up.

For landing the petrol cock was set to RESERVE and the fuel booster pump switched on. The flaps were then set to the 260mph (418km/h) notch, and when speed had dropped to 195mph (314km/h) the undercarriage was lowered. The flaps were then set in 172mph (277km/h) notch and the 150mph (241km/h) notch (fully down). The elevator trimmer was wound well back and a deck landing type approach made at 98mph (158km/h). Lateral control at this speed was very spongy, but the rate of roll was acceptable when judged in conjunction with the good view provided and the fact that the wing could be picked up readily with slight application of engine power. The long sloping nose of the aircraft provided a handy attitude datum.

As soon as the throttles were cut at touchdown the Tigercat pitched forward on to its nose wheel, but the undercarriage behaviour was excellent, there being no tendency to bounce or swing.

A baulked landing could normally be dealt with at half throttle power, but the use of increasing amounts of power beyond that value gave a fairly violent nose-up change of trim, and as the aircraft was normally trimmed full nose up on the approach, this assumed dangerous aspects since it involved as much as full forward stick movement and high stick forces to counteract it. There was no directional or lateral change of trim with increase of power.

The main British interest in the Tigercat was to see how it could cope with a single-engine deck landing, and in this respect the power boosted rudder was the focal point of our attention. On the ground there was a fair amount of friction in the rudder control circuit with the hydraulic power boost off, but this disappeared when the power booster was put on, giving complete smoothness in application of control. The booster was claimed to give 30% feedback to furnish the pilot with control feel, but the rudder was amazingly light and there was no noticeable build up of control force with speed and only a slight build up with increasing rudder displacement. It certainly gave me the impression that the rudder was probably too powerful in effect at high speeds and could cause structural failure if misused.

On the other hand, without power boost, the rudder was very heavy indeed throughout the speed range, and in fact was almost immoveable above 460mph (740km/h).

The effect of the power boost was illustrated by cutting the port engine at take-off power of 44in (1.1m) Hg. boost, 2,550rpm. With boost on, the swing could be held at a steady minimum speed of 182mph (293km/h) and, without power boost, at 230mph (370km/h). In the first case the foot load was quite light and could be held for a sustained period, but with the power boost off it became extremely heavy and could only be held for a few minutes.

In the event, a single-engine deck landing was not a practicable proposition, as at an approach speed of 109mph (175km/h) at a reasonably low power setting the aircraft had run out of both rudder and aileron trim, and consequently out of elevator travel since no more power could be used to keep the nose up.

On the whole the Tigercat was a delightful high performance aircraft to fly, with the exception of the heavy aileron control at high speeds. From a deck-landing viewpoint the Tigercat was superior to the Mosquito mainly on the strength of its good take-off characteristics, its tricycle undercarriage arrangement, slightly better lateral control on the approach, and improved power-on stalling characteristics. However, it was inferior to the Sea Hornet, mainly because of its critical CG restriction on effective elevator travel during the approach, and its dangerous baulked landing longitudinal trim change.

There has really been only one successful solution to single-engine deck-landing of a twin propeller driven aircraft, and that is the contra-rotating co-axial airscrews layout as in the Fairey Gannet.

However, the Tigercat's tricycle undercarriage and power-boosted rudder were useful contributions to the general problem, although not the solution.

Strangely enough I was to meet the Tigercat some six years later in a most interesting new guise with a supine piloting position. This F7F-2N was located at the Naval Air Test Center at Patuxent River, and when I first saw it in the hangar I could scarcely believe my eyes. It had been modified by installing a pilot's seat in the position normally occupied by the radar operator. The seat was adjustable for position from the fully upright to the supine, and had two upright hand grips, the right one of which was an auto-pilot control stick and the left a master throttle lever. There was a periscope sight for use when supine. The normal pilot's seat in the aircraft was used for carriage of a safety pilot.

I was eventually given a chance to fly this strange beast, and found the take-off and landing in the supine position a hair-raising experience. In normal flight it was still uncomfortable, and positively alarming in aerobatics in the looping plane when I found myself going vertically uphill standing on my head. After some experimenting with the seat I selected the three-quarter supine position as the optimum compromise for comfort and 'g' resistance. Of course the Navy's intention was only to use the supine position for long range cruising, and the three-quarter position for combat, and the upright position for take-off and landing. Personally I much prefer the prone position in a fighter, although it is tiring for lengthy flights.

The prominent Pratt & Whitney Double-Wasp engines of the Tigercat gave excellent performance across the full range.

23 GRUMMAN WILDCAT

Forerunner of the Hellcat and a worthy family member. A great carrier aircraft, but touchy on land. A nippy little fighter in its day.

ERIC BROWN

Martlet Is of 804 Squadron. Aircraft A, (BJ562), was one of the two Martlets involved in shooting down the first German aircraft by an American aircraft in British service, on 25 December 1940.

THE DESIGN of any combat aircraft involves a measure of compromise, and that of the shipboard single-seat fighter, perhaps more than most. A masterpiece in combining the contradictory factors called for in a fighter suited to the naval environment was the corpulent but rugged and pugnacious little Grumman Wildcat.

Introduced into the Fleet Air Arm in 1940, with the singularly uninspiring name of Martlet, at a time when that service had a far from impressive fighter armoury comprising the Sea Gladiator, the Blackburn Skua and Roc, it was like a gift from heaven. I was overjoyed to learn I had been posted to 802 Squadron at Donibristle to participate in the formation of the second FAA squadron to be mounted on this new Grumman fighter.

I first set eyes on the Martlet in November 1940, when it had still to be dubbed Wildcat by the US Navy, with which it had not yet entered service. Indeed our first aircraft in 802 were actually export versions of the G-36A for France's Marine Nationale and diverted to Britain on the fall of France. At first sight I thought this barrel-like little fighter, of 38ft span, looked like a venomous bumble-bee, with its sturdy fuselage, stubby mid-wing, squat undercarriage, powerful radial engine and wide-chord propellor blades. It had two features not previously seen as equipment on British-operated aircraft – its 0.5in (12.7mm) Colt-Browning machine-guns and its sting-like arrester hook. The cockpit held its quota of surprises. It was unexpectedly roomy and all the instruments were calibrated in metric units for its originally intended Gallic recipients. Its unique features included gun cocking handles, tailwheel lock, and toe brakes on the rudder ped-

als. From my point of view the cockpit seemed to have been tailored for someone a size larger than me, for everything was at full stretch as far as I was concerned, making take-off and landing a somewhat tricky operation. Fortunately this hazardous situation was relieved after a few months when the solid rubber-tyred tailwheel was replaced by a much larger pneumatic type which raised the tail about 9in (23cm) and unblanked just enough of the rudder from the fuselage in the ground attitude to ease the directional control problem. Another feature requiring circumspection, especially in a crosswind or when taxying round corners, was the tendency for the aircraft to roll on its remarkably soft narrow-track undercarriage, with the risk of a wing-tip contacting the ground.

Two other areas requiring sharp attention of the pilot were lack of automatic boost control, and manual control of the undercarriage. This required approximately 28 turns of the crank to raise or lower the wheels, usually resulting in a roller-coaster climb out.

However, these shortcomings were forgiven once the Wildcat, as it came to be called, became airborne. Here, it showed it was capable of competing on almost equal terms with contemporary fighters, but it needed plenty of stick handling by

the pilot to get the best out of it. Its main advantages were its steep climb, excellent turning circle, completely innocuous stalling characteristics and the exceptional view from the cockpit.

Our Martlet Is were powered by a 1,200hp Wright R-1820-G205A Cyclone, which gave a top speed of 310mph at 15,000ft and a rate of climb of 3,300 ft/min which was outstanding at that stage of the war. In addition to this, its 1,100 mile range was ideal for its role in convoy protection.

In September 1941 No. 802 Squadron embarked on the world's first operational escort aircraft carrier, HMS *Audacity* with six Martlet Is. This small carrier had no hangar, so the aircraft were permanently out in the open on the flight deck. The groundcrew had to carry out maintenance whilst braving all that the Atlantic weather could throw at them. The pilots were grateful too for the sting hook, since their ship had only two arrester wires fitted, and also for the efficient wing flotation-bag system at their disposal, which saved many a pilot when forced to ditch in the sea.

The Martlet Mk II arrived with 802 in the summer of 1941 and differed from the Mk I in that it was powered by the two-row Pratt & Whitney S3C4-G Twin Wasp engine, rather than the single-row Wright Cyclone. This was a real improvement

Top: The first export Grumman G-36A, ordered for France's Marine Nationale but diverted to the UK as Martlet Mk I (AX753).

Above: The third G-36A in British colours and delivery markings of NX-G3, prior to becoming Martlet Mk I, AL231.

Above: One of the French contract Grumman G-36As, BJ513, after delivery to the Royal Navy as Martlet Mk Is.

Right: An early folding-wing Martlet Mk II (AM968), on the lift of an escort carrier.

as the latter had proved less than reliable. They were also fitted with folding wings which freed up a great deal of space on an otherwise cramped flightdeck. Later versions were equipped with six 0.5 machine-guns; this armament was not supplied to 802 for *Audacity*, although we did eventually acquire one such six-gunner.

Performance with the Twin Wasp was virtually identical to the Cyclone, except in the rate of climb where the Mk IIs 13% escalation in overall weight took its toll.

Operationally, the Martlet got off to a good start with the FAA, forcing down a Junkers Ju 88 in the Orkneys while serving with 804 Squadron on 25 December 1940. This success was extended by 802 Squadron, flying from *Audacity*, which accounted for five Fw 200 four-engined Kuriers. *Audacity* was eventually sunk in the Bay of Biscay on 21 December 1941, but had by then already proven the value of the escort carrier, which went on to be used extensively by both Britain and the United States, throughout the war. The Americans used the Wildcat as its main fighter with both the US Navy and the Marines operating in the Far East, against the formidable Japanese Zero fighter.

After the demise of *Audacity*, Martlets continued to be supplied to the Royal Navy under Lend-Lease arrangements with America. These aircraft were 220 Mk IVs and 312 Mk Vs – generally similar to the Mk II, except the Mk IV had six guns instead of four. The Mk IV was built by Grumman and the Mk V by the General Motors Corporation.

Early in 1942 I was launched into my test flying career with a posting to the Service Trials Unit at Arbroath. There I became reunited with the Martlet in early September, carrying out catapult tests, using the American single-point system, aboard the American-built escort carrier HMS *Biter*. This catapult system was new to British carriers. All previous FAA aircraft had been catapulted from a cradle arrangement, which involved a tedious loading process. This also required ugly, heavy steel spools – sticking out of the aircraft at four points – which fitted into the claws of the four-legged cradle. However, the Martlet, using the American system, had only a small steel hook under its belly, to which one end of a wire strop was attached while the other end went around a shuttle fitted almost flush into the catapult slot in the forward end of the carrier's deck. This innovation brought simplicity in catapult design and a

Above: Grumman Martlet (NXG-2). *RAF Museum Hendon.*

Left: The Martlet Mk V, alias Wildcat Mk V, was an Eastern Motors-built FM-1 with a Twin Wasp engine and only four wing guns.

Grumman Martlet I, EJ569/F, Nº 804 Naval Air Squadron, FAA, March 1941. © *Richard Caruana* (scale 1:48).

A Cyclone-engined
F4F-4B, designated
Martlet Mk IV by the
Royal Navy, on test
with British Mk I rocket
launchers under the
wings.

The final model of the
Wildcat, the Eastern
Motors-built FM-2.
It was designated
Wildcat Mk VI in Royal
Navy service.

A fixed-wing Martlet
Mk II (AM980), one of
ten accepted by the
Royal Navy to avoid
delivery delays.

weight and drag saving on the aircraft. A further important advantage was that the aircraft got airborne at an angle of attack which gave it maximum lift without the pilot having to rotate it immediately after launch.

The flow of Martlets continued with an improved Cyclone-engined Mk VI, probably the most satisfactory to fly because it was lightened for small carrier work. It could also be spun with impunity, whereas this was banned on all previous marks. Add to this the bonus that in January 1944 the Admiralty finally dropped the name Martlet and standardised on the US appelation of Wildcat.

British Wildcats were mainly used on convoy protection duties, operating with Swordfish from escort carriers. They saw action from larger carriers in Madagascar, the Mediterranean, the Allied invasion of North Africa and the South of France. They were also used as escorts for Baracudas in the attacks against the battleship *Tirpitz* in Norway, the Allied landings at Salerno in Italy and the D-Day landings in Normandy. After the war in Europe ended our Wildcats continued to see service in the Far East with the British East Indies and Pacific Fleets.

I have, of course, an emotional tie with the Martlet/Wildcat, but would still assess it as the outstanding Allied naval fighter of the early war years. Its ruggedness suited the hurly-burly of carrier operations, and it was at its best in the naval environment, to such a degree indeed that it was easier to take-off or land on a carrier than on a runway, where it was inclined to be fickle about the direction it took up. With its excellent patrol range – I actually flew one sortie of four and a half hours in a Martlet II – and fine ditching characteristics, for which I can vouch as a matter of personal experience, this Grumman fighter was, for my money, one of the finest shipboard aeroplanes ever created.

24 HANDLEY PAGE HAMPDEN

Nicknamed 'the flying suitcase',
and it flew like one. ERIC BROWN

THE HAMPDEN MEDIUM BOMBER was an unusual looking aeroplane with its new, narrow, deep flat-sided fuselage and slender tail boom carrying twin fins and rudders, a layout earning it the nickname of 'flying suitcase'. It was powered by two 1,000hp Bristol Pegasus XVIII nine-cylinder radial air-cooled engines, driving three-bladed de Havilland constant speed airscrews.

The object of the fuselage layout was to provide a maximum field of defensive fire in the vulnerable rear area. The design allowed a gunner in a position above the fuselage over the trailing edge of the wings, and one below the fuselage at the break in the lower fuselage line.

The Hampden was designed to Air Ministry Specification D.9/32, and made its first flight at Radlett on 21 June 1936.

It was ordered in quantity by the Air Ministry in August 1936 and so was very much in the front line at the beginning of World War II with ten operational squadrons totalling 160 aircraft. It was unique in that, in a four crew fuselage, the pilot was seated in a fighter type cockpit that conceded something of its bomber role in having a spectacle type handwheel instead of a stick type control column. It had automatic slots on the outer half-span of each wing leading edge, while the inner half-wing trailing edge carried 20 per cent chord slotted flaps. Internal bomb load was 4,080lb (1,851kg), and a 500lb (227kg) bomb could be carried under each wing.

I first got a chance to fly the Hampden at the Aircraft and Armament Experimental Establishment at Boscombe Down at the end of 1943. By that time the aircraft had been relegated to the minelaying and torpedo-dropping roles and was being gradually phased out as obsolescent.

Entry to the cockpit was by way of a short ladder, the peg on the top rung of which was inserted in a hole in the trailing edge fillet, and this gave access to a walkway on the port wing and thus, via a footstep, to the cockpit hood aperture. Once installed in the office, the view was good and the cockpit layout very logical in its groupings of instruments and controls, with the standard British T-layout of blind flying instruments.

It was typical of the speeds of that design era that a hinged window was fitted in each side cockpit window to provide clear view if necessary. In really bad visibility conditions the front bottom panel on the port side of the cockpit hood was secured in such a manner that it could be knocked out by the fist and jettisoned.

All flying controls and the flaps were fabric covered. The ailerons were each fitted with a trimming tab, that on the starboard aileron being pre-set on the ground, whilst the port trimming tab could be controlled in flight from the cockpit.

My purpose in flying the Hampden was to get experience in its well known rudder overbalance characteristics, which had proved an operational limitation in evasive manoeuvres. The directional

Handley Page
Hampden B.Mk I,
L4032 'Hampden' (1st
production aircraft),
Radlett, June 1938.
© *Richard Caruana*
(scale 1:96).

Pilot's notes: Handley Page Hampden 1

Fig. 2

Pilot's instrument panel – later type

37 Combined nose and tail heavy indicator and pressure gauge, for automatic controls

41 Flap position indicators

47 Push-button for calling wireless operator

48 Oxygen delivery altitude gauge

49 Oxygen delivery contents gauge

55 Fuel pressure gauges

56 Instruction panel

58 Time-of-flight clock

87 Identification lamps switchbox

96 Blind flying panel suction gauge

97 Compass lamp

98 Three-position head lamp switch for signalling or independent use of headlamps

99 Lorenz beam-approach indicator

100 Hinged clear vision panel

101 Switches for Graviner fire-extinguishers (where applicable)

Fig. 3

Port side of pilot's cockpit

9 Pilot's seat

12 Firing button for fixed gun

14 Aileron control wheel

15 Brakes thumb lever

17 Magnetic compass

23 Mixture control lever for both engines

24 Two-speed super-charger gear lever

25 Master fuel cocks

26 Port and starboard throttle levers

28 Airscrew control levers

30 Pilot's bomb firing switch

31 Landing lamps switch

32 Resetting switch for automatic controls

33 Automatic control cut-out switch

34 Landing lamps dipping lever

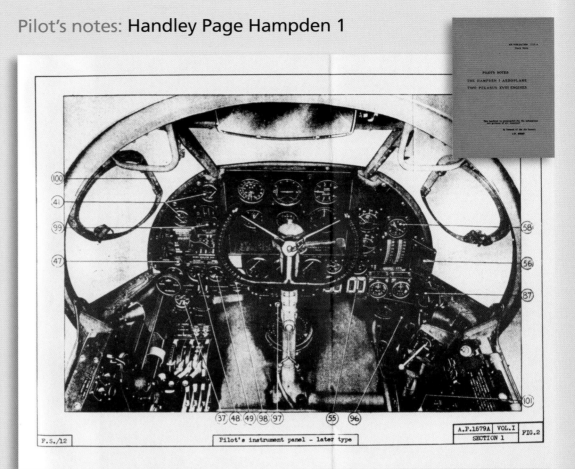

Pilot's instrument panel - later type

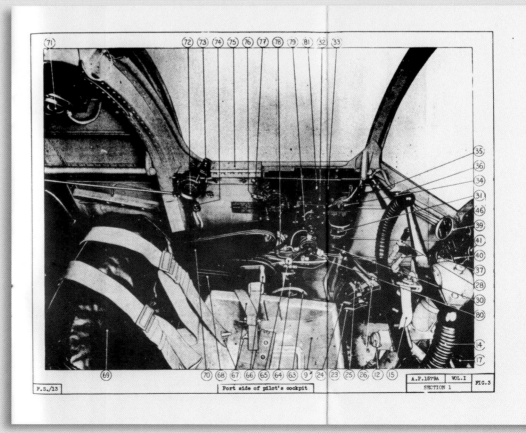

Port side of pilot's cockpit

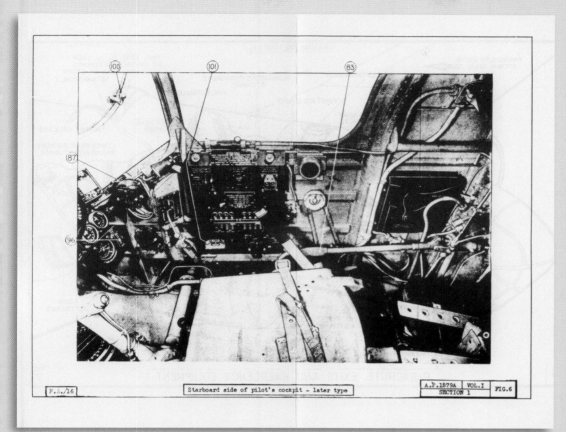

Starboard side of pilot's cockpit – later type

A.P.1579A VOL.I SECTION 1 FIG.6

P.S./16

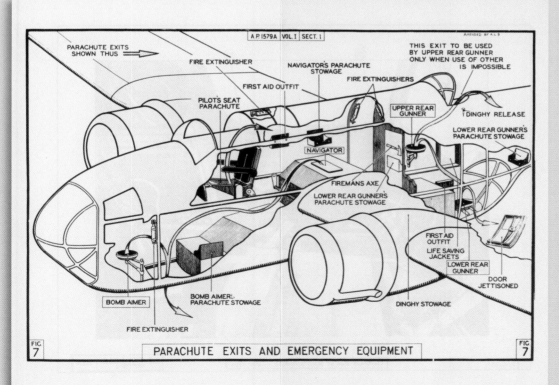

PARACHUTE EXITS SHOWN THUS

FIRE EXTINGUISHER

FIRST AID OUTFIT

PILOT'S SEAT PARACHUTE

NAVIGATOR'S PARACHUTE STOWAGE

FIRE EXTINGUISHERS

THIS EXIT TO BE USED BY UPPER REAR GUNNER ONLY WHEN USE OF OTHER IS IMPOSSIBLE

UPPER REAR GUNNER

DINGHY RELEASE

LOWER REAR GUNNER'S PARACHUTE STOWAGE

NAVIGATOR

FIREMAN'S AXE

LOWER REAR GUNNER'S PARACHUTE STOWAGE

FIRST AID OUTFIT

LIFE SAVING JACKETS

LOWER REAR GUNNER

DOOR JETTISONED

BOMB AIMER

BOMB AIMER'S PARACHUTE STOWAGE

FIRE EXTINGUISHER

DINGHY STOWAGE

A.P.1579A VOL.I SECT.1

AMENDED BY A.L.9

FIG. 7

FIG. 7

PARACHUTE EXITS AND EMERGENCY EQUIPMENT

35 Cockpit lamp
36 Dimmer swtich for (35)
37 Combined nose and tail heavy indicator and pressure gauge, for automatic controls
39 Aileron trimming tab control
40 Starting magneto switches
41 Flap position indicators
46 Alighting gear indicator lamps
63 Elevator trimming wheel
64 Elevator trim indicator
65 Carburettor air intake heater lever, both engines
66 Cowl gill control handle
67 Pilot's harness
68 Release handle for back of pilot's seat
69 Back of pilot's seat
70 Seat arm-rest
71 Warning horn, wheels position
72 Volume knob, wireless remote control
73 Switch lever, wire-less remote control
74 Tuning lever, wire-less remote control
75 Footstep
76 Speed lever for automatic controls
77 Steering lever for automatic controls
78 Clutch lever for automatic controls
79 Attitude control for automatic controls
80 Control clock for automatic controls
81 Automatic control main switch

Fig. 6
Starboard side of pilot's cockpit – later type

83 Handle of hydraulic handpump
87 Identification lamps switchbox
96 Blind flying panel suction gauge
100 Hinged clear vision panel
101 Switches for Graviner fire-extinguishers (where applicable)

147

A Hampden of 408
Squadron, Royal
Canadian Air Force.

stability was markedly low, and there were large changes of directional trim with change of speed. This could lead to sideslip, and this in turn produced a powerful tendency to bank, which the heaviness of the ailerons made it impossible to overcome directly at high speeds, so that rudder had to be used to remove it. This situation was compounded by the nose heaviness produced by sideslip.

At low and moderate speeds large sideslips could cause the rudder to lock over, and the overbalance could only be overcome by increasing speed – altogether a very unpleasant experience at low altitude. The greatest danger, of course, occurred in the single-engine situation when the footload to counteract the asymmetric condition could become tiring even when full rudder trim applied, and could be inadvertently eased off, thus allowing sideslip to develop. It was also important not to use large aileron angles at low speeds, as their yawing tendency caused sideslip.

This otherwise innocuous aeroplane therefore had a very nasty sting in its tail, and although much of the pain could be taken out of it by training, it could still shock under operational stress. Altogether 413 aircraft were lost to enemy action and 194 to other causes.

Because the production rate of the Pegasus engines was unlikely to meet the demand in the timescale required, a version of the Hampden with Napier Dagger VII air-cooled 'H' in-line engines was built by Short Brothers and Harland at Belfast, and renamed the Hereford. However, the Dagger engines proved unsuitable for operational use, being prone to overheating while taxying and overcooling in cruising flight, so the Hereford was relegated to operational training only.

Altogether the production totals were 1,430 Hampdens and 150 Herefords. In its service with Bomber Command the Hampden made 16,541 bombing sorties to drop 9,115 tons (9,261 tonnes) of bombs. Twenty-three of the type saw service with the Soviet Air Force.

The Hampden grew up alongside the Wellington, as both were designed to the same specification, and the Hampden undoubtedly suffers in comparison with its better known contemporary. However, I have to admit that, having been brought up as a fighter pilot, the Hampden appealed more to me than the Wellington; it was slightly faster and lighter, and then there was that cockpit that almost seemed like home to me.

Handley Page
Hampden I of 455
Squadron, RAAF, 1942.
RAF Museum Hendon.

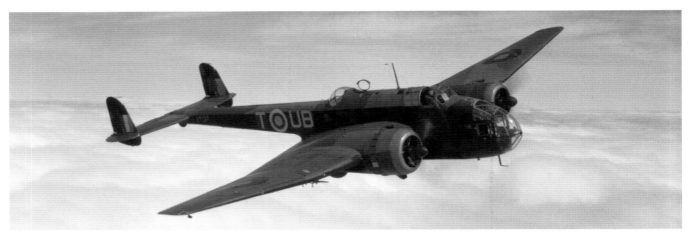

25 HAWKER P.1052

A link between the Sea Hawk
and the Hunter. ERIC BROWN

HAD ALWAYS ENJOYED FLYING Hawker piston-engined aeroplanes, and so it was with great anticipation that I awaited their first attempt at a jet aircraft. I was certainly not to be disappointed with the beautiful P.1040 which had the aesthetic beauty of the line that was the hallmark of Chief Designer Sydney Camm.

I flew the P.1040 on 1 November 1947, being the second pilot to fly the prototype, and it was clearly a winner all the way. Already I knew that a research specification E.38/46 had been issued for application of a swept wing to the P.1040, and this was to become the P.1052, which made its first flight on 19 November 1948.

It arrived at RAE Farnborough on 1 June 1949, and looked a real beauty with its 38° sweepback. VX272 was powered by a Rolls-Royce Nene 2 engine of 5,000lb (2,268kg) static thrust, and the aircraft had an all-up weight of 9,900lb (4,491kg) for the first series of tests.

The all-round view from the cockpit was excellent, although the curved front side panels gave a distorted effect to anything seen through them. The aircraft was easy to steer during taxying except if a very tight turn had to be made, when harsh braking and high engine power were required to supply the necessary turning moment to the narrow track undercarriage.

Hawker P.1052,
(VX279), August 1949.
RAF Museum Hendon.

On revving up for take-off the brakes began to slip at 11,500rpm, before the full 12,300rpm were reached. With the elevator trim neutral and no use of flap the nosewheel could be lifted off easily at 92mph (147km/h) and the aircraft would unstick at 132mph (212km/h), but if unstick was made below 150mph (241km/h) then there was a tendency to wallow, and lateral control was rather sloppy. On raising the undercarriage the trim change was negligible.

Climb at 345mph (555km/h) at 12,000rpm required no change in the take-off trim setting and revealed the aircraft was just stable longitudinally and neutrally stable laterally – just about perfect for a fighter.

The P.1052 had to be trimmed nose down into cruising flight at 506mph (814km/h) at 7,000ft (2,134m), using 11,500rpm. Harmony of control was very good and stability was longitudinally just neutral, laterally neutral, and directionally positively stable. This was the perfect fighter formula and the damping of yaw oscillations was the best I had experienced up to that time on a jet aircraft.

The real purpose of the P.1052's existence was to be a pressure-plotting high-speed swept wing aircraft for test purposes at the RAE, so from my very first flight I was collecting transonic data, both in level flight and dives.

From 45,000ft (13,716m) in a dive the first compressibility effects appeared in the form of a tremor vibration of moderately high frequency on the rudder at M=0.845. At that speed a light left foot force was required on the rudder bar, and that built up steadily with increase in indicated airspeed. At M=0.877 an appreciable nose-up pitching moment became apparent, which also built up with Mach number. At M=0.893 there was an onset of harsh rudder vibration of fairly low frequency and this was almost immediately transmitted to a less harsh degree to the whole airframe. This rudder judder and aircraft buffet built up markedly at M=0.898, and at M=0.91 the nose-up pitch was strong enough to require full nose-down elevator trim and a heavy push force on the stick. The left foot force at this stage was only moderately heavy. All the controls heavied up appreciably, particularly the rudder, above M=0.877, but it was possible to carry out turns at M=0.887.

By increasing altitude, and thereby reducing the control forces, it was possible to push the aircraft up to M=0.935, which was the maximum I ever reached in the P.1052.

On the other hand reduction in height increased all the compressibility characteristics in intensity except the harsh rudder judder and airframe vibration, which disappeared below 20,000ft (6,096m). At M=0.808 at 8,000ft (2,438m) I could even perform slow rolls.

The P.1052 was fitted with dive recovery flaps, whose operation gave a positive nose-up change of trim and, when released, a sharp nose-down pitch. Obviously they were useless for recovery from a high Mach no. dive as the aircraft was already limited by a strong nose-up change of trim.

Level speed performance runs made at 20,000ft (6,096m) at maximum continuous cruising and climbing power gave the following results:

- 11,500rpm gave 444mph (715km/h) IAS and 0.825 IMN (=M 0.838 true).
- Elevator position was three-quarter division nose-heavy.
- 12,000rpm gave 468mph (753km/h) IAS and 0.865 IMN (=M 0.88 true).
- Elevator trim position was full nose-heavy, plus a slight push force.

A series of forced landings delayed VX272's deck-landing trials on HMS *Eagle* until May 1952, by which time they had lost much of their significance.

Hawker P.1052,
(VX279), August 1949.
RAF Museum Hendon.

The stalling characteristics were checked at 10,000ft (3,050m) with 180gal (818 litres) of fuel evenly distributed between the front and rear tanks. Engine power was set at 7,000rpm.

The all-up stall occurred at 120mph (193km/h) when the starboard wing dropped sharply to about 25°, and simultaneously there was a sharp twitch on the ailerons and the nose also dropped away. The only stall warning was a very slight lateral rocking, which set in at 132mph (212km/h) and was present right down to the actual stall.

The all-down stall occurred at 108mph (174km/h) when the starboard wing dropped very sharply to about 45° and the nose followed, so that the aircraft tended to spiral gently. From 155mph (249km/h) the ailerons oscillated in the disturbed outflow from the flaps, but otherwise there was no stall warning.

It was the Royal Navy's intention to make the first landing of a British swept-wing aeroplane on an aircraft carrier with the P.1052, so I was asked to check out its deck landing characteristics to see if it was suitable for the task.

A circuit speed of 207mph (333km/h) was comfortable, and the undercarriage could be lowered at that speed with negligible trim change. The flaps could then be lowered in two stages, the first movement giving a slight nose-down pitch and the second a nose-up pitch, the total trim change being slightly nose-up. The full flap position produced mild buffeting.

The turn on to the final approach was made at 172mph (277km/h) with the flaps at the first position and then full flap lowered and the speed eased to 150mph (241km/h). The view on the approach was excellent, even though the powered approach angle was flat in order to keep the rate of descent within moderate limits. The ailerons were very light and effective, the elevator very light but rather ineffective, and the rudder moderately light but better at producing roll than yaw.

Landing was easy, provided the final approach speed was kept at 150mph (241km/h) so that a check could be given to the high rate of descent that developed as soon as the power (about 7,000rpm) was cut. It later became a matter of standard deck landing technique with swept-wing aircraft to maintain a constant attitude/rate of descent right down to contact with the flight

The P.1052, forerunner of the P.1081 and the Hawker Hunter, shows off its 38° swept-back wings.

deck, thus enabling a lower speed and steeper angle of approach to be used.

For airfield landing it was easier to use a slightly higher approach speed as the aircraft decelerated quite quickly after touch-down, since the nose-wheel could be held off the ground right down to 70mph, and thereafter the brakes were very good.

VX272 had a history of forced landings after I last flew it on 12 July 1949. These delayed the deck-landing trials aboard HMS *Eagle* until May 1952, when they had by then lost much of their significance as the US Navy was operating a number of swept-wing types from aircraft carriers. For the *Eagle* trials VX272 was fitted with a long stroke Sea Hawk undercarriage.

The P.1052 was undoubtedly a delightful aeroplane to fly and pointed the way ahead to the splendid Hawker Hunter by way of the P.1081, which abandoned the bifurcated jet pipe layout for the straight-through exhaust. The P.1052 also made its own small contribution to British naval aviation history, albeit a little too late to make the impact it could have made.

The elegant P.1052, the first swept-wing aircraft to land on an aircraft carrier.

26 HAWKER SEA FURY

A truly great aeroplane, the counterpart of the American Bearcat. ERIC BROWN

I N APRIL 1943 the Naval Staff issued Specification N.7/43 for a naval interceptor fighter to replace the Seafire. Hawker's were already designing a fighter to Specification F.2/43 and Sydney Camm felt that the same design with an uprated Centaurus XII engine could meet the naval requirement.

Early in 1944 the naval specification was upgraded to N.22/43 and that same year a contract for 200 of the aircraft was placed. Of them, 100 were to be built by Boulton Paul, who had had the responsibility for preparing the prototype and production drawings for the N.7/43. However, the imminent end of World War II caused the Boulton Paul order to be cancelled and the Sea Fury X prototype was delivered to Hawker's for completion in January 1945.

The Sea Fury prototype, SR661, flew on 21 February 1945, fitted with a Centaurus XII engine, driving a Rotol four-blade airscrew, and a deck arrester hook, but retained fixed wings. The second prototype, SR666, flew on 12 October 1945, powered by a Centaurus XV engine driving a five-blade Rotol propeller and with folding wings.

I first flew SR661 on 17 May 1945, just nine days after VE day. The aircraft had come to Farnborough to assess the rudder control for carrier deck operations. This was found to be critical for correcting the powerful swing to starboard, and the situation was aggravated by the fact that it was a spring tab rudder lacking feel and therefore prone to mishandling. Thus, initially, if left rudder was applied as soon as the take-off run was started, the powerful effect of the spring

Hawker Chief Test Pilot, Bill Humble, flying the prototype Sea Fury, NX802.

153

The racy Sea Fury in plan form. It later distinguished itself in the air races held at Reno, Nevada.

tabs invariably led to over correction and setting up of a slight swing to port. The subsequent correction with starboard rudder then occurred just at a time when the characteristic late swing of Bristol-engined aircraft developed (Rolls-Royce-engined aircraft were characterised by their early swing). This situation became more critical with the use of 30° flap for take-off.

On the overshoot from a missed landing approach the rudder would only hold the aircraft straight with maximum climbing power, but not with full power.

The Sea Fury was also very unstable directionally on the landing run, where the rudder was ineffective, so the harsh use of brakes was necessary to keep straight. In consequence I recommended the fitting of a tail-wheel lock.

The stall characteristics also showed a loss of lateral control at 98mph in the landing configuration, while the elevator control still remained positive down to 88mph. This ineffective aileron control showed up on simulated deck-landing approaches, but elevator control was excellent.

The engine was fitted in rigid mountings and gave bad vibration at speeds below 1700rpm, which meant this roughness was present throughout the landing approach. Propeller overspeeding was very noticeable with any sudden application of power, especially in the baulked landing case.

SR661 came back to the RAE on 5 July 1945, fitted with a five-blade propeller, redesigned rudder, and 0.44 airscrew reduction gear. The most noticeable effect of the modifications was the vastly improved take-off distance, while the rudder control had now attained an acceptable standard for deck landing trials, although only marginally so. The five-blade propeller had increased the braking effect on touch-down and this, together with the pleasantly soft undercarriage, made for a safe deck arrival without bounce.

A Sea Fury gets the batman's 'cut' to land on a carrier.

A Sea Fury takes off from a carrier deck.

Pilot's notes: Hawker Sea Fury 10 & 11

Fig 1:

Cockpit – front view

1   Undercarriage position indicator
2   Throttle and rpm controls friction nut
3   RI compass indicator
4   Ignition switches
5   Undercarriage position indicator switch
6   Supercharger warning light
7   Contacting altimeter switch
8   Flaps position indicator
9   Rpm control lever
10 Contacting altimeter
11 Throttle lever
12 Gyro gunsight selector dimmer control
13 Ventilating louvre
14 Undercarriage warning light
15 GGS master switch
16 Gyro gunsight skid indicator
17 Cine-camera master switch
18 Cloudy/sunny selector switch
19 Gyro gunsight
20 Emergency lamp
21 Cockpit lamps dimmer switch
22 Guns/RP selector switch
23 Gyro gunsight skid indicator
24 Cockpit lamps master switch
25 Emergency lamp switch
26 Windscreen de-icing pump
27 UV lamps dimmer switch
28 Generator failure warning light
29 Sliding canopy control
30 Engine cooling shutters control

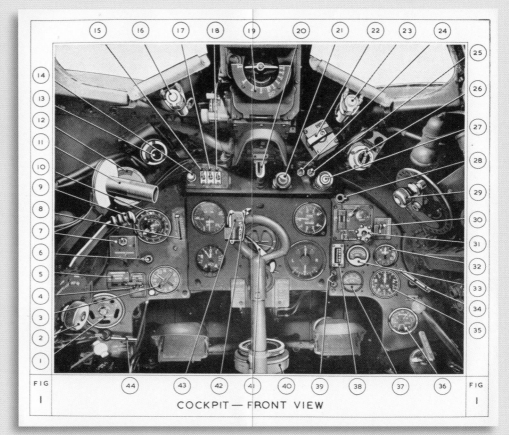

COCKPIT — FRONT VIEW

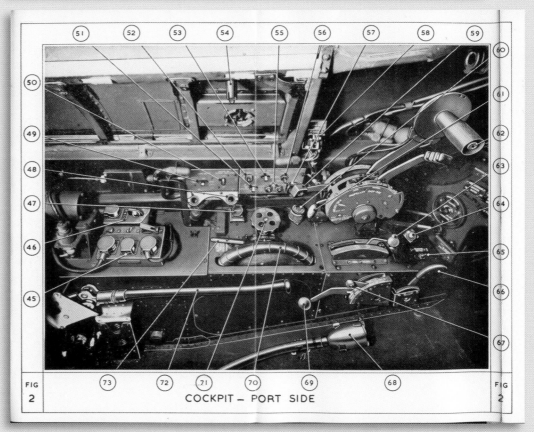

COCKPIT — PORT SIDE

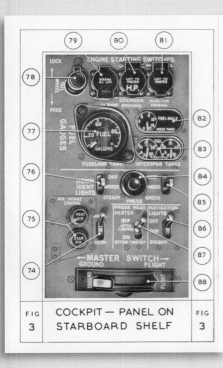

FIG 3 COCKPIT — PANEL ON STARBOARD SHELF FIG 3

31 Oxygen regulator
32 Boost gauge
33 Oil temperature gauge
34 Canopy jettison control
35 Engine speed indicator
36 Triple pressure gauge
37 Cylinder temperature gauge
38 Oil pressure gauge
39 Spare bulbs for gyro gunsight
40 P11 compass
41 Parking brake lever
42 Press-to-speak switch
43 Firing button
44 Starter re-indexing control

Figs 2, 3 and 4

45 IFF control unit
46 IFF selector unit
47 RATOG jettison push-button
48 Flare door warning lights
49 Flare doors operating switch
50 Camera container master switch
51 Fusing switch
52 Pairs/salvo switch
53 RP/bombs selector switch
54 Canopy locking control
55 Port/starboard selector switches

56 Single/salvo switch
57 SC jettison push-button
58 RATOG master switch
59 Supercharger gear change control
60 Cockpit (port) lamps dimmer switch
61 Fuel cut-off control
62 RATOG firing button
63 Flaps selector lever
64 Arrester hook indicator light
65 Arrester hook training switch
66 Arrester hook control
67 Undercarriage control lever safety catch
68 Sanitary bottle
69 Undercarriage control lever
70 Elevator trimming handwheel
71 Rudder trimming handwheel
72 Hydraulic handpump
73 Bomb rack jettison control
74 Air-intake filter control
75 Air-intake filter control warning lights
76 Downward identification lights signalling switch
77 Main tank fuel gauge
78 Fuel level warning light

79 Cartridge starter and booster-coil push-button
80 Cylinder priming push-button
81 Injector priming push-button
82 Nose tank fuel gauge
83 Interspar tanks fuel gauges
84 Downward identification lights signalling push-button
85 Downward identification lights colour selector switch
86 Navigation lights switch
87 Pressure-head heater switch
88 Ground/flight switch
89 Locking pin for emergency hydraulic selector levers
90 Flaps emergency selector lever
91 Undercarriage emergency selector lever
92 Main fuel cock
93 Drop tanks jettison control
94 Drop tanks selector lever
95 'Window' launcher override control unit
96 Mixer box
97 'Window' launcher speed control unit
98 Safety harness locking control
99 VHF control unit
100 ZBX control unit
101 IFF auxiliary control unit
102 Watch holder
103 Clock holder
104 Oil dilution push-button
105 Fuel pump circuit breaker
106 Fuel pump ammeter test push-button
107 Fuel pump ammeter test socket
108 Ignition booster-coil test push-button
109 Air-intake heat control
110 Wing folding control lever
111 Wing folding control safety lever
112 Oxygen pipe
113 Map case
114 Chartboard container
115 See Fig. 3
116 Tailwheel locking control
117 Cockpit heating control
118 Signal pistol stowage
119 Fuel tank air pressure gauge

FIG 4 COCKPIT — STARBOARD SIDE FIG 4

Head-on view of the sleek (unhooked) Sea Fury.

I still felt there was a strong case for fitting a tail wheel lock, not only to stabilise the landing run directionally, but also to help retraction of the tail wheel, which it seldom did because of a bad self-centering device.

In the first half of July I also proofed the Sea Fury on arresting tests up to three 'g' at 15ft off centre on the arrester wires at Farnborough, before returning the aircraft to Langley on 20 July. I had some misses on the wires due to poor arrester hook damping efficiency, but a quick modification by Hawker's saw the aircraft returned to RAE on 27 July and satisfactorily cleared by the end of the month.

I had been alerted to do initial deck-landing trials on the Sea Fury X, but these coincided with the Sea Hornet initial trials. It was considered I had too much on my plate with both, so the Sea Fury was handed over to A&AEE at Boscombe Down, whither I flew it on 2 August.

The Sea Hornet and Sea Fury flew on to HMS *Ocean* on 10 August and both sets of trials went smoothly in the Western Approaches.

Almost a year went past before the second prototype, SR666, came to Farnborough for accelerating proofing on the RAE catapult. The tail-down method was used and on the initial launch on 19 July 1946 the tail wheel collapsed at 2.2'g'. I therefore flew to Langley to land on the grass and return the aircraft direct to Hawker's. No further damage was done as I held the tail up throughout the landing run. All this had the salutary effect of speeding up my long standing recommendation to fit a tail-wheel lock.

SR666 returned to Farnborough on 25 September with a temporary modification which allow-

ed the tail-wheel to be locked, but prevented its retraction, so a speed limit of 200mph was imposed on the aircraft. However, the tail-wheel lock was a great success and allowed the accelerating proofing to be done in two days on 3 October and 5 October.

The Sea Fury was in fact the first British aircraft with a single towing hook to which the catapult launching strop was affixed. This arrangement introduced a certain amount of directional instability into the launching process as compared with twin towing hooks. Hence the benefit of the tail-wheel lock.

On 18 March 1947 I put the fourth production Sea Fury X, TF989, through its accelerating proofing trials and then flew it on to HMS *Illustrious* on 24 March for side-wing catapult launches. I repeated the shipboard trials on 31 March with the sixth production aircraft, TF900, which had a new type rigid sting arrester hook fitted. This hook was also longer than the original and its rigidity improved directional stability on the deck after wire pick-up. The short hooks had given trouble during intensive deck landing trials on HMS *Victorious* by the Service Trials Unit.

In November and December 1947 I took Sea Fury X, VR920, to Farnborough for arresting proofing of the type with a variety of external stores, and returned again in August for its RATOG proofing. The carriage of RPs (Rocket Projectiles) caused a hiccup in the arresting programme as the shear pins kept failing at high 'g' off-centre landings, causing the missiles to dislodge themselves from the wings and skid away haphazardly along the deck. This problem was not solved until October of that year.

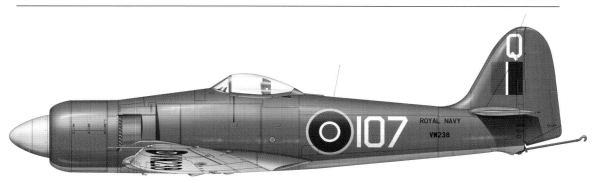

When I eventually left the RAE in August 1949 to return to Fleet Air Arm fighter squadron service, I went first to the School of Naval Air Warfare at St Merryn, equipped with Sea Fury XIs, and from there became Senior Pilot of 802(F) Squadron at Culdrose, again flying Sea Fury XIs. The Squadron was assigned to HMS *Vengeance* as part of the 15th Carrier Air Group.

In May 1950 the squadron was detached to RAF Wunstorf in Germany and there received its first Sea Fury Trainer 20 for instrument flying training. This variant was so similar in performance and flight characteristics to the parent model that it was often flown on normal squadron duties. The view from the rear cockpit was also surprisingly good in spite of being set far back on the fuselage, aft of the wing trailing edge.

802 Squadron was selected to provide the Royal Navy's Festival of Britain formation aerobatic team to give displays all over the UK and in Europe, and I was ordered to form a team of four and work them up to display standard. Within the squadron were three young pilots with above average flying ability, who were the obvious choice – Lt 'Boot' Nethersole and Commissioned Pilots Johnny Walker and Bill Newton. They proved to be excellent material and we had an excellent aeroplane for the job.

We were fortunate to be in the Mediterranean, aboard *Vengeance*, in the late autumn of 1950 to enjoy amiable weather for the work-up. The team rehearsed a routine that involved an initial box formation, changing into a close line astern formation stepped down so that the airscrew was just behind and below the tail of the aircraft ahead. In line astern we carried out a very low level barrel roll, which meant that the circle described by the leader was accentuated back along the line until the 'tail-end Charlie' was using full throttle to keep up with the hunt, while the leader was only at half-throttle.

This demanding manoeuvre was made with 'Boot' as No. 2, Johnny as No. 3 and poor Bill in No. 4 position. I have never seen it copied by any formation aerobatic team, certainly not in piston-engined aircraft.

To this gimmick we added that of taxying out for take-off before the spectators with wings folded and then spreading them as we turned on to the runway. This was always a good curtain-raiser, and we had a good finalé with a low fly-past in box formation, with myself inverted in the lead position and the other three zooming vertically up into a Prince of Wales feathers.

We were fortunate as a team to be able to stay together throughout the summer season of 1951,

Sea Fury FB.11, VW238/107/Q, No. 802 NAS, HMS *Vengeance*, Cape Town (South Africa), January 1949. © *Richard Caruana* (scale 1:72).

Sea Fury, WF619, entered service with 805 Squadron in 1951, eventually being sold to the Cuban Air Force.

Hawker Sea Fury

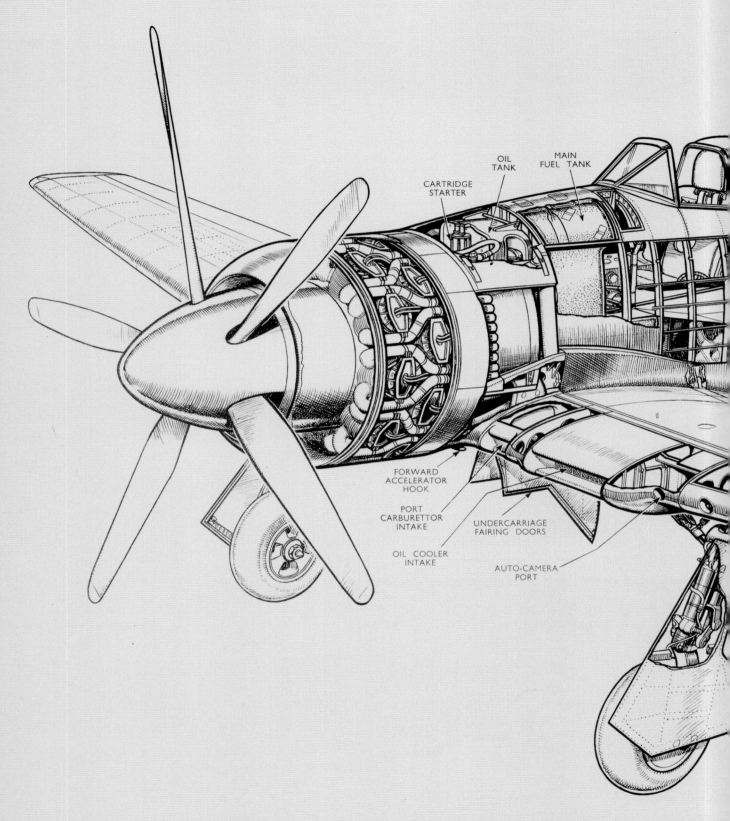

OIL
TANK

MAIN
FUEL TANK

CARTRIDGE
STARTER

FORWARD
ACCELERATOR
HOOK

PORT
CARBURETTOR
INTAKE

UNDERCARRIAGE
FAIRING DOORS

OIL COOLER
INTAKE

AUTO-CAMERA
PORT

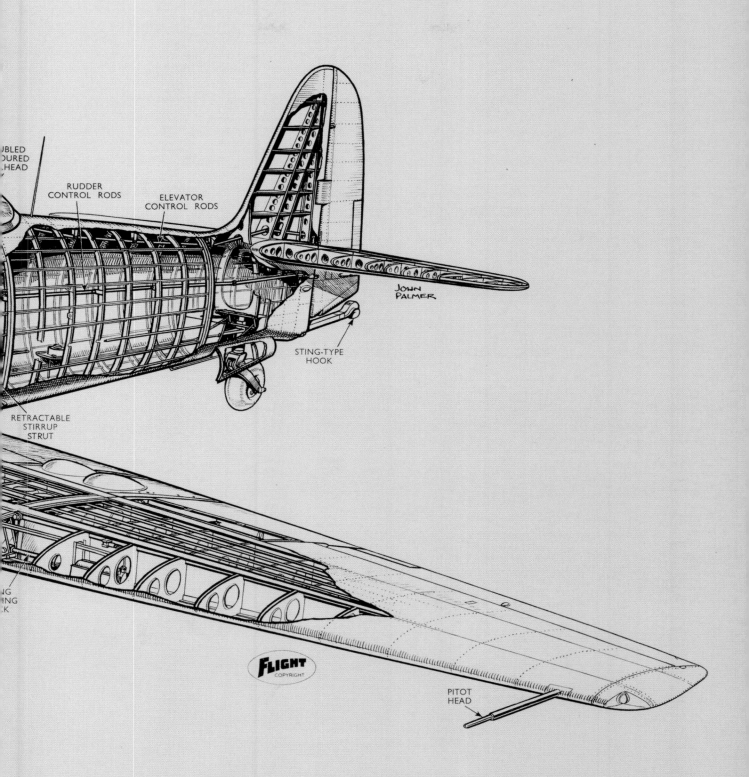

UBLED
OURED
HEAD

RUDDER
CONTROL RODS

ELEVATOR
CONTROL RODS

JOHN
PALMER

STING-TYPE
HOOK

RETRACTABLE
STIRRUP
STRUT

NG
NG
K

FLIGHT
COPYRIGHT

PITOT
HEAD

before a posting to the Korean War removed Bill Newton. I soon followed on appointment as resident British test pilot at the US Naval Air Test Center, Patuxent River. It was the end of my very happy acquaintance with the Sea Fury.

Although I enjoyed the delightful handling characteristics of the Sea Fury in aerobatics, the major part of our squadron flying involved combat weapon training. Its effectiveness in that role was all-important, especially in the light of the Korean War in which it was to play such a prominent part.

To give an idea of the squadron standards achieved, I have extracted the following from my log books as my best weapon results, while emphasising that these were not necessarily the squadron best:

Air to air firing (on towed drogue) – 52.9%

Low level bombing	– MRE =	13.3yds (12m)
30° dive bombing	– MRE =	15yds (14m)
55° dive bombing	– MRE =	25yds (23m)

Air to ground firing (on 10ft (3m) target) – 41%

15° R/P firing	– MRE =	6yds (5.5m)
30° R/P firing	– MRE =	5yds (4.6m)
45° R/P firing	– MRE =	18.5yds (17m)

All mean radial errors are for four missiles released singly.

These results show that the Sea Fury was an excellent weapon platform, and it distinguished itself as such in the Korean conflict.

There is no doubt that the Sea Fury was a good looking aircraft, with those fine lines so typical of the famous Hawker designer, Sydney Camm. It also gave an impression of strength, which is an essential quality of any carrier-borne aircraft.

Entry to the cockpit was by way of a retracting footstep in the port side of the fuselage, behind the wing. When the footstep was pulled down it opened the cover over a hand-hold behind the cockpit, to allow the pilot to pull himself up to the spring-loaded footstep in the wing root. From there another footstep in the side of the fuselage gave final access.

The cockpit was very comfortable, with orderly layout of the instruments and controls, good all-round vision in spite of the long nose with its cowled engine, and especially well positioned rudder pedals, which could be adjusted to give 'g' resistance to the pilot.

Starting the engine was by the Coffman cartridge system, and was fairly reliable, although the starter breech occasionally jammed when trying to index a fresh cartridge.

Take-off checks were made that the elevator trim was neutral, rudder trim fully left, airscrew in fully fine pitch, main fuel cock ON, wings locked

Hawker Sea Fury T.20 (VX302 77/M G-BCOV). *RAF Museum Hendon.*

spread, flaps at TAKE-OFF and tail-wheel locked. Lift-off in the tail-down position was often so speedy that it occurred before full throttle could be achieved. For catapult take-off the flaps were set to the MAX LIFT position and the elevator trimmed slight nose-up. Retraction of undercarriage and flaps gave a nose-up change of trim.

Once airborne the rpm control lever was moved to AUTO before reducing boost from +9½–+4lb/sq in and rpm fell from 2,700 to 2,400 for the climb. The rate of climb was good, with 30,000ft (9,144m) being reached in just over ten minutes, using a climbing speed of 213mph (343km/h) up to 20,000ft (6,096m) and thereafter reducing by 6mph for each 4,000ft (1,219m) increase in height. The supercharger had to be changed from low to high gear when the boost fell to +1¾ lb/sq in.

In level flight the aircraft was marginally stable about all three axes, and the controls were light and effective. There was just a slight tendency to tighten in turns at high altitudes. Maximum speed was 460mph (740km/h) at 18,000ft (5,486m). There was a large change in directional trim with alterations in speed and power, and such changes in directional trim induced variation in longitudinal trim. Operation of the engine cooling shutters also

produced a marked change of trim, being nose down as they opened and nose up as they closed.

The Sea Fury was an easy aircraft in which to perform individual aerobatics, but in formation the directional trim changes made it hard work for the team, especially in the looping plane.

The circuit for a deck landing was made at 138mph (222km/h) after having lowered the undercarriage at 172mph (277km/h) and the flaps to max lift at 150mph (241km/h). The arrester hook was then lowered, tail wheel unlocked and rpm control lever set to give 2,400rpm. The turn-in was made at 120mph (193km/h) after lowering the flaps fully, and this required zero boost. On coming out of the turn on to the final approach the throttle was eased to -2 boost and the speed allowed to decay to 104mph (167km/h). On getting the 'cut' signal from the batsman the throttle was closed and the control column eased back to maintain the three-point position for touchdown. View on the approach was surprisingly good.

In essence the Sea Fury was a first-class naval aircraft that proved itself as an effective fighter-bomber in the Korean War. It was well liked by Fleet Air Arm pilots and I personally remember it with affection.

Hawker Sea Fury T.20, (VX818), January 1949. *RAF Museum Hendon.*

27 HAWKER SEA HAWK

Aesthetically beautiful, docile and delightful to fly, but could do with some beef-up in performance. ERIC BROWN

MY FIRST ASSOCIATION with the Sea Hawk began in its prototype form, the P.1040, which I flew on 1 November 1947, being the second pilot to fly a Hawker jet aircraft. When I set eyes on it I was enthralled by the beauty of its aerodynamic lines, which were the hallmark of Chief Designer Sydney Camm.

The P.1040 first took form on paper in December 1944 with its patented bifurcated jet efflux pipe system, which was considered so unorthodox that it probably delayed acceptance by the military. It was not until October 1945, after extensive ground testing of the layout, that Hawkers issued a production order for a prototype, and not until early 1946 that Naval Staff Specification N.7/46 was issued and three prototypes ordered in May.

The P.1040 prototype VP401 made its first flight in the hands of Bill Humble at Boscombe Down on 2 September 1947. It then made several very short flights during which Bill reported airframe vibrations, which he could not quite account for, and since he had not had a great deal of jet experience he asked for a second opinion. This was how I came to fly VP401 at RAE to which Hawker's had transferred the aircraft.

The P.1040 was powered by a Nene engine, temporarily derated to 4,500lb (2,041kg) static thrust, and when I got airborne I found several marked peculiarities under normal flight conditions, all closely allied with engine handling. These peculiarities involved resonant vibrations in the vertical plane, varying from mild to severe with

The P.1040 prototype, VP401, which was passed to RAE Farnborough and tested by Eric Brown.

The 804 Squadron aerobatics team. It was in the realm of aerobatics that the Sea Hawk excelled and it says a great deal for its good handling qualities that the young pilots with no previous jet experience were able to be moulded into a first class aerobatics team.

In 1953 Eric Brown moved to RN Air Station, Lossiemouth to train the pilots of 804 Squadron on the Sea Hawk F1.

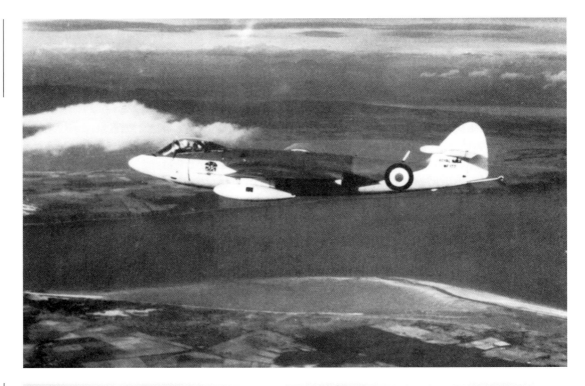

VP413 was the second of three prototype jet fighters developed for the Royal Navy as the Hawker P.1040. It was put into production looking more or less the same as seen here, as the Sea Hawk. Probably on display at Farnborough in 1949, it was later used in 1953 in connection with the infamous flexible deck trials. As the second jet fighter type to enter service with the Fleet Air Arm, the elegant aircraft was a considerable improvement over the Attacker, proving to be highly successful and popular with both air and ground crew. *Barry Ketley.*

increase in engine rpm and accompanied by strange sound effects emanating from well behind the cockpit. There was also directional snaking, increasing with reduction in engine rpm. It took me 1 hour 15 minutes to thoroughly investigate these characteristics and this one flight doubled the total flight time to date on the aircraft.

As a result of these findings the rectangular heat shield fairings which protected the rear fuselage skin from the jet efflux were replaced by pen nib fairings to cure flow breakaway. An acorn fairing was fitted at the intersection of the fin and tailplane. These modifications cured the problems beautifully.

I made my first acquaintance with the navalised N.7/46 prototype, VP413, on 5 April 1949. This air-craft had several changes from the P.1040, such as wing-folding, catapult hooks, arrester hook, and full gun armament of four 20mm cannon in the nose. The first job was arresting proofing of the type, as I had already catapult proofed the P.1040 which had returned to RAE with catapult strong points fitted a few days earlier.

The brutal work having been done, I now got down to the general handling and deck landing assessment of the N.7/46 and what a delightful task that proved to be. VP413 had the full rated Nene of 5,000lb (2,268kg) static thrust and was at an AUW of 10,500lb (4,763kg).

The all-round view was excellent, although the curved windscreen side panels gave a distorted effect to anything seen through them. This was

Four aircraft of the 804 Squadron aerobatic team making a box formation landing.

cured in production aircraft by a modified hood shape. The cockpit layout was first class and the seating very comfortable.

For taxying the hydraulic brakes were not so powerful as the pneumatic type fitted to P.1040, but were adequate to control the weathercocking tendency in a cross wind. On lining up for take-off the brakes would only hold the aircraft up to 11,500rpm before they started to slip. But from that point the engine could be instantaneously opened up to the full 12,350rpm without any adverse effects on jet pipe temperature.

The take-off run even with the use of the TAKE-OFF flap setting of 27½ degrees was surprisingly long. Using two divisions of nose-up elevator trim and with the stick held fully back the nosewheel would not come off the ground until a speed of 110mph (177km/h) was reached, and the unstick occurred at 120–125mph (193–201km/h).

After unstick there was no appreciable change of trim with retraction of the undercarriage, although raising the flaps gave a strong nose-up pitch which could be comfortably held whilst re-trimming. Undercarriage retraction was rather slow.

In cruising flight the ailerons were light and effective, although not so good as on the P.1040. The elevation and rudder were also light and effective; stability was neutral both laterally and longitudinally, and positive directionally. The aircraft did snake in rough air, and damping was somewhat sluggish but as good as I had met on a jet to date.

The all-up stall occurred at 125½mph (202km/h)

and was preceded by a gentle buffet at 130mph (209km/h). At the stall itself there was a gentle port wing drop of some 10–15 degrees. The all-down stall, with the engine set at 10,000rpm as for a deck landing approach, displayed similar characteristics except that there was slightly less stall warning with buffeting at 110mph (177km/h) before the stall occurred at 107mph (172km/h). With the flaps thus lowered to the full drag position of 86½ degrees, there was a continuous tremor to be felt all the time before it developed into the pre-stall buffet.

With the flaps in the maximum lift position of 53½ degrees, the only difference in stalling characteristics was a reduction in the buffet speed to 109½mph (176km/h) and increase in the stalling speed to 107½mph (173km/h), and the absence of the continuous tremor.

Opening the hood raised the stalling speed by one knot, but gave an unpleasant updraught of dirt from the cockpit floor as well as an oppressive thrumming noise emanating from an airflow burble round the open cockpit. This was cured in production aircraft by a modified hood shape. A reduction of 60gal of fuel gave a corresponding reduction of 3mph (5km/h) in stalling speed.

The landing characteristics of the N.7/46 were superb, with perfect view, good control characteristics, and a soft tricycle undercarriage. In the circuit it was difficult to reduce speed because this prototype had no dive brakes; the type to be fitted had not yet been decided. For this reason no dive tests were conducted on the N.7/46

167

Pilot's notes: Hawker Sea Hawk

Fig 1:

Cockpit – port side

1. Rudder and aileron trim position indicator
2. Rudder and aileron trim control
3. HP cock lever and relight button
4. Camera oblique/ vertical switch
5. Wing fold control switch
6. Elevator trim control
7. Flaps emergency air pressure gauge
8. LP cocks levers
9. Triple pressure gauge (when Mod. N246 incorporated)
10. Undercarriage/ arrester hook emergency air pressure gauge
11. IFF master switch
12. Hood lock release lever
13. Hood control switch
14. Hood motor de-clutching lever
15. Throttle lever and press-to-transmit switch
16. Airbrakes control
17. Armament master switch
18. GGS guns/RP switch
19. RP selector switch
20. Arrester hook emergency control
21. Undercarriage emergency control
22. Flaps emergency control
23. Flaps control
24. Outer bomb selector switches
25. Inner bomb selector switches
26. Bomb distributor switch
27. Bomb jettison push-buttons
28. Bomb fusing switch
29. Bomb control panel fuse holder
30. Bomb fuse warning light
31. Cockpit heat control

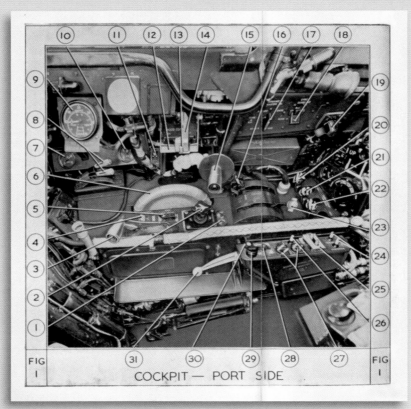

COCKPIT — PORT SIDE

A Sea Hawk of 804 Squadron.

FIG 2 — COCKPIT — FORWARD VIEW — FIG 2

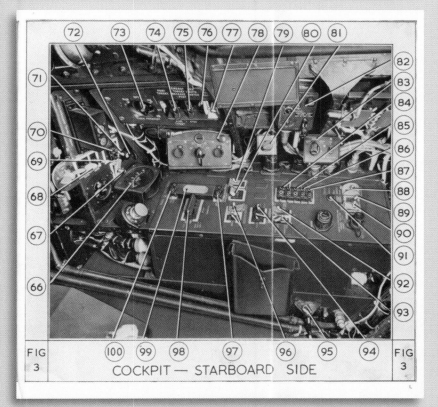

FIG 3 — COCKPIT — STARBOARD SIDE — FIG 3

Fig 2:

Cockpit – forward view

32 Anti-G control panel
33 GGS selector/dimmer control
34 Air temperature gauge
35 Undercarriage position indicator
36 Undercarriage selector push-buttons
37 Flaps position indicator
38 Undercarriage warning light
39 RATOG push-button
40 Arrester hook green light
41 Arrester hook switch (training switch outboard)
42 Hood jettison control
43 Deck landing ASI
44 Fuel tanks fire warning light
45 GGS master and retraction switch
46 Top generator failure warning light
47 Bottom generator failure warning light
48 Fuel pressure warning light
49 GGS emergency lowering control
50 E2 compass
51 Engine fire warning light and extinguisher button
52 Port and starboard demister switches (inoperative)
53 G45 camera aperture switch
54 Front fuel contents gauge
55 Rear fuel contents gauge
56 Cockpit pressure altimeter
57 ARI.18049 indicator
58 Inverter reset relay switches
59 Windscreen demisting control
60 Oxygen contents gauge
61 Windscreen de-icing pump
62 Turn and slip indicator emergency switch
63 Mk 17 oxygen regulator
64 Bomb/RP push-button
65 G45 camera push-button

Fig 3:

Cockpit – starboard side

66 Jpt gauge
67 Engine starter switch
68 Engine starter master switch
69 Engine igniter switch
70 Engine igniter circuit breaker
71 HP fuel pump isolating valve switch
72 HP fuel pump isolating valve switch warning light
73 Cockpit pressure control
74 Target release selector switch
75 Target emergency release switch
76 Red lamps master switch
77 Emergency lamp switch
78 VHF control unit
79 Cockpit pressure warning horn cut-out switch
80 Pressure head heater and G45 camera master switches
81 VHF/ZBX mixer box
82 ZBX control box
83 ARI.18049 control box
84 Flight instruments circuit breakers
85 GGS circuit breaker
86 Hood motor circuit breaker
87 Cockpit pressure circuit breaker
88 Battery isolating switch
89 Ailerons power control switch
90 RATO master switch
91 Ailerons power warning light
92 Aileron power/aileron manual trim switch
93 Inner pylon jettison/safe switch
94 Navigation lights switch
95 Identification lights switches
96 Emergency oxygen bottle manual control
97 Rear booster-pump circuit breaker
98 Booster-pumps control switch
99 Booster-pumps warning light
100 Forward booster-pump circuit breaker

although I had dived the P.1040 up to M=0.84, without dive brakes. It showed progressive nose-up trim change from M=0.79.

For deck landing the optimum approach speed was 118mph (190km/h) at 10,500lb (4,763kg) and 115mph (185km/h) at 10,000lb (4,536kg) and the use of full drag flap kept the engine rpm well above the Nene's 'flat spot'.

In the event of a baulked landing the maximum lift flap setting could be selected instantaneously on opening up the throttle using the flap trigger switch located on the throttle. This retraction action gave a nose-down pitch, while further retraction to the closed position gave a nose-up pitch, which cancelled out the first stage trim change.

After touch-down the landing run necessitated full use of brakes, for the nose-wheel could not be held off the ground for long by use of elevator.

At the conclusion of these tests my assessment was that the N.7/46 was undoubtedly an outstanding aircraft and certainly fit to undertake its deck-landing trials even in prototype condition. These were successfully carried out on HMS *Illustrious* at the end of April.

In July the wing span was increased by 30 inches, giving 12sq ft (1.1m²) more wing area,

and a second series of deck landing trials on HMS *Illustrious* took place in November.

The second N.7/46 prototype, VP422, had provision for RATOG, the undercarriage retraction period shortened, and a lengthened arrester hook. This aircraft, together with VP413, now commenced a series of trials with different dive brakes schemes.

The first production Sea Hawk, WF413, first flew on 14 November 1951, and suffered from aileron oscillation. This led to the introduction of power-assisted ailerons as a remedy on the fifth production aircraft.

My first contact with a production Sea Hawk occurred in October 1953, when I was seconded to the first operational unit, No. 806 Squadron at Brawdy, before taking command of No. 804 Squadron at Lossiemouth. The 806 Sea Hawks were Mk F 1s, built by Armstrong-Whitworth.

In November 1953 I moved to RN Air Station Lossiemouth to re-equip No. 804 Squadron with twelve Sea Hawk F 1s. The entire complement of squadron pilots except myself had never flown a jet aircraft, so I had the task of converting them with the aid of two Vampire trainers and two qualified flying instructors attached to the squad-

Starting up the Sea Hawks of 804 Squadron in unison was a spectacular affair; as the turbo-starter cartridges fired, jets of smoke spurted skyward from the fuselage behind the cockpit.

ron. This conversion experiment was successfully conducted without any problems, and became the pattern for other re-equipping units at this stage of the Fleet Air Arm's history.

The Sea Hawk F 1 differed from the N.7/46 prototype in the following details: (1) the maximum rpm of the Nene 101 were 12,500. (2) Airbrakes were fitted. These consisted of trailing edge flaps, the lower surfaces being the landing flaps. They were controlled electro-hydraulically by a small lever on the throttle control. Pressing the lever aft opened the air brakes, the upper surface to 20 degrees and the lower to 30 degrees. Releasing it returned them to the closed position. The air brakes could be retained in the open position by pressing the control further aft until a catch engaged. The catch had to be tripped to close the air brakes.

Because of the presence of air brakes I was able to check the high speed characteristics to the full. The ailerons and elevators heavied up considerably at high indicated airspeeds. At high altitudes the controls remained light up to M=0.78 but at M=0.79 a nose-down change of trim set in and increased rapidly to a strong pull force at the limiting M=0.80.

The AUW of the Sea Hawk F1 was 13,200lb (5,988kg) with full internal fuel and ammunition. Maximum landing weight was 12,100lb (5,489kg), at which weight the all-down stall occurred at 104mph (167km/h). The deck landing speed, with 60–70gal (273–318 litres) of fuel remaining and no ammunition, was 115mph (185km/h).

It was in the realm of aerobatics that the Sea Hawk excelled and I had an aerobatic team of seven aircraft in 804 Squadron, which gave me one of the most enjoyable periods of my flying career. Even starting up in unison was a spectacular affair as the turbo-starter cartridges fired and a jet of smoke spurted skyward from the fuselage behind the cockpit.

It says a lot for the good handling qualities of the Sea Hawk that the young 804 Squadron pilots, with no previous jet experience, were able to be moulded into a first class aerobatic team in a matter of two months. We produced a routine that included a finger four take-off (virtually line abreast on the runway), a seven aircraft loop, and a box landing with four aircraft. In the latter manoeuvre the man in the box position touched down first and called 'contact' to the leader who continued the approach to touch down with his

wing men just ahead of the box man. I am led to believe that some, if indeed not all, of these manoeuvres were innovatory in 1954.

To make our display team easy to follow we affixed smoke containers to the arrester hooks, and the smoke could be fired electrically from the cockpit.

Having been promoted to Commander just after taking over 804 Squadron, becoming the senior Squadron Commander in the Fleet Air Arm, it was obvious I would have to move on soon. This I did

on 14 July, flying for the last time with my team to Brawdy in Wales to take over as Commander (Air).

There were three Sea Hawk squadrons at Brawdy – No. 806 with F.2s, No. 897 with FB 3s and No. 899 with FGA 4s, so I was able to sample their variations. The F 2 had hydraulically-powered ailerons with spring feel and this in particular improved its handling at high Mach numbers. The FB 3 could carry either two 500lb (227kg) bombs or mines in place of the 90gal (409 litres) drop tanks for which provision was made on all

Five squadron Sea Hawks in line abreast.

804 Squadron Sea Hawks taking off in formation. Eric Brown was appointed to command the squadron on 30 November 1953.

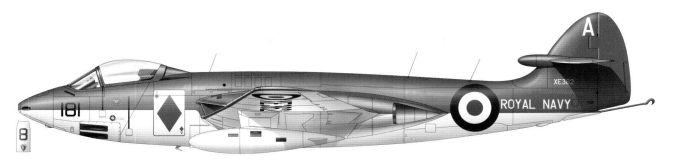

marks. The F.G.A.4 could carry ten 60lb RP's or four 500lb (227kg) bombs.

The Marks 2, 3, and 4, exhibited the same compressibility characteristics as the Mark 1, up to M=0.80. They could be taken beyond this point with a continuing nose-down trim until, at M=0.82, a strong nose-up trim change occurred; this could not be held above M=0.84 with full forward stick movement.

For reasons of performance the Sea Hawk was in fact a better ground attack aircraft than a fighter, rather in the same stamp as the US Navy's Grumman Panther. This shortfall in performance led to the introduction of the Nene 103, uprated to 5,300lb (2,404kg) static thrust. Sea Hawk F.B.3s thus modified became F.B.5s, while F.G.A.4s became F.G.A.6s. The latter type re-equipped 897 Squadron, and my first flight in one of their aircraft on 16 May 1956 was both unexpected and unusual. A report was received that a captive barrage balloon had broken away from Aberporth Guided Weapons Range and was drifting east towards populated areas. I was despatched to shoot it down while still over the wilds of Wales. I intercepted it at 13,000ft (3,962m), 15 miles (24km) west of Hereford and ended its wanton journey with a burst of 20mm cannon fire.

After I left Brawdy in November 1956 my next meeting with the Sea Hawk was in Germany, whither I had been sent on 10 March 1958 as Head of the British Naval Air Mission, with the task of training the newly formed German Naval Air Arm. Exactly one year later I flew my first Sea Hawk 100, serial no. VB133, at Schleswig-Jagel airfield, and on 20 April my first Sea Hawk 101, serial no. RB242.

The Mk 100 was a day interceptor. Thirty-two were ordered by the Germans, followed by a further thirty-two Mk 101s, which had Ekco radar fitted in a large underwing pod to give it an all-weather reconnaissance capability. Both these marks had their own particular modification in the form of increased vertical tail surface area

The Ekco 38B underwing radar proved a somewhat taxing device on the Sea Hawk's electrical generators, and was of limited tactical use because it could only be operated with the hydraulically-powered ailerons switched off. Otherwise the aircraft could rapidly assume a dangerous attitude while the pilot was peering in the radar scope. However, it did pick up ships in the Baltic with notable clarity, even through cloud.

From April to June 1960 I was seconded to the Focke-Wulf company at Bremen to replace the Chief Test Pilot who was temporarily removed for security vetting. Focke-Wulf did the assembly and flight testing of newly arrived Sea Hawks, as well as repairs and overhauls. The factory was operating in only a small rebuilt area amidst the ruins of its former glory. But it was a fascinating experience to work with the former colleagues of the great German aircraft designer, Kurt Tank, and to hear their high opinion of the Sea Hawk design.

Certainly the Sea Hawk was the perfect fighter aeroplane for the German Naval Air Arm to start its rehabilitation. It was a delight to fly, very reliable, and an efficient weapon platform. It instilled confidence in everyone who had a part in its operation.

After I returned to the UK to become Deputy Director of Naval Air Warfare I renewed acquaintance with the Sea Hawk 6 at Lee-on-Solent. This was merely for the joy of flying again a pilot's aeroplane and at the same time cementing 15 years of happy relationship.

It will be obvious that I have a very high regard for the Sea Hawk in all its forms, but that is from the handling viewpoint rather than the performance one. Between my test flying spell on the Sea Hawk and my operational time with it I had flown the North American F-86 Sabre, which set a standard I still regard as superb. This was therefore the inevitable basis for my comparison of the Sea Hawk. It says much for the Hawker product that it came out of this analysis with flying colours, although matched against a contemporary fighter of the highest calibre.

Sea Hawk FGA.Mk 6, XE362/181/A, No. 806 Naval Air Squadron, HMS *Albion*, early 1960. © *Richard Caruana* (scale 1:72).

28 HORTEN IV

A tailless sailplane incorporating
some of the more extreme
Horten design ideas. ERIC BROWN

THE HORTEN BROTHERS, Walter and Reimar, were high performance sailplane designers who first came into prominence in pre-war Nazi Germany. Their designs incorporated many advanced features including prone pilot positions, sweptback wings, and no vertical or tail surfaces, all with the aim of eliminating parasite drag.

I first heard of the brothers from Major General Ernst Udet in 1936 and again in 1938, for he was intrigued with the novelty of their tailless designs. The Ho I, built in 1933, was only partially successful, because lateral control was unsatisfactory, mainly due to adverse yawing moments from the ailerons, and longitudinal control was very ineffective at low speeds.

The Ho II, although an improvement, still had some serious shortcomings. In spite of these, Udet had one of the four Ho II sailplanes fitted with a small 80hp Hirth engine, driving a pusher propeller. He got the famous aviatrix, Hanna Reitsch to test it at Rangsdorf airfield in November 1938.

Hanna's report, especially with regard to its stalling characteristics, was encouraging enough to get official backing for further development work. Thus the Horten brothers, who were then studying at Bonn Technical High School, organised construction of the Ho III at Berlin's Tempelhof Airport. The Ho III differed from its predecessor in having increased span and aspect ratio, and also landing flaps. The basic design underwent many modifications in development, and one example was fitted with a small 32hp Volkswagen engine, whose propeller blades folded to reduce drag in gliding flight.

The Ho IV was built in 1941 to investigate the effects of high aspect ratio, which at 21.3 was twice that of the Ho III, although the span of 65.6ft (20m) was the same for both models. There were five examples of the Ho IV that survived the end of World War II and one of these,

found at Göttingen, came to RAE Farnborough, while four eventually went to the USA. The RAE aircraft was designated LA-AC and had flown some 500 hours since its construction in 1942.

I really found the Ho IV a weird looking bird, with its praying mantis position for the pilot in the wing centre section, with a retractable skid under the cockpit nose and a fixed skid under the well that contained the pilot's legs. The whole was supported by an incredibly long and narrow wing with 17° sweepback and 5° dihedral. The total fore-and-aft length of the sailplane was only 12ft 3½in (3.7m), and the empty weight 440lb (200kg). Loaded weight was 660lb, giving a wing loading of 3.3lb/sq ft (16kg/m²).

The cockpit was very snug, even for one of my modest stature and proved quite inaccessible for anyone taller than about 5ft 9in (1.75m). Since Heinz Scheidhauer, the Horten Chief Test Pilot, was a small man it would appear that either he influenced this component of the design or was chosen to fit in with a fait accompli.

When prone in the cockpit the pilot's weight was taken mainly on the chest and knees. The knee-well could be adjusted for varying pilot size within a limited range, and an adjustable chin rest

was provided. Security of position was ensured by shoulder rests, and the thighs against the knee-well, as well as a harness consisting of a single broad strap passing under the buttocks. This was released by a red knob on the right hand side of the cockpit, while a similar knob on the left-hand side jettisoned the access cover. The parachute was stowed in a pocket on the cover and connected to the pilot's harness by short straps, so that he was relieved of the weight.

Flying instruments included a low reading airspeed indicator driven by a venturi, electrical turn and bank indicator, sensitive variometer, and a high reading variometer. Oxygen equipment could be fitted with provision for electrically heated clothing.

The pilot's feet controlled pedal-operated wing tip spoilers on the upper and lower surfaces immediately ahead of the outer control flap. These could be used individually as drag rudders by pressing with the toes, moving the feet from the ankle against a spring feel fitted to the pedals, thus opening the rudders. They could also be used together as spoilers by pressing both feet together to open the rudders simultaneously and so give extra drag for glide control. A hand lever

The high position of the Ho IV in towed flight above the Fieseler Storch.

on the left hand side of the cockpit was available to operate large spoiler-type dive brakes, which were used for landing and which could also be used to give variable drag for glide path control.

The elevon control surfaces, which were operated by a spectacle-type control wheel, were subdivided into three flaps, the gearings of which were arranged to provide a gradual change in effective wing twist, giving optimum lift distribution for minimum drag and the prevention of tip stalling. The outer flaps worked in effect as up-going aileron, while the middle flaps gave climbing elevator action, and the inner flaps diving elevator. Down-going aileron, needed to neutralise pitching moments, was effected by the inner and middle flaps working together.

Take-off in the Horten IV was the most difficult part of flying it. By trial and error I found it was vitally important to get perfectly lined up at the end of the 120–150yds (110–137m) tow rope, dead behind the tug and dead into the wind. At RAE we used a Fieseler Storch as a tug. Other important points were to ensure that the compression strut of the nose skid was somewhere between 25–35 atmospheres and not over that pressure: that one-quarter to one-half up elevator deflection was used; and on no account to use the foot pedals to keep straight on the ground.

The wing tips, or at least one tip, had to be held up very lightly on the take-off run, and it was essential that the holder or holders did not drag on the tip by not keeping up with the tug's initial acceleration. In the take-off learning routine I had a success rate of about 1 in 3, and in the process must have trained many potential Olympic sprinters.

My first take-off was in the evening of 13 May 1947, in flat calm conditions and, in accordance with the notes given to me by Scheidhauer during interrogation, I pulled up above the tug as quickly as possible after unsticking. At the same time I pulled the handle on the right side of the cockpit to retract the skid and jettison the nose wheel in one movement.

Once the tug had unstuck I settled some 50ft (15m) above it. The Storch towed at a steady 62mph (100km/h), and on the advice of Scheidhauer I used the drag rudders as little as possible as this set up a Dutch roll. Any reduction in tow speed resulted in a mushy sort of waffling motion, whilst an increase to 87mph (140km/h) caused periodic oscillations due to wing bending. The latter could be countered by deflecting both wing tip spoilers simultaneously.

I cast off from the tug at 5,000ft (1,524m) and spent a few minutes getting the feel of the unusual controls, especially the drag rudders. Certainly the Ho IV had only marginal directional stability, and use of the drag rudders gave yaw and pitch together, which set up a lazy sort of Dutch roll motion. Lateral control was sluggish but produced no adverse yaw. Longitudinal control was surprisingly light and effective in comparison with control about the other axes and gave good circling characteristics.

A stall was made at 3,000ft (914m) and it

required a lot of elevon deflection to achieve the requisite angle of attack before the nose dropped gently and straight at 38mph (61km/h). Little height was lost in the recovery and it was obvious the wing tips were not stalled.

I carried out a succession of stalls to check a strange burbling noise to be heard as the stall was approached. This seemed to come from an area just behind my head, but was most distinctive and intensified as the angle of attack was increased.

The gliding ratio at 34mph (55km/h) seemed good, and although the aircraft generally felt sluggish in response to control movements it did not require large control displacement to get initial response. The rate of descent at 62mph (100km/h) was 200ft/min (61m/min) and at 34mph (55km/h) was 106ft/min (32m/min).

Landing the Ho IV was an exhilarating experience because of the prone position layout. The view was superb and the spoiler dive brakes exceptionally effective in controlling the glide path at 44mph (71km/h), although they could not be locked out, the hand lever having to be continuously held to keep them open.

However, when holding off at 10ft (3m) off the ground the spoilers had to be closed and speed reduced to 37mph (60km/h), otherwise a heavy landing resulted. The actual touch-down could be made with great precision due to the effective longitudinal control and bird's eye view of the ground. It was certainly possible to convert the expression 'a daisy cutter' into reality. The landing run was short and the wings could be held level virtually to a stop.

Subsequent flights I made were mainly aimed at further assessment of the prone pilot position, but some involved flying in turbulence and these showed up some of the more unpleasant stability and control characteristics of the Ho IV. In free flight in gusty air the bending of the wings caused almost continuous hunting about the horizontal axis, giving an unpleasant feeling of inherent instability, although Scheidhauer had assured me these fluctuations or wiggles, as he called them, were due to sweep back and not instability.

I also did some gentle dives to assess the control effectiveness at speed, but these had to be curtailed due to wing tip flutter above 87mph (140km/h).

The Horten brothers progressed their design work through a series of unpowered and powered tailless aircraft up to the Ho XIV. The most interesting of these was the Ho IX, a single seat fighter bomber with twin Jumo 004 jet engines. When I first heard of this aircraft I had assumed it would have the prone pilot layout, so favoured by the Hortens. In fact the pilot seating was of the normal type on the partially completed V3 model found at Friedrichroda.

The Ho IX was designed for a normal acceleration of 7'g', combined with a safety factor of 1.8. What little testing was done on the V2 model showed the aircraft to be probably faster then the Me 262. Estimated top speed was 590mph (950km/h) at sea level, and rate of climb 4,300ft/min (1,311m/min) at sea level.

The Horten brothers were probably the greatest exponents of pure tailless aircraft design, possibly because they persevered where others gave up. I only wish I could have shared their enthusiasm and faith, but my short experience of the Ho IV left me unconvinced that this was the way ahead. However, one thing the Ho IV certainly did for me was to whet my appetite for the prone pilot position.

The innovative cockpit design in the Ho IV.

29 LOCKHEED LIGHTNING

A good performer at low levels, but a poor fighter at high altitude. Had a great combat record against the Japanese. ERIC BROWN

THE LIGHTNING was a fascinating aeroplane in every way; it was unusual in its design layout, it was the first American production aircraft capable of 400mph (644km/h) in level flight, and it was also one of the first military aircraft equipped with a tricycle undercarriage. It had a startling combat record, flying in every combat theatre of World War II, and producing some 160 American aces. It certainly had charisma in plenty, for it was the aircraft that shot down the Japanese war leader, Admiral Yamamoto, at a range of some 450 miles (724km) from its island base. America's top two fighter pilots, Majors Richard Bong and Thomas McGuire, also flew Lightnings exclusively to score their respective 40 and 38 kills.

The P-38 Lightning was designed to a 1936 specification and first flew on 27 January 1939. Of course it went through a series of refinements throughout its full wartime career. I first flew it at Farnborough on 18 February 1945, by which time it had acquired power-boosted ailerons. The model was an F-5E with the serial no.44-24365, and it was a photo-reconnaissance version of the P-38L. It was fitted with two Allison V-1710 twelve-cylinder liquid-cooled engines, each rated at 1,520hp and driving oppositely rotating Curtiss Electric constant-speed, full-feathering airscrews.

Our interest in the Lightning F-5E at RAE was mainly in its hydraulically powered ailerons and high Mach number dive recovery flaps, although

The P-38 was the 'steed' of America's top scoring fighter aces.

A dramatic shot of the P-38 Lightning's twin tailboom layout. The turbo superchargers mounted just aft of each engine gave it sufficient power to compete, but it was far from racey.

my own interest went much deeper than those areas.

The cockpit was entered via a ladder on the port side, and provided me with my first disappointment. It was a large cockpit by British standards, and instead of the fighter type stick, the control column was cranked to the pilot's right with a half spectacle wheel. Also, in spite of being a 'trike', the view ahead was impaired by the long nose.

Take-off was delightfully easy with no swing and good acceleration. Rate of climb was very good, but of course, this PR version was several hundred pounds lighter than the fighter version. It also proved to be some 10mph (16km/h) faster, with a top speed of 414mph (666km/h) at 25,000ft (7,620m).

This aircraft had a fairly high wing loading of 54.9lb/sq (268kg/m^2) ft but the stalling speed was

Lockheed P-38 Lightning

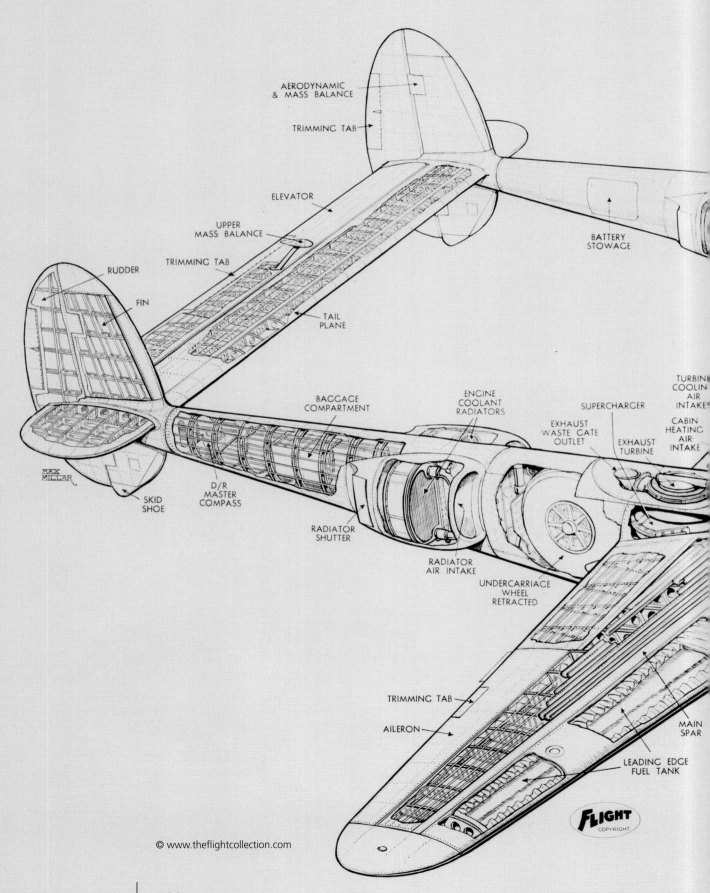

AERODYNAMIC
& MASS BALANCE

TRIMMING TAB

ELEVATOR

UPPER
MASS BALANCE

TRIMMING TAB

RUDDER

FIN

TAIL
PLANE

BAGGAGE
COMPARTMENT

ENGINE
COOLANT
RADIATORS

BATTERY
STOWAGE

TURBINE
COOLING
AIR
INTAKE

SUPERCHARGER

EXHAUST
WASTE GATE
OUTLET

CABIN
HEATING
AIR·
INTAKE

EXHAUST
TURBINE

MAX
MILLAR

SKID
SHOE

D/R
MASTER
COMPASS

RADIATOR
SHUTTER

RADIATOR
AIR INTAKE

UNDERCARRIAGE
WHEEL
RETRACTED

TRIMMING TAB

AILERON

MAIN
SPAR

LEADING EDGE
FUEL TANK

FLIGHT
COPYRIGHT

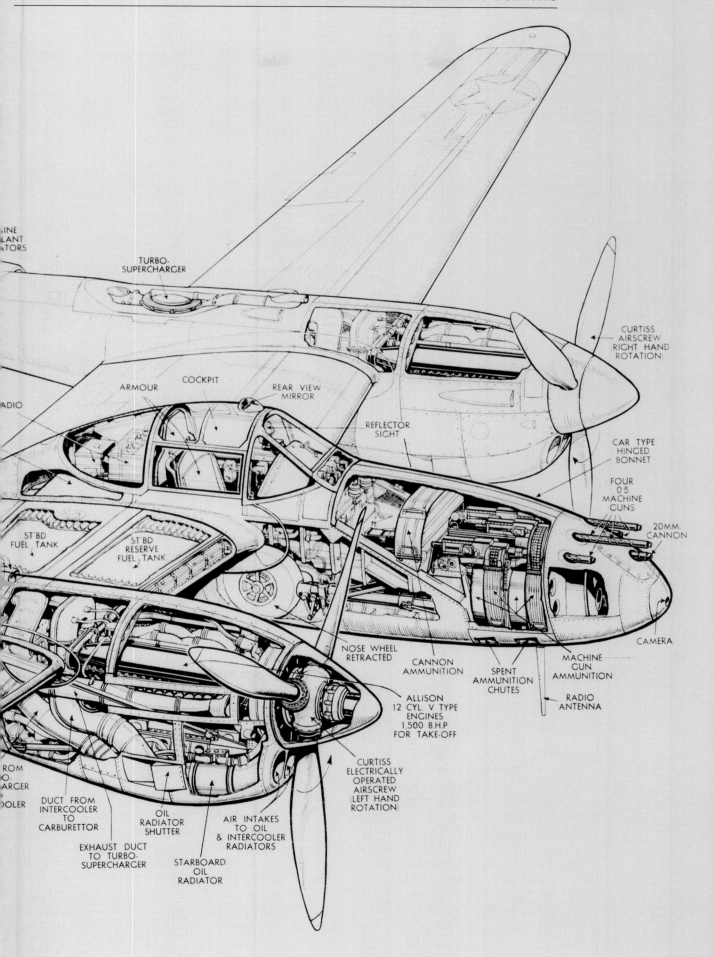

TURBO-
SUPERCHARGER

INE
LANT
ATORS

RADIO

ARMOUR

COCKPIT

REAR VIEW
MIRROR

REFLECTOR
SIGHT

CURTISS
AIRSCREW
RIGHT HAND
ROTATION)

CAR TYPE
HINGED
BONNET

FOUR
0·5
MACHINE
GUNS

20MM
CANNON

ST'BD
FUEL TANK

ST'BD
RESERVE
FUEL TANK

CAMERA

NOSE WHEEL
RETRACTED

CANNON
AMMUNITION

SPENT
AMMUNITION
CHUTES

MACHINE
GUN
AMMUNITION

RADIO
ANTENNA

ALLISON
12 CYL. V TYPE
ENGINES
1,500 B.H.P.
FOR TAKE-OFF

ROM
O-
ARGER

OLER

DUCT FROM
INTERCOOLER
TO
CARBURETTOR

OIL
RADIATOR
SHUTTER

AIR INTAKES
TO OIL
& INTERCOOLER
RADIATORS

CURTISS
ELECTRICALLY
OPERATED
AIRSCREW
(LEFT HAND
ROTATION)

EXHAUST DUCT
TO TURBO-
SUPERCHARGER

STARBOARD
OIL
RADIATOR

In the latter stages of World War II the Lightning was competing for survival with fast piston-engined planes and the early jets.

remarkably low at 94mph (151km/h) all up, and 78mph (126km/h) with undercarriage and flaps down. Since the stall was mild this all augured well for good manoeuvrability, but the early Lightnings had been handicapped by a poor rate of roll. Not so this baby – it rolled like a dingbat.

Hydraulically powered controls were still very much a rarity in 1945, and we were experimenting with them at RAE on a Firebrand IV (ailerons only) and a Lancaster. It soon became apparent that the Lightning system was very unsophisticated, because its ailerons lacked feel in that they had a constant force for any amount of stick displacement, increase in speed, or rate of application. Such lack of feel is disconcerting to the combat pilot, and can be disturbing in instrument flight, particularly if the control column does not self-centre after displacement as indeed it did not in the case of the Lightning. However, the Sperry A-4 automatic pilot was standard equipment in the model F-5.

The Lightning lived into the transonic era of

flight, so in the later stages of World War II it was competing for survival with very fast piston-engined aeroplanes and the early jets. Not only had speeds risen significantly but so had heights at which both fighters and bombers could fly, and in that region airspeed was replaced with Mach numbers.

As examples of the maximum safe flight true Mach numbers of contemporary aircraft before compressibility effects set in and limited control, the Mustang's was 0.78, the Tempest V's was 0.80, the Meteor I's was 0.80, and the Me 262's was 0.83. The pre-war Lightning was very low in this league table at M=0.68.

Obviously all these aircraft could be flown at various small increments above these Mach numbers before going out of control, and it was the task of research establishments such as RAE Farnborough to probe into these difficult areas. In the case of the Lightning we wanted to know why dive recovery flaps had been fitted, and how effective they were. These flaps were electrically operated, positioned outboard of the engine nacelles and hinged to the under surface of the wings beneath the main spar.

Dives were started from 32,000ft (9,754m) and increased from M=0.65 to 0.68 when vigorous buffeting was accompanied by a strong nose-down pitch. Recovery could be made on elevator alone but required a very strong pull force. Use of the dive recovery flaps alleviated this situation considerably.

It was decided to increase the Mach number by increments of .01 until recovery could no longer be affected without use of the dive recovery flaps. It was clear that I was reaching my physical limit of pull around M=0.70, but I just managed to pull out at M=0.71. However, at M=0.72 I met my Waterloo and no amount of pull could prevent the nose dropping. At M=0.75 I decided to pop the dive recovery flaps and the nose began to rise gradually at first and then more positively.

There is no doubt that without the dive recovery flaps such a runaway dive would have fatal results, but of course the pilot would normally have ample warning from the heavy buffeting. In the heat of combat the situation could easily get out of hand, hence the decision to fit the recovery flaps.

Landing the Lightning was child's play, whether on two engines or one; the latter case was made easier by the powered ailerons.

This short acquaintance with the Lightning left me with the feeling of having enjoyed it, but wondering how the earlier models had been so successful in combat. Certainly the earlier shortcomings had been improved sufficiently to keep this likeable aeroplane in good enough shape to survive in 1945, so I suppose it must have been very good when it first joined the battle scene, in 1942.

The clean lines of the Lightning are clearly shown.

The twin-tail layout of the P-38 was almost unique in WWII.

30 MARTIN BAKER MB 5

An outstanding fighter except for the lateral control. Arrived too late to participate in World War II. ERIC BROWN

JIMMY MARTIN, later Sir James Martin of ejector seat fame, entered the field of aircraft design in 1929 and after an initial drawing-board venture produced his first practical aeroplane, the MB 1, in 1935. This was a good looking, small, cheap two-seater, with a simple but highly ingenious method of construction using round-section thin-gauge steel tubing throughout the structure. It was powered by a 160hp Napier Javelin engine, with electrical starting, and had a neat enclosed cockpit with a sharp V windscreen.

The first military machine designed by Martin was the MB 2, which first flew on 3 August 1938, powered by a Napier Dagger 24-cylinder H-type engine, driving a fixed-pitch two-blade propeller. It had a fixed undercarriage with beautifully clean trouser-type fairings, and carried eight Browning 0.303 machine-guns in the wings, thus making it the first British eight-gun fighter.

The next design, the MB 3, was powered by a Napier Sabre, a development of the Dagger, giving 2,000hp, driving a de Havilland variable-pitch

A fighter with great potential, which arrived just too late for World War II.

three-blade propeller. It was armed with six 20mm cannon, thus making it the heaviest armed fighter in the world. Unfortunately an engine failure soon after take-off on 12 September resulted in a fatal crash involving the test pilot, Captain Valentine Baker.

The MB 4 was a drawing-board project only, but was followed by the magnificent MB 5, a low-wing monoplane powered by a 2,340hp Griffon 83 engine, driving a pair of three-bladed contra-rotating propellers.

Although I first saw and admired the MB 5 at RAE in October 1945 – when it appeared in the static park along with a collection of captured German aircraft at a post-war exhibition and flying display – it did not come to Farnborough for testing until the spring of 1948.

I carried out handling flights in April of that year on the prototype R2496. By this time the original Rotol contra-props had been replaced by DH ones. The fuselage was of the Martin-Baker patented steel tube system of construction, with the covering in the form of quickly detachable metal panels. The power-plant installation was particularly clean, with the coolant and oil radiators and intercooler grouped together in a laminar-flow duct under the rear fuselage. The AUW of the aircraft was 11,500lb (5,216kg) and the wing loading was 44lb/sq ft ($215kg/m^2$). Starting was by Coffman cartridge.

Ease of entry to the cockpit from the ground was unusually good, and the cockpit itself was outstandingly well designed. It was the acme of simplicity, with a single fuel control lever, absence of any undercarriage emergency lowering system or intermediate flap position, and an exceptionally clean floor. Instrument grouping was logical, thus enabling swift and easy routine checking. It all added up to perfection.

The cockpit was midway along the wing chord, but the view provided was very good indeed for taxying, except for a narrow sector dead ahead. The undercarriage seemed springy when moving over grass, but very pleasant to steer on a smooth surface as the brakes were quite powerful and the aircraft had no tendency to nose heaviness.

Take-off was most impressive, there being no swing. The aircraft unstuck nicely in a three-point attitude in a very short distance without the use of flap and with the trimmers set neutral.

There was no noticeable change of trim with undercarriage retraction and initially climb was very good. But then the rate appeared to fall off more rapidly than I had anticipated with a two-stage, two-speed, supercharged engine.

In cruising flight at medium altitude the longi-

The Martin-Baker MB 5 was the ultimate development of a series of prototype fighter aircraft built during the Second World War. R2496 shown here, is believed to be pictured in 1944. *Air Team Images*.

tudinal stick-free stability was very positive, the directional almost neutral, but the lateral unstable in spite of good control self-centering in all cases after displacement.

All the spring tab controls were light throughout the speed range and the rudder too much so. Both the elevators and rudder were very effective, but the ailerons were out of harmony with the other controls by their ineffectiveness and the rate of roll was disappointing but could be significantly aided by rudder application. The all-round view was particularly good during manoeuvres and was the best of any single-piston engine, high perormance fighter of that era. Range at 224mph (360km/h) was 1,236 miles (1989km).

The all-up stall occurred at 93mph (150km/h) without any warning other than a slight tendency for the aircraft to get port wing heavy. At the stall the port wing dropped about 15°. In high 'g' turns at the stall the aircraft snapped into a port wing drop of about 30° without warning.

The all-down stall gave a 20° starboard wing drop at 78mph (126km/h) without any warning, but there was absolutely no tendency to spin and recovery was straightforward.

Landing was delightfully easy, with the undercarriage being lowered at 167mph (269km/h) and flaps at 155mph (249km/h). Lowering of the pneumatically-operated trailing edge split flaps gave a nose-up change of trim, which could be countered by opening the radiator flap to give moderate nose-up change of trim. A final approach speed of 104mph (167km/h) gave a perfect three-point attitude, and on touchdown the undercarriage felt very soft. With the marked airscrew braking effect on throttling fully back the landing run was extremely short and without swing.

In bumpy weather there was a feeling of lateral insecurity on the approach, due to the spongy feel of the ailerons at very low speed and partly to the inherent lateral instability of the aircraft.

In my test report I wrote as my conclusions 'In my opinion this is an outstanding aircraft, particularly when regarded in the light of the fact that it made its maiden flight as early as 23 May 1944. It is certainly open to improvement in regard to lateral handling qualities, but in my brief experience of this aircraft I should say any other point for criticism would be hard to find. My lasting impression will always be one of stepping into a strange aeroplane for the first time, and yet immediately feeling so completely at home with it, that I might have already flown hundreds of hours in it – a compliment I could pay to no other new type of advanced aircraft I have flown to date.'

The name of Sir James Martin is irrevocably linked with the ejection seat, and for his achievements in that field he has become the patron saint of military jet pilots. But I am bound to wonder what his talents might have given to aviation if he had not forsaken aircraft design in a somewhat disillusioned frame of mind because the superb MB 5 had not been chosen for production and because his friend and business partner had been killed in the MB 3.

A pilot's aeroplane, which was a delight to fly.

31 MARTIN MARAUDER

A smart performer, but a bit edgy when it came to landing – particularly on one engine.

ERIC BROWN

MUCH HAS BEEN WRITTEN of the Marauder, but I want to just say a few more words about it, because there was something especially appealing to me in this aeroplane. It had that splendid combination of looking both lethal and beautiful at the same time. It also flew beautifully but could be lethal if mishandled in certain circumstances.

The prototype B-26 Marauder first flew on 25 November 1940 and by the end of 1944 over 5,000 had been delivered. There were inevitably a number of different models of the aircraft developed, but these mainly involved changes to the engines and armament.

This shoulder-high wing aeroplane had a voluptuous but elegantly smooth shape and the big Double Wasp engines oozed power. It bris-tled with guns, the Mk II version carrying eleven 0.5-inch calibre machine-guns, and its internal bomb-bay housed 4,000lb (1,814kg) of bombs.

I first got my chance to fly a Marauder on 30 October 1944 at Farnborough. It was a Marauder II, serial number FB482, fitted with the 2,000hp engines, with the area of the vertical tail surfaces increased, and with a wing span of 71ft (22m), increased from the original 65ft (20m). Normal crew was seven.

The aeroplane came to RAE so that we could investigate its single-engine flying characteristics. A considerable number of crashes had occurred to Marauders returning to their bases in Britain after the loss of an engine and in the final phases of the landing.

This aircraft had a high wing loading for its

Martin Marauder II on a high-speed low level test flight.

Seen at the A&AEE at Boscombe Down in March 1944, Marauder II FB482 still carries its USAAF serial on the fin. At the time it was undergoing trials with a large smoke-bomb with an attached parachute. *Barry Ketley*

day, being over 58lb/sq ft (283kg/m^2) at full load, and about 43lb/sq ft (210kg/m^2) for landing, so the approach speed was 135mph (217km/h).

I found the Marauder II very nice to fly, responsive to the controls, very stable, and very manageable on one engine in cruising flight. However, when it came to a normal landing, the limiting speed of 170mph (274km/h) for lowering the undercarriage was so low that this could only be done on the straight in final approach. In consequence a wide circuit had to be made to allow a long final leg. Also the view was bad, in spite of the twin-engined layout, due to the nose-up attitude for landing.

A single-engine landing aggravated this situation since the approach speed with one-third flap had to be at least 150mph (241km/h). The undercarriage took longer to extend, and the final leg tended to become a long drawn out knife edge affair. Add in as an extra ingredient the vagaries of the British weather, and the problem could be compounded to a dangerous degree – as indeed it often was.

The only modification that proved possible to improve these characteristics was introduced in the Marauder III, whose wing incidence was increased by 3½ degrees. This improved the view at low speed and reduced the exaggerated nose-up attitude in cruising flight.

The Marauder is a prime example of a basically good design with an Achilles heel in the form of a structural limitation that did not affect its combat efficiency but could hit the pilot hard at a *moment critique*. It may seem surprising that something was not done about this flaw, but in a war where the stakes were high the delay that could be caused by extensive redesign of the undercarriage was unacceptable.

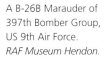

A B-26B Marauder of 397th Bomber Group, US 9th Air Force. *RAF Museum Hendon.*

32 MILES M.20

A brilliant concept as a Battle of Britain stopgap, but was never needed.

ERIC BROWN

I N JANUARY 1942, as a young Fleet Air Arm pilot fresh from operations in a fighter squadron, I received an unexpected assignment to go to RAE Farnborough and fly a new fighter, to compare it with the Martlet (Wildcat) and Hurricane as a prospective naval combat aircraft. My report to the Admiralty was to be given verbally and I was to regard the assignment as SECRET.

At Farnborough I was briefed by Flight Lieutenant J.R. Tobin of Aero Flight and shown over what was designated the Miles M.20, bearing the serial no. DR616. My first impression was of something that looked somewhat of a cross between the Hurricane and Spitfire, with a smaller wing span and a more pugnacious nose than either. However, the two eye-striking features were the fixed undercarriage and the bubble type cockpit hood, the latter to become commonplace in fighters, but at that time a rare innovation. Closer inspection also showed the aircraft to be of wooden construction, which didn't surprise me as I was familiar with the Miles Master trainer. The engine was the well tried Merlin XX of Hurricane and Spitfire fame.

Having climbed aboard and settled in the well laid out cockpit I was amazed at the beautiful view from the bubble hood. However the ground angle of the M.20 and the comparatively long nose defied even this clear view canopy and the view dead ahead was not good for taxying.

The Merlin started with its usual efficiency and was soon warmed up to allow taxying to start. Because of the poor view ahead the aircraft had to be swung from side to side. I had been warned not to use the brakes harshly as the aircraft had a tendency to tip up – and there was not too much propeller ground clearance.

The take-off was made with 30° flaps down, and this gave a strong swing to the left that needed at least three-quarter opposite rudder and full right rudder trim to counteract it – and the foot force required was considerable. The run was longer than I had expected and there was a lot of pushing and pulling required to unstick.

The initial rate of climb was surprisingly good, for I had rather expected it to be sluggish on account of the fixed undercarriage and the all-up weight being in excesss of that of the contemporary Hurricane and Spitfire. The even bigger surprise was its level flight turn of speed, which was in excess of the Martlet at 335mph (539km/h). In cruising flight the nose of the M.20 was 5° below the horizon, so the pilot had superb all-round view.

The stalling speed with flaps up was 93mph (150km/h), and with flaps fully down 72mph (116km/h). There was little warning of the stall involving a wing drop.

The harmony of control was quite good but the controls were all heavier than those of the Hurricane, Martlet, or Spitfire.

For this test a Hurricane flown by Tobin had come up to dog fight with me and it was obvious the Hurricane was more manoeuvrable and had a much smaller turning circle. In attempting to follow the Hurricane in a steep turn I flicked out of control at 140mph (225km/h) without any warning. The Hurricane could also change direction faster and accelerated faster, although the M.20 was itself no slouch.

In flicking out of the steep turns I had been advised to use caution in recovery as the M.20 had exhibited some recalcitrance in spin recovery while under test with the parent company. But I found no particular difficulty in the flick recovery.

Landing was of course an important part of the test if the M.20 was ever to be a carrier-borne aircraft. After a normal approach at 100mph (161km/h), which seemed to give a rather steep nose-down attitude, I started easing the speed

The cleverly conceived Miles M 20 was surprisingly nippy in performance but did not match the Hurricane or Spitfire for manoeuvrability.

off to 90mph (145km/h), then finally to 85mph (137km/h), which seemed about right for a powered carrier approach. At this speed the attitude of the aircraft gave poor forward view, and there was barely sufficient backward elevator trim available. The controls felt sluggish, particularly the ailerons. On cutting the power for touchdown the nose dropped quite sharply and firm backward stick had to be applied to prevent the aircraft hitting main wheels first and bouncing. Half a dozen more landings convinced me that this would not be an ideal deck landing aircraft.

In essence my report to the Admiralty, which apparently was considering the M 20 to meet Naval Staff specification N.1/41, expressed the view that the M 20, although surprisingly nippy in performance, could not match the Martlet, Hurricane, or Spitfire for manoeuvrability. It did not offer enough speed performance superiority over the Martlet or Hurricane to give an offsetting advantage.

For deck landing the M 20 was not in the same class as the Martlet, but was probably somewhere between the Hurricane and Spitfire. Certainly the

wheel spats would have to be removed for deck work and this would adversely affect performance. However, my biggest misgiving was whether the wooden airframe of the M 20 could withstand the punishment of arrested landings.

What I did not know at that time was that the M 20 was designed, built, and flown in 65 days. This being made possible by using standard Master parts wherever possible, the elimination of hydraulics, and of course the fitting of a fixed undercarriage. The concept was to offer a fighter capable of speedy production if we suffered heavy fighter losses in the Battle of Britain. Such a fighter would, of course, also have to offer near comparable performance with the Hurricane and Spitfire, and indeed the M 20 had some very attractive advantages in that it could carry twelve .303 Browning machine-guns in the wings, 5,000 rounds of ammunition, and 154gal (700 litres) of fuel – virtually double the fire power and endurance of the Hurricane and Spitfire. Viewed in that light, the M 20 was indeed a brilliant concept, and typical of the genius of the Miles team.

33 MILES M.39B LIBELLULA

Another Miles oddity, but not really a starter as a naval aircraft.

ERIC BROWN

WHEN I FIRST JOINED the RAE as an experimental test pilot in January 1944, I was fascinated by the line up of types that was always to be seen outside 'A' Shed, alongside the Control Tower. We used to call this area the Heinz Hangar, because of the association of 57 varieties possibly being parked there.

In my six years at the RAE I saw many weird and wonderful aircraft there, but none stranger than the Miles M.39B Libellula which inhabited 'A' Shed. To my delight it was one of the first experimental aircraft on which I became project pilot.

The reason for this was that George Miles had designed the Libellula to test out some ideas on improving naval aircraft. The Royal Navy's Fleet Air Arm had been plagued with aircraft ill-suited to the demands of landing on a carrier, and as a result was collecting for itself an unenviable deck-landing accident rate. Indeed my predecessor at Farnborough had been killed while landing a Seafire on a carrier.

The essential requirements for a good carrier aircraft were view, a robust undercarriage, and small span to enable it to be stowed in the ship's hangar and transported there on a lift.

It appears that while George Miles was giving thought to these problems he visited Boscombe Down in the winter of 1941 and saw the Westland Delanne there. This was a modified Lysander with an extra large tailplane to allow a Boulton Paul four-gun turret to be fitted in the tail. Thus grew the idea in his mind of a tandem-wing layout.

Such an arrangement would permit the pilot to be located in the nose with unobstructed view, while the engine was in the tail. Furthermore the layout of two sets of wings would enable the span to be kept to the limited dimensions of a carrier's lift. These limits on span were normally achieved by wing folding, which meant an increase in all-up weight or some compensating reduction in fuel or ammunition.

These were the specialised advantages claimed, although there were others such as the increased manoeuvrability from the small size of the air-

The prototype of the Miles Libellula, U-0244, showing the tail plane in front and the wing behind.

191

craft, and the more efficient coefficient of lift from both wings.

The idea was rapidly translated into fact by the industrious George Miles and his M.35 Libellula was born. It was of wooden construction, with a 130hp Gipsy Major, mounted in the tail, driving a pusher propeller. The forward wing was on top of the fuselage, immediately behind the cockpit, and carried the elevators. The larger rear wing was attached to the bottom of the fuselage and carried the ailerons and fins and rudders at each tip. Both wings were fitted with flaps. The span and length of the aircraft were about the same at 20ft (6m).

These were the facts as I learned them once I delved into the history of the Libellula. The M.39B differed considerably from its predecessor in that the front wing was now lower, while the rear wing had become the upper component. The pusher layout had given way to two conventionally mounted Gipsy Major 1c engines of 140hp each. The rear wing was also of considerably greater span than the front wing, these being 37½ft (11m) and 25ft (8m) respectively. The length was still only 22ft 2in., but the weight had grown to 2,800lb (1,270kg), i.e. 1,000lb (454kg) heavier than the M.35.

The M.39B first flew on 22 July 1943, bearing the registration U-0244, and some six months later arrived at the RAE, where it acquired the serial number SR392, in August 1944.

By the time I first flew the M.39B on 30 June 1944, it had already had two mishaps at Farnborough – an inadvertent belly landing, and it had been blown on to its back by an aircraft running up ahead of it.

However, what interested me more was that rumour had it that George Miles had had a dicey first flight in the M.35 due to serious instability. I remembered also that Herr Wulf, of the famous Focke-Wulf firm, had been killed in the tandem-wing Focke-Wulf *Ente* in 1928. The history of the 'canards' was not reassuring; but George Miles had learned a lot on the M.35 and had had no trouble with the first flight of the M.39B.

The flight test programme I carried out on the Libellula was mainly concerned with stability and control rather than performance. The aircraft was more of a test bed to prove the tandem-wing configuration than a serious operational prototype.

Taxying was very easy because of the steerable nosewheel tied in with the rudder bar. Since it could not be disconnected, however, it made for some problems in landing.

The flaps were operated manually by two levers and both the front and rear flaps could be moved five notches. The front flaps had a particularly powerful nose-up effect on trim and were

generally counteracted by the rear flaps, so it was normal to operate them in turn one notch at a time. There were no control trimmers fitted to the aircraft.

Take-off was normally made at a flap setting of 3/0 when the Libellula would fly itself off at 68mph (109km/h) in 435ft (133m), with the elevator held neutral. The flap could be left at this setting for climbing once the undercarriage was retracted, and then to 1/0 for cruising. Rate of climb was 1,100ft/min (305m/min).

In cruising flight the effect of the front flap on control was to make the ailerons heavier without affecting the rudder or elevator control. The rear flap further affected the ailerons so that they became very sluggish and the elevator also lost some of its effectiveness while rudder control remained unaffected. The maximum speed reached in level flight at the 1/0 flap setting was 164mph (264km/h).

The Aerodynamics Department was particularly interested in the stalling characteristics of the Libellula and I carried out extensive tests in this region of the flight envelope. On these flights a 60ft (18m) trailing static pitot, which looked something like a needle-nosed 11lb (5kg) practice bomb, was released from the underside of the fuselage to give readings on a widely graduated low-scale airspeed indicator in the pilot's cockpit. This meant that the ASI reading was always from a pitot source in undisturbed air, irrespective of the angle of attack of the aircraft wings. The height for the tests was normally 5,000ft (1,524m).

The test basically covered the range of front flap settings and of rear flap settings and then the combinations of both.

With no flaps used the aircraft could not be stalled but settled in a steady descent at 81mph (130km/h) with the stick fully back. It was not until the 2/0 setting that a stall could be produced, and at the 5/0 setting the stall speed was down to 63mph (101km/h). The stalling characteristics with front flap were, in general, gentle and straightforward, with the nose dropping increasingly sharply as more flap was used until an angle of 50° was reached at the 5/0 setting.

All the controls lost an increasing amount of their effectiveness as the front flap setting increased and particularly the ailerons. The elevator remained the most effective and the aircraft tended to self-recover immediately after the nose drop at the stall. This characteristic, combined with the steep nose drop at the 5/0 setting, could set up an unpleasantly violent porpoising motion. This could only be stopped by pushing the control column firmly forward as the self-recovery

began, or by taking off the front flap setting. The height loss in the stall was very small – 200–300ft (61–91m) – because of the self-recovery characteristics. The stalling tests using rear flap were all made with the front flap at the maximum extension. This was necessary, otherwise there would not have been enough backward elevator power to stall the aircraft. Even at a flap setting of 5/1 the stick was about two-thirds of full backward travel to produce the stall. At the 5/3 setting the

stall could just be produced at 60mph (97km/h) with the stick fully back. All these stalls with rear flap occurred without warning and gave a sharp nose drop. As the rear flap setting increased, the ease of inducing any fore-and-aft porpoising motion got less until it was completely eliminated at the 5/3 setting. The height loss in the stall was a mere 100ft (30m) as the nose drop, although sharp, was shallow.

At the 5/4 and 5/5 settings the aircraft would

The Libellula's unorthodox layout is clearly visible from this overhead view of SR392.

The Libellula – a weird aircraft. The flight test programme carried out at RAE was primarily concerned with stability and control, rather than performance.

not stall but settled into a stable descent at increasing airspeed as the rear flap setting increased.

Use of the trailing static revealed a large position error in the pilot's normal airspeed indicator, which at 90mph (145km/h) was under-reading by 27mph (43km/h), and at 60mph (97km/h) by 18mph (29km/h). Therefore the true 60mph stall recorded at the 5/3 setting was showing a reading of some 43mph (69km/h) on the aircraft's normal ASI.

With the knowledge that the stalling characteristics of the Libellula were surprisingly mild, it became possible to investigate single-engine flying in depth, i.e. to the point of loss of control.

Because of the direction of rotation of the propellers the loss of the port engine was less critical than the loss of the starboard. An abrupt cut of the port engine, while in the cruise with a 1/0 flap setting, immediately set up a 15° bank to port with a moderately fast swing in the same direction, accompanied by a rapid drop off in speed so that the nose began to drop and the bank increased to about 35° and developed into a steep 'graveyard' spiral. A starboard engine cut accentuated all these features and the bank increased rapidly to 50° before a steep spiral commenced.

If corrective action was taken the aircraft could only be held straight and level with full throttle on the live engine and full opposite rudder to the direction of swing. But the airspeed fell off to just above 80mph (129km/h) with the port engine

failed, and just below 80mph (129km/h) with the starboard engine failed.

With this 'all stops pulled out' situation the aircraft was on a knife edge as regards control and was particularly unpleasant in bumpy conditions. With the good engine at full power and the pilot having a heavy rudder load, it was obvious that the continuance of straight and level flight was dependent on both modes of power holding out together.

Landing the Libellula was a very straightforward affair, with the approach being made engine-assisted at 75mph (121km/h) with a flap setting of 4/2. The view was superb and the controls, except the rudders, effective. However, a crosswind made this simple process somewhat hazardous because of the sloppy rudder control, and the fact that the steerable nose wheel was directly connected to the rudders. Thus, if a rudder corrective movement was made just before touch-down, the nose-wheel would contact the ground off-centre. The violence of the self-centering action could burst the tyre or give the pilot's ankles a good wrench on the rudder bar.

I thoroughly enjoyed flying this unusual aircraft because it was so much out of the ordinary run of conventional design. But I could never really see it as a serious test vehicle for a naval operational aircraft.

34 MITSUBISHI ZERO-SEN

Japanese philosophy on aerial combat gave a highly manoeuvrable aeroplane, but one that afforded its pilot little protection. ERIC BROWN

ALTHOUGH during and for a period after World War II, I had the opportunity to fly almost every type of British, American, and German operational fighter, I felt there would be little or no hope of ever getting my hands on a Japanese fighter for comparison.

The chance came in an unexpected way when I was despatched to Renfrew Airfield in April 1946 to deliver a US Navy Grumman Tigercat, which had been on loan to RAE Farnborough, and was to be prepared for return to America on a ship already in the Clyde. It was also my brief to examine a captured A6M5 model of the infamous Zero, which had established a formidable reputation in

the Pacific theatre. This aircraft had arrived some days earlier aboard the same ship that was to carry the Tigercat. The Americans had given permission for it to be disembarked for examination and any necessary anti-corrosive treatment, before it was reshipped to cross the Atlantic.

The shipment preparation was being undertaken by a small detachment of US Navy mechanics, assisted by a party from the nearby Royal Naval aircraft repair yard at Abbotsinch. I soon found that there were no specific instructions that the Zero was not to be flown, although it appeared to be the US Navy's intention to test fly it in America. Indeed it might already have been flown by the

The ubiquitous and highly successful Japanese Zero with a kill loss ratio of 12:1.

The Zero could turn
tighter than virtually
any other fighter in
World War II.

Americans as it had some of their instruments replacing Japanese ones in the cockpit.

The situation was therefore ripe for the Nelsonic eye treatment, and this was not difficult in the circumstances. I arranged for a couple of engine run-ups to be carried out in the afternoon, so that any engine noise in the evening would not cause curious investigation. These run-ups gave an ideal opportunity to familiarise myself with the cockpit layout and engine starting procedure, and the Zero was then left outside the hangar to show it was still being worked on. Thus the scene was set

for the dog watches when most law abiding citizens had departed for home or the nearest bar. As party to the plot, the Zero had no nationality markings. These had been obliterated by the aircraft's captors and not replaced so far with their own.

The Zero was to my mind a beautiful looking aeroplane, very reminiscent of the Fw 190. This impression was further strengthened by the wide track undercarriage and layout of the cockpit, from which a very good view was obtained round the neatly cowled 1,130hp Nakajima Sakae 21 air-cooled radial. The view was enhanced by the absence of bullet-proof glass in the windscreen.

The fourteen-cylinder engine had a gear-driven two-speed supercharger and a downdraught carburettor with automatic mixture and boost control. It drove a Hamilton-type three-blade constant speed airscrew, and purred very smoothly on start-up.

The aircraft had split-type ailerons, and split-type wide-chord flaps which could extend to 60°. The latter feature was needed in a shipborne aeroplane, and another advantageous point for a deck-lander was that the propeller had a large ground clearance of 2ft (61cm) with the tail down, so there was little chance of the blades striking the deck during arresting. All controls were unsealed and fabric covered and there was a small horn on the rudder. For take-off there was a tailwheel lock fitted.

The cockpit layout was good and generally followed the British pattern. Fore-and-aft adjustment of the seat and rudder pedals was excellent, as was the position of the plain uncluttered control column. The brakes were of the toe-operated type, but the main criticism I had of the cockpit was the crude hood lock, which would have been suspect under catapult acceleration or arrested deceleration.

The Zero was principally a naval aircraft and I looked at it critically from that aspect. The view for deck landing was good average, rather similar to the Wildcat, and I liked the large throttle quadrant as well as the conveniently positioned elevator trim. There was no friction in the control circuits and I generally felt very comfortable and that I was in a pilot's aeroplane. In this particular example of the Zero there was no arrester hook fitted, although normally it would lie just forward of the tail wheel.

The most astonishing features of the Zero were its lack of armour for the pilot's seat, and its three non-self-sealing fuel tanks, one in the fuselage just forward of the cockpit, and one in each inner wing, with a total capacity of 130gal (591 litres).

This was all part of the design philosophy employed by the American-trained designer Jiro Horikoshi to keep the Zero's weight down to a minimum to obtain the fighter manoeuvrability demanded by the Japanese Naval Air Staff as their prime requirement. Such a philosophy was almost traditional Japanese thinking that attack is the best form of defence. Although it paid great dividends in the Chinese conflict and in the initial stages of the Pacific war against the Americans, it was to prove an Achilles heel when the American aircraft increased their fire-power and performance.

Part of the technique of keeping down the Zero's weight involved the liberal use of the newly created ESD (extra super duralumin) to lighten the airframe. Other technical tricks were employed in the lightweight aim, but these were to prove a hindrance to mass production.

The Zero made its first flight on 1 April 1939 and the date was perhaps significant in that its early success in air combat over the Chinese mainland lulled the Japanese into thinking they had got the magic formula for fighter success.

The original models of the Zero had foldable wing tips for stowage in the confined hangars of aircraft carriers. But since these same models suffered from poor aileron control at high speeds, the wing tips were permanently removed to alleviate this fault.

The A6M5 was such a clipped version and had the Allied code name 'Hamp', although it later became generally known as the Zeke 52. It first appeared in operational service in the autumn of 1943, and more of this model were produced than of any other Zero sub-type.

On a walk around the aircraft I noted some of its main features. The elevators and rudder were fabric covered, and although the elevators had controllable trim tabs, the rudder trim tab was only adjustable on the ground. Shades of the Me 109! There were two 7.7mm guns in the engine cowling. synchronised to fire through the airscrew, and two 20mm cannon in the wings. Each wing had two watertight compartments, and there

The Mitsubishi Zeke 52 was outclassed in performance and firepower by many American fighters. However, its light weight made it highly manoeuvrable.

The pilot looks comfortable in this Zero, but for most Japanese pilots it was virtually a 'tin coffin'.

was a canvas bag in the rear fuselage for flotation. The deck arrester hook lay flush with the fuselage just forward of the tail wheel, which was partly retractable. The most striking feature of the aircraft, however, was the incredibly thin gauge of the fuselage alloy skin. The wing skin seemed of a heavier gauge.

The cockpit layout was neat, with only two unusual features. There was no canopy emergency release, and there was a flotation valve which was normally kept open, but in emergency when ditching was imminent it was closed by the pilot to trap air at atmospheric pressure in the entire flotation system. However, these functions would hopefully only be of academic interest to me.

I have seldom awaited a flight with greater anticipation, partly because of the enviable reputation of the Zero, and partly because the propriety of the situation was somewhat dubious.

When all activity on the airfield seemed to have ceased I taxied out hoping I looked like a Sea Fury in disguise, and took off very smartly in every sense of the word, for the take-off run was incredibly short. Hydraulic retraction of the undercarriage was not particularly fast, but once it was up, the rate of climb was high for a piston-engined fighter, probably of the order of 4,500ft/min (1372m/min).

Time was short, so I did not climb above 10,000ft (3,050m), but the other reason was that my oxygen tube did not match the Japanese socket. I did a flat out run at that height and was not overimpressed with the result, clocking around 300mph (483km/h).

However, it was manoeuvrability I was most interested in, and this was superb. I stalled it first to check whether there were any violent characteristics, but this proved very straightforward, so the Zero could be pulled into very tight turns and

'g' stalled with little likelihood of a resultant spin. Acrobatics in the looping plane were beautiful to execute, but the overall control characteristics were not as good as I had expected. The ailerons produced only a moderate rate of roll, and there were considerable directional trim changes with power and speed so that constant use of a rather sensitive rudder was necessary. The other disappointment was the rather slow acceleration in the dive which must have been a combat shortcoming.

In manoeuvring this nippy little fighter my lasting impression is of the noise emanating from the fuselage, rather like the sound produced when one pushes on the side of a biscuit tin. This was presumably due to the panting of the light alloy skin, but was somewhat disconcerting.

For landing I was of course interested in the Zero as a carrier-borne aircraft. It was very good indeed with a surprisingly good view, effective lateral control, a responsive throttle, draggy flaps, and a good resilient undercarriage. The landing speed was 81mph (130km/h) on the US-fitted airspeed indicator.

A half-hour flight is hardly the basis on which to deliver judgement on a high performance fighter, but I'll stick my neck out and say that this was one of the most enjoyable aeroplanes I have ever handled. When it came into service in 1943 the Zeke 52 was already outclassed in performance and firepower by the American Hellcats, Corsairs, Thunderbolts, Mustangs, and Lightnings. But never excelled by any in manoeuvrability. The Zero must indeed have been a wonderful fighter in its early days, and the feeling of invincibility of the Japanese pilots is easy to understand. But that same aeroplane was to become a tin coffin for these same pilots in the later years of World War II because of its total vulnerability to cannon fire.

Sic transit gloria!

35 NORTH AMERICAN MUSTANG III

Best escort fighter of World War II, with a fine combat record. Quite tricky to land. ERIC BROWN

THE MUSTANG I single-seat fighter was a good looking aeroplane, more angular than the Spitfire, but with the same sleek appearance of a thoroughbred. It was powered by an Allison V-1710-F3R twelve-cylinder liquid-cooled engine of 1,150hp driving a three-blade airscrew, so was comparable to the Spitfire V.

We had a Mustang I at RAE Farnborough for performance and handling trials. These showed it to be considerably inferior to the Spitfire V at high altitude, and also in its manoeuvrability, particularly with regard to rate of roll, although these faults were magnificently improved in the superb Mustang III.

The standard for fighter rate of roll in World War II had really been set by the Focke-Wulf 190, and in an attempt to find the correct lateral control formula the RAE Mustang I, AG393, was fitted with linearly geared aileron tabs. I flew this aircraft at five different gearing ratios, and on the fourth attempt the magic formula was found and we had a set of ailerons even lighter and more effective than those of the Fw 190.

By the time these experiments were made the

North American Mustang I (AG633) of 2 Squadron, 24 July 1942. *RAF Museum Hendon.*

North American Mustang

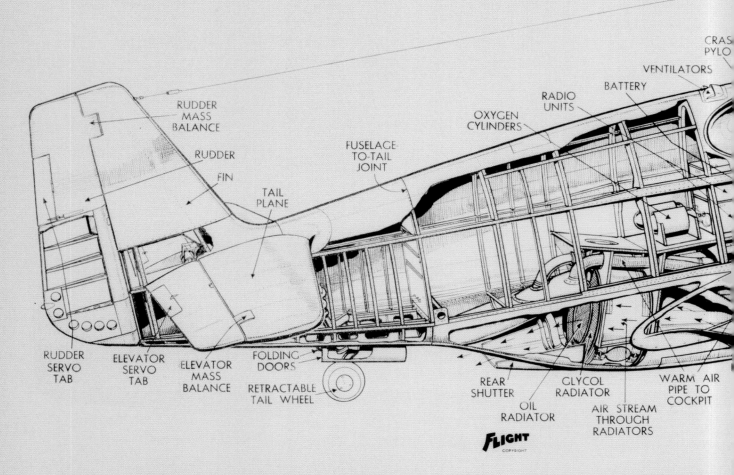

RUDDER MASS BALANCE

RUDDER

FIN

TAIL PLANE

FUSELAGE-TO-TAIL JOINT

OXYGEN CYLINDERS

RADIO UNITS

BATTERY

VENTILATORS

CRAS PYLO

RUDDER SERVO TAB

ELEVATOR SERVO TAB

ELEVATOR MASS BALANCE

FOLDING DOORS

RETRACTABLE TAIL WHEEL

REAR SHUTTER

OIL RADIATOR

GLYCOL RADIATOR

AIR STREAM THROUGH RADIATORS

WARM AIR PIPE TO COCKPIT

In the tests on the Lightning, Thunderbolt and Mustang at RAE early in 1944, only the P-51B Mustang achieved a Mach number comparable to the Me 109 and Fw 190.

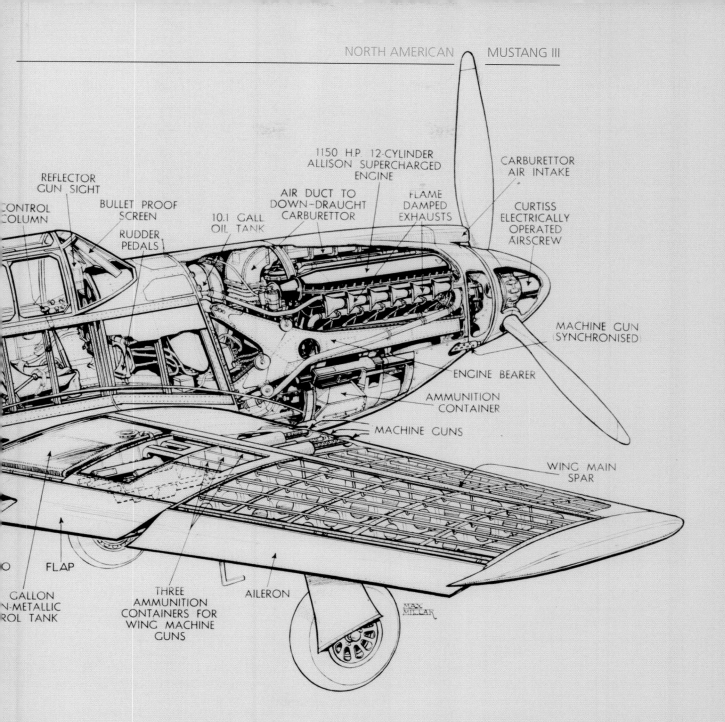

REFLECTOR
GUN SIGHT

CONTROL
COLUMN

BULLET PROOF
SCREEN

RUDDER
PEDALS

10.1 GALL
OIL TANK

AIR DUCT TO
DOWN-DRAUGHT
CARBURETTOR

1150 H.P. 12-CYLINDER
ALLISON SUPERCHARGED
ENGINE

FLAME
DAMPED
EXHAUSTS

CARBURETTOR
AIR INTAKE

CURTISS
ELECTRICALLY
OPERATED
AIRSCREW

MACHINE GUN
(SYNCHRONISED)

ENGINE BEARER

AMMUNITION
CONTAINER

MACHINE GUNS

WING MAIN
SPAR

FLAP

GALLON
N-METALLIC
ROL TANK

THREE
AMMUNITION
CONTAINERS FOR
WING MACHINE
GUNS

AILERON

MAX
MILLAR

201

The P-51B Mustang III with the Merlin engine, proved to be the finest escort fighter in the European war theatre.

Mustang III was already in service, and it had a rate of roll only slightly inferior to the Fw 190. However, the greatest advance in the Mk III over the Mk I was the fitting of the Merlin engine and a four-blade airscrew. The original conversion was made in Great Britain by Rolls-Royce by the installation of a Merlin 63 in a Mustang II (a slightly higher powered Allison version of the Mk I).

The success of the conversion was such that North American redesigned the P-51 to take the 1,520hp Packard V-1650-3 (Packard-built Merlin 68, with two-speed two-stage supercharger and aftercooler). The airframe was strengthened to take the new engine, the radiator installation redesigned, and new ailerons fitted. The new P-51B first went into action in mid-December 1943. Then followed the P-51D Mustang IV with the blister-type sliding hood and a modified rear fuselage, including a small dorsal extension to the fin.

Actually the RAF's Mustang IIIs had already been modified in Britain by the introduction of the Malcolm backward-sliding bulged cockpit hood, which was a very marked improvement on the original hinged canopy.

A Mustang III, serial No.KH505, was allocated to RAE for high speed research, and this showed up some unpleasant compressibility effects. Indeed the aircraft was eventually lost in failing to recover from a high Mach number dive, killing the Canadian pilot, Sqn Ldr E.B. Gale.

In such dives compressibility effects set in at M=0.71 with a slight vibration of the aircraft and buffeting of the controls, accompanied by a slight nose-down pitching moment. These symptoms increased in intensity up to M=0.75, which was the limit imposed for service use. Above M=0.75 a porpoising motion started and increased in intensity together with the other effects up to M=0.80, when the nose-down pitch became so strong that it required a two-handed pull force for recovery.

However, the Mustang III was an effective fighter over Europe and a pleasant aeroplane to fly. The cockpit was neatly laid out and not the usual over-large American style. View ahead on the ground was poor, so for taxying the nose had to be swung from side to side, but this was made easy by virtue of the tail-wheel being capable of being locked to the rudder controls and steered over a range of six degrees either side. This steerable position was achieved by holding the control column past the neutral position.

For take-off the elevator was trimmed five degrees back, the rudder five degrees right and the ailerons neutral. The fuel cock was set to MAIN TANKS and the master booster pump to EMERGENCY. The supercharger was set to AUTO, the carburettor air intake to RAM AIR and the radiator and oil cooler shutter to AUTOMATIC.

The stick was held back as the engine was opened up to 61in Hg boost, 3,000rpm, and this helped eliminate swing. The aircraft was very blind forward during the early part of the take-off run, but got off smartly in the tail-down attitude. Actually a normal take-off could be comfortably made using only 46in boost.

The master booster pump was switched to NORMAL before commencing the climb at 160mph (000km/h). The aircraft was positively stable about all three axes, and rate of climb at 46in. boost, 2,700 rpm was high.

The performance in level flight will be commented on later, but suffice it to say at this stage that the Mustang III was very nippy indeed. The Americans in Europe used the aircraft as long range escort for their daylight Flying Fortress raids and for this purpose it carried a 71gal (323 litres) auxiliary tank in the fuselage. This made the Mustang longitudinally unstable, and the Mk III had a strong tendency to tighten up in turns. The stability problem was not eased by having sensitive elevator trim tabs, but it was considerably alleviated in the Mk IV by having an inertia weight fitted in the elevator control circuit.

The stalling characteristics of the Mk III were mild without fuel in the fuselage tank, with slight tail buffeting at some 3–4mph (5–6km/h) before the actual all-up stall at 90mph when the right wing dropped gently. The all-down stall occurred at 75mph (121km/h). With full fuselage tank there was no buffet stall warning, but a series of stick reversals just before the wing fell sharply.

The Mk IV with full fuselage tank stalled at 105mph (170km/h) (all up) and 96mph (154km/h) (all down). In high speed stalls either wing could drop very rapidly, preceded by pronounced juddering.

Landing the Mustang was much trickier than the Spitfire. The flaps were lowered 20 degrees at any speed below 275mph (443km/h) until speed was reduced to 170mph (274km/h) when the undercarriage and full flaps were lowered, and the master booster pump set to EMERGENCY. Approach on the Mk III was made at 105mph (170km/h); at this speed the view was very bad, and non-existent ahead when holding off to land. The high rebound ratio undercarriage made a three-point landing a very tricky proposition. Thereafter the aircraft was directionally unstable on the landing run, although good brakes and a tail wheel lock helped to ease these skittish tendencies.

In the summer of 1944 a new menace appeared in the British skies when the Germans launched the V-1 flying bomb, dubbed the 'doodlebug' by the long-suffering English. It flew at about 1,000ft (305m) at around 400mph (644km/h) and posed a nasty problem to our air defences. It was a small target, equalling or exceeding the top speed of our current fighters so that they had to be in an advantageous position to overtake it. Furthermore our fighters were all piston-engined and the V-I had an impulse duct engine – in effect a crude jet engine. The V-1 was also not easily detected by radar because of its size and low height.

The 'doodlebug' chaser squadrons of Spitfires, Mustangs, Tempests, and Mosquitoes were polishing their paintwork and fairing all excrescences in the faint hope of picking up a few mph in speed. But the real hope lay in improved engine performance, so a crash programme was started at RAE Farnborough in conjunction with the engine manufacturers.

In the main the engines were given an emergency rating based on a short burst of full throttle using 150 octane aromatic fuel and giving a boost much greater than that used for take-off.

This was a very exciting test project because it meant full-power level flight runs at 200ft (61m) until the aircraft's speed had settled at a maximum. I found the whole thing rather exhilarating, like doing a series of World Speed Record runs in a hot rod version of a standard production fighter. However, it had its hairy moments and I had to bale out of a Tempest V when the engine blew up and caught fire.

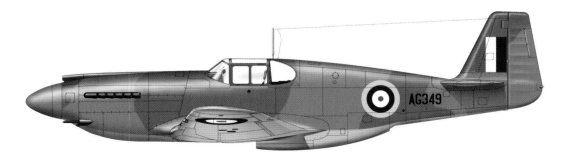

North American NA-37 Mustang Mk I, AG349, fifth production aircraft delivered to UK, late 1941. © *Richard Caruana* (scale 1:72).

Pilot's notes: North American P-51B III

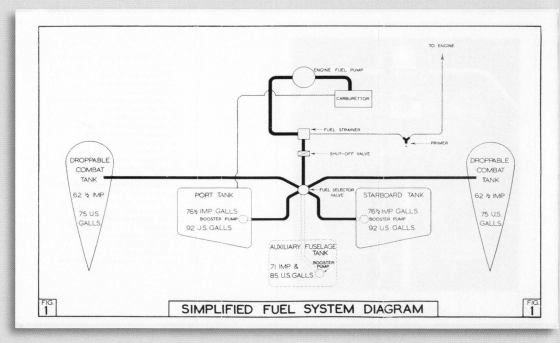

Fig 2:

Instrument panel

1. Bomb control handle
2. Boost override (inoperative)
3. RI compass
4. Undercarriage warning light test button
5. Undercarriage warning light
6. Bomb release button
7. Oxygen EMERGENCY control
8. Oxygen AUTOMIX control
9. Oxygen demand regulator
10. Oxygen pressure warning light
11. Fluorescent lights rheostat
12. Hydraulic pressure gauge
13. Undercarriage emergency knob
14. Supercharger gear-change warning light
15. Supercharger gear-change switch

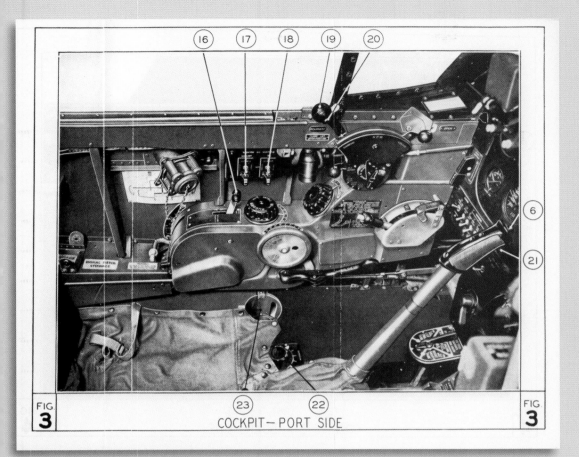

COCKPIT—PORT SIDE

FIG. 3   FIG. 3

Fig 3:

Cockpit – port side

6 Bomb release button
16 Carburettor air intake control
17 Coolant radiator manual switch
18 Oil cooler manual switch
19 Throttle lever
20 Press-to-transmit switch
21 Gunfiring button
22 Windscreen defroster control
23 Fuel contents gauge for left main tank

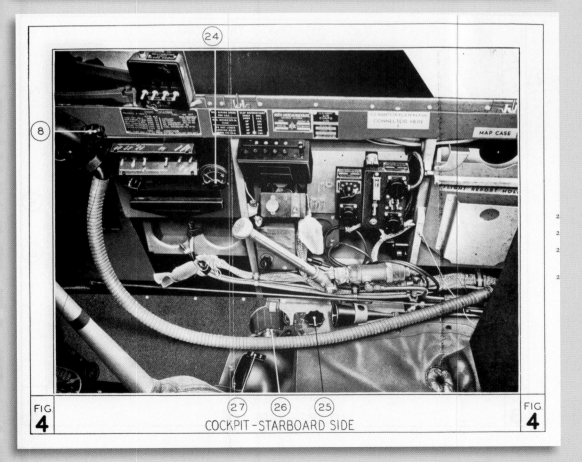

COCKPIT–STARBOARD SIDE

Fig 4:

Cockpit – starboard side

8 Oxygen AUTOMIX control
24 Ammeter
25 Cabin warm air control
26 Fuel contents gauge for right wing tank
27 Cabin cold air control

The comparative results I achieved on the three single-engine day fighters are worth recording. The Spitfire XIV with its Griffon boosted to +19lb (8.6kg) reached 365mph (587km/h), the Tempest V with its Sabre boosted to +10¼lb (4.6kg) managed 405mph (652km/h), but the Mustang III with its Merlin boosted to +25lb(11.3kg) peaked at 420mph (676km/h).

The Mosquitoes used were Mk XIXs with radar in the nose, but their Merlins were only boosted to +18lb (8.1kg), since they operated at night when an engine failure is less desirable. The night interception problem was helped by both their own AI radar and the flashes of flame from the V-1's tail cone, making up to some extent for the Mosquito's top speed of 330mph (531km/h) at 1,000ft (305m).

Although the Mustang III stole the laurels for speed as a 'doodlebug' chaser, the standard Spitfire XIV was in fact faster than the standard Mustang III and IV at operational height, but only by some 10–15mph (16–24km/h). However, the fastest of all the Mustangs may have been the twin fuselage version, which was an experiment aimed at solving the fatigue problem of long-range escort flights. Both pilots had sets of controls, one pilot to fly the long legs and the other to take over in the combat zone. No one has said what happens if the ferry pilot gets nervous in the heat of combat and thinks the combat pilot should be taking evasive action in the opposite direction. A mind boggling prospect!

The US Navy did limited deck landing trials on an aircraft carrier with a Mustang, but these were abandoned due to the aircraft's obvious unsuitability for the role. The appalling view on the approach and high rebound ratio undercarriage made it a non-starter as a naval aircraft.

Certainly in any listing of the great single-engine, single-seat fighters of the piston engine era, the Mustang must rank in the top five. It was nice to fly and a delight to fight in and its combat record speaks for itself. In the European zone it was respected and indeed feared by an enemy that itself had some superb fighter designs. It was undoubtedly the finest fighter produced by the United States in World War II, as was evidenced by the fact that 15,586 were built. This was an extraordinary record when one considers that the NA-73 prototype was designed and the airframe built in 117 days. The result was an aeroplane with an outstanding performance in terms of both speed and range.

The first Merlin-engined Mustang, AL975/G, flew on 13 October 1942.

One of the P-51Ds supplied to the RAF and RAAF in 1944/45 under Lend-Lease. Its bubble canopy and cut-down rear fuselage greatly improved visibility for the pilot.

36 NORTH AMERICAN F-86 SABRE

Great harmony of control, which reached handling perfection in the F-86E with the flying tail. ERIC BROWN

A s soon as I saw the F-86 Sabre I instinctively knew I was looking at the Spitfire of the jet age. It had the same sleek aerodynamic lines and elegance of a true thoroughbred. The place of our meeting was the Naval Air Test Center at Patuxent River in the USA, and this aircraft was an F-86A-5, kept for chase plane duties and general handling in Flight Test. In consequence I had the pleasure to fly it many times, starting with my first on 26 September 1951.

The Sabre was a 35 degree swept low-wing single-seat interceptor fighter, powered by an axial flow J47-GE-13 jet engine, which in the A-5 model produced 5,200lb (2,359kg) static thrust. The wing span of 37.5ft (11.4m) was only eight inches more than that of the Spitfire. With an

The F-86E Sabre with its 'flying tail', which consisted of the tail-plane and elevator combined as one unit.

North American Sabre Mk 4

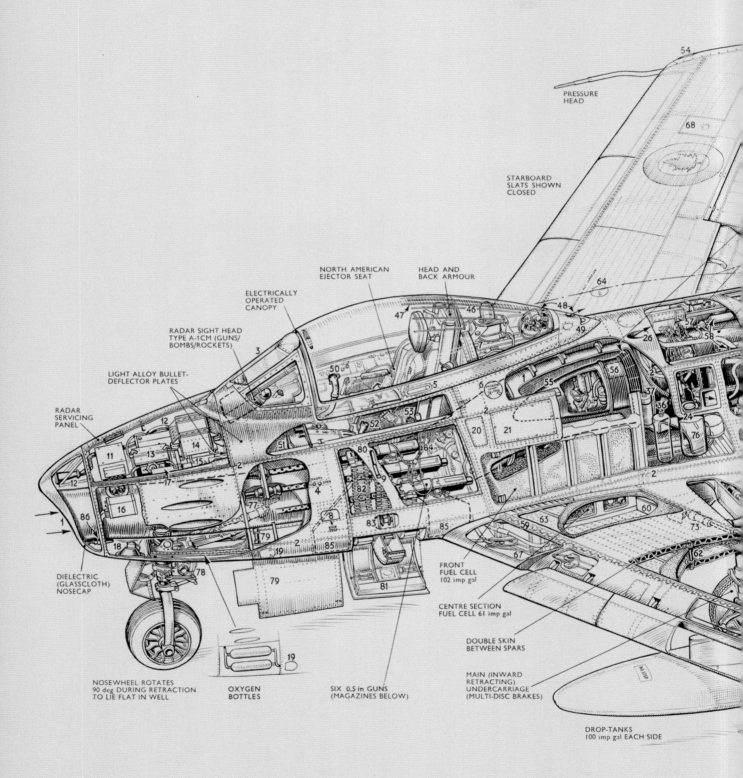

54

PRESSURE
HEAD

68

STARBOARD
SLATS SHOWN
CLOSED

NORTH AMERICAN
EJECTOR SEAT

HEAD AND
BACK ARMOUR

64

ELECTRICALLY
OPERATED
CANOPY

48

47

46

49

RADAR SIGHT HEAD
TYPE A-1CM (GUNS/
BOMBS/ROCKETS)

26

57

3

58

LIGHT ALLOY BULLET-
DEFLECTOR PLATES

50

5

6

55

56

37

RADAR
SERVICING
PANEL

12

53

52

51

20

21

36

24

76

11

13

14

15

2

80

84

2

2

12

17

81

9

2

79

82

85

60

73

16

77

8

83

85

59

63

1

86

18

19

85

67

62

DIELECTRIC
(GLASSCLOTH)
NOSECAP

78

79

FRONT
FUEL CELL
102 imp gal

81

CENTRE SECTION
FUEL CELL 61 imp gal

DOUBLE SKIN
BETWEEN SPARS

NOSEWHEEL ROTATES
90 deg DURING RETRACTION
TO LIE FLAT IN WELL

OXYGEN
BOTTLES

19

SIX 0.5 in GUNS
(MAGAZINES BELOW)

MAIN (INWARD
RETRACTING)
UNDERCARRIAGE
(MULTI-DISC BRAKES)

DROP-TANKS
100 imp gal EACH SIDE

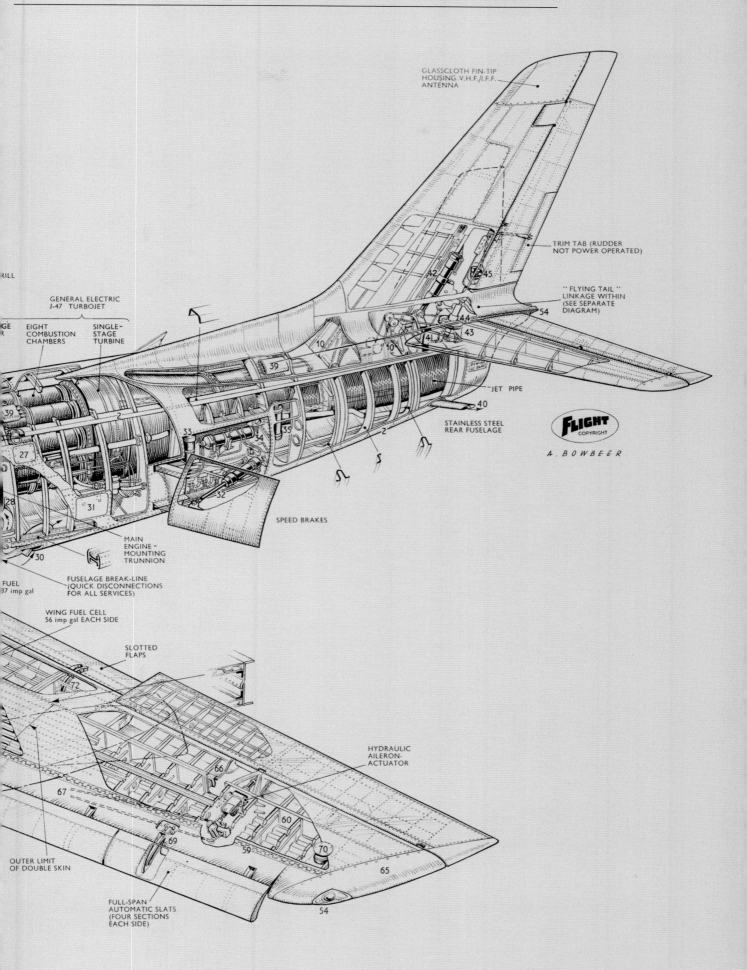

GLASSCLOTH FIN-TIP
HOUSING V.H.F./I.F.F.
ANTENNA

TRIM TAB (RUDDER
NOT POWER OPERATED)

GENERAL ELECTRIC
J-47 TURBOJET

EIGHT
COMBUSTION
CHAMBERS

SINGLE-
STAGE
TURBINE

"FLYING TAIL"
LINKAGE WITHIN
(SEE SEPARATE
DIAGRAM)

42

45

44

54

43

41

10

10

39

39

JET PIPE

40

27

33

34

35

2

STAINLESS STEEL
REAR FUSELAGE

2

31

32

28

FLIGHT
COPYRIGHT

A. BOWBEER

30

MAIN
ENGINE-
MOUNTING
TRUNNION

SPEED BRAKES

FUEL
37 imp gal

FUSELAGE BREAK-LINE
(QUICK DISCONNECTIONS
FOR ALL SERVICES)

WING FUEL CELL
56 imp gal EACH SIDE

SLOTTED
FLAPS

72

HYDRAULIC
AILERON-
ACTUATOR

66

67

60

69

59

70

OUTER LIMIT
OF DOUBLE SKIN

65

FULL-SPAN
AUTOMATIC SLATS
(FOUR SECTIONS
EACH SIDE)

54

An F-86A Sabre.
Eric Brown flew the
F-86A Sabre at the US
Naval Air Test Center at
Patuxent River.

AUW of 14,100lb (6,396kg) the wing loading was 49lb/sq ft (239kg/m^2) It was fitted with full-span slats, variable position speed brakes, power-boosted ailerons (50:1 ratio) and elevators (7:1 ratio), and an adjustable tail-plane whose angle of incidence could be varied between +1 degree and -10 degrees, and which was very powerful in altering longitudinal trim. Only the ailerons had manual reversion in case of power-boost failure, for there was no need for it on the elevators in view of their low boost ratio and the adjustable tail-plane.

My first flight was like an initiation ceremony because the Flight Test pilots were all daring me to boom the base commander's house in a super-sonic dive. This is easier said than done because the sonic bang does not hit where the aircraft is pointed, so I reckoned the Admiral's house was safe.

I climbed this lovely bird like an eagle to 43,000ft (13,106m) and half rolled into a 60 degree dive right over the huge airfield. As speed rose to M=0.91 there was a slight nose-down trim change, and at M=0.94 a wing heaviness occurred which required about half aileron deflection to prevent roll, but aileron position returned to normal at M=0.97. At M=0.99 a slight longitudinal instability was felt, but this rapidly disappeared at M=1.0.

Due to position error from the location of the pitot head in the standard Sabre, it was necessary to dive to an indicated Mach number of 1.15 to actually exceed the speed of sound. However the Flight Test Sabre had a modified boom pitot which reduced this error and an indicated M=1.12 gave the magic sonic bang. To me that was the achievement of a goal I had been struggling to attain for at least five years.

There was a slight aftermath to this event that made it more unforgettable. I didn't get the Admiral's house with my sonic bang but unfortunately got a bull's eye on his garden hothouse. I had only been on the base a week and had not yet met Admiral Davis, so my interview was accelerated. He knew of the transonic work I had been doing at Farnborough so was very sympathetic, but discipline had to be upheld so he fined me twenty dollars for the damage to Navy property. However, the Flight Test boys decided to pay up their bets and so I was in surplus on the whole deal, and the Admiral, who had arrived on the base the same day as myself, invited me to become his ten-pin bowling partner. No wonder I feel affectionate towards the Sabre.

I should go on to say that recovery from a sonic dive required use of the variable incidence tail-plane, because of the ineffectiveness of the elevator. Recovery could actually be made on elevator alone, but this required very large angles of movement which tended to cause rivets to be shed from the trailing-edge. The speed brakes were not very effective and gave a nose-up pitch, which increased appreciably with speed, so were of some help in recovery.

Indeed the longitudinal manoeuvring of the F-86A above M=0.97 was almost completely dependent on the electrically operated trim-switch controlled adjustable tail-plane. The thumb control trimmer switch on the stick was too high geared, and although the manual trimmer control was better it was badly located.

On 20 February 1952 I was chase plane in the Sabre for some high speed demonstrations of a Grumman F9F-2, fitted with magnesium wing panels, when I had a total hydraulic failure at M=0.85 at 10,000ft (3,050m), just after having actuated the dive brakes. The first intimation of the failure was when a fairly severe left wing heaviness was felt at 450mph (724km/h). The aileron boost was immediately shut off and the wing heaviness trimmed out as speed was reduced. The effect on the elevator was a reasonably comfortable increase in force, but it could have been a more difficult situation at higher Mach numbers.

The ailerons were extremely light, but lacking in feel, and certainly too sensitive for instrument flying, particularly as they were not self-centering. Manual reversion gave sufficient lateral control below 200mph (322km/h), but later aircraft with short chord ailerons gave acceptable control in manual up to 375mph (603km/h).

The Sabre had superb handling characteristics, but lateral and longitudinal stability were neutral, which meant that instrument flying required much concentration. It did not snake as badly as most contemporary jets which made it a good gun platform. It had a perfect rate of roll, splendid manoeuvrability, and was very docile at low speed where the slats began to open at 190mph (306km/h) and were fully open at 145mph (233km/h). Its general performance was very impressive.

Even on the ground the Sabre was faultless to handle, with its beautiful view and tricycle undercarriage with nose-wheel steering. Hydraulic pressure was applied in the nose-wheel steering unit through a shut-off valve actuated by a push-button switch on the control stick grip. When the switch was depressed with the nose-wheel on the ground and the shock strut compressed, the nose-wheel could be turned approximately 21 degrees either side of centre by rudder pedal action. Before the steering mechanism could be engaged, the rudder pedals had to be co-ordinated with the nose-wheel position.

Not quite perfection, but that was on the way. The F-86E was fitted with a 'flying-tail', which consisted of the tail-plane and elevator combined as one unit, with the elevator geared to increase the effectiveness of the horizontal tail at large deflections. The 'flying-tail' and ailerons were controlled by the pilot with two independent, irreversible constant-pressure power hydraulic systems which were also independent of the normal aircraft system. The 'flying-tail' and ailerons power systems incorporated mechanical force (spring bungee) arrangements for pilot artificial feel.

The F-86E in which Colonel Ascani broke the world speed record. It had a red fluorescent nose and fuselage brakes.

Pilot's notes: North American Sabre Mk 4

Fig 1:

Cockpit – forward view

1 Undercarriage selector lever
2 Machmeter
3 Altimeter
4 Undercarriage emergency ground-lock override
5 Parking brake
6 Radio compass indicator
7 Fuel filter de-icer push-button
8 Fuel filter de-icer warning light
9 Accelerometer
10 Airspeed indicator
11 Inverter failure warning light
12 Hydraulic pressure gauge
13 Inverter failure warning light
14 Hydraulic pressure gauge selector switch
15 Inverter failure warning light
16 Control surface alternate system 'on' warning light
17 A-4 sight
18 Oil pressure gauge
19 Take-off trim indicator light
20 Jet pipe temperature gauge
21 Artificial horizon
22 Fuel pressure gauge
23 Fire warning lights
24 Stand-by compass
25 Fire warning system test push-button
26 Tachometer
27 Fuel flowmeter
28 Cockpit pressure altimeter
29 Rudder pedal adjuster release
30 Rudder pedal indicator
31 Fuel contents gauge
32 Vertical speed indicator
33 Clock
34 Loadmeter
35 Generator failure warning light
36 Voltmeter

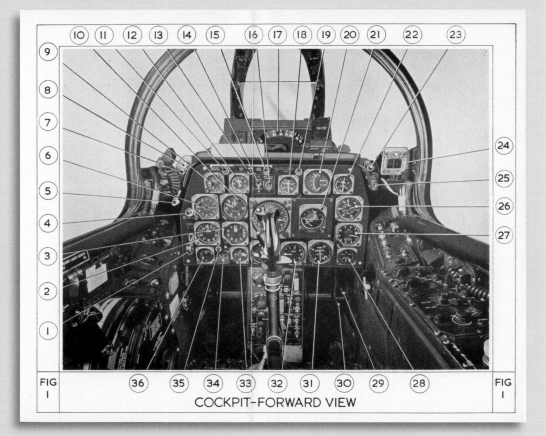

COCKPIT–FORWARD VIEW

COCKPIT–PORT SIDE

FIG 3 COCKPIT–STARBOARD SIDE FIG 3

Fig 2:

Cockpit – port side

37 Drop tanks pressurising cock
38 Ammunition compartment overheat warning light
39 Air-inlet selector
40 Ammunition compartment heat emergency shut-off
41 Circuit-breaker panel
42 Windscreen anti-ice overheat warning light
43 Cockpit air inlet
44 Windscreen anti-icing control
45 Hood auxiliary defrost lever
46 Air brakes control
47 Gunsight caging push-button
48 Rocket projector release control
49 Air brakes emergency closing control
50 Flap selector
51 Oxygen pressure gauge and flow indicator (aircraft up to serial no. XB.593)

52 Pressure head heater switch
53 Hood-operating switch
54 Undercarriage warning horn override
55 Undercarriage position indicator
56 Landing and taxy lamps switch
57 Rocket, bomb and drop tank jettison push-button
58 External load emergency mechanical jettison handle
59 Oxygen regulator pressure breathing knob (aircraft up to serial no. XB.593)
60 Oxygen regulator diluter control handle (aircraft up to serial no. XB.593)
61 Throttle friction control
62 Throttle lever
63 Pilot's press-to-transmit push-button
64 Power controls hydraulic system changeover switch
65 Stand-by longitudinal trim switch
66 Rudder trim switch

67 Stand-by lateral trim switch
68 Cockpit pressure control switch
69 Cockpit pressure selector switch
70 Cockpit temperature selector rheostat
71 Cockpit temperature control switch
Note: Emergency fuel regulator switch, directly above throttle quadrant, is hidden by hood rail.

Fig 3:

Cockpit – starboard side

72 Nosewheel steering switch
73 Target selector push-button
74 Gun-firing trigger
75 Bomb/rocket release
76 Normal trim switch
77 Power controls hydraulic system manual override
78 Exterior lights BRIGHT/DIM switch
79 Engine starter emergency-stopping push-button

80 Battery-starter switch
81 Engine master switch
82 Generator re-set switch (guarded)
83 Relighting switch (guarded)
84 Fuel densitometer switch (guarded)
85 Stand-by compass light ON/OFF switch
86 Navigation and fuselage lights selector switch
87 VHF command radio control panel
88 Radio compass control panel
89 Cockpit main lighting switch
90 Cockpit auxiliary lighting switch
91 Consoles and armament panel lighting switch
92 IFF control panel

Sabres of 92 Squadron in formation. They were replaced by Hunters and Meteors in 1956.

An electrically powered alternate hydraulic system was provided to operate the controls if the normal system functioned incorrectly. Two hydraulic cylinders in tandem actuated the surface controls, each of these cylinders being hydraulically independent of the other so that loss of pressure to one cylinder did not affect the other. The primary control was an automatic electric transfer system, which automatically changed over to the alternate system if the normal system malfunctioned. The secondary electrical transfer system permitted the pilot to select either system for test or operation. A warning light on the instrument panel illuminated when the flight controls were operating on the alternate system.

I first flew the F-86E in November 1951 and the stick force per 'g' was excessive at intermediate and low speeds, and too low at high indicated airspeeds. However, the longitudinal feel system, which gave the pilot a change in force with stick travel and 'g' was later modified to give the change in force with changes in indicated airspeed.

I flew the modified F-86E a year later and its longitudinal control was then superb. Indeed harmony of control was beautiful with a stick force per 'g' of about five pounds throughout the speed range at mid-CG. Maximum rate of roll was 20 degrees per second at M=0.68 at 10,000ft (3,050m) and 223 degrees per second at M=0.78 at 30,000ft (9,144m).

The high Mach number characteristics had been

improved over those of the earlier F-86 models insofar as the longitudinal and lateral control effectiveness were concerned. The high altitude/high Mach number buffet boundary now had a considerable useable spread, for example the onset of buffet occurred at 3.5 'g' at M=0.90 at 35,000ft (10,668m). But the aircraft could be manoeuvred tactically up to 4.75 'g' under these conditions.

Recovery from a sonic dive was now straightforward with the 'flying-tail', but the wing dropping was still present. The American National Advisory Committee for Aeronautics tried to find a solution with the use of vortex generators. These are small wings placed perpendicular to a surface in a flow field in such a manner as to create vortices with their axes aligned in the flow direction. Vortex generators of the proper size and arrangements thus provided an intermixing of the retarded flow in the boundary layer with the higher energy farther from the surface, and hence tended to delay separation.

I got the opportunity to fly an F-86A fitted with vortex generators at Langley Field. I found the rapid increase in aileron stick force and angle required to hold the wings level above M=0.92 was generally reduced and practically eliminated for 1'g' flight with an arrangement of vortex generators at 35 per cent chord. The aircraft drag co-efficient penalty incurred was negligible.

The Sabre distinguished itself in the Korean War, which suited its short range, and it produced the leading ace in Captain Joseph McConnell, USAF, with his 16 victories. Even when fitted with two 100gal (454 litres) drop tanks I found the aircraft handled beautifully up to M=0.92 between 35,000ft (10,668m) and 32,000ft (9,754m). I have yet to meet any pilot who flew this aeroplane who did not have the highest praise for it. For my money, the F-86E is the greatest jet aircraft I have ever flown from a pure handing aspect. It set standards in stability and control which are still held up as ideals to attain.

A Sabre of 92 Squadron taking off at its base at Linton-on-Ouze.

37 NORTH AMERICAN AJ-1 SAVAGE

Carrier-borne nuclear bomber. Its complex hydraulic system malfunctioned often, making it a doubly lethal aircraft.

ERIC BROWN

THE AJ-1 Savage was an unusual aeroplane designed for an unusual task – take-off from an aircraft carrier with a nuclear bomb, to drop it in level flight from high altitude. Alternatively it was to carry 10,500lb (4,763kg) of conventional bombs. For this task North American designed a high-wing, three crew, attack bomber, powered by two 2,300hp R-2800-44W Double Wasp reciprocating engines with internal, single-speed, engine-driven turbo superchargers. In addition, a 4,600lb (2,087kg) static thrust centrifugal flow J33-A-10 turbo-jet, was located in the rear of the fuselage.

The outer wing panels and vertical tail could be folded for carrier hangar storage. The main legs of the undercarriage were of the 'walking' type, i.e. they could be displaced aft about two inches of oleo drag-strut travel to absorb the impact of a fly-in landing.

Three individual hydraulic systems supplied surface boost pressure in a ratio directly proportional to the forces required to overcome surface loads. The elevator boost ratio was 27:1, the aileron boost ratio 16:1, and the rudder boost ratio 57:1.

When aileron boost was inoperative a handle could be engaged to obtain a mechanical advantage of 2:1 for ease of aileron movement. In such a case aileron travel was restricted to one-half of normal, and stick play was present at the neutral position.

An electrical rudder limiting system prevented rudder deflection beyond a safe allowable minimum by regulating the amount of rudder boost pressure available at different airspeeds. Full rudder travel of 25 degrees was available below 160mph (257km/h), but as airspeed increased, the rudder angle at which boost became ineffective gradually decreased to 10 degrees at 230mph (370km/h). Above 310mph (499km/h) the boost limiting relief valve was actuated to limit boost

pressure available to some 15 per cent of maximum. High control forces then prevented the pilot from exceeding the safe allowable maximum of rudder deflection.

Internal fuel capacity was 1,041gal (4,734 litres), and jettisonable wing tip tanks could be fitted to increase this by another 500gal (2,272 litres).

I made my first flight in AJ-1, serial no.122594, on 11 March 1952 at Naval Air Test Center, Patuxent River. I was serving in Flight Test and had been assigned to this aircraft as one of the two Project Pilots. This was a big aeroplane by aircraft carrier standards with its span of 71ft 5in (22m) and a maximum all-up weight of 53,800lb (24,404kg), but it wasn't a bad looker for such bulk.

The cockpit was the most fearsomely complex I had seen to date, considering there was only one guy up there to sort it all out. I began to realise why I had been instructed to make my first handling flight using the reciprocating engines only. Most subsequent flights were made with all engines operative and were part of the test programme involving two AJ-1s, the others being serial nos. 122596 and 124161.

The first tests involved longitudinal stability and control, and showed that longitudinally the aircraft had always to be kept in trim lest the power boost fail and give high out-of-trim forces. The elevator break-out forces were of the order of 3lb (1.4kg), and stick force per 'g' was only 4½ lb at 316mph (509km/h) at 10,000ft (3,050m) at mid-centre of gravity. This was a dangerous state of affairs when considering that at aft CG the structural limit of the aircraft was reached with a mere 10lb (4.5kg) pull force. That type of aircraft should have a 10lb (4.5kg) per 'g' stick force.

With boost off, the longitudinal forces were unacceptable in all flight conditions.

The second set of tests involved lateral and directional stability and control. The maximum

boost on rate of roll was an unsatisfactory 42 degrees per second at 230mph (370km/h), but with boost off and 2:1 mechanical ratio operative it dropped to about 4 degrees per second for a 30lb (14kg) stick force. This was totally unacceptable for landing under any conditions. There was also a lot of adverse yaw with aileron deflection.

Directional stability became unsatisfactorily weak above 276mph (444km/h).

Stalling characteristics were next investigated and showed that mild elevator overbalance occurred at some 6mph (9.7km/h) before the stall in the powered approach and cruising configurations. The stall was characterised by a mild airframe buffet 3.5mph (5.6km/h) before the left wing dropped fairly sharply at 92mph (147km/h) in the landing configuration at 38,000lb (17,237kg).

This pre-stall overbalance became a vicious condition with the elevator boost OFF. If the aircraft was kept in trim right up to the overbalance point, a sudden rapid force reversal occurred necessitating an 80lb (36kg) push to hold the aircraft just off the stall – if indeed the pilot could react fast enough to prevent the stall occurring.

Disregarding this appalling feature, the take-off and landing characteristics were acceptable for carrier operations, except for poor lateral control. Deck landing approach speed was about 95–98mph (153–158km/h) at an all-up weight of 37,000lb (16,783kg) with the jet engine idling, and could be reduced to 86mph (138km/h) at an all-up weight of 35,000lb (15,786kg). At the 'cut' signal no pushover or flare was necessary to achieve a nice landing.

The Savage shows its lethal lines in flight.

On 13 November 1952 I took the Savage aboard the USS *Coral Sea*, and after a series of normal landings made three landings with one reciprocating engine plus the jet engine only. With the jet engine running at full throttle to keep asymmetric trim to a minimum, the approach speed was only 98mph (158km/h).

Shore tests I made showed that a carrier type landing was possible on one reciprocating engine only at an AUW of 37,000lb (16,783kg), at an approach speed of 104mph (167km/h) with three-quarters flap. But the margin for error was too small for this ever to be an allowable practice.

Catapult take-offs were carried out up to 53,800lb (24,404kg) AUW. My usual procedure was to have the normal elevator boost switch OFF and the emergency elevator boost switch ON in case a boost failure should occur with its inevitable disastrous results.

The performance was somewhat pedestrian, with a top speed of 328mph (528km/h) at 30,000ft (9,144m) and a time of 27½ minutes to climb to 20,000ft (6,096m). The service ceiling was 34,400ft (10,485m), but cooling of the reciprocating engines was marginal for high altitude operation. Range was 1,127miles (1,814km) at 274mph (441km/h) at 20,000ft (6,096m).

The Savage was a curious paradox in that it was a fairly reasonable aircraft when everything was functioning correctly. Indeed it had outstanding deck landing characteristics, but could rapidly change to a most lethal machine for the pilot to cope with when the complex hydraulic system malfunctioned, as it unfortunately was so prone to do.

Frankly, I considered the AJ-1 Savage to be unacceptable for service use by British standards, but the American system was such that the aircraft was already in service with limited clearances. It was up to Naval Air Test Center to expand these clearances in conjunction with the manufacturer. In consequence Flight Test offered many projected control system modifications, so it was going to be a long painful development process before the Savage reached full fruition, if ever.

In the event 55 AJ-1s were produced, and 55 AJ-2s, which had improved reciprocating engines and increased fuel tankage. These were followed by 30 specialist photographic reconnaissance versions. This limited production run tells its own story, but in fairness to North American the role of the Savage was a fleeting sign of the times.

Below: North American AJ-1 Savage.

Bottom: The mixed powerplant, carrier-borne Savage nuclear bomber in flight.

38 NORTHROP P-61A BLACK WIDOW

Docile handling characteristics and unusual lateral spoiler system made the P-61 a useful all-weather aeroplane. ERIC BROWN

The Black Widow's twin tailboom layout is the main design feature of this all-weather fighter.

THIS SINISTERLY NAMED aeroplane had indeed a somewhat sinister appearance, but this was as much due to its all black night fighter camouflage as to its shape, although the latter was not altogether conventional.

The P-61A, which arrived at RAE Farnborough in April 1944, was a shoulder-wing monoplane with twin tail booms extending aft from nacelles, each housing a Pratt & Whitney Double Wasp R-2800-65 eighteen-cylinder engine of 2,000hp.

The reason for our interest in this aircraft was its unusual lateral control system. This consisted of two small conventional ailerons, each with a trim tab, and four retractable spoilers, two each on the upper and lower wing surfaces. These spoilers were perforated metal scoop-shaped strips, which when not in use retracted into slots near the trailing edge. When raised they spoilt airflow and reduced the lift on one wing; this

was done by mechanical interconnection with the small upgoing aileron.

I first flew Black Widow serial no. 25496 on 4 April 1944 at an all-up weight of 27,600lb (12,519kg), carrying full fuel and two crew in addition to myself. The cockpit, like most American aircraft of that vintage, was large and roomy, and the view was good as with all 'trikes' in spite of a longish nose, which housed radar equipment.

Taxying was easy and the delightful purr of the Double Wasps oozed power, which was certainly needed on this aircraft, whose take-off was somewhat pedestrian. Once the undercarriage was up and the large landing flaps retracted from the TAKE-OFF position things began to improve performancewise, but hardly to an exciting degree. The rate of climb was mediocre, with a time of 13 minutes to 25,000ft (7,620m).

Cruise performance at 5,000ft (1,524m) with

Top: Ground crew adjusting the black Widow's powerful underbelly armament.

Above: The Black Widow was a docile aircraft, completely undeserving of its sinister name.

2,150rpm, and 29in Hg boost was 210mph (338km/h), and at that speed the aircraft had neutral stability in all three planes, which was hardly ideal for a night fighter.

The harmony of control was poor, the elevator being extremely heavy, and the rudder fairly heavy. The lateral control on the spoiler system was the aircraft's outstanding characteristic, and was very effective and positive throughout the entire speed range.

The small ailerons were light except in the last part of their travel, especially at the high end of the speed range. They seemed to me to be lacking in feel, however, for I trimmed the aircraft to allow it to assume various airspeeds. I then tried to gauge these speeds by aileron feel, but could get no real indication in this way whatsoever.

The complete lack of self-centering in the ailerons was also a little disconcerting, as was the lack of response in the first few degrees of stick movement. This varied from 20 degrees at 100mph (161km/h) to 5 degrees at 250mph (402km/h).

The trimmers in the cockpit were a mess, comprising three adjacent wheels not lying in their natural planes of movement but all upright side by side, and with no neutral pointer to line them up on. Bad enough by day, but for a night fighter – terrible!

Stalls carried out at 5,000ft (1,524m) were incredibly mild under all conditions from everything up to everything down, with ample warning in the form of heavy buffeting. The stall was not sharp and clearly defined, but was a wallowing system with a nose-down pitch, giving a moderate rate of sink in a series of stalled steps. Stalling speeds were 96mph (155km/h) (all up), 79mph (127km/h) (all down), and 72mph (116km/h) (all down with landing power of 2,000rpm and 19in. Hg boost).

The Black Widow made its contribution to aeronautical knowledge by being chosen by the Americans to conduct a series of thunderhead penetrations in the 'twister' area of the mid-West of that country.

The choice of this aircraft for such a hazardous task may seem strange in the light of its neutral stability characteristics. This made it tiring to fly on instruments for long periods, but the penetrations were of relatively short endurance.

The stability aspect was compensated for by other factors, such as the structural strength of the Black Widow. It was stressed to the American fighter specification of a limit load factor of 7.3 'g'. with a design ultimate factor of 1.5; the totally docile stalling characteristics; the effective spoiler control; the built-in radar; and the useful service-ceiling of 33,000ft (10,058m).

Apart from the radar the other aspects were very similar to those that made RAE choose a Spitfire for a similar task in the UK, and indeed a task that provided me with some of the most unpleasant moments of my flying career.

Entering a cumulo-nimbus thunder cell is something to be heartily discouraged unless your life is short of excitement. In pitch blackness my Spitfire was often tossed violently around like a toy, while at the same time being bombarded with hailstones and subject to the shattering noise of thunder at close quarters. Just to complete the demoniac scenario there were blinding lightning strikes, St Elmo's Fire circling the propeller, and occasional engine cutting from icing effects. The grave danger, of course, is that all these external distractions might divert the pilot's concentration from the job in hand of controlling the aircraft.

The Black Widow, by all accounts, came out of this assignment with flying colours and only superficial damage, although the damage to the crew's nerves was more serious. Certainly they affirmed that the spoiler control had stood up particularly well to the exacting demands on it.

Certainly our own tests with the Black Widow and the account of the American thunderhead penetrations might have impressed some UK designers, for a Halifax VI, serial no. NP715, was

Despite the name, this early Northrop P-61A is finished in standard USAAF Olive Drab. Later service versions were Glossy Jet Black all over. Even so, the aircraft still packed a mighty sting. Note that only part of the armament is seen here; there were four .50 calibre machine guns in the upper turret and four 20 mm cannon in the belly. *RAF Museum Hendon.*

fitted with similar spoiler-aileron controls. The Halifax system consisted of four closely adjacent scoop spoilers of 20ft 3in. (6.1m) total span, and of an average vertical height of about 6in (15cm), issuing from each wing at a distance well back to the chord behind the transition point. The spoilers actually decreased in height as they travelled outboard in order to conform to decreasing wing thickness.

A small tip aileron of 8ft 11in. (2.7m) span lay behind the two outboard spoilers of each wing. Extra flaps were fitted where the reduced aileron span left free trailing edge area normally occupied by the long-span ailerons on standard aircraft.

The spoiler lateral control system as applied to the Halifax was meant to achieve an improved coefficient of lift for landing by virtue of the auxiliary flaps that were now possible to be fitted.

There was little difference in lateral control effect compared to the standard Halifax, and the increase in lift coefficient showed in the reduction of stalling speed by 4mph (6km/h). The lowering of the auxiliary flaps gave a strong nose-down change of trim which could not be trimmed out sufficiently to effect a three-point landing. The crunch factor, however, was that the spoiler system could not overpower the torque effect of the engines if they were opened up below 160mph (257km/h), as in the case of the baulked landing.

Doubtless the spoiler system could have been improved on the Halifax, and the latter experiment did not negate the fact that the system was successful on the Black Widow and was later applied successfully to other types of aircraft.

To sum up, the Black Widow did not have the performance to be an operational success as a night fighter. But it was a completely docile aircraft with no really bad features to damn it, except perhaps one – shocking forward vision in rain due to the fact that the front windscreen panel was so far from the pilot's eyes that any mark came into focus and affected his view. Certainly it was completely undeserving of the sinister name it bore.

Northrop P-61A Black Widow, 42-5508/313, 419th Night Fighter Squadron, USAAF, Guadalcanal (Pacific Theatre), summer 1944. © *Richard Caruana* (scale 1:96).

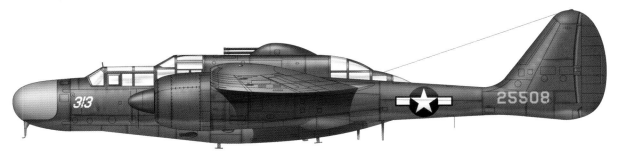

39 REID AND SIGRIST DESFORD

A docile but spritely little twin that would have made a superb primary trainer, but arrived too late for the wartime military scene. ERIC BROWN

OLLOWING the fall of the Third Reich, an abundance of revolutionary aeronautical ideas cascaded into the laps of the Allies, together with their brilliant innovators. The RAE Farnborough was a prime recipient of both and was soon putting them to work.

Two captured German aerodynamicists, who were attached to Aero Department, came up with a design study of a transonic aircraft to break through the, as yet still intact, sound barrier. It was expected to reach a Mach number of I.24 and a height of 60,000ft (18,288m). Basically the design was for a severely swept-wing aircraft built round a Rolls-Royce jet engine, with the pilot lying in a prone position in a nacelle inside the air intake duct, and with hydraulic skid landing gear.

All of a sudden our interest was concentrated on the prone piloting position. In this we had the expert advice of our next door neighbour, the RAF Institute of Aviation Medicine, and also of one of the German aerodynamicists who had

flown the prone position Berlin B.9 experimental aeroplane.

You don't need to be particularly observant to notice that birds fly in the prone position, so to speak. It was only natural that man's first attempts to fly accepted this as the natural layout to be copied. That the problem is not this simple, however, is obvious from the hard fact that nowhere in the world has a prone position aeroplane ever been put into production.

The Germans, in keeping with their astonishing range of ingenuity in aircraft design during World War II, had a good long look at the possible advantages to be offered by the prone position. Firstly they built the Berlin B.9 twin engine, prone position experimental aeroplane in 1943. The B.9 was designed by the University of Berlin, and was stressed to an ultimate of 22'g'. It was the delight of the D.V.L. Academic Flying Group in Berlin, but like so many aircraft that found their way into that establishment, it fostered

The Desford in its original intended role of dual twin-engine primary trainer.

more erudite paperwork than it produced flying hours. It never actually exceeded 8.5'g' in flight.

At the same time a number of tailless sail-planes, called the Horton IV (see pages 174–177), were built experimentally in Germany, and the pilot was in a semi-prone position as if kneeling in prayer.

I flew this glider at the RAE Farnborough. Although it was not easy to fly, this was not entirely because of the pilot position, which was in fact very comfortable and gave me my first insight into the pros and cons of the prone pilot position.

The advantages are staringly obvious. Firstly high centrifugal force can be tolerated. Radial acceleration is produced by a change of direction of the aircraft and acts through the vertical axis of the aircraft – hence the blackout or red-out conditions produced by positive and negative 'g' in aircraft with conventional pilot seating. In the prone position, high speed turns and aerobatics in the looping plane are such a pleasurable sensation that one is apt to lapse into a spirit of gay abandon and run the risk of overstressing the aircraft.

As a fighter pilot I found that in a normal upright seating position I could sustain 5'g' for about four seconds. By crouching this tolerance could be raised to 6'g' for the same length of time. However, in the prone position I have pulled 7'g' for five seconds and still not ever had a red-out. I believe that normal human tolerance in the prone position can indeed be 11'g' for 120–180 seconds.

The second great advantage offered by the prone position is that the pilot can be housed in a fuselage of much smaller diameter than would normally be possible. This decreased frontal area of cockpit is of course an attraction to any designer, and the removal of aerodynamic excrescences such as the cockpit hood produce an efficient streamlined form. However, there are attendant problems in accommodating the pilot in sufficient comfort to perform his duties efficiently.

The prone position compels the pilot to lift his head back to see forward and puts a strain on his dorsal neck muscles. His weight is also on his chest and abdomen and he thus needs a flexible support to allow for respiratory movements. But at the same time his arms must be free to move the controls, although the shoulders will need support.

The field of view of the prone pilot is restricted upwards and rearwards and so provides a tactical disadvantage. Also the pilot's head must be supported to prevent fatigue, and a chin support is unacceptable if an oxygen mask is worn.

The next problem involves the controls them-

selves. The elevator and aileron controls can be powered and geared to give full travel for small forearm movements, but rudder control is more difficult. On the Horton IV, the directional control was via toe cups operated by dorsi-flexion and extensions of the feet. The range of movement is thus comparatively small and consequently accurate control is not easy. Indeed the Horten IV was a real handful on take-off, due to the difficulty of steering it accurately on the ground run. It often took two or three attempts to get off due to ground looping, when the tow would have to be released.

An alternative method of rudder control is to make it hand operated, but this involves an un-natural movement of the control column, which would require practice to overcome.

Instrumentation needs a new look if it is not to interfere seriously with the pilot's field of view, and smaller dials are needed. Indeed, with the number of instruments present in modern aircraft, this becomes a major problem.

Although the prone position offers resistance to radial acceleration, the reverse is true of linear acceleration, such as catapulting, arrested, or crash landings. This was readily demonstrated at RAE Farnborough when I used to carry out catapult launches on a Grumman Avenger, with my dog in the rear being observed by scientists. While I could take 4'g' comfortably, it used to get a doggy blackout as its body is, of course, in the horizontal plane.

The effects of linear acceleration highlight the need for an adequate harness in the prone position. The question of escape for the prone pilot is also a difficult matter. Rocket ejection downwards, feet first, is probably practicable and was the intended method for the RAE transonic research aircraft – but the jettisonable cockpit capsule seems the safest for the pilot.

The prototype Desford Trainer, G-AGOS.

The all-round view from the front cockpit was excellent and almost as good from the rear.

And so with a lot of theoretical and a little practical knowledge I was given the task of selecting an aircraft for our first prone position trials. Obviously the conversion task would require a twin-engine layout, and also a very aerobatic, tandem seat, dual control aeroplane. Cost of conversion was a prime consideration as was also the quality of the handling characteristics, for this would very much be an experimental trainer.

With this in mind, I recalled a little twin-engine primary trainer, the Reid and Sigrist Desford, which I had seen portrayed in an aircraft journal. Its looks had appealed to me and I had read that it flew well on its RAF trials, and had only been stopped from going into production because the requirement died with the end of the war.

The RS.3 Desford, G-AGOS, was the only one built at Desford in Leicestershire in 1945, and it was known to still exist in solitary state. At a meeting in Thames House, London, on 10 May 1948, the decision was taken to go for the Desford for the first stage of the trials, and the dual control Meteor for the second stage.

And so it was to Desford airfield I flew on 1 June 1948 to try out the Desford trainer, and what a little beauty it turned out to be. Settling into the cockpit gave that 'just right' feeling, the all-round view being excellent from the front, and almost as good from the rear, cockpit.

The aircraft handled well on taxying, and take-off with the flaps set to the TAKE-OFF position (10 degrees) gave a short unstick run with slight swing to starboard.

The satisfactory all-round stability of the aircraft made it non-fatiguing to fly, but the controls were not well harmonised, although in this case it was almost a niggling criticism. The ailerons were excessively light, the rudders very light, and the elevator just right. All controls were very effective.

With controls like these aerobatics were a delight. Slow rolls could be executed beautifully at 140mph (225km/h) and loops from 155mph (249km/h), although a close watch had to be kept on the engine revs. lest overspeeding occurred. A peculiar elevator buffet always occurred at the top of a loop, when the speed was low and the control-column well back. This was not pre-stall buffet, for it occurred no matter how much the speed of entry into the loop was stepped up, and I had a feeling it might be coming from the fixed undercarriage.

The flaps-up stall occurred with just a slight buffeting warning at 68mph (109km/h), and was completely innocuous, being simply a straight nose drop. The flaps-down stall exhibited similar characteristics and occurred at a speed below the low reading limit of the airspeed indicator – probably at 50mph (80km/h).

The spinning characteristics of the Desford were excellent. It had to be forced into a spin for

half a turn, then spun fast and steeply, but recovered almost instantaneously on the application of standard recovery action, and only took about half a turn to recover on rudder alone.

With the stick fully back in the spin the same elevator buffet occurred as I had experienced in looping the aeroplane, so the undercarriage now seemed an unlikely source.

I had an excellent opportunity to test the aircraft's single-engine performance when the starboard engine stopped in inverted flight, although the propeller kept windmilling. In that condition, with myself and test observer aboard, height could only be maintained at 80mph (129km/h) with full throttle on the port engine. However, the safety speed of the Desford was virtually the stalling speed, and rudder foot loads were extremely light. A slight rate of climb was possible at 70mph (113km/h).

The landing on one engine was very simple at 80mph (129km/h), and after rectification of the fault I made some more landings, both engine off at 80mph (129km/h), and under power at 65mph (105km/h). The landing run was short with no swing, and the wheel brakes were good.

My overall assessment of the Desford was that it was an outstanding aircraft in its class, with extraordinarily fine handling characteristics, view, cockpit layout, and some good novel features. These included the automatic retraction of the flaps from the maximum drag or approach position to the maximum lift or take-off position when the throttles were opened in the event of a baulked landing.

I recommended that constant speed airscrews be fitted, especially as provision was already intended to be made for such a modification at an early stage in the development programme, and parts were readily available. The resultant freedom from overspeeding during aerobatic manoeuvres and the improvement in single-engine performance would justify the change.

On 30 June I attended a meeting at RAE to discuss the requirements for a prone piloting position on the Desford. The decision had been made about a week previously to choose this aircraft for the initial experiments. The major point of discussion was the best method for controlling the rudder, and it was finally decided to make provision for both foot and hand controls, although I personally favoured foot controls.

In May 1949 Desford G-AGOS was sold to the Air Council for modification for the prone-pilot experiments. After conversion it was redesignated the RS.4 Bobsleigh and given the service serial VZ728.

From this point until I left the RAE in August 1949 I was involved closely with the conversion work on the Desford, and it is my great regret that I never flew this fine aircraft in its new

Right & below: Reid & Sigrist RS.3 Desford Mk I (G-AGOS), of Kemps Aerial Surveys Limited. *RAF Museum Hendon.*

configuration. However, the experiments were a success and led to the prone position Meteor, which I was fortunate enough to get my hands on.

In the event the RAE's transonic research aircraft was never built, probably because it was too radical in concept, but this was very much in keeping with the excitingly progressive thinking of German aerodynamicists of the 1940s.

The prone piloting position was a fascinating idea that offered significant advantages to fighter aircraft of the post-war era, but it imposed limita- tions of all-round view on the pilots, as well as being fatiguing for anything but short flights. It was largely made obsolete when dog-fighting was replaced by guided air-to-air missiles. However, for those who flew prone it was an unforgettable experience, and I shall always be grateful that the concept was responsible for introducing me to the docile, but spritely Desford. It would have made a superb primary trainer for the Services.

40 SAUNDERS-ROE SR/A1

Unique jet fighter flying boat, which could have been useful in the Far Eastern theatre of operations, but was too late. ERIC BROWN

THE CONCEPT of a small fighter flying boat dates back to 1918 when Supermarine built the Baby as a counter to the marauding German Brandenburg flying seaplanes, which were harassing Allied patrol airships and flying boats guarding coastal convoys.

The success of the Japanese in the Pacific theatre of World War II brought the idea of a flying boat fighter to the surface again, and with the advent of the jet engine the combination had exciting potential. It certainly offered solutions to the disadvantages of the draggy and somewhat fragile seaplane designs with their difficult handling characteristics on water.

The Saunders-Roe company started work on the specification E.6/44 at Beaumaris on Anglesey, where their Design Office was located. The aircraft so conceived received the designation SR/A1, and was designed around two Metropolitan-Vickers F2/4 Beryl turbojets. These were axial-flow engines and so two could be installed side by side in a reasonable hull width.

The hull shape was of faired V-form and was entirely of metal construction as was the rest of the aircraft. The engine exhausts were toed out five degrees each side of the centre line. The cockpit was pressurised and was fitted with the first production Martin Baker ejection seat. Four

Landing in Cowes Roads, on Eric Brown's last flight in the SR/A1, it struck a piece of wood and over-turned, trapping him under-water. Eventually freeing himself, he was pulled, semi-conscious from the water. *RAF Museum Hendon.*

20mm cannon were mounted in the nose and provision was made for carrying two 1,000lb (454kg) bombs or eight rockets.

Three prototypes of the SR/A1 were manufactured at Beaumaris and then assembled at Cowes. These were TG263, fitted with two 3,748lb (1,520kg) static thrust engines; TG267, with 3,500lb (1,588kg) engines; and TG271, with 3,800lb (1,724kg) engines.

The first flight was made by Geoffrey Tyson on 16 July 1947. The second prototype went to the Marine Aircraft Experimental Establishment at Felixstowe in 1948, and was lost with its pilot who was practising for an air display in poor visibility when he crashed into the sea.

The third prototype was magnificently displayed by Geoffrey Tyson at the 1948 Farnborough Show, with some superb low inverted flying. This was the machine I was invited to fly in 1949, when commanding Aero Flight at RAE Farnborough.

I flew down to Cowes on the morning of the 12 August and had a briefing from Geoffrey Tyson. The fuel system consisted of one integral tank in each wing forward of the main spar with a total capacity of 426gal (1,937 litres) for the aircraft. The oil system was a constant loss type with a 4gal capacity tank.

The flying controls were a combination of

geared and spring tabs. Control on the water was by means of a smaller rudder, integral with the rear step. It could be locked centrally when in flight or, when on the water, linked to the rudder pedals. The wings were fitted with dive brakes, dive recovery flaps, and landing flaps.

I clambered aboard TG271, which was on beaching gear, and was gently eased down the slipway into the water. There the gear was removed and the aircraft was then towed to the starting point. Starting was controlled from the starter panel on the middle dashboard, comprising an igniter switch, starter motor switch, and engine selector. The Beryls both lit up first time without any trouble, so the tow was released.

I had already engaged the water rudder and followed the launch out into Cowes Roads to the take-off position, finding the aircraft surprisingly easy to manoeuvre. As we approached the take-off lane, I set the flaps to UP, checked the cross-balance feed OFF, master battery switch to FLIGHT, dive recovery brake OFF, and all trimmers at ZERO.

I had decided not to use TAKE-OFF flap as this only improved the run time by two seconds and gave a nose-up effect on unstick, due to the removal of the cushioning effect between flap and water.

I opened the throttles steadily to the maximum

The SR/A1 being towed to its mooring at Cowes.

This is TG263 after a final modification to the cockpit canopy, post-1948. Two other examples were built, Eric Brown almost lost his life while landing TG271 in the Solent. He was rescued in the nick of time by Geoffrey Tyson, Saunders-Roe's chief test pilot. The aircraft was never recovered. *Barry Ketley.*

7,750 rpm although the rate of opening was controlled to a set speed by a hydraulic throttle valve, irrespective of the speed at which the pilot operated the throttle levers. Acceleration was moderate and after two to three seconds the aircraft got up on the hump at about 20–30mph (31–48km/h) at a very large angle of attack (about 15 degrees), and the view ahead virtually disappeared. I had been warned not to push the stick forward of neutral otherwise porpoising might be initiated. Coarse use of water rudder was needed for directional control.

As speed increased to about 40mph (64km/h) the aircraft settled more nose down and lateral control became effective. The unstick occurred after 18 seconds or about 500yds (457m), and I retracted the floats before the limiting speed of 175mph (282km/h) was reached. These were rotated mechanically as they retracted inwards so as to lie inverted in the under surface of the wing, thus creating minimum drag. I then disengaged the water rudder so it remained locked.

Rate of climb was high at 7,600 rpm and the aircraft exhibited good stability characteristics and also good harmony of control as I climbed to 32,000ft (9,754m). At this height I throttled back to 7,400 rpm and let the aircraft settle down in the cruise. Once speed had built up I eased it into a dive to check its compressibility characteristics. Buffeting set in at an indicated M=0.79 and longitudinal pitching started at M=0.8 (M=0.83 true). I took it an increment further to an indicated M=0.82, but used the dive recovery flaps when the nose began to pitch down. This was a remarkable performance for a flying boat and compared favourably with contemporary straight wing fighters.

I then tried some clean stalls at 12,000ft (3,658m) and these occurred without warning and were accompanied by a sharp wing drop and aileron kick in either direction. I had a distinct feeling this could have been an incipient spin situation if mishandled.

I then used the height for a dive to 550mph (885km/h) at 3,000ft (914m) and found the controls did not heavy up much with the increase in speed – a very satisfactory state of affairs. At this stage I used the air brakes to decelerate and found them effective with virtually no change of trim.

As I circled over Cowes Roads for landing I noticed the launch was moving to a patrol line at right angles to that I had used for take-off. I was informed by radio that this was due to a shift in the wind direction, although the wind was only about 5mph (8km/h) and the water almost flat calm.

I eased the speed back to 150mph (241km/h) and lowered the floats, followed by the flaps, opened the cockpit hood, and approached at 110mph (177km/h). Hold-off was made slightly low and the aircraft just kissed the water before settling on its deceleration run. At this stage I noticed a black object just protruding from the surface of the water dead ahead. Then there was a tremendous crash as the piece of timber (possibly from a dismasted yacht) struck the forebody planing bottom, then shot out under compression and knocked the starboard float clean off the aircraft. The wing dipped and as the tip struck the water the aircraft cart-wheeled and skidded along the surface completely inverted.

Upside down in the cockpit the water rushed past me at first, then poured in as we came to a stop. I undid the safety straps hoping to fall out of the cockpit but was firmly held in by my parachute. Eventually I kicked free, having swallowed an enormous amount of water, and then found I could not surface as I kept hitting the wing.

Seen in Class 'B' markings, G-12-1 is the first, and now only, surviving jet-powered fighter flying boat. With the military serial TG263 it flew for the first time in July 1947, but is probably seen here in later years, possibly as part of the Festival of Britain in 1951, or later still at the College of Aeronautics at Cranfield. *Barry Ketley.*

Desperation is a great spur, and in spite of being half drowned I got clear but then felt myself losing consciousness before I could inflate my Mae West. So I did a Dutch boy act and stuck my finger in a vent hole in the side of the hull. Fortunately the launch raced up and Geoffrey Tyson leapt fully clothed from it to my aid.

The observers in the launch reported there were two holes about 3–4ft (91–121cm) forward of the main step and very near to the centre line. The forward hole was smaller than the rear which was about four feet square. The aircraft sank as I was being hauled aboard the launch, and no trace of it was ever found again.

In spite of that incident I very much enjoyed handling the SR/A1 because it was a unique aircraft of unexpected quality – well, not totally unexpected if you had seen it demonstrated by

Geoffrey Tyson. It was the sort of fighter that could have found its real operational environment in the fiords of Norway or the atolls of the Pacific, but the opportunities for that had passed and so the concept withered.

A brief resurgence of interest was sparked off by the Korean War, and tests were resumed on the surviving prototype for a short period, beginning in November 1950. This was short lived for the SR/A1's performance had been outstripped by time.

Bearing a civil registration G-12-1, the old TG263 was flown to Woolwich Reach by Geoffrey Tyson in June 1951 for display at the Festival of Britain. It was moored on the Thames within sight of the Houses of Parliament for three days before departing to its final role as a museum piece.

The SR/A1 was an aircraft of unexpected quality. TG263 was fitted with two 3,350lb static thrust engines.

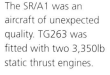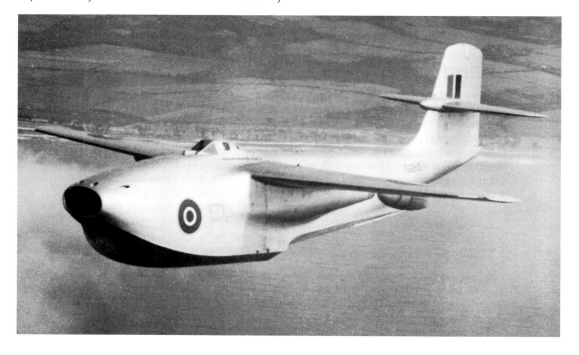

41 SHORT S.29
HALF-SCALE STIRLING

My first four-engined aircraft and the only one I have ever looped, but it didn't persuade me to take the same liberty with the full-scale Stirling. ERIC BROWN

BETWEEN my long periods of service in the Royal Navy's Service Trials Unit and at the RAE Farnborough, I had a short spell in 'C' Squadron at A&AEE Boscombe Down. It was during this last appointment that I flew my first four-engined aircraft, and a pleasantly gentle introduction it was on the half-scale Short S.29 Stirling.

The Air Staff Specification B.12/36 called for a four-engined bomber, which was essentially to operate at night. This would be Britain's first such aeroplane, so when Short's won the design competition it was thought prudent to build a half-scale flying model – which was constructed in 1937 – since the design included several novel and previously untried features.

The wings were Short S.16 Scion components with a span of 42ft (13m), and the engines chosen were seven-cylinder Pobjoy Niagara IIIs. This was a very natural marriage as the Pobjoy company acquired the licence to build the Short Scion, and in March 1938 Short Brothers acquired a large proportion of the issued shares of the Pobjoy company.

This baby Stirling, now designated the S.31, made its first flight in 1938, and soon proved the feasibility of the design so that production of the full-scale bomber could go ahead.

The S.31 was kept flying to try out modifications to the original design and thus eventually found its way to Boscombe Down. By the time I flew it in

The half-scale version known as the S.31, was powered by four Pobjoy Niagara engines, and first flew in September 1938.

The mighty Stirling, first of the RAF's wartime four-engined heavy bombers.

January 1944 it had been re-engined with 114hp Niagara IVs and had gone into semi-retirement. It bore no other registration than simply M4.

For my flight it was at all-up weight of 5,370lb (2,436kg), including myself and passenger, and had a wing loading of 16.3lb/sq ft (80kg/m²). When I looked it over externally there was a full-scale Stirling nearby, so I was able to make a direct comparison. Apart from the obviously different cowling of the power plants the only striking difference was that the full-scale Stirling's undercarriage seemed stalkier and gave the bomber a more exaggerated ground angle.

The cockpit is the one thing in a half-scale model that is out of symmetry, because the crew are full-scale. Certainly the S.31's cockpit was cosy for two.

Starting up the Niagaras was a simple procedure and all Pobjoy engines had that crackling noise as they ran, almost as if to remind the pilot of their limitations of power. But they had a reputation for reliability.

The view from the cockpit was good, and taxying only presented problems across wind, for there was a lot of keel surface to pick up side wind effect. Take-off with one-third flap was characterised by a pronounced swing to starboard. This in fact proved to be one of the difficult handling aspects of the full-scale Stirling, because the ground angle was such that the rud-

der was almost blanked by the fuselage and so was ineffective to counteract swing until the tail was raised. In this respect a few years later I was reminded of the Stirling when flying the Heinkel He 177. Indeed these two aircraft bore many similarities both in appearance and handling.

Half-scale models are of course built with the purpose of checking handling characteristics and not to assess performance, so there is little point in commenting on the rate of climb except to say it was quite lively.

In cruising flight the controls were light and well harmonised, with the ailerons being particularly light. This augured well for evasive manoeuvring by the full-scale bomber, provided there was no heavying up in the Stirling due to scale effect.

Stability proved to be neutral, both longitudinally and laterally, and this inevitably meant the aeroplane was not easy to fly on instruments and needed a lateral trimmer. However, the shortcomings in stability were to some degree compensated by there being little longitudinal trim change with throttle movement or application of flaps, and little directional trim change with speed. This latter point was very fortuitous as rudder trim was ineffective at all speeds.

The lessons learned on the S.31 were applied to the Stirling, and it was fitted with a lateral trimmer and more effective rudder trimmers.

The stalling characteristics of a bomber are very

important, both from the point of view of what can happen in violent evasive action, and the matter of the landing – especially at night in poor weather.

With everything up the little S.31 gave no warning of the impending stall (a minus mark), but when the stall did occur it was gentle and uncomplicated (a plus mark). With flaps and undercarriage down there was a sudden wing drop at the stall, but since there was barely enough elevator available to produce the stall it was unlikely to create a problem on landing.

Another matter of great importance on all multi-engined aircraft is of course the engine-out performance. In the case of a four-engined aeroplane the critical case is that of both engines on one side failing, thus giving maximum asymmetric effect. The S.31's engines could not be feathered, so such a failure represented a worse situation than should be experienced with the Stirling's fully feathering airscrews.

With two Niagaras throttled back on one side, only slight foot load was required to keep straight, and this was just as well since the rudder trim was so ineffective. However, maintaining a foot load for a short period is a very different proposition from doing so for a matter of hours, so the rudder trim needed improvement on the full-scale Stirling – as indeed it was.

Landing the S.31 was straightforward until the final stage, when it was better to wheel the aircraft on to the ground rather than attempt a three-pointer. There was barely enough elevator control available for this, and anyway too high a hold-off in such an attempt could result in a nasty wing drop.

The building of flying scale models as a forerunner to an intended full scale design has seldom been practised, because it is a doubtful cost effective exercise. It is also inevitably a delaying process in the progress from drawing board to full scale production.

In the case of the S.29, Short's were taking what was for them an innovatory step from being almost exclusively a flying boat manufacturer into the bomber business – and Britain's first four-engined bomber at that. Under these circumstances the S.31 made sense and probably paid a worthwhile dividend.

There was one feature of the S.31 that was not applicable to the Stirling – it was aerobatic, at least so I was assured. Anyway I decided to take it round a gentle loop and it behaved beautifully, although it needed quite a steep dive to get the momentum to get up and over, and those little Pobjoys were working very hard. However, if for no other reason, I shall always remember the half-scale Stirling as the only four-engined aircraft I have ever looped or am ever likely to loop. Shades of a fighter pilot's fantasy.

The lofty Stirling bombing-up for a wartime mission.

42 SHORT STURGEON

A pedestrian naval twin, which was a design attempt to solve the problem of asymmetric deck landing of a propeller aircraft – but no dice. ERIC BROWN

The Sturgeon on its deck-landing trials.

THE PROBLEM of making a successful single-engine deck landing on an aircraft carrier with a twin-engine aeroplane had occupied the minds of the Naval Staff and aircraft designers alike since the Mosquito made its historic landings in 1944.

The Mosquito, with a conventional twin-engine layout, was impossible to deck land on one engine because of lack of asymmetric control on the high power/low speed approach required for such an operation. There were also problems of take-off swing with both engines giving high power output to propellers rotating in the same direction.

The Sea Hornet, with its handed propellers rotating in opposite directions, cured the take-off swing trouble, but did nothing towards solving the single-engine landing problem.

The Grumman Tigercat with its power-boosted rudder was an attempt to solve both problems, and although it succeeded in the take-off mode, it failed with the single-engine landing.

The next attempted solution arrived in the form of the Short Sturgeon, with its contra-rotating propellers on each engine. This layout allowed the engines to be brought closer together because of

the shorter diameter airscrews, thus easing the asymmetric effect in the event of an engine failure.

The Sturgeon prototype, RK787, came to the RAE Farnborough in mid-April 1947 for arresting proofing and deck landing assessment. It sailed through the former trials with no hitches, and so on to the evaluation tests of its suitability to undertake the actual deck landing trials.

The aircraft was at an all-up weight of 18,500lb (8,392kg), with the centre of gravity on the forward limit. The reason for this CG position was to represent a similar handling condition to that of the later long-nosed production Sturgeon II at normal loading and CG.

The Sturgeon I was a purposeful, sturdy looking aeroplane and this impression of robustness had certainly been confirmed in the faultless way it went through its arresting proofing trials. However, in getting into the cockpit I was disappointed at the view provided, because the windscreen was not high enough on the sloping nose, and the overhang shields round the instrument panel encroached much too high on the windscreen side-panels.

The two 1,660hp Merlin 140S engines started with their usual efficiency, and there was a great blur created by the airscrew discs just ahead of the nose. During taxying the aircraft had a slight tendency to weathercock in a crosswind, but in spite of the brakes not being very powerful, there was no real problem in steering the Sturgeon on the ground.

For a carrier type of take-off the brakes held the aircraft up to +7lb boost before they started to slip, but then full power could be applied because of the lack of swing due to the contra-props. Using take-off flap the unstick distance in the three-point attitude was very short with +20lb boost.

The change of trim on raising the undercarriage was negligible, and that on raising the flaps only slightly nose-down. The best setting of the radiator flaps for take-off seemed to be one-quarter open, and all trims were neutral. The rate of climb was good, but the cockpit was noisy and very hot.

In normal cruising flight the aircraft exhibited marginally positive stick-free stability and that was about ideal for its strike/reconnaissance role. Harmony of control was good, and all controls were effective in response.

The stalling characteristics of a naval aircraft are particularly important in view of its low margin of speed above the stall on a deck landing approach. The essentials are ample pre-stall warning and lack of a severe wing drop at the actual stall. The Sturgeon had sufficient pre-stall buffeting and a gentle fore-and-aft oscillation before the nose dropped away squarely at 92mph (147km/h) all-up, and 86mph (138km/h) with undercarriage and flaps down. In fact the all-down stall was difficult to produce, requiring full backward elevator trim and stick movement to produce it.

The application of engine power did not alter the stalling characteristics markedly, except that if the stall was approached very gently it was possible to get through the fore-and-aft pitching and produce a starboard wing drop with a slight snatch of the stick to starboard.

The crunch test was of course the simulated deck landing. The undercarriage was lowered at 144mph (232km/h) and had little effect on trim, whilst lowering the flaps to the take-off position at 115mph (185km/h) gave a slight nose-up change of trim, and then to the down position at 103mph (166km/h) a stronger nose-down change. Opening the radiator flaps fully gave a nose-up pitch to ease the overall nose-down trim effect.

The best landing speed was 86mph (138km/h) at 0 boost, but at that speed all the controls suffered in effectiveness and particularly the ailerons, which became spongy in feel although the elevators and rudder remained light. However, longitudinal stick fix stability was excellent and this, combined with a throttle quadrant that gave adequate coarseness of engine control, enabled a well-controlled approach path to be maintained.

A hard pull back on the stick was required at the last moment to effect a three-point touchdown. Even if a three-pointer wasn't achieved, the undercarriage was so soft that no bounce was likely. There was no swing after landing, and although the brakes were not very powerful the landing run was exceptionally short.

The whole landing process with the Sturgeon reminded one vividly of the Barracuda, which

was a very good deck-landing aircraft if little else. The view ahead was good on the approach in the Sturgeon, but it was drastically affected by rain, although the rear two-thirds of the curved side screens remained clear enough to enable safe deck landings to be made.

The next step was to try an asymmetric deck-landing approach. This proved to be unfeasible because the lateral control became too heavy and spongy to bring the speed down to acceptable limits for such an operation.

The Sturgeon was really the last attempt with a twin piston-engined aeroplane to solve the single-engine deck landing problem. The axial-flow jet engine arrived on the scene and its slim shape and lack of airscrew allowed the two engines to be housed close together and so the problem solved itself with such a layout.

The Sturgeon was a pedestrian aircraft from a performance point of view, with a top speed of 370mph (595km/h). The few long-nosed Mark IIs that were produced were relegated to target-towing, a fate reserved for the 'also-rans'. Nevertheless I remember it as an interesting attempt to solve a difficult problem, and it just might have succeeded with more development time.

The Sturgeon had a rather ungainly look in flight.

Seen at the SBAC Show at Radlett in 1946, this is the unpainted first Short Sturgeon, RK787. Originally intended as a strike aircraft for the Fleet Air Arm, the end of World War II meant that it was surplus to requirements. Heavily modified into a high-speed target tug, however, it gave valuable, if unsung, service to Royal Navy gunners for ten years or so. *Barry Ketley.*

43 SIKORSKY R-4B HOVERFLY

Remarkably reliable for a first-ever mass production helicopter, although it did vibrate a lot and was pretty noisy. ERIC BROWN

WHEN I WAS in Aero Flight at RAE Farnborough in 1945, we were mainly concerned with transonic flight research. Although I had also been very involved with low speed research, this was primarily concerned with the stalling characteristics of fast aeroplanes. It therefore came as a complete surprise when I learned that we were to receive two helicopters in Aero Flight.

I had first seen a helicopter in Germany in 1938 when I witnessed Hanna Reitsch fly the Fw 61 in the Deutschlandhalle in Berlin. However, that aircraft had quite a different configuration from the Sikorsky helicopters allocated to RAE. The Fw 61 had two contra-rotating rotors on outriggers and an ordinary fin and rudder, but the Sikorsky designs had a single main rotor and a tail rotor for directional control.

I was one of the two pilots chosen to go to Speke airfield at Liverpool in February to pick up

our two helicopters and fly them to an MRU for check over before delivery to Farnborough. On arrival we found the R-4Bs, which had arrived on a freighter from America, had been uncrated, and assembled by a US master sergeant. When I enquired from this laconic gentleman who was to teach us to fly these contraptions, he stuffed a large orange coloured manual into my hand and said 'There's your instructor, bud'.

The manual was titled *Provisional Manual for Flight Training – R-4 Sikorsky Helicopter*, and I doubt if any manual has been more avidly read than by us two Aero Flight pilots that evening. My running mate even suggested it was like reading your own obituary. Our only solace was that Igor Sikorsky had made it on his own. So why shouldn't we?

Next day we had the two R-4s pushed into the middle of the airfield as far from any obstruction as possible, and well spaced from each other. We

The R-4B at RAE Farnborough.

had decided to attempt hovering first and then progress to a circuit and landing. The antics that followed can best be summed up by the master sergeant's comment that we could only improve, but would we leave as soon as possible while the helicopters were still in one piece.

Actually I did not find the experience as alarming as I expected, but then I was a light weight for the underpowered R-4, while my squadron-leader companion weighed 200lb (91kg). However, after safely delivering the Gadflies, as the RAF had designated them, we rested on our laurels and demanded a proper course of instruction before launching into a test programme.

We were assigned to RAF Andover to begin a course on 6 March. On 5 March an R-4 visited Farnborough, flown by Sub Lt Alan Bristow, who had been sent on the first helicopter course for British pilots in the USA. He gave me a demonstration flight in KK970 and this really whetted my appetite for the Andover course.

Actually the experience of the Andover instructors was very limited as they had also just returned from the American course. So it was, as one put it, somewhat akin to the blind leading the blind. However, they had been well taught in the USA and imparted their knowledge in a very professional manner. I was thus taken through the mysteries of hovering, backwards and sideways flight, quick stops, autorotation landings, precision turns, and all the other facets of helicoptering – all in 8½ hours of dual instruction, interspersed with solo practices from the four-hour stage onwards.

The R-4 was a two-seater dual-control helicopter with a single, three-bladed main rotor and a three-bladed tail rotor for torque balance. It was powered by a 185hp seven-cylinder R-550-3 Warner Scarab air-cooled engine, and fitted with a conventional tail wheel type undercarriage. The fuselage was built up from chrome-molybdenum tubing, and was fabric covered, except for the tail rotor outrigger.

Fuel was carried in a single non-self-sealing tank situated laterally across the fuselage and with a capacity of 25gal (114 litres). The oil tank was located vertically on the starboard side aft of the main gear box, and had a capacity of 2.5gal (11.4 litres). Normally only half fuel was carried.

The cockpit was quite roomy, with two standard control columns and rudder pedals, a centrally mounted main rotor pitch lever with twist grip throttle control, and above and behind it the main rotor clutch and brake lever. On the floor between the control columns were the carburettor heat control and mixture control levers, and between the two sets of rudder pedals was the wheel brakes control lever with self-locking ratchet.

The author flying the Sikorsky R-4B helicopter 'hands-off'.

There was a single row instrument panel containing eight dials, with the oil temperature gauge and main rotor pitch indicator centrally on the shelf above the panel. All electrical switches were on a panel on the port wall of the cockpit, forward of the door.

On the Andover course it had been impressed on me that the R-4 was underpowered and that overpitching could therefore land one in serious trouble. This occurs when the pilot raises the pitch lever without compensating with a power increase and thus the rotor rpm start to decay and the aircraft begins to settle into a vertical descent. The golden rule was, therefore, to lead with the throttle to keep the rpm up and then increase the pitch whilst opening the throttle to maintain the rpm. The danger of overpitching increases with increased weight and high air temperatures. Perhaps for the former reason I found myself chosen to conduct the helicopter research programme after completing the course of instruction and some familiarisation flights on our three Gadflies at RAE, serial numbers KL107, 108 and 109. Actually the flights were mainly on KL108 as KL109 was withdrawn in late March for fitting out with test instrumentation, and was followed by KL107 in April and eventually KL108 in June.

KL109 reappeared from the workshops, and the test programme started on 12 October, by which time I had the startling total of 20 hours helicopter experience. The boffin responsible for the conduct of the tests was Bill Stewart, who had been in charge of the Mosquito deck-landing trials with me in 1944.

In December 1945 the Air Ministry decided to change the name Gadfly to Hoverfly, with effect from 1 January 1946.

The initial tests were concerned with control effectiveness in normal and autorotative flight, and with exploring the limits of the CG movement which was very restricted on the R-4. Longitudinal control was light and effective with some noticeable lag in response. Lateral control was very sensitive. Directional control was moderately light and effective.

Main rotor pitch control was very sensitive, and there was a continuous stirring motion of the stick, attended by constant jarring low frequency vibration.

Stability checks showed the helicopter to be directionally stable in forward cruising flight, but lateral and longitudinal stability was pendulous.

The only trimming possible was in the fore-and-aft plane by means of a crude bungee cord fixed between the right hand set of rudder pedals and attached at the other end by a ring to the control column. The ring was moveable in a series of ratchet slots extending for about one-third of the length at the aft side of the stick.

The maximum weight for the tests was 2,800lb (1,270kg). Instrumentation specially fitted included desynn indicators giving control column position and an open scale airspeed indicator reading off a trailing static lowered some 80ft (24m) below the helicopter. The standard ASI fitted to the Hoverfly read from 30mph (48km/h) to 200mph (322km/h)!

This phase of the tests embraced stability and control in autorotation, but broke new ground in measuring longitudinal dynamic stability with the aid of an automatic observer. Some of these tests involved flying in very turbulent conditions, including a 65mph (105km/h) gale, when it was found that atmospheric gusts had very much less

Investigating the flight characteristics of early helicopters by flying in coloured smoke. The fifteen-foot-long hollow metal pole had been fixed laterally to the helicopter. But the weight and its drag forced the aircraft to go into an uncontrollable turn towards the side to which the pole was attached. It was also used vertically as depicted.

effect than that usually experienced on fixed-wing aircraft. This was a feature of the flapping blade system of the R-4B acting to some extent as an automatic gust alleviator.

During these tests we moved into a region of the flight envelope that gave rise to loss of control. This occurred frequently in zero forward air speed descents at values of collective blade pitch greater than 7 degrees and was always obtained under these conditions if the pitch was reduced. The loss of control took the form of a nose-down pitching of the helicopter and full backward movement of the control stick could not prevent the speed increasing rapidly to about 40mph (64km/h), with consequent loss of height in regaining control.

This vortex ring state had not been previously explored and was therefore not fully understood. So it was decided in the next phase of the tests to investigate the nature of the flow through the rotor disc. This involved some very innovative iron-mongery being fitted to KL108, which emerged from the workshops in mid-November 1946.

Protruding radially outwards from the top of the port undercarriage leg was a 15ft (4.6m) hol-low perforated metal pole for measuring rotor disc induced velocity by use of the smoke filament technique. This involved feeding the smoke from a smoke generator into the outboard end of the pole whose inboard end was sealed, so that smoke filaments streamed through the perforations on top of the pole and were photographed by a camera mounted on the rear fuselage.

This system, although physically tiring to fly because of the heavy lateral out-of-trim forces, was eminently successful and produced the first in-flight photographs of the vortex ring flow. However, a different system was needed for measuring flow conditions through the rotor disc in hovering flight, since the helicopter rotor had to be at least 40ft (12m) above the ground to eliminate the ground cushion effect. The pole had to be removed because of the adverse effect of its weight on this manoeuvre. The helicopter was now hovered under the jib of a 60ft (18m) crane to the end of which a smoke generator was attached. Since I could not see the jib I was totally dependent on ground signals for height control.

The induced velocity measurements in forward

In the days before the Health and Safety brigade joined up, two jolly Jack Tars were sufficient to support a helicopter. This is the second Sikorsky R4 bought by the Royal Navy, KK983, during June 1945 at Whale Island in Portsmouth Harbour, being flown by Sub/Lt K Reed. The canvas hangar used by the unit can be seen in the background. *Barry Ketley.*

flight also meant elimination of the pole because of resonance and speed limitations. The system then used was to fly through a smoke streamer from three smoke generators towed on a long wire by a slow flying Fieseler Storch. This system also produced some classic airflow photographs taken from a formating helicopter.

This phase of the tests brought us into the unusually severe winter weather of early 1947. The opportunity was taken to investigate the whiteout phenomenon caused by loose snow being picked up by the rotor circulatory flow in the hover and creating a swirling dense cloud, obliterating all outside visual reference. Since an artificial horizon had been fitted in the cockpit for test purposes I found I could cope with the attitude problem as long as I was in the hover in the ground cushion. It was just a question of easing down the collective pitch lever until ground contact was made and then dumping the collective down to the floor to avoid ground resonance developing.

We also took advantage of the cold weather to make a ceiling climb, and reached 9,170ft (2,795m), which was a respectable performance with two crew wearing parachutes. This was really the start of the performance phase of the tests, which created difficulties in achieving accurate measurement of the low air speeds below 20mph (31km/h). A trailing pitot – static universally mounted on the end of an 80ft (24m) cable, allowing it complete freedom to take up the direction of the relative air flow, proved very satisfactory in use and eliminated any position error.

At this stage the RAE work on the vortex ring state had made an international impact and the great Igor Sikorsky visited Farnborough to have a practical demonstration. He was a delightful man with an old world charm, and before our flight we swopped stories of our first solo flights. He wore a trilby hat, just as I had seen him wearing in photographs of his early flights on the VS-300, and he never took it off during our flight. I asked him if he wanted to wear a parachute, but he would have none of that, so I obviously had to follow suit. He was fascinated by our forty minute flight, and we talked for over two hours afterwards about our research work. He was tremendously interested and apparently very impressed.

A decision had been made to push into the realms of blind flying and this was started in September 1947. The main difference in blind flying a helicopter compared with a fixed-wing aircraft is in the longitudinal behaviour; laterally and directionally both types show very similar behaviour. With the pendulous longitudinal stability of the helicopter it was immediately obvious that the

standard artificial horizon was of no use for giving an absolute indication of the changes of attitude with speed or rate of climb. It does, however, respond normally to any change in attitude, e.g. due to atmospheric bumps. Therefore a more sensitive artificial horizon was used, with greater movement of the bar for equivalent attitude change. The positions of the bar thus gave a better indication of speed in the steady conditions, but the movements for arbitrary disturbances were also exaggerated, tending to cause over-corrections from the pilot. In practice I found the airspeed indicator became the master instrument for longitudinal control of the helicopter.

After some practice 'under the hood' I made the first actual cross country flight totally in cloud from Farnborough to Beaulieu on 7 October 1947, involving 45 minutes on instruments. I carried a flight observer and the whole flight was recorded by auto-observer in KL108.

As an extra-curricular activity I became an instructor to two pilots in Radio and Instruments Flight at RAE, which had been allocated KL107. Both soloed within 6 hours.

On 27 November I made the first night flight of 45 minutes in KL108. There was no panel lighting, and this omission was compensated for by a torch held by the ever trusting Bill Stewart.

In an attempt to improve stability and reduce control sensitivity, an arrangement of lateral and longitudinal trimming by four bungee cords was fitted on KL109. Lateral control effectiveness was reduced by up to one-third by altering the stick gearing. This actually allowed the R-4B to be flown hands off for periods of up to 10 seconds. Somehow that seemed to be as far as we could go with the R-4.

On 15 June 1948 I flew to an airfield glorying in the name of Horsey Toll, where the newly formed British European Airways Experimental Helicopter Unit kept a Bell 47B-3. I was checked out on this aircraft G-AKFA by Captain Jock Cameron, so that I could assess the effectiveness of the Bell-patented stabiliser bar fitted to the rotor head. This gave a very small but worthwhile improvement in stability. Indeed at that early stage in helicopter development any improvement could be termed worthwhile.

The Hoverfly must be assessed as a truly remarkable first ever production helicopter. It was comparatively easy to fly within its limitations, the main one of which was that it could not hover out of ground effect at normal weight. It was noisy and vibrated, but it was a fantastic new experience to fly. However, it was its astonishing reliability that made the greatest impression. I flew it for some 500 hours yet can never remem-

Pilot's notes: Sikorsky R-4B Hoverfly

HOVERFLY I

FIG. 1   FIG. 1

HOVERFLY II

FIG. 2   FIG. 2

Fig. 1

1 Main-rotor clutch and brake lever
2 Main-rotor pitch lever with twist-grip throttle control
3 Ventilator lever
4 EMERGENCY DOOR RELEASE levers
5 Fluorescent lights
6 Ignition switch
7 Switch panel
8 Instrument panel
9 Oil temperature gauge
10 Main-rotor pitch indicator
11 Control column
12 Wheel brakes control
13 Compass
14 Carburettor heat control
15 Mixture control

Key to Fig. 2

2 Main-rotor pitch lever with twist-trip throttle control
4 EMERGENCY DOOR RELEASE levers
5 Fluorescent lights
6 Ignition switch
7 Switch panel
8 Instrument panel
10 Main-rotor pitch indicator
11 Control column
12 Wheel brakes control
13 Compass
14 Carburettor heat control
15 Mixture control
16 Fuel endurance light
17 Main fuel cock
18 Main rotor brake

ber snagging it for other than a minor item in the whole of that time, when it was being subjected to a very demanding series of research flights.

In January 1949 Hoverfly II, KN863, arrived at RAE. This helicopter had an improved streamlined fuselage, a more powerful engine of 245hp, and many other minor refinements. AUW was only 60lb (27kg) greater than the Hoverfly I and main rotor disc area was the same.

There was a lateral bungee trimmer only fitted to the Hoverfly II, but the controls were less sensitive except directionally. However, the throttle was very sensitive indeed. Take-off was livelier with the extra power available, and vibration was notably reduced.

One noticeable effect of the redesigned fuselage was that rain did not coagulate on the moulded perspex nose of the Hoverfly II as it did on the flat panels of the Hoverfly I.

All in all Sikorsky had certainly incorporated a lot of their experience on the R-4B into making an improved helicopter in the R-6A. But it still could not be hovered out of ground effect, so it represented only a very small step forward.

The first helicopter deck landing on a British carrier.

44 SUPERMARINE ATTACKER

An undistinguished naval jet fighter, except that it was the first in Fleet Air Arm squadron service. Pity about the tail wheel. ERIC BROWN

This is the unpainted second naval prototype of the Attacker, more or less a jet-powered version of the Seafang, built to Specification E.1/45. Initial landing trials took place aboard HMS *Illustrious* on 29 October 1947. Returned to the A&AEE at Boscombe Down on 15 June 1948. It crashed a week later at Bulford and was written off. *Barry Ketley.*

I N MID-1944 Supermarine embarked on a series of laminar flow wing flight tests on a modified Spitfire XIV and these were continued on the Spiteful and its naval counterpart, the Seafang. This experience led in turn to the company being asked to marry the Spiteful type wings to the new Rolls-Royce Nene jet engine, to the Government Specification E.1/44 and this in turn was modified to E.10/44.

Three prototypes were built, the second being navalised to Specification E.1/45. It was this latter aircraft which was the first to be named Attacker. It differed from the E.10/44 in having a smaller fin and larger tailplane, modified flaps, and lift spoilers on the wing upper surface, balanced aileron tabs in place of spring tabs, modified air intakes with louvred by-pass air bleeds, extra rear fuel tanks, long-stroke undercarriage, and a Martin-Baker ejection seat.

The lift spoilers were the most interesting mod-ification and stemmed from a meeting which I attended at the Ministry of Aircraft Production on 6 March 1946. Those present included Joe Smith, Chief Designer, and Alan Clifton, Head of the Supermarine Technical Office, as well as Frank Holroyd, one of the R.J. Mitchell's original draw-ing office staff, and then Assistant Director of Naval Research and Development in the Ministry of Aircraft Production. I was the only pilot atten-ding.

The RAE viewpoint at this meeting was that the aircraft as designed, with no variable lift device and with a conventional undercarriage, would be more difficult to deck land than a Vampire or Seafire. A lift spoiler was therefore essential.

Joe Smith then proposed a scheme consisting of an upper surface spoiler situated aft of the front spar, of dimensions approximately 80in. × 3in. (203 × 75cm) RAE said the operation of the spoilers must be progressive, and estimated they would

Pilot's view of the Attacker's cockpit.

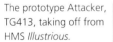

The prototype Attacker, TG413, taking off from HMS *Illustrious*.

intermediate spoiler position to regulate thrust to the minimum (35%) required during approach, without requiring the rpm to fall below the critical value. It was agreed to continue with this development on the 'belt and braces' principle.

In the event the jet spoiler was never used on the Attacker, but it was test flown in Wellington, W5518, with a tail-mounted Power Jets W2/700 engine.

The prototype Attacker, TS413, made its first flight in the hands of Mike Lithgow on 17 June 1947. Shortly afterwards it went to Boscombe Down before coming to RAE, where I first flew it on 2 September.

My task included a deck landing assessment, stability and control tests and arresting proofing. The aircraft was at an AUW of 11,030lb (5,003kg), with the CG at 1.5in (4cm). aft of the datum. The Nene turbo-jet unit gave 5,000lb (2,268kg) static thrust.

To my mind the Attacker was not a particularly good looking aeroplane, being both bulky and angular, and it just did not seem right to be fitted with a conventional tail-wheel undercarriage in the new era of the tricycle jet.

On getting into the cockpit I found the view directly ahead and on each beam was good, but only if I raised myself until my head was touching the top of the canopy, for the front windscreen was not deep enough to provide sufficient field of vision from any other eye level. Furthermore the seat was too low in the cockpit for me to achieve the desired position when wearing a parachute.

Taxying with the tail-wheel free was tricky in that once any turn was initiated it seemed to develop rapidly with the wide-track undercarriage, and harsh braking was required to counteract it. However, with the tail-wheel locked,

give a 7½% increase in approach speed. It was agreed that the operating loads should be light enough to allow mechanical linkage with the throttle, and it was suggested that this linkage should be brought into operation by the lowering of the flaps. The decision was then made to proceed with model wind tunnel tests to check buffeting of tail surfaces and trim changes.

Concurrently with the lift spoiler the meeting considered a jet thrust spoiler to overcome the problem of slow acceleration of the jet engine in the case of a baulked landing. Rolls-Royce then had under development a three-position spoiler, the positions being open, shut, and some intermediate setting, with the control separate from the throttle. The idea was to keep the jet engine at a high rev. setting from which full thrust could be attained in about one second, then use the

The Attacker taxying up the deck of *Illustrious* after landing and being unhooked.

taxying was greatly simplified, and turns up to 45 degrees could easily be made under these conditions without any apparent dragging effect being felt from the rear end of the aircraft. Rudder effect alone was useless during taxying, but weathercocking tendencies in a crosswind were only small.

For take-off the brakes would only hold the aircraft up to 10,000rpm before they started to slip. But from that point the engine could instantaneously be opened up to the full 12,350rpm without any adverse effects on jet pipe temperature. There was of course no tendency to swing with the tail wheel lock engaged, but it was not very easy to raise the tail off the ground until the aircraft was almost airborne. However, the view was good and, using TAKE-OFF flap, the run was short. The change of trim on raising the undercarriage was negligible, but raising the flaps gave a very strong nose-down pitch. By using neutral elevator trim for take-off the stick force to take up this change of trim was greatly eased.

The Attacker carried almost 300gal (1,364 litres) of fuel and so the stalling speed varied considerably with reduction in fuel load, but the characteristics were mild. The all-up stall occurred with practically no warning other than a slight twitch on the port aileron just before the nose dropped, and the port wing dropped about 15 degrees. The all-down stall was similar, but a slight air-frame vibration could be felt a few mph before the port aileron twitch. The only effect of the spoilers on the stall was to increase the airframe vibration to a definite juddering and to add some 3.5mph (5.6km/h) to the stalling speed. The stalling speeds varied by 6mph (9.7km/h) between a 250gal (1,137 litres) and 50gal (227 litres) fuel load. With the latter load these speeds were 116mph (187km/h) (all-up), 105mph (170km/h) (all-down), 108mph (174km/h) (all-down, spoilers open).

In cruising flight the controls were well harmonised and effective. Stability was neutral, both longitudinally and directionally, but unstable laterally, thus making instrument flying hard work.

The aircraft also suffered from directional snaking in any form of turbulence, which would affect its performance as a gun platform.

The spoilers had no apparent effect on control up to their limiting speed of 172mph (277km/h). They gave the impression of a slight nose-down pitch if opened above 126mph (203km/h), but this was merely a deceleration effect felt on the pilot.

With a maximum speed of 590mph (949km/h) at sea level, and maximum rate of climb of 6,350ft/min (1,935m/min), the Attacker was a useful performer.

Using an airfield, the landing characteristics of the Attacker were excellent, but it was a different matter for deck landing, due to lack of sufficient drag in the landing condition. A final approach at any speed above 1.05Vs (spoilers IN) would not give an instantaneous touch-down even when the spoilers were opened at the last moment. So there was a grave danger of floating over all the arrester wires or picking up a wire on the float and being pitched heavily on to the deck, although the long-stroke undercarriage gave a low rebound and therefore damage was unlikely to result from an airborne arrest.

In order to get the best results I evolved the constant power/constant angle approach. On turning in at 132mph (212km/h), assuming 200gal (909 litres) of fuel remaining, I set the engine at 8,000rpm, settled on to finals at 126mph (203km/h) and regulated the approach angle by the spoilers until settled 'in the groove' at 120mph (193km/h). Then I closed the spoilers and eased back on the stick to reduce speed to 115mph (185km/h) for the last 50ft (15m), finally opening the spoilers fully and easing further back on the stick for touch-down. The only effect of picking up an arrester wire with power on was a slightly longer pull-out of the wire, but no build-up in deceleration.

In the event of a baulked landing full-power could be applied instantaneously. This gave a strong nose-up trim change which was dangerous at such low speed, but if only 10,000rpm were applied the aircraft would climb away slowly, without much change in longitudinal trim.

After this rather unfavourable deck landing assessment, I started the arresting proofing of the Attacker on the RAE arrester gear on 11 September. This ended with the arrester hook V-frame being torn out of the aircraft at 3'g' and the aeroplane being swung violently to port off the runway, but fortunately without further damage. Next day I flew it to Chilbolton airfield for repair.

Supermarine certainly did not let the grass grow under their feet. TS413 returned with a strengthened hook within three days, and the first stage of arresting proofing was satisfactorily completed this time.

MAP called a meeting on 18 September at Boscombe Down to review progress to date. At this meeting there were A&AEE pilots and Supermarine's Jeffrey Quill and Mike Lithgow, in addition to those who had been at the first meeting in 1946. The outcome was a decision to increase spoiler travel by 30% and measure its effect on the baulked landing case with the spoilers open.

The spoiler modification was made with the usual Supermarine speed and efficiency, and I started the assessment on 23 September. The increased travel had increased stalling speed by 1mph (1.6km/h) and gave a marked buffet near the stall. Rate of sink with full spoiler had also increased considerably, so the right effects had been produced.

Unfortunately, when flying the aircraft at high cruise speed, the spoilers got partially and unevenly sucked out of the wing because suction was still present over the spoilers behind the transition point of flow over the laminar flow wing. This caused the aeroplane to roll smartly and caused slight distortion damage to the spoilers.

However, we were soon back in business and

The prototype Attacker (TS409) on a low-level test flight.

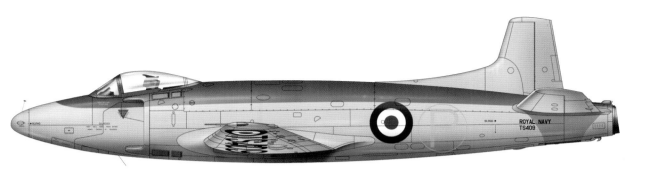

the next flight I made on 26 September was to assess the efficiency of the spoilers on touchdown. They now gave a much more positive contact on opening at 1.05Vs and even at 1.1Vs. It was also clear that by leaving 8,000rpm on the engine at touch-down, an immediate getaway on a baulked landing was possible by closing the spoilers first and then opening the throttle.

On 30 September and 1 October, I finished off the arresting proofing with runs up to 3.35'g' on centre and 2.9'g' at 15ft (4.6m) off centre. It is interesting that the tail came up above the horizontal on catching a wire.

On 2 October the MAP held a final meeting at Boscombe Down, at which it was agreed that the

deck landing trials should go ahead on HMS *Illustrious*.

The first deck landing of the Attacker was made by Mike Lithgow on 15 October, off the Isle of Wight. This was done at the specific request of Supermarine for publicity reasons and was a break with the normal routine of naval test pilots doing the initial landings. However, Mike was an ex-naval pilot, so it was not an unreasonable request. After landing he handed the Attacker over to me for the first take-off and subsequent landing. The trials involved a total of twelve landings on two days, carried out by an RAE, Supermarine and A&AEE pilot. Only three landings were made on the first day, as it was found that during a tail-first

Top: Supermarine Attacker prototype, TS409, in its final form with fin fillet attached. © *Richard Caruana* (scale 1:72).

Above: Supermarine Attacker F.1 aircraft of 800 Sqn, 5 June 1952. *RAF Museum Hendon.*

Attacker, WA498, on final approach for a carrier deck landing.

touch-down the tail wheel oleo did not absorb the vertical energy imposed on it. The resultant rebound threw the aircraft fuselage into an almost horizontal attitude and unless a wire had been picked up at the point of contact the arrester hook rode above the next few wires until the tail started to drop again. The aircraft was therefore flown back to Chilbolton and Supermarine increased the energy absorption qualities of the tail wheel by about 20%, and increased the angle of trail of the hook so that it was some two inches lower than in the original condition.

The trials recommenced on 28 October, and on my four landing I sought to progressively step up the approach speed to test the effectiveness of the spoilers. In fact these proved to be very effec-

tive, but the pilots criticised having to operate a separate spoiler control in addition to the throttle. This moved Supermarine to abandon the spoilers and seek more drag effect by simple use of drag-producing airbrakes. Other later modifications included a dorsal fin to obviate rudder overbalance propensities, especially when fitted with an external long range tank, flat-sided elevators, and lighter aileron controls.

The first production Attacker was flown on 5 May 1950, and the first squadron formed on 17 August 1951. Thus the Attacker had the distinction of being the Royal Navy's first operational jet aircraft, and for that, if for little else, it will always be remembered..

The Attacker folds its wings after landing on HMS Eagle.

45 SUPERMARINE SEAFANG

A vicious stall of its laminar flow wing ruled it out as a naval aircraft. Also it had little to offer over the mighty Seafire 47. ERIC BROWN

THE ADVENT of the laminar flow wing from America in the early 1940s caused a considerable stir in aeronautical engineering circles in Britain. The newly developed wing profiles were intended to reduce skin friction by maintaining substantial areas of laminar flow by locating the maximum aerofoil thickness much further aft than on previous conventional wing sections. The pursuit of reduction in drag was going hand in hand with the race to break the sound barrier.

Supermarine were, of course, world leaders in high speed flight with the incomparable Spitfire so it was to this aircraft that they turned for their first laminar flow wing experiments. Specification 470 was written in November 1942 'to raise as much as possible the critical speed at which drag

increases, due to compressibility, become serious; to obtain a rate of roll faster than any existing fighter; to reduce profile drag and thereby improve performance.'

The Type 371 wing was developed with the aid of the National Physical Laboratory. The maximum thickness was at about 42% of the chord. Wing area was 210sq ft (20m^2) with straight leading and trailing edges. This wing was fitted to Spitfire XIV, NN660, and first flew on 30 June 1944. On 13 September Supermarine test pilot Frank Furlong, a former Grand National winning jockey, was killed in NN660 while conducting a mock dog fight with a standard Spitfire XIV near High Post airfield. The hybrid Spitfire flicked out of a high 'g' turn on to its back at a fairly low height,

The Seafang 31 prototype, (VG471), which came to Farnborough early in 1946.

This view of the Seafang
Mk 31 prototype,
VG471, clearly shows
the different wing
planform compared to
the Seafire. Although
the Seafang never
entered Royal Navy
service, the wing
design, attached to a
vastly different fuselage
and powerplant, did so
as the first jet fighter for
the Fleet Air Arm,
namely the Supermarine
Attacker. *Barry Ketley.*

and this may have been a pointer to the short-coming of the Type 371 wing – its vicious stalling characteristics.

NN660 was, in effect, the prototype of Speci-fication F.1/43 to be named Spiteful. This new fighter was to have the laminar flow wing, whose shape allowed a conventional two-spar construc-tion, unlike the single-spar wing of the Spitfire.

The first true Spiteful prototype, NN664, first flew on 8 January 1945, and the first production version, RB515, in April 1945. At about this stage the Royal Navy issued specification N.5/45, which was a navalisation of the Spiteful, whose two-spar wing made the provision of wing folding an easier proposition than with the Seafire. It also allowed an inwards retracting undercarriage, thus extending, by some 4ft (1.2m), the narrow track of the Seafire. Spiteful F.14, RB520, became the interim prototype Seafang.

Seafang 31 prototype, VG471, came to RAE Farnborough in February 1946 for its arresting proofing trials and failed them when the rudder skin wrinkled during off-centre arrests at 2.7'g' retardation.

Repairs were made, but on the next set of off-centre runs the rudder horn split open, and after further repairs the rudder skin wrinkled again. And so, on 16 March, I delivered VG471 back to Supermarine's at High Post, so that modifications could be incorporated to cure this series of set-backs.

These tests gave me my first acquaintance of the Seafang, which was a good-looking aircraft, rather like a Seafire 46 on a lower, wider track undercarriage, but of course distinguished by the more angular lines of its laminar flow wings.

The cockpit layout was also similar to the Seafire 46, but there the similarity ended. The lower ground angle of the Seafang gave a better view ahead, although the nose was still very long to house the Griffon 69 and its five-bladed airscrew. The aircraft was directionally unstable on the ground, but excellent brakes and a tail wheel lock got around this difficulty in the main.

Take-off at +18lb boost was easier than with the non-contra-rotating propeller version of the Seafire 46, because the swing could be held more easily and there was no torque roll effect, due to the wide undercarriage. Full power could be held on the brakes without the tail rising if the stick was held just aft of central. Indeed it was advisable to keep the tail down during the take-off run as the airscrew ground clearance with the aircraft's horizontal datum level was only ten inches. It was also advisable to select the positive open coolant radiator setting rather than auto, for if the radiator shutters opened they gave a noticeable nose-down change of trim, which could be disconcerting if unexpected.

The Seafang had beautiful controls, all light and effective in the normal speed ranges, but it had an Achilles heel – a vicious stall. Actually I had been given a chance to try out Spiteful RB521, one of the first production types, which had three degrees less dihedral and sharper mainplane lead-ing edges than the later production types. The clean stall on the Spiteful occurred at 109mph (175km/h), preceded very early on by a large amount of lateral pecking of the wings and finally a very sharp port wing drop to about 80 degrees. The all-down stall at 101mph (163km/h) was even more vicious and showed incipient spin tenden-cies.

A 5in (12.7cm) length of cord, about ⅛in (3mm) diameter, was fitted to the leading edge of the starboard wing tip for a later flight on the

Supermarine Seafang (VG471) in flight, High Post, 30 January 1946. *RAF Museum Hendon.*

Seafang FR.Mk.32, VB895, deck landing trials on HMS Illustrious, May 1947. © *Richard Caruana* (scale 1:72).

The prototype Seafang 32, VB895, with contra-rotating propellers. Eric Brown flew this aircraft in 1947.

Spiteful in an attempt to cure the port wing drop. The effect was to reduce the wing drop to 20 degrees and reduce the stalling speed by about 3mph (4.8km/h).

Seafang VG471 had three degrees more dihedral than the early Spiteful and more rounded leading edges on the mainplanes. Both these changes were incorporated in later production Spitefuls. VG471 had been given an 8in. (20cm) length of spoiler cord, of ¼in. (6.4mm) diameter, fixed to the starboard wing tip leading edge. The stalls exhibited the same general characteristics as Spiteful RB521 when modified with spoiler cord, but the speeds were 7mph (11km/h) higher.

The view for landing was comparable to the Firefly. Lowering the undercarriage and flaps gave a very strong nose-up change of trim; the aircraft felt generally unsafe at approach speeds less than 110mph (177km/h) and indeed, below 120mph (193km/h) in bumpy air, due to the pre-stall characteristics and ineffectiveness of the rudder. Obviously an entry speed of about 120mph (193km/h) into the aircraft carrier's arrester gear would have to be allowed for. Since arrester gears in service at that time were only designed to cope with an absolute maximum entry speed of 75mph (121km/h), a severe operational limitation of always having at least a 46mph (74km/h) wind over the flight deck would be imposed on the aircraft. It would also always be undergoing high acceleration loads on being arrested under such conditions.

The Seafang 31 passed its arresting proofing trials finally on 30 April 1946, and I carried out its deck landing assessment on 1 May.

The inevitable conclusion I formed at this stage was that the Seafang left a lot to be desired as a deck landing aircraft. This fact, when allied to the small improvement in performance over the Seafire 47, really left the latter clearly the preferable carrier-borne aircraft.

On 2 May I returned the aircraft to High Post and that was virtually the end of the Seafang as far as the Royal Navy was concerned. Although 150 had been ordered, only 8 were in fact built. Actually Mike Lithgow, Supermarine Test Pilot and ex-Fleet Air Arm, landed a Seafang aboard a fleet carrier, more as an act of defiance than of hope, so some thought. However, there was more to it than that, for the new Supermarine ship-borne jet fighter, the Attacker, was about to start its acceptance trials, with the Seafang's laminar flow wing incorporated in its design, so much was at stake.

A year passed before I flew the prototype Seafang 32, VB895, with contra-rotating propeller and on which an all-out effort was being made to improve the lateral control characteristics at low speed – all part of research aimed to benefit the Attacker.

In March 1948 I flew Seafang 31, VG474, with power-operated ailerons which had 30% feedback of feel and they were superb except that the build-up in force with speed above 460mph (740km/h) was excessive. In July I again flew this same aircraft, fitted with a pair of Attacker ailerons, which were actually the same as standard Seafang ailerons except that spring tabs replaced the balance tabs of the latter. The result was near perfection in lateral control, from the stall to the limiting diving speed.

The Seafang, like the Blackburn Firecrest, was an unnecessary and abortive attempt to extend the performance of an operational aircraft by a minimum of redesign. In the end more was lost on the swings than was gained on the roundabouts. In some ways it marked the beginning of the end of the charisma surrounding the Supermarine name. Certainly the Attacker, Swift and Scimitar that followed the Seafang, lacked that mark of greatness that Mitchell stamped on the Spitfire.

46 SUPERMARINE SEAFIRE

The Spitfire in the difficult environment of shipborne aviation had its problems, but never when once unleashed into its natural freedom of operation. The Seafire 47 was a thunderous example of success against the odds. ERIC BROWN

A Seafire III, BL676, fitted with a tropical filter.

THE NAME SPITFIRE conjures up an image of lethal beauty that became an immortal aviation icon as it fought worldwide to uphold the cause of freedom. It first impacted on the aviation world during the Battle of Britain in 1940, and the Royal Navy looked on both it and the Hurricane with envious eyes.

Since the Hurricane was the earlier and sturdier design it was decided to go ahead and equip it with an arrester hook for carrier operations on the large fleet size carriers. These were successful, but a hooked Spitfire would be a different proposition because it was faster to land and had an even worse view for landing. Added to this, its airframe and undercarriage were much less robust and less suited to the high vertical velocities of deck landing, the severe acceleration of catapulting and the rapid deceleration of arrested landing.

Despite this, it was decided to initiate shipboard trials, and it fell to Cdr H. P. Bramwell, the CO of the Navy's Service Trials Unit to undertake this task on the fleet carrier *Illustrious*, in late December 1941. The trials were successful, but Bramwell recommended that a curving approach technique be adopted to compensate for the limited cockpit view when landing. He also expressed some doubt as to the Spitfire's suitability for operation from US-built 'Woolworth' escort carriers.

At this stage in history I was returning to the UK after the sinking of the tiny escort carrier *Audacity*, which had been highly successful in operating Grumman Martlet/Wildcat single-seat fighters. After a short spell of survivor's leave, I was selected to carry out initial trials of the Sea Hurricane on the Woolworth carrier *Avenger* in May 1942, followed by Seafire trials on the Woolworth *Biter* on 11 September. Contrary to Peter Bramwell's earlier recommendations, I adopted a straight final approach with the aircraft crabbed to starboard so that I could have a good

clear view to port of both the deck and the batsman. This method is considered by some aviators
to be rather risky, but I can only say that it has
stood me in good stead for some 570 Seafire deck
landings, many under rather extreme trials conditions.

The original hooked Spitfires, which became
Seafire IBs were conversions from the Spitfire VBs,
and, apart from the introduction of a retractable

V-frame arrester hook, were almost identical to
their RAF counterparts. They had the fixed 'B'
type Spitfire wing with two 20mm cannon and
four .303 machine-guns.

The next variant of the Seafire was the Mk IIC,
with the 'C' type Spitfire wing which had provision for one 500lb (227kg) bomb under the fuselage or two 250lb (113kg) underwing bombs.
Two versions of the Mk IIC were built – the F Mk IIC

A Seafire L Mk IIC,
fitted with a four-
bladed propeller,
serving as a trials
aircraft for 60lb (27kg)
rocket projectiles.

A Seafire L Mk IIC of
899 Squadron, taking
off from HMS *Hunter*
during the Salerno Bay
operations in
September 1943.

Seafire L Mk IICs of
Nos 879 and 886
Squadrons, flying off
HMS *Attacker* at the
start of the Salerno Bay
operations.

A Seafire Mk XVII, (SX194), in post-war service with No. 781 Squadron. This version became the Seafire FR Mk 17 in 1947.

The fourth Seafire Mk 47, (PS947), picking up the arrester wire.

by Supermarine and the L Mk IIC by Westland. The latter was specially produced for low-altitude operations and its Merlin 32 engine drove a four-blade airscrew instead of the three-blader on all earlier Seafires.

Up to this point no Seafire had folding wings, which was a severe limitation for seaborne operations, especially for the smaller escort carriers. This was remedied with the Seafire F.R.III and L.F.III, all of which could be fitted with RATOG (rocket-assisted take-off gear), and were produced with both clipped and full-span wings.

The first significant operation involving Seafires was Operation Torch, the Allied invasion of North Africa in November 1942, and it saw the first air victory claimed by a Seafire. However, this overall operation showed that the Mk IIC was some 15–17mph (24–27km/h) slower than the Mk IB at all altitudes. This was due to the heavier 'C' wing, the added weight of local strengthening, coupled with the greater drag of the wing and the catapult spools. The resultant performance deficiency of the Mk IIC led to the development of the L Mk IIC, and this arrived at the Service Trials Unit at Arbroath about the same time as I did, in late 1942.

The Seafire L Mk IIC was the most exciting aircraft I had flown up to that time. Its initial climb rate and acceleration were little short of magnificent, and there was quite a dramatic reduction in take-off distance. On 15 December 1942 I took this Seafire aboard HMS *Activity* for deck landing and take-off trials, and the aircraft's performance was such that the decision was taken to convert all Merlin 46-engined Seafire Mk IICs to the L Mk IIC standard.

During this time, Joe Smith, who had succeeded the late R. J. Mitchell as Chief Designer for Supermarine, began to take special interest in the Seafire and its special requirements for shipboard use. Firstly he realised the undercarriage on RAF Spitfires was normally only subjected to a vertical velocity of 8ft/sec (2.4m/s), but on carrier landings this could rise to 15ft/sec (4.6m/s), so he beefed up the landing gear on production Seafires, and also designed a manual wing folding arrangement with a weight penalty of only 125lb (56.7kg). The wing fold was incorporated in all Seafire IIIs, which were also fitted with a Merlin 55 engine with automatic boost control and barometrically governed full throttle height.

The Seafire III displayed almost identical handling qualities to those of the Mk IIC but was 20mph (32km/h) faster at all altitudes. However, this model was replaced on the production line by the LIII with a low-altitude Merlin 55M with a

Pilot's notes: Supermarine Seafire 45 & 46

Fig 1:

Instrument panel

1 Pneumatic supply and brakes pressure gauge
2 Tailwheel indicator light
3 Ignition switches
4 Arrester hook indicator light
5 Undercarriage position indicator
6 Oxygen regulator
7 Gyro gunsight – RP/guns selector (Mk 46 only)
8 RP (PAIRS – SALVO) switch (Mk 46 only)
9 Flaps selector control
10 Gun and cine-camera firing push-button
11 'Press to transmit' push-button
12 Gyro-gun-sight
13 Gyro-caging push-button
14 Cine-camera independent push-button
15 Engine speed indicator
16 Supercharger gear-change switch
17 Supercharger high gear warning light
18 Boost gauge

19 Oil pressure gauge
20 Oil temperature gauge
21 Coolant temperature gauge
22 Fuel contents warning light
23 Rear tank fuel contents gauge (Mk 46 only)
24 Fuel pressure warning lamp
25 Priming selector cock
26 Cylinder priming pump
27 Main tanks fuel contents gauge
28 Engine starter re-indexing control
29 Engine starter push-button
30 Lower fuselage tank cock
31 Brakes lever
32 Compass
33 Generator failure warning light (Mk 46 only)
Note: on Mk 45 this light is on electrical panel below the trimming tab controls
34 Elevator trimming tab indicator
35 RATOG carrier jettison

control (Mk 46 only)
36 Gyro gunsight master switch (Mk 46 only)
37 RATOG master switch (Mk 46 only)
38 RATOG firing push-button (Mk 46 only)
Note: on Mk 45 this push-button is used for release of bombs

Fig 2:

Cockpit – port side

39 RP auto selector control
40 General purpose radio controller
41 Rudder trimming tab control
42 Elevator trimming tab control
43 Door handle
44 Bomb selector and fuzing switches
45 Vertical and oblique camera controls (FR Mk 46 only)
46 Fuel cut-off lever
47 Throttle control
48 Ground/flight switch (Mk 46 only)
49 Rpm control lever

50 Throttle friction damper lever
51 Fuel transfer cock
52 Wing combat tanks jettison levers (Mk 46 only)
53 Air-intake filter control lever
54 Rear fuselage tank cock (Mk 46 only)
55 Oil dilution push-button
56 Radiator shutters – test push-button
57 Supercharger test push-button
58 Rear tank booster pump test push-button
59 Main tanks booster pump test push-button
60 Fuel booster pumps ammeter test socket
61 Fuel booster pumps master switch
62 Navigation lamps switch
63 Pressure-head heater switch
64 Cine-camera master switch

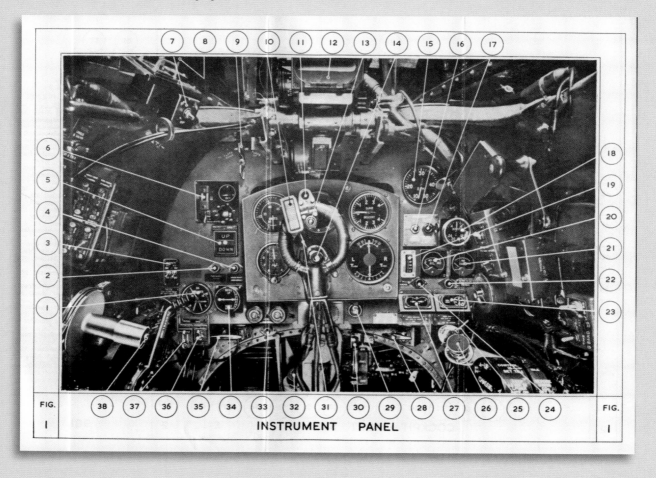

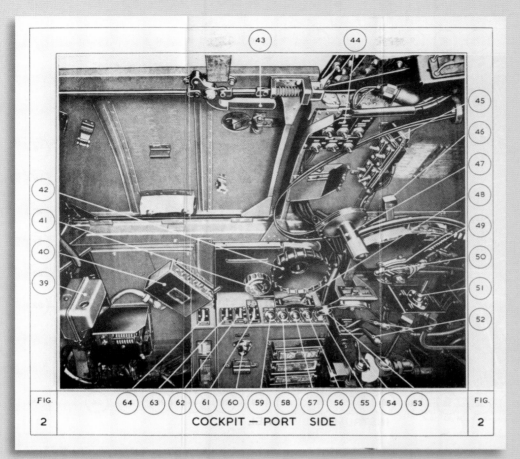

COCKPIT — PORT SIDE

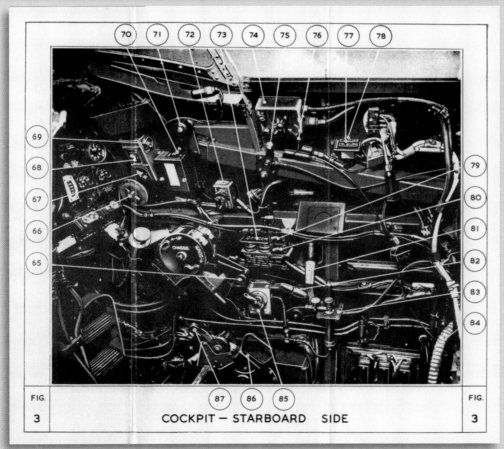

COCKPIT — STARBOARD SIDE

Fig 3:

Cockpit – starboard side

65 Undercarriage selector control
66 Gyro gunsight selector dimmer*
67 Identification lamps colour selector (Mk 46 only)
68 Identification lamps master switch (Mk 46 only)
69 Identification lamps morse push-button (Mk 46 only)
Note: on Mk 45 the identification lamps are controlled by a switchbox mounted in place of items (67) (68) and (69)
70 Telephone junction box*
71 Sliding hood winding lever (Mk 46 only)
72 IFF auxiliary control unit (Mk 46 only)
73 IFF demolition switches
74 Homing control unit*
75 Vertical camera mud flap release (FR Mk 46 only)
76 Pilot's harness release
77 Heated gloves switch (Mk 46 only)
78 Heated boots switch (Mk 46 only)
79 IFF 'D' switch
80 IFF 'F' switch
81 Undercarriage emergency control
82 Deck hook release
83 Windscreen de-icing pump
84 Oxygen supply tube
85 Windscreen de-icing cock
86 Fuselage drop tank jettison handle
87 Fuselage drop tank fuel cock

* These items are mounted in slightly different positions on Mk 45 aircraft, because of the absence of the sliding hood winding lever (71).

A disastrous landing on HMS *Attacker*. During the first day of the Salerno Bay operations, 38% of the Seafires were put out of action due to deck landing accidents.

NS487 being landed aboard HMS *Indefatigable* by Eric Brown on 26 March 1944.

Eric Brown landing NS490 on HMS *Pretoria Castle*, 20 November 1944.

258

cropped supercharger impeller. It was built in larger number than any other Seafire variant, and began to reach the squadrons in quantity during the spring of 1944.

In July 1943 I was involved in landing trials on escort carriers to ascertain the minimum acceptable windspeed at which a Seafire could be operated. By early August I had completed 35 low windspeed landings with a Seafire IB on three small carriers, without any untoward problems. All this was in preparation for Operation Avalanche on 9 September 1943 when five escort carriers with 106 Seafire L Mk IICs were to cover the landing of Allied forces in the Bay of Salerno in southern Italy. The weather was flat calm and the carriers were operating at virtually their own top speeds of about 20mph (32km/h). The assault landings ashore were totally successful, but at a price of 42 Seafires being written off due to deck landing accidents in the low wind speed conditions. This cataclysmic event inevitably led to the strengthening of the arrester hook on the Seafire.

The Seafire still had some heavy tasks facing it, namely providing fighter cover for Force H, mounting Operation Husky, the invasion of Sicily, launched on 10 July 1943, and also Operation Dragoon, the invasion of the South of France in August 1944. In additon, Seafires were involved with the Desert Air Force in Italy, and with the Second Tactical Air Force in Normandy.

A new phase was now in store for the Seafire with the advent of the powerful Rolls-Royce Griffon engine. I first saw a Griffon-engined Spitfire when Jeffrey Quill, Supermarine's Chief Test Pilot, flew into Arbroath on 21 February 1943 with a Mk XII, and I was moved on to this new type right away. I was most impressed with this aircraft, and loved the throaty growl of the Griffon III engine, the superlative low-level speed and the very fine roll rate, owing much to its clipped wings. All these features combined to produce sheer magic, and many years later when reminiscing with Jeffrey about our extensive Spitfire experience, we both agreed that for

sheer pleasurable flying the Spitfire XII was our favourite.

I took the hooked Mk XII, serial number EN226, for landing trials on HMS *Indomitable* on 9 March 1943 and completed 15 deck landings without any trouble. One year and five weeks later I landed the first prototype (NS487) of the Griffon-engined Seafire XV on HMS *Indefatigable* for the first time. This prototype had a Seafire L Mk III airframe which had been mated with the wing root fuel tanks of the Spitfire IX, the enlarged vertical tail surfaces of the Spitfire VIII and a Griffon VI engine. This amalgam was maintained in production versions of the Seafire XV.

Although the nose was lengthened as a result of the longer engine, the forward view was not noticeably inferior to that of the Merlin-engined models, owing to the Griffon's lower thrust line. The Griffon was 'left-handed' as opposed to the Merlin, and the incidence of the wing of the Mk XV had to be reversed to help balance out the torque effect, which posed serious problems on take-off if full take-off power was used.

Discussions about the possible conversion of the Spitfire 21 for naval use were taking place, and it was agreed that a contra-rotating propeller should be introduced at the earliest opportunity. A further stage in the refinement of the Spitfire XV was reached on 12 May 1944 when I made the first tail-down catapult launch with the first prototype. The next refinement was the fitting of a sting type arrester hook and I again took the first prototype (NS487) for successful landing trials on HMS *Implacable*, but this time with a sting hook.

The next step in our quest for perfection was to lengthen the sting hook and fit a five-bladed propeller to assist braking in the landing configuration. Because the Seafire was such an aerodynamically clean aircraft with excellent stalling characteristics, it tended to float over the arrester wires if the landing speed was a little fast.

A long overdue modification was to appear in the next variant, the Seafire XVII, fitted with the

Seafire Mk IIc, LR753/HL, No. 807 Naval Air Squadron, FAA, HMS *Hunter*, November 1943. © *Richard Caruana* (scale 1:48).

Top: The prototype Seafire Mk 47 (PS944), showing the wing-fold arrangement.

Above: A Westland-built Seafire Mk II (NF545), with standard Merlin 55 engine and four-bladed propeller.

Mk XV. However, the increase in power of the two-stage Griffon 61, driving the five-bladed propeller meant it had to be handled somewhat carefully on take-off. This aircraft was essentially a development model and only 50 were built.

The Mk 46, an adaptation of a Spitfire 22, again embodied minimum navalisation, but the most important innovation was the Griffon 87 engine, driving two three-bladed contra-rotating propellers. On 12 July 1945 I took it aboard *Pretoria Castle* and found it by far the easiest Seafire of them all to operate from a deck.

The war now being over there was little urgency to getting the ultimate Seafire 47 into carrier service, but when it finally arrived it proved a thunderous climax to the Seafire's career. It was powered by a direct injection Griffon 88, and after the first 14 fighters of this type appeared with manual wing folding, this was then updated to hydraulic actuation. The supreme feature of the Mk 47 was its superlative harmony of control which, combined with its performance, rendered it an outstanding combat fighter. It was the easiest of all Seafires to deck land, although strangely enough it was probably the most difficult to land ashore due to its marked nose-heaviness.

Only one Fleet Air Arm squadron was to gain the distinction of taking the Seafire 47 into action in the Far East and Korean War, embarked in the carrier HMS *Triumph*. The Mk 45 had twice the power, was twice the weight, was 100mph (161km/h) faster, had a staggering rate of climb, had three times the range and had five times the rate of roll of the first RAF Spitfire. The data speaks volumes for the versatility of Joe Smith and the Supermarine design team, and of course the Rolls-Royce team.

markedly superior long-stroke undercarriage. All these changes meant a considerable number of deck landing trials on various carriers through the latter half of 1945 into the beginning of 1946.

The Seafire was now reaching the apogee of its design career with the Mk 45, whose prototype was the slight adaptation of a Spitfire 21 to its nautical role by adding a sting hook and slinging points. I took this aircraft for its initial trials on the carrier *Pretoria Castle* on 23 November 1944, and found it easier to deck land than the

The second production Seafire Mk 46 (LA542).

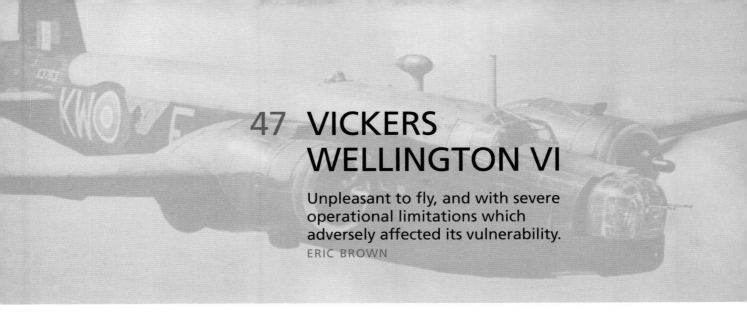

47 VICKERS WELLINGTON VI

Unpleasant to fly, and with severe operational limitations which adversely affected its vulnerability.
ERIC BROWN

THIS WAS a comparatively rare bird, because of 11,461 Wellingtons built only 64 were the specialist high altitude types designated Mks V and VI.

In the autumn of 1938 the Air Staff requested Vickers to investigate the possibilities of using the Wellington as a high altitude bomber, to operate at 35,000ft (10,670m) with a maximum ceiling of 40,000ft (12,200m). Obviously the geodetic construction of the Wellington did not lend itself to pressurisation, but the problem was ingeniously solved by building a cigar-shaped pressure capsule of 18ft 3in. (5.6m) length, with a diameter of 5ft 5in. (1.7m), and attaching it by means of integral feet anchored to the nodal point of the geodetic structure. This allowed the capsule to expand and contract independently of the rest of the structure. It was pressurised to 7lb/sq in. (0.5bar), thus giving an equivalent cabin altitude of 10,000ft (3,050m).

The cabin housed three crew (pilot, navigator, radio operator) and entry was by a 3ft 2in. (.97m) circular pressure-tight door at the rear end of the capsule. There was a circular opening on the top of the capsule to which was fitted a double-skinned perspex dome, which could be tilted to afford a clear view through the gap under its forward edge for take-off or landing in restricted visibility. An optically flat double circular window for the bomb-aimer was situated at the lower forward end of the capsule and was inclined at about 30 degrees to the line of flight. There were rectangular windows along the top of the cabin to enable the navigator to obtain sextant readings.

The early marks of the Wellington were powered by 1,000hp Bristol Pegasus XVIII radial engines.

Wellington bomber, X3595, came off the production line as a MkIII and served with 75 (New Zealand) Squadron. It was later converted to Mk X standard.

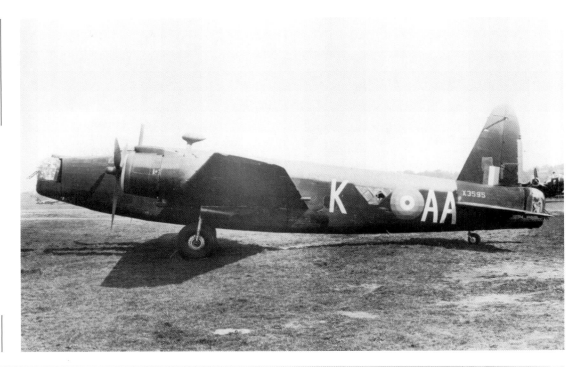

Vickers Wellington Mk III being loaded with a blockbuster bomb.

All windows and the pilot's dome were of double sheets with hot air passed between the panes to prevent misting and frosting internally.

Before flying trials had begun on the Mk V, the Air Staff issued specification B.23/39, incorporating two-speed two-stage supercharged Merlin 60s of 1,600hp. Basically the Wellington VI, as this new version was known, was a Mark V airframe with new engines.

I first flew Mk VI, W5802, on 8 February 1944, by which time a great deal of flying and trouble had been experienced at A&AEE Boscombe Down, from whence I had recently arrived to join RAE Farnborough. We had two Mk VIs at RAE for tests quite extraneous to the aircraft's operational task but utilising its high altitude capability. The Structural and Mechanical Engineering Department was testing a series of turret heaters at 35,000ft (10,670m), and the Physiological Laboratory was measuring strain on aircrew during evasive manoeuvring at high altitude.

The Mk VI had a strange looking forward fuselage profile, due to the pressure capsule, and the dome looked like a transparent pea on a pod. Entry was by a door in the starboard aft side of the fuselage and thence forward to the cabin. As soon as I entered it I realised why this version of the Wellington had earned the unenviable nickname of 'The Flying Coffin'. Obviously the chances of baling out of this metal tomb were slim indeed. The pilot sat on the port side near the centre of the capsule, with the wireless operator behind him, while the navigator, who also acted as bomb-aimer, was forward, nearer the starboard side.

Once settled into the pilot's seat I found the view ahead blind because of the length of the nose, but otherwise it was good. The throttles were difficult to reach and indeed to see.

Take-off required full right trim and rudder and differential throttling to counteract the strong swing to port. The climb at 130mph (209km/h) showed the aeroplane to be longitudinally unstable, and required a lot of concentration to fly in cloud, unless the auto-pilot was engaged.

In level flight at 35,000ft (10,670m) the aeroplane was still unstable and took a lot of flying if not on auto-pilot. The heater we were testing was to make the rear turret habitable at altitude. The original idea of locking the turret in position at altitude and operating it by remote control from the pressure cabin – and sighting from a periscope on the aft underside of the fuselage – was found to be impracticable.

On the second such flight, on 9 March, the heater burst into flames internally and started emitting a fine paraffin spray from a pipeline union on to the fabric of the aircraft. We were still on the climb, so a rapid change to descent was made while the three technicians at the rear of the fuselage pulled off their flying clothing and used it to smother the flames – on the principle it was better to freeze than fry. In the event we landed with the three technicians almost suffocated from the pungent smoke that filled the fuselage, while the wireless operator and I were safely cocooned in our pressure cabin.

At 35,000ft (10,670m) the cabin always maintained its pressure and was very warm, but there

The unarmed prototype of the Wellington (K4045), first flew at Weybridge on 15 June 1936.

Top: Wellington VI, DR484, west of Salisbury in January 1943. It has the extended nose, with the escape hatch (not visible); a footstep has recently been introduced below the fuselage roundel. Note the faired rear fuselage, the original cockpit cover and pilot in his peaked No. 1 SD hat (A&AEE rec.123)

Above: The high altitude Wellington VI.

was a tendency for a thin blue haze of oil fumes to permeate the air, probably coming from faulty oil seals in the cabin blower. The pilot's dome suffered a small amount of icing, but the other windows all froze over consistently.

Contrary to what I expected, landing presented no particular problems, except that the airspeed indicator and flap indicator were difficult to see on the approach, and the undercarriage and flap controls were not easy to reach. However, I should imagine a landing at night or in poor visibility would present its fair share of problems.

The second Wellington VI, W.5800, was used for evasive manoeuvring tests at 15,000ft (4,572m) and 30,000ft (9,145m) and showed the severe limitations in the high altitude operational phase

of such an aircraft. The controls invariably tended to freeze up at the higher altitude, and in consequence it was a real battle of strength to even move them. This, combined with the inherent longitudinal instability of the aeroplane, made it clear that a fighter attack at 30,000ft (9,145m) should be viewed with great apprehension – so it was safer to fly above 35,000ft (10,670m), out of the fighter's operational height band.

To sum up, the Wellington VI was not a pleasant aeroplane to fly and indeed had a dangerously high single-engine safety speed of 130mph (209km) on take-off. It obviously had severe operational limitations in the matter of vulnerability, and in bad weather I should imagine it was a very dicey proposition to either take-off or land.

However, it made an invaluable contribution to pressure cabin installation in this country and in the USA, to which all relevant data was sent. In fact it is probably no exaggeration to say that the pressure capsule designed for the Mk V laid the ground rules for the application of pressure cabins to many other aircraft.

48 VICKERS WINDSOR

Unusual four-wheel undercarriage.
A hairy ride in bumpy weather at low
level emphasised its specialised design as
a high altitude bomber. ERIC BROWN

THE VICKERS COMPANY is probably best known in aviation for its pioneering work with geodetic construction, the brain child of Barnes Wallis, the chief structures designer. Wallis drew on his design experience on the R.100 airship to devise a lattice work system, which was stress balanced in all directions and offered great weight saving.

The system was first used in the Wellesley medium bomber in 1935 and then in the famous Wellington and the later Warwick heavy bomber. The tremendous success of the Wellington was not matched by the Warwick because the latter never received the high-power units for which it was designed.

Rex Pierson, Vickers' Chief Designer, was aware that to exploit the physical characteristics of the geodetic concept to the full, it was necessary to apply it to very large aeroplanes. His chance came with the issue of specification B.5/41 for a high altitude heavy bomber to be equipped with a pressure cabin. Thus was born the Windsor, which was basically a Warwick with wingspan extended by 20ft (6.1m) and fuselage by 4ft (1.2m), fitted with four Rolls-Royce Merlin 60s, and with the unusual undercarriage arrangement of one wheel and leg assembly in each engine nacelle.

Before the prototype was built the specification was revised to B.3/42 with four 1,635hp Merlin 65s, and take-off weight of 68,000lb (30,845kg), carrying 12,000lb (5,443kg) of bombs. However, the main change was abandonment of the pressure cabin requirement.

The first prototype, DW506, made its maiden flight from Farnborough on 23 October 1943. It broke its back in a forced landing on 2 March 1944 after some 34 hours total flying.

The second prototype, DW512, had Merlin 85 engines with off-centre annular radiators and cowlings as opposed to the bearded radiators and cowlings of the first prototype. It was also heavier because of armour plating and minor modifications. It was first flown on 15 February 1944, and the more extensive tests with it revealed deformation of the fabric covering of the wings; this had a severe effect on the stalling characteristics of the aeroplane. Eventually the wings were recovered with a thin glass-cloth-backed fabric to cure the ballooning effect.

The only other Windsor to fly was NK136 which first flew on 11 July 1944 and was designated a Mark IIA. It was stressed to 70,000lb (31,752kg) and there were no speed restrictions as had been applied to its predecessors. A wire-mesh-backed heavyweight fabric replaced the lightweight material of the two previous Windsors. Other modifications included leaving the wings unsealed to reduce billowing, and the fuselage utilised four longerons instead of the previous three to stiffen lateral deflection.

I was brought into the Windsor testing programme at RAE Farnborough in 1944 with NK136, which I first flew on 9 October of that year. We were mainly concerned with the performance aspects as Vickers had reported this aircraft to be 25mph (40km/h) slower than DW512.

The first time I saw the Windsor I thought how good looking it was for such a large aeroplane. Somehow the undercarriage arrangement contributed to this impression, for each unit was comparatively small and neat as opposed to the massive dual pieces of ironmongery found on such heavy bombers as the Stirling.

The whole fuselage seemed unusually close to the ground, and there was a pronounced droop of the shapely elliptical wings. With the cockpit perched on top of the massive fuselage it reminded me vividly of the Wellington VI.

The cockpit was well laid out and the view was superb from this lofty perch, which was just as

265

The second Vickers Windsor prototype, DW512 – a high-altitude experimental bomber.

well because considerable care had to be taken in taxying, not only because of the large span but also because the track of the outer wheels of the undercarriage was 50ft (15m). This was a tight fit indeed for taxiways of that era.

The performance tests consisted of take-offs and landings at increasing weights, and measuring the cruising performance at various heights. On 24 October I had made a flight in foul weather and on returning to Farnborough was twice baulked on the landing approach by smaller aircraft sliding inside me before the weather clamped down. These baulked landings showed up the Windsor in a good light because it was obvious that the drag of the four units undercarriage was much less than expected.

Eventually, on 14 November, I made a take-off at the maximum weight of 68,000lb (30,845kg) and had my first visual introduction to aeroelastic distortion. This phenomenon consisted of flexing of the wing tips up and down through a 6ft (1.8m) arc, which looked extremely frightening from my line of sight. The sweep of the arc decreased somewhat in the cruise, but still gave the impression of a giant bird flapping its way through the air.

This was quite an eventful flight for other reasons, because we ran into severe icing at 23,000ft (7,010m) which rapidly made the cockpit hood

go opaque. Power had to be substantially increased to maintain level flight as the ice built up on fuselage and inner wings, although the outer wings were doing their own de-icing due to the continuous flexing motion.

After almost 2½ hours in such conditions we suddenly got a big drop in electrical power as the generator drive shaft on three engines sheared virtually simultaneously. This situation necessitated a rapid descent to below freezing level and I returned to base to land. As we turned on to the cross-wind leg I tried to lower the undercarriage but the hydraulic pump had failed so we had to resort to the emergency system. This only succeeded in lowering three of the legs fully to the locked down position, but the starboard outer unit failed to lock.

The landing was being made at the maximum allowable all-up weight of 60,000lb (27,216kg) so this was an unprogrammed test of the severest nature for the undercarriage strength. As we touched the runway the loosely dangling outer unit kicked back as its wheels hit the tarmac, but it remained intact and I braked the Windsor gently to a halt. The maintenance crew then appeared and locked the offending unit with ground locks before I taxied it off the runway.

The deterioration of performance in NK136 was largely caused by increase in weight from the

modifications, and increase in drag from manufacturing imperfections. As a result a proposal was made for a new type of covering for a geodetic structure known as Geosteel, which consisted of steel strips, 1,000th of an inch thick (.025mm) and 2in. (51mm) wide, woven into a homogenous sheet.

NK136 was next allocated for armament trials with a novel defensive system comprising rearward-firing nacelle barbettes remotely controlled from a tail-sighting gunner's station, and each barbette mounting twin 20mm Hispano cannon. Further development plans for the Windsor included installing propeller turbine engines, and also civil adaptations, but all these came to nought with the conclusion of World War II.

It is clear that the Windsor could have been developed into a useful very long range bomber for use in the Far East theatre of war. In my short experience of the prototype I found it pleasant to handle, but I am bound to say I would not have relished getting into a tropical towering cumulus-nimbus cloud with those flapping wings.

Perhaps the Windsor is best remembered for its unique four-unit undercarriage, whose four-wheel differential braking system meant that on the inside of a turn the inboard wheel was locked, while the outboard one was travelling in reverse. However, the system had a built-in five second

lag between brake application and operations which led to continuous over-braking and under-braking. But there is no doubt that the undercarriage layout aided directional stability on the ground, especially in a cross-wind and on take-off and landing.

Another feature that I will remember the Windsor for and which it seemed to have inherited from the Wellington VI was the awkward position of the throttles. These were set so low that they had to be pulled rather than pushed open and this made differential throttle handling very awkward.

My own overpowering memory, however, is of flying the Windsor at low-level in bumpy weather, with everything vibrating, the wings and fuselage flexing violently and the control column see-sawing continuously with no corresponding control movement. Definitely not recommended as a low-level bomber.

In flight the Windsor's wings flexed continuously like those of a large bird. This prototype, NK136, was designated a Mk IIA, and was first flown by Eric Brown on 9 October 1944.

267

49 VULTEE VENGEANCE IV

An excellent dive-bomber which redeemed the considerable design faults of earlier versions.

ERIC BROWN

ALTHOUGH of American origin, the Vultee Vengeance owed its existence to the British. It happened like this. The RAF's Air Staff had been so impressed with the blitzkrieg effectiveness of the Stuka dive bombers, that it decided it must go into the dive-bombing business, and so in 1940 the British Purchasing Commission initially ordered 400 of Vultee's dive bomber design, the V-72 or Vengeance. Most of these early Mk I and II aircraft went to the Royal Australian and Indian Air Forces, and the few that came to Britain were primarily for performance and handling assessment.

The USAAF purchased 600 Mk IAs, Mk IIs and Mk IIIs, for Lend-Lease and also retained some Mk IIs for their own operation. A decision to continue purchasing V-72s for Lend-Lease led to some redesign. The zero wing incidence was changed to reduce the aircraft's nose-up flight characteristics, and the armament changes saw 0.50in. (12mm) guns replace the four 0.30in. (9mm) wing guns, and a single 0.50in. (12mm) replace the two 0.30in. (9mm) guns in the rear cockpit. This was designated the A-35A, and 99 were built for the USAAF.

The significance of the different marks of Vengeance was that the Mk I was built by Northrop on direct British contract, the Mk IA by Northrop on USAAF contract, the Mk II by Vultee on direct British contract, the Mk III by Vultee on USAAF contract.

Further modifications were introduced in the RAF Vengeance IV and USAAF A-35B. Wing armament was increased to six guns, the bomb load doubled to 2,000lb (907kg) and a more powerful version of the Wright Cyclone installed. A simplified fuel system was fitted, together with spring tabs to all control surfaces.

We received Vengeance IV, FD218, at RAE Farnborough in August 1944 for comparison with other types of dive-bomber we were testing, and also to assess the effects of the design improvements over the Mk I. This had four major faults, namely poor take-off, bad view in normal flying attitude, a complex fuel system, and heavy out-of-trim rudder foot loads in the dive.

My first impression of the Vengeance was that it was big for a single-engined aeroplane, and its mid-wing had a most unusual platform. The flat centre section had marked sweepback on the

The Vengeance Mk II built on direct British contract.

The Vengeance Mk III built on USAAF contract.

leading edges, while the trailing edges were straight. The outer wing panels, which were set at a slight dihedral angle, had straight leading edges, while the trailing edges swept sharply forward to squared-off wing tips. Dive brakes were fitted both above and below the outer wing panels, hinging upwards and backwards, and forward and downwards respectively.

The Vengeance cockpit was in the roomy American style, but instrumentation layout was haphazard, with no thought given to rational grouping for the operational task.

The controls consisted of statically and aerodynamically balanced fabric-covered elevators and rudder, with controllable trim-tabs in the rudder and port elevator, while the differentially-operated metal ailerons both had electrically operated trim-tabs.

Starting up the Cyclone produced that powerful throaty growl I have always associated with that engine, which in this case drove a Hamilton Standard Hydromatic constant-speed airscrew.

The undercarriage – in spite of its laborious gyration backwards through 90 degrees to lie flat beneath the wings in 'bathtub' fairings – retracted remarkably smartly, and the tail wheel partially disappeared into the tail cone. Once the ironmongery was raised and the slotted trailing edge flaps followed suit, the rate of climb became fairly respectable, with stability neutral round all three axes.

At 10,000ft (3,048m) I levelled off into the cruise at 215mph (346km/h) and again stability was neutral. View dead ahead was poorish, due to the slightly nose-up normal flying attitude of the aircraft, but the controls were quite well harmonised.

Then up to 15,000ft (4,572m) to check the stalling characteristics, which were remarkably mild, with slight buffet some 8mph (13km/h) before the nose dropped gently.

And so to the main objective – to assess the Vengeance IV as a dive bomber. On the run-in a shallow dive is usually entered to build up speed

and at this stage the bomb doors are opened, so the higher their permitted operating speed the better. The Vengeance had a high restricting speed of 335mph (539km/h), thus allowing great operational flexibility in that respect. In the light of the poor view ahead I found it best to approach the target keeping it in sight on either bow until it drew abeam to disappear under the wing tip, and then peel off on to it.

On entering the dive the ailerons on FD218 were surprisingly light and the elevator force small, but the aircraft soon started to yaw to starboard and this had to be trimmed out. Speed build up to 270mph (435km/h) was quite fast, requiring constant directional trimming to avoid skid, but the rudder foot load was light because of the spring tab.

At that speed I popped the dive brakes, which opened rapidly without affecting trim. However, to open the brakes necessitated removing one's hand from the throttle, as the control was at one's left elbow. Also the actuating lever had to be returned to neutral after completion of the operating movement.

Terminal velocity, with the dive brakes extended, was 300mph (483km/h), and this was also the restricting speed for operating the brakes – a significant operational advantage. Although the elevator force built up progressively after 270mph (435km/h) it never reached a force that could not easily be held by pushing on the stick without using the trimmer. The yaw to starboard still required constant trimming to avoid skid. Any corrections for line on the target were made by rolling in the dive, and the Vengeance IV's ailerons remained delightfully light and effective throughout the speed range.

In the actual dive the view over the nose was excellent for the top cowling was flat and smooth, and the front windscreen panel wide enough to accommodate a dive bombing sight without completely obliterating direct vision sectors.

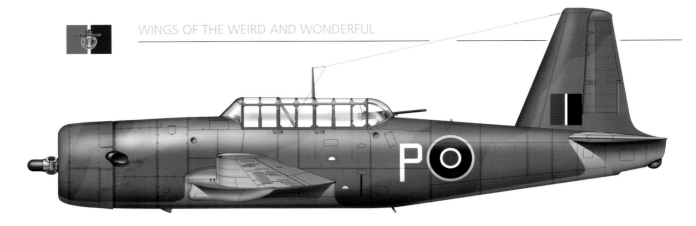

Vultee Vengeance Mk IV, 'P' (serial unknown), No. 8 Squadron, Indian Air Force, Spring 1944. © *Richard Caruana* (scale 1:72).

The Vengeance's natural dive angle seemed to be about 70 degrees, which feels to the pilot more like 90 degrees. Pull-out after bomb release only required a light stick force per 'g' so that it was easy for the pilot to black himself out. However, the aeroplane was so highly stressed there was little fear of causing structural damage.

The dive brakes were closed immediately the bombs were released and pull-out commenced. But the bomb doors were only closed on resuming level flight so as to avoid trapping the bomb displacement gear; their action was very quick, thus speeding up the vital getaway.

The whole dive bombing sequence was so efficient with the Vengeance IV that it seems incredible that items such as trimmers should be so inefficiently designed in the cockpit. There was no indicator for the aileron trimmers, that of the rudder a mere electric bulb which lit up when the trimmer was at full nose right setting, while the elevator trim position was crudely painted on a disc above the operating handle.

In my opinion the trimmers for dive bombing should be low geared wheels, working in the conventional sense and placed on a level with the pilot's seat on the left-hand side. They should have pointer indicators marked in degrees of tab setting to each side of neutral.

The internal bomb bay accommodated two 500lb (227kg) bombs, and as overload two further 250lb (113kg) bombs could be carried on external wing racks. This gave the Vengeance a useful punch which, delivered with high accuracy because of the aircraft's good dive-bombing characteristics, made it a potentially powerful attack weapon.

Surprisingly, the Vengeance had a reputation of being somewhat difficult to land. But one must remember that it was being operated mainly in hot and high conditions, and often from hastily prepared strips hewn out of the jungle and of limited dimensions.

Actually the approach speed of 125mph (201km/h) was quite high, but a lot of speed could be killed off in the last 100ft (30m) of height before touch down at 105mph (169km/h). Indeed the dive brakes could be extended at 10–15ft (3–5m) off the ground to give a positive sink on to a three-point landing and at the same time act as drag brakes to reduce the landing run. However, once on the ground the view ahead vanished and the pilot had to keep his wits about him to keep straight on a narrow strip on an aircraft with comparatively narrow track undercarriage.

I have read a number of pilot impressions of the Vengeance I; the great majority of these are far from enthusiastic. So Vultee did a great improvement job on the Mk IV, albeit a little late for it to reap the operational benefits.

After the Ju.87, the Vengeance IV is the best dive bomber I have flown. The irony of this aeroplane is that, although it was a vast improvement on the previous marks of the type, only the latter saw operational service. The Mk IV arrived at a time when the Air Staff had gone cool on dive bombing; so it was relegated to the ignominious task of target towing. The early Vengeances earned themselves a bad reputation, and therefore it is a great pity the Vengeance IV was not given a chance to redeem that situation.

Head-on view of the Vengeance with dive-breaks extended.

50 WESTLAND (EAGLE) WYVERN

A precursor of the turbo-prop version. Big, draggy, and heavy. In the event of engine failure it glided like a streamlined brick. ERIC BROWN

Westland Wyvern S.4s (VZ758 188, VZ757 187, VZ852 182, VZ753 183 VZ783 184 and VZ762 192) of 813 Squadron, flying in formation, Ford, 25 August 1953. *RAF Museum Hendon.*

THE WYVERN began life as a strictly Westland proposal, which attracted the Naval Staff and so eventually was designed to specification N.11/44 as a single seat torpedo-strike-fighter aircraft. Because the specification was written around the Westland proposal it was not put out to competitive tender by other manufacturers. It was intended for turboprop power, but such engines were not available until 1948, so the five prototypes and ten pre-production Mk 1s were fitted with the Rolls-Royce Eagle 22 sleeve-valve, liquid-cooled piston engine of 2,690hp, driving an eight-bladed, 13ft (4m) diameter contra-rotating airscrew.

The Eagle was a huge 24-cylinder engine still under development, and so the Westland Chief Test Pilot, Harald Penrose, was faced with a formidable combination of new engine and new airframe. They really gave him some hairy moments after the first test flight at Boscombe Down on 16 December 1946.

Certainly when I saw the third prototype, TS378, flown in to Farnborough in mid-September 1947, I mentally put it in the Firebrand class of oversize,

single-seat aircraft. It looked huge and ungainly, with an engine that appeared to have been an afterthought, as indeed it was. Altogether, not very impressive aesthetically.

It was fitted with Youngman three-position flaps across the centre section, and plain split-flaps on the outer wing panels inboard of the ailerons.

As usual with a prototype naval aircraft, RAE Farnborough undertook its arresting proofing trials, followed by a deck landing assessment. The all-up weight of the aircraft was 18,060lb (8,192kg), with the centre of gravity 1ft 11in. (58cm) forward of the datum (undercarriage down).

There was a slight problem connected with the arrester hook fairing during the arresting proofing trials, but modification action was relatively simple.

The first striking impression on getting into the cockpit was the view which, with a 15 degree angle down over the nose, was the best I had ever encountered on any piston-engined aircraft of conventional single-engined layout. It even surpassed that of the tricycle Bell Airacobra.

Starting the Eagle engine was like setting a gigantic threshing machine in motion as the

Westland (Eagle) Wyvern

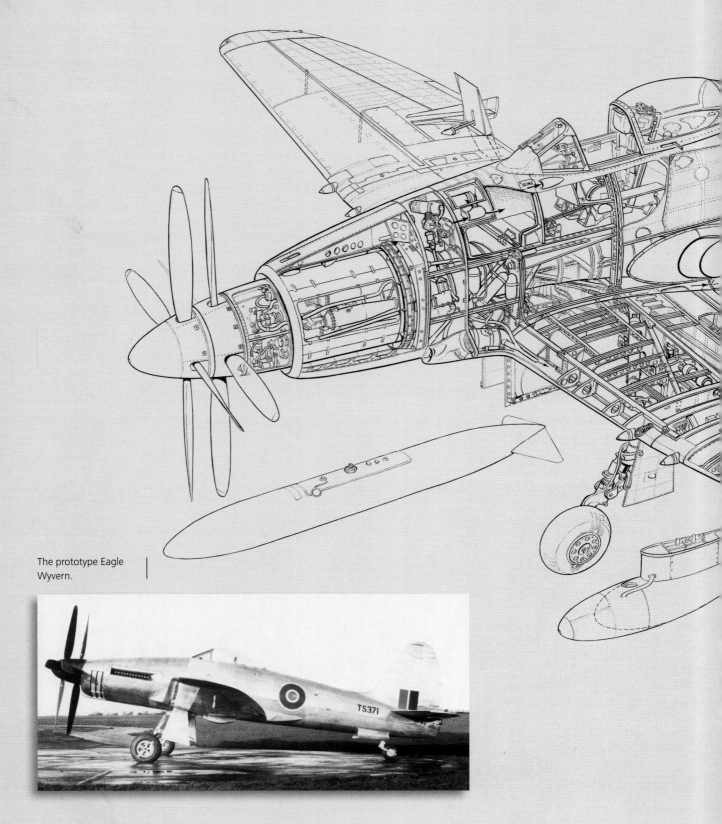

The prototype Eagle
Wyvern.

© www.theflightcollection.com

A. BOWBEER.

The Wyvern S.4
in flight.

Westland Wyvern S.4s (VZ758 188, VZ757 187, VZ852 182, VZ753 183 VZ783 184 and VZ762 192) of 813 Squadron, flying in formation past Beachy Head Lighthouse, 25 August 1953. *RAF Museum Hendon.*

mighty contra-props came to life. Cockpit layout was generally satisfactory, with electric trimmers on the rudder and aileron.

The aircraft had slight weather cocking tendencies during taxying in a cross wind. Although the brakes were good, one had to be careful not to use them too harshly, as once a turn was initiated it tended to develop rather quickly, due to the wide track undercarriage.

For a carrier type of take-off the brakes would only hold the aircraft up to +14lb boost before they started to slip. Using the TAKE-OFF flap setting, the unstick distance was rather long with the full +18lb boost applied. The change of trim on retracting the undercarriage was slightly nose-up, and that on raising the flaps slightly nose-down, so trimming was unnecessary to settle into the climb. The radiator flap setting could be left at AUTO from starting to stopping the engine, as cooling was excellent under all flight conditions.

The undercarriage had been designed to withstand a vertical velocity of 14ft/sec (4.3m/s), and in consequence the pre-compression system was used to shorten the long main leg oleos as they retracted. The Wyvern was one of the first aircraft to employ this technique.

In normal cruising flight the aeroplane was lon-gitudinally stable, laterally just stable, and directionally very stable. However, there was a slight hunting on the elevators in anything other than dead calm air and this suggested too much horn balance.

And so on to the stalling tests. I had done so many of these on so many different types of aircraft that I could sense the difficult ones, and the Wyvern gave me that feeling. The all-up stall occurred with very little warning other than a kicking on the port aileron at 119mph (191km/h), followed by a snatch to port on the stick as the port wing dropped sharply at 115mph (185km/h) and the aircraft tended to spiral steeply.

The all-down stall produced a warning at 104mph (167km/h) with kicking on both ailerons, followed by a snatch to starboard on the stick as the starboard wing dropped sharply at 88 knots and the aircraft tended to spiral steeply.

The sharpness of the stalls could catch the unwary as the stall itself would undoubtedly develop into a spin if the stick was not eased forward at once.

In manoeuvring the aircraft as a fighter it was apparent the stick force per 'g' was very high to an unacceptable degree and the spring tab elevators still hunted in steep turns. The ailerons were also fitted with spring tabs but fairly heavy, though very effective in giving a good rate of roll, and they did not heavy up much with increase in speed. The rudder was light and effective. Altogether not the harmony of control one would seek in the strike-fighter role.

The best deck landing speed for the Wyvern was 115mph (185km/h), using engine power in the range of +2 to +4lb boost. The view on the approach was very good indeed, but a hard pull back on the stick was required to effect a three-point touchdown, otherwise the aircraft tended to pitch nose down on to the main wheels.

However, the long-stroke undercarriage was very soft and absorbed potential bounce beautifully. But in spite of this I recommended keeping power on right down to actual contact as float was unlikely with this aircraft up to 1.2Vs (1.2 times the stalling speed) due to the discing effect of the contra-prop when the throttle was eventually cut.

The baulked landing had to be handled cautiously as there was a marked nose-up pitch with application of full power, which involved moderately high stick forces. But the aircraft could climb away satisfactorily at power considerably below full throttle.

The Eagle Wyvern was undoubtedly a very easy aircraft to deck land and in many respects was comparable in its characteristics to the Short Sturgeon. However, it hardly matched up to my idea of a strike-fighter. It was big, draggy, and heavy – more fitted to carrying a torpedo than a fighter pilot. Indeed, when engine failure was simulated, the aircraft assumed the gliding angle of a streamlined brick, with that large contra-prop giving the drag effect of a perforated disc. Actual failure in fact showed that if the engine seized and the massive propeller stopped dead, then a full flat plate drag effect took the streamlining out of that brick. In such circumstances a forced landing was fraught with very high risk of disaster. Indeed two Westland test pilots and the Armstrong-Siddeley chief test pilot were killed in this way during development flying.

The Wyvern T.F.2 was the first variant with a turbo-prop power plant. It was powered by a Rolls-Royce Clyde of 4,030shp, and was to be a torpedo-fighter. The Clyde gave a beautifully streamlined look to the aircraft, but the marriage of the turbo-prop to the contra-prop brought a new batch of troubles in the matter of the finely tuned lift control required for deck landing. The only Clyde-engined prototype made its first flight on 18 January 1949.

Re-engining the Wyvern with the 4,110shp Armstrong-Siddeley Python turbo-prop somewhat diminished the aesthetic look of the Clyde version and did nothing to help the lift control problem. This was not solved until four years later by the installation of the Rotol inertia controller. The maiden flight of the Python-engined version took place on 22 March 1949.

The Wyvern T.F.4, as the Python version was originally known, was redesignated the S.4, thus throwing off any fighter pretensions and settling for the role of a dedicated strike aircraft. It was the first Wyvern to reach operational status, and this had taken nearly seven years to achieve since the maiden flight of the Eagle version, and ten years from the inception of the design.

The S.4 featured a cut-back engine cowling to permit cartridge starting, stiffened cockpit canopy, modified aileron tabs, and auxiliary tail fins on a dihedral tailplane. Ninety production models were built and seven T.F.2s converted to S.4 standard. After entering service it proved to accelerate so fast in a dive that perforated air brakes were introduced below the centre section.

The Wyvern S.4 took part in the Suez campaign in November 1956, but this was too short lived an affair to make an in-depth assessment of its strike capabilities. Seventy-nine sorties were flown and two aircraft were lost, but only one of these to enemy action. It carried a useful load of four 20mm cannon and 16 rocket projectiles or three 1,000lb (454kg) bombs. Its alternative weapon was a single torpedo.

In the final reckoning I was just about as impressed with the Wyvern as I was with the Firebrand. That was not saying much, although one must concede that the Wyvern was a much more daring design that was plagued with development problems.

Westland Wyvern S.4, VZ766/273, No. 813 NAS, FAA, 1957. © *Richard Caruana* (scale 1:72).

51 WESTLAND WELKIN

An unimpressive but not totally unsuccessful attempt at producing a high altitude interceptor. Poor transonic flight limits.
ERIC BROWN

Westland Welkin I, (DX318), 20 April 1944. *RAF Museum Hendon.*

IN 1941–42 the German Ju 86P and 86R high-altitude reconnaissance bombers made their appearance over Britain and sparked off a mild panic because they operated at altitudes the RAF fighters could barely reach. The Junkers aircraft were fitted with pressure cabins and were normally unarmed because their operating altitude gave them virtual immunity.

As an interim defence measure, Fighter Command formed a high altitude Spitfire flight, manned by specially trained pilots. However, they were flying unpressurised aircraft and consequently suffered the physical discomfort of gas generated in the stomach and intestines. In order to minimise these effects the pilots were restricted to a special food diet, and operated on a shift basis of one day on, two days off.

On the rare occasions when contact was made with the bombers, attack was usually made impossible by windscreen icing. Even when the first Spitfire with a prototype pressure cabin got within striking distance of a Ju 86P at 36,500ft (11,125m), the fighter was so near the limits of its altitude performance that it stalled on opening fire.

It was in this background situation that the Welkin was conceived as a single-seat high altitude fighter, with a pressure cabin as a basic part of the design. This automatically pressurised cabin consisted of a relatively small self-contained unit made of extremely heavy gauge bullet-resisting

Seen in its element high above Somerset, most early Welkins were similar to this one. By the time it was ready for service, however, the high-altitude German bombers it was intended to counter had long gone and the day of the jet was dawning, so none ever saw service with the Royal Air Force. *Barry Ketley.*

light alloy and bolted to the front face of the main spar, with an armour steel bulkhead at the rear and a special openable bulkhead at the nose.

To reduce as far as possible the necessity for a number of pressure glands to give egress from the cabin to numerous small controls, an electrical system using grouped and pressure-tight junction boxes was adopted, and a special remote control unit devised to operate all trimtabs and fuel cocks.

Concurrently with the development of this cabin, extensive research was necessary to produce a coupé top with a wide field of vision. This not only had to take the abnormal loads of pressurisation but also had to be both suitable for ingress and jettisonable. A sandwich system of glazing evolved in which the thick inner shell retained the pressure, and an outer shell acted as a fairing, leaving a space between which warm air could be circulated to prevent icing and misting.

The design of the aeroplane called for a high aspect ratio wing, and the Welkin had a span of 70ft (21m). It had two 1,650hp Merlin 72 and 73 engines with two-speed, two-stage superchargers, each driving a Godfrey fixed displacement-type compressor to provide air for the cabin. Rotol four-blade constant-speed full-feathering airscrews were fitted.

In spite of its large span there was something about the look of Welkin, DX328, that appealed to me, probably the association of coming from the same stable as the Whirlwind. The cockpit was high off the ground, but once settled in it the view was excellent, and the layout was neat and functional.

Taxying was easy, with a good view of the wing tips and powerful brakes to compensate for the

ineffective rudder. Once lined up for take-off a pleasant surprise then awaited me for the Merlins accelerated the large Welkin faster than any non-tricycle undercarriage aeroplane I had ever flown up to that date – 24 March 1945. Engine response to throttle movement was excellent, the amount of quadrant travel being fairly small for full power. There was a slight tendency to swing to port, and the aircraft flew itself off in the three-point attitude without any tendency of the tail to rise. Raising the undercarriage gave no noticeable change of trim, but raising the flaps from the TAKE-OFF position gave a strong nose-down effect. This was not embarrassing as the flap setting was normally maintained for the climb, since the flaps were directly connected to the radiator flaps.

The climb at 150mph (241km/h) with +12lb

The Welkin had a span of 70ft (21m). The pressurised cabin, made of extremely heavy gauge bullet-resisting light alloy, was bolted to the front face of the main spar. *RAF Museum Hendon.*

The Welkin, like the Arado 240, proved to be an unimpressive high altitude interceptor.

boost, 2,850 rpm, was very steep, thus impairing the view badly. Longitudinal and lateral stability in the climb were neutral.

Cruise speed at 10,000ft (3,050m) was 260mph (418km/h) with +7lb boost, 2,650rpm. Again longitudinal and lateral stability were neutral, with directional stability remaining positive. Harmony of control was good.

In a dive up to 330mph (531km/h) all stick forces remained light but the rudder and ailerons were not very effective. The elevator, however, remained very effective.

Failure of an engine gave no drastic effects, but once trimmed in single-engine flight there was very little rudder travel left for manoeuvre. Also, if speed dropped below 150mph (241km/h), the ailerons became increasingly sloppy in effect, and full rudder was necessary.

Having thus established that the Welkin had the essential attributes of a fighter at a medium-low altitude, it was now time to see how it behaved at the high altitude for which it was designed, so up to 40,000ft (12,200m) we headed. The rate of climb remained remarkably good to 30,000ft (9,144m), then began to fall off gradually up to 35,000ft (10,670m) and then quite markedly to 40,000ft (12,200m).

On the climb cabin pressure and temperature were automatically controlled and at 40,000ft (12,200m) the cabin pressure showed an equivalent altitude of 21,000ft (6,431m). So the cockpit environment was very comfortable, with no icing or misting of the windscreen or canopy.

After retracting the flaps and settling into level flight at full throttle the indicated airspeed was 190mph (306km/h) – 385mph (620km/h) true airspeed. It was difficult to trim the aircraft longitudinally at that speed, but it could be manoeuvred gently without loss of height, sufficiently to get it into an attacking position on a bomber.

In the event that it might have a height advantage over the enemy I dived it to find its limiting Mach number but this was only a disappointing M=0.72. At about M=0.66 the aircraft began to porpoise longitudinally, and this was accompa-

nied by lateral lurching and a nose-down pitch. The limiting factor was the amplitude of the porpoising, which appeared to be a series of 'g' stalls, thus making pull-out a difficult task.

Although this limit was disappointingly low in 1945, it was not too bad for a piston-engined fighter of that size in 1941. By comparison the Lockheed Lightning's limit was M=0.68.

The landing approach at 110mph (177km/h) was uncomfortable, due to the very ineffective lateral and directional control. But the elevator control was so good that a three-point touchdown was easy to effect, and the undercarriage seemed to have a low rebound ratio.

The Welkin was destined never to see operational service, because just as it became ready the Ju.86s ceased their high altitude raids, which were ineffective because the persistent cloud over Britain obscured the targets. Just over 60 of the type were built, so the Welkin was a comparatively rare bird, which made its own special and important contribution to high altitude flight technology. It was a very respectable attempt to combat a special menace in Britain's skies, and it would probably have proved effective in that role. It is never easy to design an aeroplane's controls to work effectively throughout the speed and height range of its performance envelope, and the Welkin left much to be desired at the low speed end, both laterally and directionally.

Perhaps the only aircraft I can fairly compare with the Welkin is Germany's Arado Ar 240, because it was meant for the same task of high altitude interception and was almost contemporary in terms of time.

Unlike the Welkin the Ar 240 was a two-seater, with the crew seated back to back in a pressurised cabin. It was more heavily armed than its British counterpart, although smaller in size.

My flight experience of the Ar 240 was too curtailed to explore its full flight envelope, but it was obviously a considerably slower aeroplane than the Welkin, nor did it have the latter's ceiling. However, it had similar controls at low and medium altitudes, but handled better in the single-engine case. From the standpoint of stability, the Ar 240 was again remarkably like the Welkin, especially longitudinally at high altitude.

In summary, neither the British nor the German efforts to produce a twin-engine, high altitude interceptor could be assessed as very impressive. But in my view the Welkin would have had more chance of operational success than the Arado 240 above 30,000ft (9,144m).

52 WESTLAND WHIRLWIND

A good looker, whose looks belied its performance.
It just never had the right engines fitted.
Disappointing manoeuvrability. ERIC BROWN

THERE IS A CERTAIN LOOK about some aeroplanes that is utterly compelling. To me such aeroplanes as the Messerschmitt 163, the Mitsubishi Zero Sen, the de Havilland Hornet, and the Grumman Skyrocket come into that category. The Westland Whirlwind should undoubtedly be added to the list. To me it was sleek, yet pugnacious, and its engine layout gave a strong suggestion of power.

The Westland P9 fighter was designed to the Air Staff specification F.37/35, which called for a single-seat, twin-engine day and night fighter, armed with four 20mm cannon. Westland chose a low-wing monoplane design, powered by two Rolls-Royce liquid-cooled, twelve-cylinder Peregrine engines, and it was remarkable for its low frontal area. The competitive Bristol design bore a striking similarity, except that it was powered by radial engines and had its guns under the fuselage rather than in the nose.

The P9 won the day and two prototypes were ordered in 1937, launching Westland into its first metal monocoque construction under designer Teddy Petter of later Canberra fame. However, before building commenced some redesign took place, eliminating the original twin rudders to ensure the tailplane was clear of turbulent airflow when the big Fowler-type flaps were lowered.

Westland Whirlwind I, (P7048), 20 April 1944. *RAF Museum Hendon.*

The first flight took place on 11 October 1938 at Boscombe Down, in the capable hands of Harald Penrose. But, from the outset there were problems. The engines were prone to overheating on the ground, the Exactor-type hydraulic throttles gave inexact and spongy response, there was heavy pre-stall buffet, and the controls were badly harmonised. However, the main drawback was a design idiosyncrasy in that Petter had led the engine exhausts through the petrol tanks in the wings to reduce parasite drag. That such a built-in vulnerability factor was ever even envisaged seems incredible.

From that point, until I flew a later production version, the Whirlwind and its Peregrine engines underwent a programme of continuing modification. The Westland test schedule had also progressed into the high speed sector and revealed undesirable compressibility effects, although they were not identified as such in this subsonic era. The sum total of these problems was such that the first production aircraft did not fly until 22 May 1940.

My opportunity to fly a Whirlwind came in July 1942 at North Weald by the good grace of a Group Captain relative of mine, who made the arrangement with my squadron commander on the basis of a swop flight on a Grumman Martlet.

At that stage of my flying career I was about to join the Navy's Service Trials Unit, so was getting myself psyched up for my embryo test pilot role. I therefore took my two Whirlwind flights as a sort of rehearsal for this role and took copious notes.

The aircraft I flew bore the serial number P7117 and was powered by two 885hp Peregrines, driving de Havilland three-bladed constant speed airscrews. The engines were supercharged and housed in streamlined underslung nacelles midway between the fuselage and the extremities of the centre section. Totally enclosed ducted radiators were in the leading edge of the centre section, between the nacelles and the fuselage. The original exhaust layout had been changed to a nacelle ducted system. The rear extremities of the engine nacelles, which projected beyond the wing trailing edge, were hinged to move with the flaps to which they were attached.

The tailplane was mounted half way up the fin with a torpedo-shaped fairing at the intersection of the two surfaces. The undercarriage retracted aft into the rear part of the engine nacelles, and the tail wheel was fully retractable.

The cockpit was set over the trailing edge of the wing and this, coupled with the fairly long nose, meant that the view on the ground was not very good. The cockpit layout was neat and relatively simple.

Starting the engines was easy and they really did sound like baby Merlins. Taxying was complicated by the inexact hydraulic throttles, the mediocre view, and the proneness of the engines to overheat. Take-off was longish but once the tail was raised the view improved immensely. The climb

was good in comparison with contemporary fighters, and the aircraft was neutrally stable about all three axes.

In cruising flight at 9,000ft (2,743m) with +2 boost, 2,350rpm, and 220mph (354km/h) IAS, the neutral stability persisted, but the harmony of control left much to be desired. The elevator was heavy, the ailerons moderately heavy, and the rudder light. The effectiveness of the controls matched the force required to move them.

At 10,000ft (3,048m) I carried out some stalls. With everything up, considerable tail buffeting set in at 150mph (241km/h) and there was a marked decrease in elevator control at that speed. At 108mph (174km/h), with the control column fully back, the aircraft settled into a stabilised descent with a rapid rate of sink and heavy buffeting. In recovery the buffet continued up to 170mph (274km/h).

With everything down, tail buffeting started at 98mph (158km/h), and with the control column fully back at 95mph (153km/h) a rapid sink developed with a tendency to drop the left wing. In recovery the buffet persisted up to 115mph (185km/h).

Single-engine flying was delightfully simple, with a very mild swing and nose drop when an engine was cut. Straightforward level flight could be held with one-quarter rudder and about one-eighth aileron with the starboard engine cut, and with slightly more application for a port engine cut. The rudder load could easily be trimmed out with the powerful trimmer. There was a slight tendency for the aircraft to become nose heavy when flying on one engine.

The manoeuvrability of the Whirlwind was brought into question by the tendency to buffet badly in tight turns, and with a wing loading of 40lb/sq ft (195kg/m^2) this was a crippling restriction. Also in dives from 25,000ft (7,620m) above 350mph (563km/h) a longitudinal pitching set in. If speed was allowed to increase there was a distinct loss of elevator effectiveness at 400mph (644km/h) at 15,000ft (4,572m) and a very strong pull force was required for recovery. These characteristics made the Whirlwind a poor bet as a fighter, and so it was given a fighter-bomber role in service and proved less than effective in that form.

The aircraft was not easy to land because speed had to be kept up to provide sufficient elevator control for hold-off. This therefore gave a long run-out – not the best characteristics for all-weather operations.

All in all the Whirlwind could be said to be a contradiction of the dictum that 'if it looks good it should fly good'. Certainly I was profoundly disappointed with its handling qualities in all but

single-engine flying. It is just as well that it had the latter blessing, for the Peregrine engine had its fair share of problems. From a performance point of view it was also about 10mph (16km/h) slower than the contemporary Spitfire Mk 1, although about 25mph (40km/h) faster than the Hurricane Mk 1.

It must be remembered that the Grumman Skyrocket, another good looker, was a failure but generated the successful Tigercat. However, the Westland Welkin, undoubtedly inspired by the Whirlwind, failed to rise above mediocrity.

The full aesthetic beauty of the Whirlwind shown to good effect.

Pilot's notes: Westland Whirlwind

Fig 4:

(Aeroplanes P.6984 and subsequent)

1   Airscrew speed controls (port and starboard)
2   Mixture control
3   Rudder bar pedal
4   Undercarriage and tail wheel position indicator
5   Throttle controls (port and starboard)
6   Change-over switch for undercarriage indicator
7   Main switch for undercarriage position indicator
8   Ventilator lever
9   Clock
10   Port dimmer switch for cockpit lamp
11   Magneto switches
13   Navigation lamps switch
14   Instrument-flying panel
16   Reflector gun sight lamp switch
17   Reflector gun sight and mounting
18   Cockpit lamps
20   ASI correction card holder (hidden by wireless remote controller handle)
21   Engine speed indicators
22   Starboard dimmer switch for cockpit lamp
23   Boost gauges (port and starboard)
24   Oil temperature gauges (port and starboard)
26   Oil pressure gauges (port and starboard)
28   Coolant temperature gauges (port and starboard)

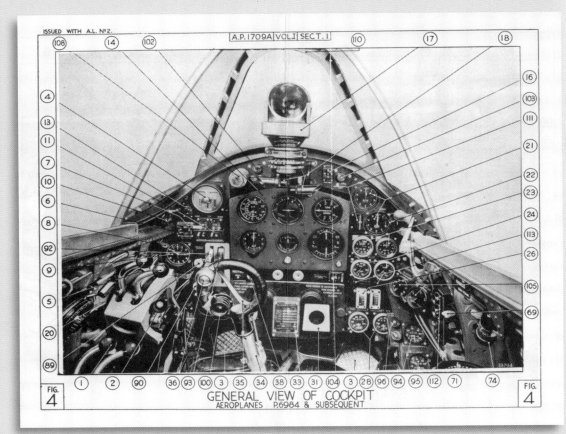

GENERAL VIEW OF COCKPIT
AEROPLANES P.6984 & SUBSEQUENT

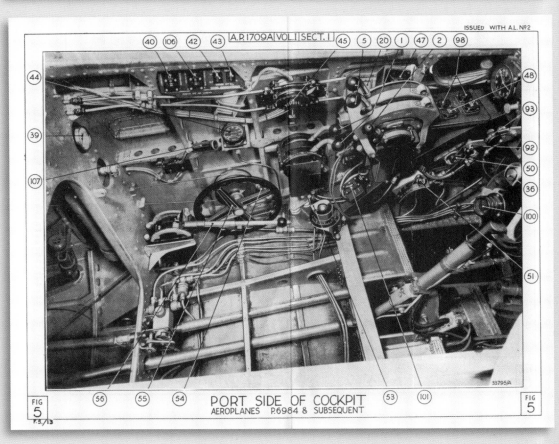

PORT SIDE OF COCKPIT
AEROPLANES P.6984 & SUBSEQUENT

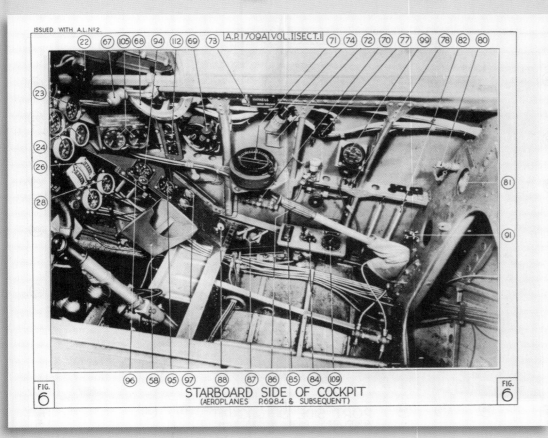

ISSUED WITH A.L.Nº2.

A.P.I709A VOL.I.SECT.I

FIG.
6

FIG.
6

STARBOARD SIDE OF COCKPIT
(AEROPLANES P.6984 & SUBSEQUENT)

81 Emergency air cylinder pressure gauge
82 First-aid outfit stowage
84 Suction pump change-over control
85 Suction gauge
86 Hydraulic pump handle
87 Flare release controls
88 Rudder bar adjustment control
91 Clip for stowage of hydraulic pump handle
94 Port tank fuel contents gauge
95 Starboard tank fuel contents gauge
96 Carburettor cut-out controls
97 Fire extinguisher push-buttons
99 Pneumatic cannon-firing and cine camera pressure
106 Oxygen regulator
109 Airscrew de-icing control rheostat
112 R.3003 switch and push-buttons

31 Camera gun footage indicator wedge plate mounting
33 Engine data plate
34 Control column
35 Brakes lever
36 Cannon firing push-button
38 Cockpit heating control
69 Signalling switchbox
71 Compass
74 Lamp for compass
89 Flap emergency lowering control
90 Undercarriage emergency lowering control (hidden by spade grip)
92 Flap control lever (hidden by spade grip) see fig. 5
93 Undercarriage control lever (hidden by spade grip) see fig. 5
94 Fuel-contents gauge (port tank)
95 Fuel-contents gauge (starboard tank)
96 Carburettor cut-out controls
100 Cine camera control push-button
102 Station-keeping lights port switch

103 Station-keeping lights starboard switch
104 Recognition-lights switch
105 Oxygen regulator
108 Windscreen de-icing pump
110 Rear view mirror (at the top of cockpit hooding)
111 Automatic recognition device control
112 R.3003 switch and push-buttons
113 Fuel pressure indicators

Fig 5:

(Aeroplanes P.6984 and subsequent)

1 Airscrew controls (port and starboard)
2 Mixture control
5 Throttle controls (port and starboard)
19 ASI correction card holder (hidden by port throttle control)
36 Cannon firing push-button
39 Hydraulic accumulator pressure gauge
40 Camera gun master switch

42 Master contactor switch
43 Remote contactor switch
44 Hydraulic system pressure gauge
45 Wireless remote controller
47 Voltmeter
48 Engine starting push-buttons
50 Port fuel tank cock control
51 Starboard fuel tank cock control
53 Rudder trimming tab handle
54 Elevator trimming tab position indicator
55 Elevator trimming tab handwheel
56 Landing lamp dipping lever
92 Flap control lever
93 Undercarriage control lever
98 Booster coil switches (port and starboard)
100 Cine camera control push-button
101 Landing lamp switch
106 Pressure head heater switch
107 Microphone-telephone socket

Fig 6:

(Aeroplanes P.6984 and subsequent)

22 Starboard dimmer switch for cockpit lamp
23 Boost gauges (port and starboard)
24 Oil temperature gauges (port and starboard)
26 Oil pressure gauges (port and starboard)
28 Coolant temperature gauges (port and starboard)
58 Map case
67 Hood operating handle
68 Hood-handle locking quadrant
69 Signalling switchbox
70 Spare filaments for reflector gun sight
71 Compass
72 Compass deviation card holder
73 Sutton harness release
74 Lamp for compass
77 Dimmer switch for compass lamp
78 Control locking clip (starboard)
80 Emergency air cylinder inflation valve

283

53 WINTER ZAUNKÖNIG

As near foolproof as an aeroplane is ever likely to get. ERIC BROWN

MANY DESIGNERS of light aircraft have pursued the elusive goal of a foolproof aeroplane. There have been some with excellent safety features such as a non-spinability. But I believe there was one aeroplane that came very close to the claim of being foolproof and certainly the nearest that I ever flew.

This was the German Zaunkönig or Wren (in English), a parasol high-wing monoplane designed by the creator of the Storch, Professor Dr Ing H. Winter, and built by his students at the Technical High School at Brunswick. Professor Winter's objective was to provide a foolproof single-seat trainer in which anyone could be sent solo in safety after only one half-hour's ground instruction. For those who had already flown sailplanes, this time could be reduced to five minutes.

The aircraft arrived at RAE Farnborough in a crate, having been captured at Brunswick, where it is believed to have made a few flights in the hands of Professor Winter. I was to make the first

flight after assembly in this country, so I watched the erecting process with interest.

The Zaunkönig was powered by a Zündapp 29-92 engine of 51hp, driving a two-bladed airscrew. It had flaps on the inboard trailing edges of the wings and as they lowered to the full 40 degrees so the ailerons drooped 15 degrees.

I made the first flight in D-YBAR, or VX190 as it was later designated, at the RAE on the 18 September 1947. The weight of the aircraft was 800lb (363kg) with a wing loading of 8lb/sq ft (40kg/m^2).

To start the engine a yellow knob on the right side of the cockpit had to be pulled down and back to turn on the fuel. The throttle was then pumped three or four times until petrol ran out under the engine to show it was primed. A key on a chain on the left wide was inserted in the single magneto and a ground crewman then cranked the starter by hand until the little Zündapp purred into life.

The aircraft was simple to taxi, the view being

The Winter Zaunkönig, probably the closest example of a foolproof aircraft there has ever been.

Published for the first time, this picture of the unique Zaunkönig (Wren) was taken at White Waltham in 1948. Designed as an essay in slow, safe flying by students at the aviation academy at Brunswick in Germany, under the direction of Professor Winter, it first flew in 1943, registered as D-YBAR.

good and the rudder effective. Foot brakes were fitted, but tended to be too powerful for such a light aeroplane.

There was no noticeable tendency to swing on take-off, the drag of the tail-skid probably acting in effect as a tail-wheel lock to negate any slight slipstream effect. With the stick held just aft of neutral the aircraft flew itself off at 45mph (72km/h) (flaps up) and 31mph (50km/h) (flaps down). The take-off distances under such conditions were approximately 110yds (101m) and 55yds (50m) respectively in a 4mph (6.5km/h) wind.

If the aircraft was pulled off it unstuck at 42mph (67km/h) and 30mph (48km/h) respectively. In the cases of take-off with the flaps fully lowered the main wheels seemed to unstick first. Then, when the aircraft became completely airborne, it did so at a steep angle of attack and a fair push was required on the stick to assume a comfortable climbing attitude.

There were no trimmers on this aircraft, but a climb speed of 47mph (75km/h) at 1,850 rpm gave a comfortable attitude with only a slight pull force. At its cruising speed of 53mph (85km/h) at 1,700 rpm a very slight pull force was required on the stick. Harmony of control was good in manoeuvring, and stick free stability was laterally neutral and directionally positive, with controls self-centering rapidly after release. A dive to the maximum permissable speed of 99mph (160km/h) showed that in order to hold that speed a slight pull force was required, whilst a dive to the limiting speed of 75mph (120km/h) with flaps down required a fair push force. No vibration or buffeting was apparent at these speeds.

The aircraft could not be stalled normally. With flaps up, a steady rate of descent was held at a minimum speed of 38mph (61km/h) and, with flaps wound down, at 31mph (50km/h). In each case the rate of descent seemed very small and probably reasonable enough to allow a heavy landing to be made straight off it.

The elevator was the heaviest of the three con-

trols, but only heavied up slightly with speed. The ailerons were very light up to 62mph (100km/h) after which they began to heavy up slightly, but they remained effective at all speeds. The rudder was extremely light, but ineffective at low speeds.

Landing was extremely simple and straightforward. Approach speeds (engine off) of 47mph (75km/h) (flaps up) and 40mph (65km/h) (flaps down) allowed sufficiently for the rate of sink to be checked easily, and touch-down occurred at 3mph (5km/h) below approach speed. There was no tendency to bounce, as the long-stroke undercarriage absorbed the rebound energy fully, and there was no swing experienced after touch-down.

There were two noticeable points about the landing. Firstly there was a marked increase in lift as the flaps were lowered and this was not just an impression caused by the nose-up change of trim. Secondly the spring loaded throttle lever tended to open itself unless the friction nut was screwed up fairly tightly.

And so this delightful little aeroplane poses the question – did Professor Winter achieve his objective? In essence I would say he did, although I should always have qualms about sending off a complete beginner after only half an hour's ground instruction.

I actually did send off a very famous aerodynamicist on his first solo in the Zaunkönig, but he had already had two or three hours dual in a Miles Magister, and in this case I had not the slightest worry about his safety. It is just as well, as he later became a prominent member of the Concorde design team. Linking the Zaunkönig in any remote way with Concorde almost tempts me to say 'from the ridiculous to the sublime', except that the little Wren was anything but ridiculous. At a point in time other than the vacuum after a world war it could have revolutionised private flying in Europe, and succeeded where the Flying Flea of immediate pre-war years failed. Certainly it proved its durability because it was still flying 40 years later, after many changes of owner.

Index